Adapted from the Original

EDITED BY LAURENCE RAW
AND DEFNE ERSIN TURAN

The Adaptation of History:
Essays on Ways of Telling the Past
(McFarland, 2013)

ALSO BY LAURENCE RAW

Character Actors in Horror
and Science Fiction Films, 1930–1960
(McFarland, 2012)

Adapted from the Original

Essays on the Value
and Values of Works
Remade for a New Medium

Edited by Laurence Raw

McFarland & Company, Inc., Publishers
Jefferson, North Carolina

The author died on June 27, 2018,
after completing the manuscript for this book.

ISBN (print) 978-0-7864-7872-9
ISBN (ebook) 978-1-4766-3287-2

LIBRARY OF CONGRESS CATALOGUING-IN-PUBLICATION DATA

BRITISH LIBRARY CATALOGUING DATA ARE AVAILABLE

Front cover image © 2018 massimo1g/iStock

Printed in the United States of America

McFarland & Company, Inc., Publishers
www.mcfarlandpub.com

This collection is dedicated to the memory of
Nehir Sert, my erstwhile office-mate and head
of the Department of English Language Teaching
at Başkent until 2015, who sadly passed away
in late 2016 well before her 60th year.

Table of Contents

Part II. Ontology

Acknowledgments

I am eternally grateful to the medical and nursing staff of Başkent and Hacettepe university hospitals in Ankara for their professionalism and sympathy during a recent stay.

I am also eternally grateful to a number of people at Başkent University who offered invaluable support. They include the founding rector, Prof. Dr. Mehmet Haberal; the current rector, Prof. Dr. Ali Haberal; the former rector, Prof. Dr. Kenan Araz; assistant rector Prof. Dr. Kadir Varoğlu; the dean of the Faculty of Education, Prof. Dr. Sadegül Akbaba Altun; the immediate past dean, Prof. Dr. Füsun Eyidoğan; and my head of department, Prof. Dr. Gülsev Pekkan. Their generosity in arranging cover for my professional duties will not be forgotten.

Colleagues such as Senem Kaya, Defne Tutan, Gordon Marshall, Santiago Vaquera-Vásquez and Jason Mark Ward offered good counsel both face-to-face and online, even if they were not necessarily aware of it. Tony Gurr has always been around ever since we did *Adaptation and Learning* in 2013. Other colleagues from *The Journal of American Studies in Turkey*—Marshall, Özlem Uzundemir, Meldan Tanrısal, and Tanfer Emin Tunç—have been extremely kind.

I have also benefited from the generosity and sympathy of Adrian Thomas and Peter Wiseman, both stalwarts of Beckenham Cricket Club in southeast London, where I spent many years as a member during my teenage and 20-something years. I reconnected with them after a 27-year hiatus. My cousin Steve Colling has also been very helpful in ways that cannot really be explained.

This book would not have come about without colleagues I first encountered at the annual Southwest Popular Culture Association conference in Albuquerque. I am grateful to Lynnea Chapman King and her highly competent staff for providing such a fruitful occasion to discuss adaptation with colleagues young and old. I pay tribute to the organizers of the Association of Adaptation Studies conference, especially Deborah Cartmell, Jeremy

Strong, and Jamie Sherry, for providing a similar forum within the United Kingdom and Europe.

Many of my ideas for the introduction were worked out in the online journal *Dialogue: The Interdisciplinary Journal of Popular Culture and Pedagogy* (journaldialogue.org). I am grateful to co-editors Lynnea Chapman King and A. S. Cohen Miller for commissioning material from me. I also thank Ann Larabee, editor of the *Journal of Popular Culture*, for permitting me to write a regular column.

This collection would never have been completed if it had not been for the support offered by my wife Meltem, who combined the task of caring for me with her full-time post at the Department of American Culture and Literature at Başkent University. Quite how she managed to accomplish the task is a wonder to behold, especially as I am seldom a very good patient.

Introduction

LAURENCE RAW

Values in Adaptation Studies

Our constructions of value have been shaped by two distinct theoretical traditions—the economic and the psychological. The conservative economist Adam Smith argued in *The Wealth of Nations* (1776) that the value of any product depends on labor and supply costs. The distinction between short- and long-term value is an important one: short-term value is determined through goods' potential usefulness in daily life, while long-term value is more specialized. Smith uses that distinction to claim that there are two important notions of value—value in use and value in exchange. Value in use covers those goods required for daily existence, while value in exchange pertains to luxury goods (for example, diamonds). Value in exchange enables us to purchase other luxury items whose price perpetually fluctuates. The things that carry value in use have no value in exchange; those that carry value in exchange have no value in use (De Gupta 105–15). A century later theorists such as John Stuart Mill reinterpreted Smith's theories by claiming that exchange value depends on goods' usefulness. Use value determines the price as well as production costs, supply and demand (de Vivo 67–69). Goods are either utilitarian or marginal and form the backbone of economic activity while remaining largely stable in terms of price; marginal goods depend on market value (Lichtenstein et al. 54–67).

Psychologically speaking, value inevitably asks questions of us: How do we feel when we make the act of valuation? What are the conditions determining that feeling? Who exactly are "we"? Values are subjective and internal, often intimately connected to motivation; they are cognitive, permitting us to seek out knowledge about what matters to us; and they involve the imagination and desire as well as experience. They are conditional and subject to perpetual change throughout our lives. If distinctions have to be drawn, we

1

can say that psychological values are either intrinsic or instrumental. An intrinsic value relates to personality traits or other aspects of our character, while an instrumental value related to an object or item that attracts us (Lewis 89–111).

Although originating from different disciplines, there are palpable links between the two traditions. Marginal goods might carry instrumental value (for example, family heirlooms), while value in exchange might be interpreted psychologically as well as materialistically. Fans choosing to alter their appearance, their name or their outlook on life might be an example. Each year at the Southwest Popular Culture Conference in Albuquerque a group of aca-fans (known as "dead-headers") listen to papers while paying tribute in music and sound to the Grateful Dead. For three days, they set aside their daily identities and subject their past selves to re-evaluation in the present. For the organizers, the event is highly profitable, due to the number of participants involved, thereby promoting value in exchange as well as instrumental values.

Adaptation studies is one of those disciplines that requires us to consider both theoretical traditions. We are all familiar with certain issues of value, such as the relationship between literature and film. George Bluestone's pioneering *Novels into Film* (1957) looks at the MGM version of *Pride and Prejudice* (1940), which he claims did not enjoy the financial success it deserved on account of Aldous Huxley's script that omitted most of the Austenian ironies (145). The text's instrumental value had been overlooked in the process of transforming the novel into film. The film's release led to soaring sales of a Pocket Book version of the source text—a good example of value in exchange (filmgoers so enjoyed the screening that they were persuaded to find out more for themselves).

In the ensuing six decades, there has been a tendency among adaptation critics to favor psychological rather than economic values. The central issues of fidelity and their consequences for filmgoers interested in literature have been extensively debated in collections such as *True to the Text* (2011) and continues in recent issues of *Adaptation* (DiCecco 161–75). Yet we have already discussed how psychological values reject absolute notions (that "fidelity" exists as a universally acknowledged term) and concentrate on subjectivities instead. Any critical judgment on an adaptation tells us more about the writer's preoccupations (or prejudices) rather than the text ostensibly under analysis. Consider David Thomson's reactions to Baz Luhrmann's remake of *The Great Gatsby* (2013), where he adopts the persona of Gatsby's spirit gazing down from heaven:

> I am speechless, so you, Nick, are the only one who can spread the word round that I am mad as hell and won't take it anymore. Tell them not to make any more films about me…. It wasn't until I saw this Leonardo that I heard myself saying what I

never thought possible, "That Redford fellow isn't really such a hopeless actor...."
[The film] is stupefying, it's vulgar, it's demeaning—it's dull and there's nothing like
the dullness that is pretending to be a sensation.

The critique is based on two assumptions: (1) that the film's unfaithfulness to its source renders it an inferior piece of work; and (2) it insults our
memories of Gatsby, as mediated through the novel's previous adaptations,
or other adaptive forms. What Thomson deliberately ignores is what we might
call the value-added characterization of Leonardo DiCaprio as Gatsby. In
terms of the film's box-office potential, he fulfills a far more useful function
than the script. Likewise Baz Luhrmann's presence as a director is an attraction in itself. In financial terms both of them possessed inestimable use value,
as their presence in the credits justified the film's $105 million budget and
played a major part in rendering it profitable (three months after its opening
it had taken $144 million globally). Way back in the early 80s Lillian Hellman's
The Little Foxes (1939) opened for a limited run in London. The critics panned
the production as both archaic and unfaithful to the source text, but their
judgments counted for little due to Elizabeth Taylor's value-added presence
in the leading role, making her West End debut. To see her in the flesh had
considerable instrumental value for theatergoers of a certain generation,
while producer Zev Buffman must have enjoyed the exchange value of Taylor's
performance.

The success of both productions should remind us that film adaptations
are predominantly commercial enterprises based on market value, with the
presence of star actors and directors taking precedence over artistic issues.
Simone Murray addresses this point in detail in *The Adaptation Industry*, as
she shows how producers, distributors, investors, agents and marketing per-
sonnel exert considerable influence over the way a film is planned and exe-
cuted. Her arguments echo those that were first put forward more than a
century ago by Vachel Lindsay, who identified the producer's principal duty
to attract "the man in the audience" through spectacle, stars and incident—
the kind of visually striking material not found in books or newspapers. By
such means democracy and the "photoplay business" could operate in tandem
to enhance Hollywood's prestige both home and abroad (Lindsay, 137–38).

In an age of globalization where big-budget productions attract finance
as well as talent from a variety of sources, it becomes increasingly difficult
to separate commercial, artistic and psychological notions of value in adaptation, especially big-budget franchises such as *Lord of the Rings, The Hobbit,*
and *Harry Potter*. Each movie in the series offers the pleasures of familiarity
and difference, of well-loved characters involved in different situations. This
represents one of the films' major box-office attractions. The most recent
reboot of *The Man from U.N.C.L.E.* (2015) provides filmgoers of a certain generation with the nostalgic thrill of comparing younger actors (Henry Cavill,

Armie Hammer) in familiar roles with the original television actors (Robert Vaughn, David McCallum). This film is a prime example of convergence culture, wherein director Guy Ritchie doesn't exactly remake the original television series but offers a contemporary riff on the source material. Its value for filmgoers lies in the similarity and difference between source and target texts.

Yet value does not necessarily depend on this kind of comparison. The entire output of the digital radio station BBC Radio 4 Extra is designed for aficionados, nostalgia buffs and the curious listener. Comedies and dramas dating back to the late 40s are regularly broadcast and re-broadcast, most of it provided by BBC radios 4, 3 and 2 (known as the Home Service, the Third and the Light Programme until 1967). Adaptations feature prominently in the station's output, ranging from the hour-long *Classic Serial*, half- and full-hour episodic versions of classic detective thrillers, and half-hour realizations of classic comic novels past and present. The value of familiarity intersects with value for money: repeats are cheap to air (especially if the performers are no longer around to claim royalties), while providing listeners with a 24/7 service. Even if we miss a program at a specific time, we can always listen to it later or use the BBC iPlayer.

While not so extensively analyzed in recent literature, there are other constructions of value in adaptation that assume equal significance in our daily lives. In 2010 I co-edited a two-volume collection of essays on pedagogy—*The Pedagogy of Adaptation* and *Redefining Adaptation Studies*. This was followed in 2014 by *Teaching Adaptations*, edited by Deborah Cartmell and Imelda Whelehan. Each volume offers a variety of interventions of how to use adaptations in the classroom at secondary and tertiary levels. Although very different in terms of content (reflecting different disciplinary specialisms), they share a concern for the development of learners' creative abilities. Finding out about how adaptations are created for film and television proves an ideal means to develop communicative abilities through group work and negotiation. Timid learners can be encouraged to overcome their fears and take pleasure in participation. Meanwhile educators can rethink their roles within the classroom: Should they be "sages on the stage," offering a course of lectures, or should they assume a more advisory role akin to that of a sports coach? The learning experience becomes an opportunity for everyone to rethink their intrinsic values, how they view themselves and their relationship to the world and whether that relationship can be more precisely defined. The classroom functions as a site for pedagogical and personal adaptation (Raw and Gurr).

The purpose of this collection is to illustrate the polysemy of value in adaptation through a series of case studies whose subjects range from Korean and Finnish films to pedagogy, British television history, and stylometrics in

Jane Austen. In 2000 Robert E. Ray described this kind of approach as symptomatic of the undertheorized assumptions of New Criticism that persisted in spite of the influence of Derrida: "Without benefit of a presiding poetics, film and literature scholars could only persist in asking about individual movies the same unproductive layman's question (How does the film compare to the book?)" (44). Every case study rehearses similar arguments, leaving readers to ask, "So what?" This collection asks different questions, based on the conviction that book-to-film comparisons is only one mode of judging the value of a text. We should understand why value assumes such profound significance in adaptations of all kinds across a variety of contexts and/or historical periods. The case study method is the best means to achieve this task, as it demonstrates that a concern for value involves everyone, whether working in front of or behind the camera or learning about different forms of adaptation in education.

Drawing on the insights of literary critic Robert J. Meyer-Lee, I propose an evaluative model comprised of two strands—the ontological and the genealogical. The ontological covers what we might term the psychological aspects of value judgment, shaped by educational, material and cultural backgrounds. It might help to explain why professional critics such as David Thomson have historically exerted more influence over readers than over ordinary filmgoers. On the other hand, in a world of convergence cultures, filmgoers' ontological perspectives carry considerable weight through websites, blogs, and social media, prompting us to reflect on whether professional critics are a dying breed.

The genealogical aspect of value judgment helps us to evaluate the relationship between past, present, and future. Comparing one version of a classic text to another prompts us to reflect on our accumulated knowledge of television and film history as well as our cinematic autobiographies. The experience of watching James Ivory's *The Europeans* at the Curzon Cinema in London's Mayfair district in 1979 made me realize—perhaps for the first time—how my private education had led to emotional repression in its determination to "make me a man" (whatever that meant). The genealogical approach determines fidelity judgment as we measure one adaptation against another (for Thomson the 1974 version was much better than the 2013 effort). While planning a new adaptation, producers make genealogical value judgments: stars and directors are chosen on their recent box-office power as well as their reputations; designers are encouraged to come up with opulent representations of the past; and filming locations are selected on the basis of suitability for the material, a task that often involves considerable worldwide scouting, especially for historical adaptations. Other aspects of the *mise en scène* such as music, sound, and photography are subject to similar judgments. Meyer-Lee draws an important conclusion about evaluations of the past:

"[They] have always been valued by diverse agents ... ad infinitum ... by professional scribes, royal patrons, abbots, etc." (339). Those involved in adaptations of all kinds perpetuate this tradition.

Distinguishing the ontological from the genealogical might seem arbitrary: "each position ... in its very limits seems to implicate the other" (Meyer-Lee 339). Nonetheless, both positions are useful as they tell us how we *ought* to value adaptations from a pluralist perspective. Most critical evaluations, including those published here, draw on both strands but in different ways, depending on authorial stance. The structure of each essay remains loose, thereby permitting readers to construct their own evaluations. For Lisa Bunkowski collaborating on ethnographic research in Texas, looseness and flexibility are mandatory, so that the results reflect the diversity of her history learners. Dennis Rothermel's discussion of the Finnish director Aki Kaurismäki's adaptations of *Hamlet* and *Crime and Punishment* (among others) emphasizes the director's elusive style, which draws in yet frustrates our need to make snap judgments. What renders these films valuable is the way they challenge our ontological constructions as well as how the past functions in terms of the present and vice versa.

Of equal significance in making value judgments is the *frame* in which these cinematic events take place. We need to conduct contextual inquiries into production and reception issues to understand their intrinsic value (the value a text possesses "in itself") as well as their economic and commercial value. The frame helps us understand people's needs and wants, ranging from producers to audiences, as well as reminds us of the constructed nature of all value judgments. The intrinsic value of *The Great Gatsby* to DiCaprio's legions of fans worldwide in 2013 was very different from that of David Thomson. We need to consider the position of the valuing agent and their relationship to the frame—as Matt Hills among others has argued, die-hard fans have a very different relationship to their object of obsession, whether it be a film, a star, or another creative artist (Hills). As Simone Murray observes, most producers and distributors have very different notions of intrinsic value, chiefly measured by the adaptation's box-office performance as well as the finances accrued through subsequent releases on DVD or through various streaming services (*The Adaptation Industry, passim*). Comparing the reaction of the fan with that of the producer prompts critical reflection on the relationship between text and commerce and how it varies across different frames.

This seems an especially propitious time to examine issues of value in a world where previously established hierarchies of judgment are perpetually subject to question. Professional critics still ply their trades in major newspapers and film journals, but we are more likely to consult viewer evaluations on Amazon or composite sites such as Rotten Tomatoes that express in percentage terms whether viewers and critics like a film or not. Fans have the chance to express their views on specialist sites—for example, The Republic of Pemberley (for Austen aficionados). Social media offer a further outlet for people to express themselves. In an increasingly globalized world, where the Asian box office assumes equal if not greater significance than its American counterpart, producers try to open big-budget adaptations on as many screens as possible worldwide. The validity of John Stuart Mill's distinction between use and market value might be questioned, especially if a film attracts global publicity and mass audiences. The consequences of convergence culture are discussed in Kenneth A. Longden's essay in this collection; he shows how previously understood conceptions of what a remake might be, and how it can be distinguished from a reboot, are subject to question. Nor should we believe in the existence of two types of product—conceived for film and television—possessing distinct structures of value judgment. Convergence cultural products are often complex for producers and audiences alike, involving ontological as well as genealogical issues.

This collection is roughly divided into two parts using Meyer-Lee's distinction between the genealogical and the ontological while recognizing the porousness of both categories.

Genealogy

The first part begins with Kenneth A. Longden's discussion of the development of convergence cultures. He argues with some conviction that definitions such as the remake, which might have seemed fixed in the past, have been challenged by new constructions such as the reboot, to describe a text situated at a specific moment in time and informed by digital and global criteria. The industrial and marketing aspects of an adaptation assume as much significance as the artistic, which suggests a coming together of ontological and genealogical issues. Longden identifies a particular species of films made from televisual sources, the MFTVM (made-from-television movies), designed to appeal to a substantial nostalgia market (favoring genealogical issues) while offering different forms of wish fulfillment (ontological). These films are self-reflexive cultural phenomena, products of a pluralized media universe dedicated to multiplicity and textual plurality. Longden's essay not only emphasizes the complexities of planning an adaptation, as the various creative workers attempt to strike a balance between commercial and artistic interests, but also suggests the difficulties we experience in making value judgments on the finished product. His emphasis on multiplicity further justifies the decision to base this collection on a series of case studies.

Next is Allen H. Redmon's fascinating take on biblical adaptation. For those of us whose religious knowledge has been shaped by Mel Gibson's *The*

Passion of the Christ or (perish the thought!) *Monty Python's Life of Brian*, it comes as something of a wake-up call to discover that the Bible is not a single source text but a collection of books that encourage an almost limitless variety of adaptations. Redmon cites the reviews of Darren Aronofsky's *Noah* (2014), most of which castigated the director for alleged unfaithfulness to the book of Genesis. This is a false value judgment, telling us more about the writers' prejudices rather than the film itself. Redmon raises an issue that runs throughout this collection, that professional critics should be treated as just one of a variety of interest groups involved in the cinematic event. The ideal adaptation should be one that creates a "negative space" on the past, enabling us to make reflective interpretations on our own. With its plurality of source texts created by different scribes, generating an equal amount of responses from readers past and present, the Bible offers apparently limitless potential for establishing "negative spaces." Not one story delivers an effective essence.

The need to reinterpret the past as a sign of value dominates Rebecca M. Pauly's essay on Francophone novels and their cinematic adaptations. Too often scant attention is paid to non–English-language filmmakers in adaptation studies; this essay redresses the balance with a survey of the major figures in the 20th century. Although employing different forms of the French language, these artists are not trying to please anyone—especially the representatives of mainstream cultures—but become voices of their people and for their people, by employing dialects and sharing tales transmitted orally from generation to generation over hundreds of years. Familiar notions of value such as originality and fidelity do not matter; they are inspired by the *griot*, the mythical storyteller of the African diaspora. Tales of male coming-of-age rites of passage are adapted to the postcolonial context, with characters trying to construct value systems while coping with the inevitable clash of races and cultures. Francophone novels and films throughout the previous century have summed up these conflicts. This is especially pertinent to Muslim women artists, who have used films as well as novels to adapt themselves to globalization as well as local cultures.

Leslie McMurtry's work on adaptations of Gaston Leroux's novel *The Phantom of the Opera* (1910) might seem superficially very different in terms of subject matter. Taking up Kenneth Longden's point, McMurtry argues that *The Phantom* has been frequently adapted by different media—theater, film, radio and television—as well as become a globalized phenomenon through Andrew Lloyd Webber's musical (1986). Its market value matters, especially to investors. McMurtry argues that the majority of audiences since the early 20th century have constructed value systems out of the source text that might be very different from what Leroux intended. They have identified with the eponymous central character as a marginalized figure ignored by mainstream society, despite his ugly appearance. The enduring popularity of the source text can be explained through its potential to assist audiences and readers in forging new identities out of apparently unpromising origins. Sometimes this transformative power has been questioned, especially by critics viewing the 2004 film of the Lloyd Webber musical, but this example of convergence culture continues to inspire fan communities past and present.

A pair of contributions examine the popular adaptive strategy of neo-Victorianism. Ela İpek Gündüz looks at two versions of Sarah Waters' novel *Fingersmith* (2002), one by the BBC, the other by Korean director Park Chan Wook. She is most preoccupied with the relationship between past and present—although very different in terms of setting and script, both films are keen to emphasize how our understanding of the world, especially in terms of politics and gender, has been shaped by past value systems. We might consider ourselves more liberal than our ancestors, but Gündüz shows we are still capable of mental and physical cruelty. Dorota Babilas looks at two television dramas, both aired towards the end of 2016: *Victoria* (ITV) and *The Crown* (Netflix). Both draw on the stylistic conventions associated with previous films centering on the royal family, while humanizing the main characters for mass audiences. As with the adaptations of *The Handmaiden*, they draw on the past to comment on the present, especially the relationship between the public and private identities of a reigning monarch. Can queens Elizabeth and Victoria enjoy any sort of personal life or do they have to commit themselves to the highly public values of the crown? Does duty always have to predominate?

It is not just contemporary monarchs who have to cope with oppressive value systems. Özlem Özmen's essay on Edward Bond's *Lear* (1971) examines the dystopian world of the Shakespearean reboot. I call it a reboot because the text is redolent of its specific conditions at the end of a turbulent decade when the Soviet empire seemed virtually impregnable, with disturbances (for example, in Czechoslovakia) being brutally suppressed. Lear is transformed from a "foolish, fond old man" into a despot, while his three daughters are preoccupied with power and violence. Whereas Lear realizes what he has done, he cannot be allowed the security of redemption. He ends up being shot as he tries to destroy a wall separating his kingdom into separate fiefdoms (shades of the Berlin Wall, perhaps?). As with *The Phantom*, critics thoroughly disliked this reboot, condemning it for its overt stage violence and negative conclusion. Yet Bond is not trying to remake the text or even modernize it, but trying to offer a shocking example of how actions committed in the past have a destructive influence over present value systems.

Suzanne Diamond analyzes different versions of the shocking events of 15 November 1959, when four members of the Clutter family were murdered in cold blood at home in Holcomb, Kansas. The bulk of her attention centers on Truman Capote's 1966 novel *In Cold Blood*, the action of which she compares with accounts of the actual murder investigation. She explains how there is no such thing as historical truth: facts are shaped and re-shaped according to the individual perceiver. The Clutter murders have acquired mythic status, which leads to positive and negative consequences. Film adaptations of the event (for example, the 1996 version) benefit from the value-added advantage of the audience's prior knowledge of the events as well as the Capote novel. Conversely, the mythic associations might encourage us to set aside our day-to-day values of good and bad and overlook the consequences of the events for a small-town community left stunned by the sheer callousness of the deed. Like Özmen, Diamond emphasizes the oppressive influence of the past in a world of historical and ontological relativity, forcing us to adapt our values where necessary.

The first part of the collection ends with Hülya Yağcıoğlu's comparison of objects and their significance in Edith Wharton's *The Age of Innocence* and Orhan Pamuk's *The Museum of Innocence*. Despite the 88-year gap separating the publication of the novels (1920, 2008), they are both concerned with objects as witnesses to history. Both novels feature inveterate collectors of ephemera, the bulk of which is put on display for various purposes—to show off one's elevated social status, to satisfy one's material desires, or to preserve the past. These examples represent classic exemplifications of Adam Smith's principle of value in exchange. Both authors examine the genealogical consequences of material possessions; for Wharton the objects denote a lost world of *fin-de-siècle* New York, when class divisions were readily identifiable and deference an accepted way of life. It was certainly an "age of innocence" for those who could afford it, but what about the majority of New Yorkers? Wharton looks at the ways in which the characters nostalgically yearn for a world now past, where they were once sure of their identities. Pamuk's objects, now collected in a public museum in Istanbul as well as discussed in the novel, take him back to his childhood, which seemed so much more innocent than the present. On the other hand, the objects acquire new values as they help Pamuk's characters to make sense of their existences, especially in adverse circumstances. Yağcıoğlu's essay reminds us of the link between the imagination, genealogy and material objects, whatever their value, and how they have positive as well as negative effects on the psyche.

Ontology

The second part of this collection begins with Hui Wu's analysis of the Taviani Brothers' *Caesar Must Die* (*Cesare deve morire*) (2012). A complex film with several narrative layers, it focuses on what happens when a group of long-term prisoners rehearses and performs Shakespeare's *Julius Caesar*. Juxtaposing the experiences of their daily lives with the rigors of learning and reciting blank verse, the film attests to art's transformative power. The inmates remain incarcerated, doomed to spend most of their days in cramped cells, but at least they have a vision of a more optimistic future, where their contributions to the success of the performance are valued. Filmed on a low budget with non-professional performers, *Caesar Must Die* offers hope for everyone.

Agata Holobut and Jan Rybicki offer a suggestive variant on a familiar theme, as they use computer analysis to explore the extent to which the screenplays of Jane Austen's books imitate her authorial style. Their statistical approach might seem somewhat difficult for non-statisticians to follow, but their conclusions emphasize the extent to which adaptations cross-pollinate the source and target texts as well as embodying the preoccupations of the various adapters (Fay Weldon, Andrew Davies, etc.). This essay offers convincing evidence of the adapter's creative powers as he or she forges a new structure designed for television and/or cinema audiences out of an historical text. (We might argue with justification that recent Austen adaptations are as much of a reboot as the recent *Man from U.N.C.L.E.*)

The theme of creative adaptation is continued in Dennis Rothermel's treatment of Aki Kaurismäki's "outrageously improvisatory" versions of Shakespeare and Dostoyevsky. Rothermel successfully shows how our familiar expectations of the source texts are deliberately frustrated in unexpected ways. We are positively goaded into reflection about the source texts' potential to generate new meanings in the present, and how they might affect our values, ethical as well as literary.

The same phenomenon is also evident in Terry Gilliam's *The Brothers Grimm*, a film which delves into the world of fairy tales in a refreshingly different manner. Wickham Clayton argues in persuasive fashion that Gilliam's narrative thrives on forming coherence out of incoherence—provided, of course, that we are willing to accept such unorthodox moves. Christopher Wydler offers a reworking of Thomas Leitch's distinction between adaptation and allusion, prompting us to speculate on the nature of the source text in the adaptive process. Is it as fundamental to the adaptive act as we might previously have assumed? Or does it fulfill an allusive rather than an adaptive role; in other words, has it been decentered in favor of other intertexts? This question returns us to the issues posed by Longden at the beginning of this collection, where he claims that adapters have realigned their value systems in a world dominated by convergence cultures. By doing so they have revaluated their creative powers.

Continuing the theme of personal transformation, the next two contributions offer contrasting accounts of pedagogic practice. Drawing on

Louise Rosenblatt's transactional theories, Charles R. Hamilton shows how his undergraduate learners acquired personal connections to the texts they were reading by means of reflective questioning and discussion. In doing so, they learned to reconsider their notions of friendship and enmity: everyone in the classroom has an equal right to contribute their views. In a non-threatening environment, all learners can evaluate their personal value systems while offering fresh and often startling interpretations of familiar material. Educators such as Hamilton did not feel the need to guide the class in a certain direction through lectures; rather he educated himself through listening to his learners, thereby discovering how his own pedagogic values underwent a process of change. The "negative space" advocated by Redmon is highly achievable in the classroom, provided we are prepared to cede some of our authority to the learners. By doing so, we come to understand how a viewer's interpretation of an adapted text is as valid as that of any other creative talent.

Lisa Bunkowski arrives at a similar conclusion through her ethnographic research into how a class of undergraduates responded to her history class. This form of empirical research is relatively rare in adaptation studies (the only other text I can recall is Claire Monk's *Heritage Film Audiences* [2011]), but Bunkowski skillfully marshals her evidence to prove how historical adaptations are valuable tools in prompting reflection on the past and its relationship to the present. American history becomes something more than just a subject for study, but relates directly to the learners' conception of themselves as citizens in a fast-changing world. The class offered apparently limitless potential for transformation, with learners coping with "incidents of disequilibrium" in a supportive environment. Bunkowski makes an important point about "negative spaces": while they are to be encouraged as a means of redefining our individual value systems, they can also prove traumatic, especially for those wanting in self-confidence. Spaces should be established gradually, with plenty of support available from educators, parents, guardians and close acquaintances.

The collection ends with a remarkable autobiographical account by Jillian Saint Jacques about his personal journey of transformation as he grew up uncertain about his sexuality, became a transsexual and returned to his masculine identity. He shows how gendered distinctions are socially constructed—so much so, in fact, that they create prejudices against those embracing different sexual identities. This might seem familiar to readers, but what Saint Jacques manages to do is link the personal with the textual, which is precisely what this collection tries to achieve. While the distinction between the genealogical and the ontological serves as a convenient organizational framework, we have discovered that these two poles are indivisible. When we adapt ourselves through psychological discovery, we are altering our relationship to the worlds we inhabit and the people around us. There is no going back: our value systems require redefinition.

I have thoroughly enjoyed putting this collection together. From a personal angle the experience has helped me through a lengthy period of illness, providing me with the chance to reflect on my understanding of what the term "adaptation" signifies as well as offering alternative opportunities for evaluation that do not involve that old canard of "fidelity." Secondly, I welcomed the opportunity to incorporate such a diversity of essays emphasizing the importance of accommodation; even if I was unacquainted with the subject matter, I could understand how it contributed to the discussion on value judgments involving the issues outlined above. I realized the importance of fairness, not only as an attribute of adaptation (in the ontological sense) but also as a way of forging a community of purpose from all corners of Europe and the United States. In an age of subject specialization, this might seem rather an eccentric statement to make, but I believe that adaptation studies has always possessed the power of transdisciplinarity as well as transhistoricity. I hope this collection helps to convince readers to think in similar fashion.

WORKS CITED

Austen, Jane. *Pride and Prejudice*. Film tie-in ed. New York: Pocket Books, 1940. Print.

Bluestone, George. *Novels into Film: The Metamorphosis of Fiction into Cinema*. 1957. Berkeley: University of California Press, 1968. Print.

Bond, Edward. *Plays Two: Lear*. London: Methuen, 1972. Print.

The Brothers Grimm. Dir. Terry Gilliam. Perf. Matt Damon, Heath Ledger, 2005. Dimension Home Video (USA), 2005. DVD.

Caesar Must Die. Dir. Paolo Taviani and Vittorio Taviani. Perf. Cosimo Rega, Salvatore Striano, Giovanni Arcuri. Kaos Cinematografica, Stemal Entertainment and Le Talee, 2012. DVD.

Capote, Truman. *In Cold Blood: A True Account of a Multiple Murder and Its Consequences*. New York: Signet, 1966. Print.

Cartmell, Deborah, and Imelda Whelehan, eds. *Teaching Adaptations*. Basingstoke: Palgrave Macmillan, 2014. Print.

The Crown. Dir. Stephen Daldry et al. Perf. Claire Foy, Matt Smith, Vanessa Kirby. Netflix, 2016. Television.

Cutchins, Dennis, Laurence Raw, and James M. Welsh, eds. *The Pedagogy of Adaptation*. Lanham: Scarecrow, 2010. Print.

_____. *Redefining Adaptation Studies*. Lanham: Scarecrow, 2010. Print.

De Gupra, A.K. "Adam Smith on Value." *Indian Economic Review* 5.2 (August 1960): 105–15. Print.

De Vivo, Giancarlo. "John Stuart Mill on Value." *Cambridge Journal of Economics* 5.1 (1981): 67–69. Print.

DiCecco, Nico. "State of the Conversation: The Obscene Underside of Fidelity." *Adaptation* 8.2 (2015): 161–75. Print.

The Europeans. Dir. James Ivory. Perf. Lee Remick, Tim Woodward, Wesley Addy. Merchant-Ivory, 1979. Film.

The Great Gatsby. Dir. Jack Clayton. Perf. Robert Redford, Mia Farrow, Sam Waterston. Paramount, 1974. Film.

_____. Dir. Baz Luhrmann. Perf. Leonardo DiCaprio, Carey Mulligan. Warner Bros., 2013. Film.

Harry Potter. Dir. Chris Columbus et. al. Perf. Daniel Radcliffe, Emma Watson, Rupert Grint. Warner Bros., 2001–11. Film.

Hills, Matt. *Fan Cultures.* London: Routledge, 2002. Print.

The Hobbit. Dir. Peter Jackson. Perf. Martin Freeman, Ian McKellen. New Line Cinema, 2012–14. Film.

Leroux, Gaston. *The Phantom of the Opera.* Trans. Lowell Bair. New York: Bantam Classics, 1990. Print.

Lewis, David. "Dispositional Theories of Value." *Proceedings of the Aristotelian Society Supplementary* 63 (1989): 89–111. Print.

Lichtenstein, Donald R., Richard G. Netemeyer, and Scot Burton. "Distinguishing Coupon Processes From Value Consciousness: An Acquisition-Transition Utility Theory Perspective." *Journal of Marketing Theory* 54.3 (July 1991): 54–67. Print.

Lindsay, Vachel. *The Art of the Moving Picture.* 1915. New York: Modern Library, 2000. Print.

The Little Foxes. Dir. Austin Pendleton. Perf. Elizabeth Taylor, Maureen Stapleton. Victoria Palace Theatre, London, 11 March 1982. Theater Performance.

The Lord of the Rings. Dir. Peter Jackson. Perf. Elijah Wood, Ian McKellen. New Line Cinema, 2001–03. Film.

MacCabe, Colin, Kathleen Murray, and Rick Warner. *True to the Text: Film Adaptation and the Question of Fidelity.* Oxford: Oxford University Press, 2011. Print.

The Man from U.N.C.L.E. Dir. Guy Ritchie. Perf. Henry Cavill, Armie Hammer. Warner Bros., 2015. Film.

Meyer-Lee, Robert J. "Towards a Theory and Practice of Literary Valuing." *New Literary History* 6.2 (Spring 2015): 335–55. Print.

Monk, Claire. *Heritage Film Audiences: Period Films and Contemporary Audiences in the UK.* Edinburgh: Edinburgh University Press, 2011. Print.

Monty Python's Life of Brian. Dir. Terry Jones. Perf. John Cleese, Eric Idle, Michael Palin. HandMade Films, 1979. Film.

Murray, Simone. *The Adaptation Industry: The Cultural Economy of Contemporary Literary Adaptation.* Abingdon: Routledge, 2012. Print.

Noah. Dir. Darren Aronofsky. Perf. Russell Crowe, Jennifer Connelly, Anthony Hopkins, Paramount, 2014. Film.

Pamuk, Orhan. *The Museum of Innocence,* Trans. Maureen Freely. New York: Vintage, 2009. Print.

The Passion of the Christ. Dir. Mel Gibson, Perf, Jim Caviezel. Icon Productions, 2004. Film.

The Phantom of the Opera. Dir. Trevor Nunn. Perf. Michael Crawford. Her Majesty's Theatre, London, 12 October 1986. The Really Useful Group. Theater Performance.

_____. Dir. Joel Schumacher. Perf. Gerard Butler, Emmy Rossum, Patrick Wilson. Warner Bros., 2004. Film.

Pride and Prejudice. Dir. Robert Z. Leonard. Perf. Greer Garson, Laurence Olivier. MGM, 1940. Film.

Raw, Laurence, and Tony Gurr. *Adaptation and Learning: New Frontiers.* Lanham: Scarecrow, 2013. Print.

Ray, Robert B. "The Field of 'Literature and Film.'" *Film Adaptation.* Ed. James Naremore. 38–53. New Brunswick: Rutgers University Press, 2000. Print.

Smith, Adam. *An Inquiry into the Nature and Causes of the Wealth of Nations.* 1776. Books I–III. Ed. Andrew Skinner. Harmondsworth: Penguin, 1982. Print.

Thomson, David. "Gatsby Speaks." *New Republic* 7 May 2013. Web. 23 Mar. 2017.

Victoria. Dir. Daisy Goodwin et al. Perf. Jenna Coleman, Tom Hughes, Rufus Sewell. Mammoth Productions, 2016. Television.

Waters, Sarah. *Fingersmith.* London: Virago, 2002. Print.

Wharton, Edith. *The Age of Innocence.* 1920. London: Penguin Classics, 1996. Print

The Agency and Value of Remakes

The Television-to-Film Adaptation

KENNETH A. LONGDEN

The transition of popular television programs to film is a familiar route, but one that has had mixed results. The list of examples is extensive, but in terms of either commercial success or popularity, the experience is uneven. For Verevis ("Cinematic") or Klein and Palmer (1), the television-to-film remake is just one phenomenon that speaks of a larger and largely postmodern culture of repetition, a culture where texts are "variously described as adaptations, updates, homages, remakes, recyclings, re-creations, resurrections, sequels and spin-offs" (Verevis, *Remakes* 38) and more recently as "reboots" ("Cinematic"). What all of these descriptive terms suggest is that what seems to be a simple process of adaptation from one medium to another is anything but, at least in terms of how these films are received and understood by fans, audiences, and critics. There are potentially any number of reasons why some of these television-to-film transitions are deemed to be successful and why some are deemed to be failures, but agency—the reasons behind why some television programs make the transition to film—will be the focus here, because agency prompts questions of value.

In short, the process, the particular texts involved, the phenomena that attends the transition of television programs to film is largely determined and understood by a variety of factors, some of which we can discern through the terms applied. The term "remake," for instance, draws attention to both the act of repetition and of change and very often it is the changes made or perceived in these films that cause the most contention. Similarly, the term "reboot," as Verevis observes, is a term not only used to describe a specific and "legally sanctioned" kind of remake or adaptation, but also a text situated in a moment in time informed by digital and global dimensions. Reboots can also be understood as adding "new associations" to an "existing (serial) property" (Verevis "Cinematic"). In all of these respects, this essay will consider the television-to-film remake/adaptation as both an equivocal and desirous object—equivocal because their textual and cultural integrity is often questioned, and desirous because they can extend the viewing experience for eager audiences but also provide extra income for producers. In these respects, they are objects surrounded by issues of quality, even issues of authenticity and fidelity. These issues are nearly always related to concepts of value in adaptation. The argument proposed here is that the concept of value in the television-to-film remake/adaptation can largely be understood and informed by agency because agency serves to describe cultural, industry, textual, or economic factors.

Most recently, Guy Ritchie's remake of *The Man from U.N.C.L.E.* (2016) offers an example that not only highlights both the complex relationship between television and film, the history behind this process and phenomenon, but also issues of value and agency in remake culture and the television-to-film remake/adaptation in particular. From 1965 to 1968, the producers of the original television series, *The Man from U.N.C.L.E.*, released eight feature films alongside and at intervals during the television broadcasts. This was partly as a result of television networks exploring new forms for creating extra revenue (economic), partly as an attempt to imitate and potentially exploit the hugely popular James Bond franchise (cultural/textual), and partly as a novel attempt to reverse the then trend of "made-for-television-movies" (cultural/economic) (Davis 215). Further, a shortfall in feature film production in the 60s persuaded producers of the show as well as cinema exhibitors that there was room for these types of film adaptations or extensions. In all of these respects, we might therefore consider the recent Guy Ritchie remake of *The Man from U.N.C.L.E.* a very different animal both in film terms and in terms of adaptation. The agency behind the original television-to-film adaptations serves to provide a hitherto unexplored history of the television and film industry, but it also allows us to consider how such histories impact upon and help to describe the adaptations themselves (textual content).

The film versions of the original series were designed to keep the television series in the popular imagination while off-air, to exploit a market that seemingly enjoyed spy films (James Bond), and to keep the money coming in. Their value as adaptations lay primarily in these reasons. The films were what we would now call transmedia extensions of the story world (the series also spawned board games and other promotional material). However, the commercial and cultural pressures (agency) that influenced the original television to film remakes/adaptations of the series differed from those of the more recent remake/ adaptation, not least because the series is no longer broadcast or produced, but also because of other factors such as the absence of the original cast in the more recent version. As Ina Rae Hark points out in her essay "Translating Embodied Television Characters to Other Media" (2013): "When a television series is produced in a big-screen version, the challenges are substantially different [to other types of adaptations]. The appeal of a television series lies less in its narratives than in its continuing characters and general situation" (172). If Hark's theory is right, then we can add "star value" as an agency for these television-to-film remakes/adaptations. Clearly, therefore, while the original series and films pandered to this dynamic, the more recent film does not. The appeal of the new project, and its value, therefore, lies elsewhere, in it being something else. Consequently, the agency behind Guy Ritchie's more recent film remake of *The Man from U.N.C.L.E.* raises a host of questions regarding authenticity, fidelity, quality, and value. The retention of the original cast does not come into play, and the film does not promote or extend an existing television series.

In these respects, Blair Davis (1999) offers a useful description for more contemporary television-to-film remakes of television series that are no longer broadcast. Davis observes a distinction between MFTVMs (made-from-television movies), such as *Sex and the City* (2008, 2010), *Absolutely Fabulous* (2016), and *Twin Peaks: Fire Walk with Me* (1992), etc., and "*inspired by television movies*" (198), of which Guy Ritchie's *The Man from U.N.C.L.E.* (2016), *The Addams Family* films (1991, 1993), and the popular film franchise *Mission Impossible* (1996, 2000, 2006, 2011, 2015, 2018) are prime examples. The latter films, while initially trying to appeal to and therefore exploit a well-established nostalgia market, have since become valuable cultural products in their own right, although we can certainly see the nostalgia industry as an agency for some of these remakes. These latter remakes and adaptations also pay lip service to what Elsaesser (1998) sees as two related strategies of media repetition—"Serialization and Multiplication" (Verevis, *Remakes* 37)—strategies made even more significant in a globalized entertainment industry. As Verevis observes, "Remakes are often thought of as commercial products that repeat successful formulas in order to minimise risk and secure profits in the marketplace" (37), although another interesting feature of these latter films is their only cursory reference to the source texts. In these last respects, these films can be considered reboots—an authorized adaptation, but one that exists in and is informed by completely new conditions of production, reception, and knowledge.

The television-to-film transition/remake is not a consistent process or form, nor is it a recent phenomenon. Although this practice dates back to the 50s, when close bonds were forged between the television and film industries, as already observed, producing films based on television shows has been one of the major trends in American filmmaking, certainly since the

1990s, and one partly influenced by the lucrative nostalgia market, television and film reruns and channels dedicated to a variety of television histories in programmatic form. However, more recent contemporary examples also highlight some significant differences to the longer-established MFTVMs. Reworked film versions/adaptations of old television shows, with new casts, are often made up of a generation of directors and script writers who have grown up with the originals, and who have considerable influence over the adaptations. Self-reflexivity has become one of their most distinctive features. These shows hardly ever try to conceal their nature as a recycled product and even celebrate it. The value of this form of adaptation lies not so much in its fidelity to the source text, but in its potential as a cultural product and as a cultural phenomenon. By taking into account global and digital forces, these adaptations can not only be seen as part of a global millennial culture of "multiplicities and textual pluralities" (Klein and Palmer 1), but can also show a discursive shift where new values around such adaptations are seen as significant. As Verevis observes, new industry discourses frame "publicity more positively around a new film's 'remake' status by ascribing value to an earlier version" then positioning the new remake as a culturally, authorially, and technologically enhanced or transformed object with "value added" (Verevis "Cinematic").

Verevis' observations of film remakes in general, and television movies in particular, provides a commercial if not cultural logic for these adaptations, and as such, suggests that most of these recent television-to-film remakes, adaptations, reboots, should be accepted on their own terms. However, Davis' other remake format, MFTVMs (made-from-TV movies), such as *Sex and the City* (2008, 2010), *Absolutely Fabulous* (2016), and many others, seem to exist in different conditions and with different expectations surrounding them. Here, the concept of "value added" can also apply, but the dynamics are different. The transition of a television program to the big screen was and is largely seen as a sign of the program's commercial success and popularity, but issues of fidelity, at least to the original television experience if not the text itself, do seem to be important to audiences and therefore does play a part in their value. Their agency, however, does tend to be variable depending on cultural and historical factors.

These dynamics and variables have been pointed out by Richard Hewett in his study "Big Screen Spinoffs of British Sitcoms" (Hewett 2). The agency behind these particular adaptations are complex, but had much to do with the uncertain state of the British film industry in the early Seventies. British studios needed low-cost productions that "could guarantee audience attendance" (7). One of the solutions, according to Hewett, was to make a big-screen version of London Weekend Television's situation comedy *On the Buses* (1969–1973). At a cost of £90,000, the film went on to make more than a million pounds, two more movie adaptations, "and paved the way for a series of cinematic sitcom spin-offs" (Hewett 10). Although other British sitcoms followed the trend—*Steptoe and Son* (1972, 1973), *Bless This House* (1972), *Dad's Army* (1971), *Rising Damp* (1980), and others—and were equally commercially successful, they have since been regarded poor quality, largely parochial novelties. This said, their value to a flagging British film industry at the time was significant, although their value now may rest in their contribution to a film and television history. However, although this trend largely ended in the 1980s, it is worth noting that the sitcom-to-big screen adaptation has made a small comeback in more recent years. The reason for this return to the trend may lie in a pervasive remake culture or in other more contemporary factors to do with changes in the broadcasting industry.

The agency behind these adaptations is specific to a certain time and place, and something which is arguably embodied in the films/adaptations themselves. Clearly, these factors are not present or significant in other and more recent MFTVMs such as HBO's *Sex and the City* (2008, 2010) or the BBC's *Absolutely Fabulous* (2016). We could argue that the agency behind these more recent adaptations lies not only in a persistent economic sense of value, but also in a more empowered and influential fan culture whose loyalty and appetite for extending the viewing experience has helped encourage contemporary industry transmedia strategies. Although 1970s television programs such as *On the Buses* had a large fan base, their engagement with the television programs and the films was largely in the hands of producers, whose policy and practices, as explained here, were themselves largely determined and influenced by other commercial pressures. The various and imaginative strategies, platforms, not to mention the time and resources created and provided by producers to meet more contemporary audience/fan demands serves not only to highlight a new media landscape, but to nullify the once-common belief that these and other remakes were indicative that Hollywood had exhausted its creative potential. Contemporary MFTVMs, as Constandinides suggests, now exist as part of "the cultural logic of convergence culture" (24), and almost certainly of late capitalism. Taking into account convergence culture as well as the agency of fandom the value of these contemporary television-to-film remakes lies not only in their ability to empower an audience who often believe they have had a say in their production and remediation, but also in their potential to eradicate traditional hierarchies or boundaries that have often seen the adaptation or remake as inferior or secondary to the source text. In a contemporary global mediascape filled with remakes, reiterations, spin-offs, and reboots, the contemporary television-to-film remake or adaptation is perfectly capable of existing in its own right as a cultural event and also as a means of cultural negotiation.

Works Cited

Absolutely Fabulous: The Movie. Dir. Mandie Fletcher. Perf. Jennifer Saunders, Joanna Lumley, Julia Sawalha. Fox Searchlight Pictures, 2016. Film.

The Addams Family/Addams Family Values. Dir. Barry Sonnenfeld. Perf. Anjelica Houston, Raul Julia, Christopher Lloyd. Paramount Pictures, 1991, 1993. Film.

Bless This House. Dir. Gerald Thomas. Perf. Sidney James, Diana Coupland, Terry Scott. Rank, 1972. Film.

Constandinides, Coatas. *From Film Adaptation to Post-Celluloid Adaptation: Rethinking the Transition of Popular Narratives and Characters across Old and New Media.* New York: Continuum, 2010. Print.

Dad's Army. Dir. Norman Cohen. Perf. Arthur Lowe, John Le Mesurier, John Laurie, Ian Lavender. Columbia, 1971. Film.

Davis, Blair. "Made-from-Television-Movies: Turning 1950s Television into Films. *Historical Journal of Film, Radio, and Television* 29. 2 (1999): 197–217. Print.

Elsaesser, T.P., and Kay Hoffmann. *Cinema futures: Cain, Abel or Cable?* The Screen Arts in the Digital Age. Amsterdam: Amsterdam University Press, 1998. Print.

Hark, Inn Rae. "Translating Embodied Television Characters to Other Media." *Adaptations: From Text to Screen, Screen to Text.* Ed. Deborah Cartmell and Imelda Whelehan. 172–84. London: Routledge, 2013. Print.

Hewett, Richard. "Big Screen Spinoffs of British Sitcoms." MA paper, School of History of Art, Film and Visual Media, Birkbeck College, University of London, 2006. Print.

Klein, Amanda Ann, and R. Barton Palmer, eds. *Cycles, Sequels, Spin-offs, Remakes, and Reboots: Multiplicities in Film and Television.* Austin: University of Texas Press, 2016. Print.

The Man from U.N.C.L.E. Dir. Shane Ritchie. Perf. Henry Cavill, Armie Hammer, Alicia Vikander. Warner Bros., 2016. Film.

Mission Impossible. Dir. Christopher McQuarrie, Brad Bird, J.J. Abrams, John Woo, Brian De Palma. Perf. Tom Cruise, Jon Voight, Ving Rhames, Rebecca Ferguson. Paramount Pictures, 1996, 2000, 2006, 2011, 2015. Film.

On the Buses. Dir. Harry Booth, Brian Izzard. Perf. Reg Varney, Anna Karen, Doris Hare, Stephen Lewis. MGM/EMI, Hammer Films, 1971, 1972, 1973. Film.

Rising Damp. Dir. Joseph McGrath. Perf. Leonard Rossiter, Frances De La Tour, Don Warrington. ITC Entertainment, 1980. Film.

Sex and the City: The Movie/2. Dir. Michael Patrick King. Perf. Kim Cattrall, Kristin Davis, Cynthia Nixon, Candice Bergen. HBO Films/Warner Bros., 2008/2010. Film.

Steptoe and Son/Steptoe and Son Ride Again. Dir. Cliff Owen. Perf. Harry H. Corbett, Wilfrid Brambell, 1972/1973. Film.

Twin Peaks: Fire Walk with Me. Dir. David Lynch. Perf. Sheryl Lee, Ray Wise. New Line Cinema, 1992. Film.

Verevis, Constantine. "The Cinematic Return." *Film Criticism* 40.1 (2016): Z1.

_____. "Remakes, Sequels, Prequels." *The Oxford Handbook of Adaptation Studies.* 267. Oxford: Oxford University Press, 2017.

_____. "Remaking as Industrial Category." *Film Remakes.* 3–10. Edinburgh: Edinburgh University Press, 2005. Print.

"I make all things new"

Describing the Ongoing Adaptation in the Judeo-Christian Bible

ALLEN H. REDMON

Mel Gibson places an emotional encounter between Jesus (Jim Caviezel) and his mother, Mary (Maia Morgenstern), at the center of his plot for *The Passion of the Christ* (2004). Jesus has just been condemned to die. The Romans drape him with a cross and begin to lead him toward Golgatha. Jesus' most faithful followers—Mary Magdalen (Monica Bellucci), and John (Christo Jivkov)—watch their Messiah from a crowd that either hurls insults and rocks or watches in disbelief. Eventually, the path turns and the three followers can no longer track Jesus' movements in the way they have been. Mary turns to John and asks that he "help [her] get near him." John obliges, and the three run down an ally that puts them back in contact with Jesus at just the moment he stumbles to the ground for a second time. Mary stands frozen for a moment. The camera carries the viewer to an earlier memory presumably playing in Mary's mind: a young Jesus stumbles to the ground and his younger mother runs to comfort him. The memory moves the now older mother to run toward her son again. Gibson intercuts shots of both events as the Mary along the road to Calvary makes her way to her condemned son. In one image, Mary bends to help her adult and bloodied son to his feet; in the next, she lifts her young son. In both, she utters one phrase "I am here." The adult Jesus responds with his own declaration: "See, Mother, I make all things new."

This comment assigned to Jesus entertains a bit of irony and it does so in a couple of ways. For one thing, the encounter is not something new, and Gibson has carefully crafted the above sequence to ensure that it is not seen as something new. Each of the above events represent one of the fourteen

21

Stations of the Cross identified in Catholic liturgy. The moment shared between Mary and Jesus represents the fourth station of the cross. Virtually anyone familiar with this liturgy would recognize this moment as such. Those unaware of the liturgy might also sense a strange familiarity with the exchange. Gibson frames the entire sequence and saturates the colors in this scene in such a way that it looks like so many paintings of Mary's encounter with her son. The scene feels familiar even it if is not, which means it is not something new in the strictest sense.

Just as ironic is that a great many in the religious community praised Gibson's film for its accuracy rather than its ability to make something new. Gibson's film had, in fact, at least for a time, the highest stamp of authenticity possible: Pope John Paul II was reported to say upon seeing the film "it is as it was." Gibson's production company even began to use the statement in its marketing. The pope's private secretary, Archbishop Stanislaw Dziwisz, denied the pope ever praised the film in this way, but the denial never gained the attention the alleged approval did. Gibson's movie circulated with the pope's approval, and the presumed statement set the tone for how audiences perceived the film. Christians attended screenings of *The Passion* as though doing so were itself an act of worship, as though Gibson were taking them on a religious pilgrimage. For a great many, Gibson's film became something of "a fifth gospel," not something new.

Several excellent anthologies have given readers some reasons to reject the idea that Gibson is faithfully adapting Christ's passion. Kathleen E. Corley and Robert L. Webb, Zev Garber, or Paula Fredriksen offer three worthy examples. The common refrain is that Gibson's project contains serious historical inaccuracies. What these excellent discussions miss is the reasons why achieving historical accuracy should be avoided. In short, any attempt to recreate the biblical record faithfully, which is to say without modification or adjustments, violates the spirit of that record. The Judeo-Christian Bible is, after all, from cover-to-cover, an adaptation of itself. No one part of the literary text stands on its own. Gerald L. Bruns describes the situation as such: "despite its textual heterogeneity, [the Bible] can be read as a self-glossing book. One learns how to study it by following the ways in which one portion of the text illuminates another" (626). Bruns further explains that the biblical writers constructed the text to work in just this way. The parts are meant "to relate to one another reflexively, with later texts, for example, throwing light on the earlier, even as they themselves always stand in the light of what precedes and follows them" (627). In this way, the Judeo-Christian Bible frustrates attempts to reconstruct textual histories or to work "back to an original ... the whole orientation of Scripture is toward its future, not toward its past" (627).

When set within the concerns of adaptation studies, Bruns' description of the Judeo-Christian Bible captures an unexpected value of adaptation, one that challenges the presumed authority of any one textual expression, and that reveals the significance a series of adaptations of the same story can amass. The Bible routinely presents more than one version of its stories. This is true even of its most critical narratives, the creation, the gospel accounts, and the visions of the final judgment. Even in these decisive moments the formers of the Judeo-Christian Bible choose adaptation over strict adherence. As such, no one version can claim authority of the others. The most authoritative account, in fact, would seem to emerge between tellings, and only then temporarily. Every emerging story depends, after all, on the textual, cultural, and personal points of significance each reader brings to the texts. The only "faithful" adaptation is the one that participates in the ongoing process of adaptation the final form of the biblical record favors, a process that champions playful reinterpretation over reverential repetitions. In this way, the essence of the Judeo-Christian Bible is something never entirely expressed. Some alternate significance emerges the moment some new reader or community of readers sees it and expresses it. Every adaptation pushes the boundaries of the referents in any one expression in some new way. The only way to make the biblical record new, which is to say an extension of the biblical record, itself, is to reimagine rather than repeat what has been expressed. The essence of the biblical record always eludes readers; it waits to be realized anew in the next adaptation.

Adaptation scholars have for some time been working to shift discussions of adaptations in a way that moves the essence of a text, whatever that is, beyond any one textual expression. Robert Stam, for instance, provides scholars and spectators a reason to look for the essence of a source text somewhere beyond that text in his insightful essay "Beyond Fidelity: the Dialogics of Adaptation." One has to wonder, though, the extent to which Stam's ideas have reached popular audiences, and especially audiences of religious films. Some correlation between Stam's idea and the biblical record itself might help bring the former to the latter. Stam begins his insightful chapter by admitting that every text would appear to have some "fundamental narrative, thematic, and aesthetic features" (54). Those who know a text and recognize these features as essential are likely to feel betrayed should an adaptor not recreate those features in the adapted text. Disenchanted consumers might contend that a beloved text has been deformed, violated, vulgarized, or desecrated (54). Stam counters these claims by identifying some of the ways that a strict recreation of a source text is impossible. For one thing, readers have their own ideas of how a text should be realized. An adapter is highly unlikely to construct a text in the way a member of the audience would, and that same adapter has no chance of constructing a text in the various ways an audience of multiple people would construct it. Every audience member that knows a text enters the theater with his or her own idea of how a text should be realized. The adaptor cannot meet all of these expectations. Nor can an adapter bring a text in one medium into another without some adjustments. The images and ideas represented in a novel, for instance, cannot be realized in film without some alteration. The shift from the "single-track" medium of the novel to a "multitrack medium" of film introduces a variety of effects in the latter that would not be fixed in the former (56). Stam further explains, "The 'cinematization' [of a novel] generates an inevitable supplement" (55). The filmmaker makes choices the novelist never considers. As such, the final image on the screen is sure to differ from the image on the page.

Some might concede the difficulties of bringing every detail of an earlier text to an adaptation of that text. These more tolerant debaters might ask only that the essence of a text be preserved in an adaptation. Stam warns that this more general demand is just as difficult to meet as the more specific expectations above problematized. Where would one locate the "essence" of the text: "to the plot ... the physical descriptions of the characters ... the author's intentions ... to the style of a work" (57–58)? An adapter cannot conserve these any more than he or she can honor the expectations of every reader. The essence of a text is just as elusive. Stam explains: "The literary text is not a closed, but an open structure ... to be reworked by a boundless context ... which is seen through ever-shifting grids of interpretation" (57). Every adaptation provides a new grid of interpretation, which makes an anthology like the Judeo-Christian Bible particularly interesting for adaptation scholars.

The Bible is above all a collection of books and stories that encourages narrative exploration over preservation, and that locates the essence of its stories in the space between competing (or more accurately, complimentary) versions of these stories. No one version holds the whole of any one story. The full value of a text emerges across a series of texts that extend earlier versions in unexpected ways. One sees examples of this idea throughout the Bible, but a succinct example occurs in moments in the Gospel where Jesus tries to articulate abstract ideas like "the kingdom of God." Luke 13:18–21 offers one such example (all quotes taken from the New Revised Standard Version): "He said therefore, 'What is the kingdom of God like? And to what should I compare it? It is like a mustard seed that someone took and sowed in the garden; it grew and became a tree, and the birds of the air made nests in its branches.' And again he said, 'To what should I compare the kingdom of God? It is like yeast that a woman took and mixed in with three measures of floor until all of what it was leavened'" (104 NT). The idea of the kingdom of God does not reside in one articulation; rather, it emerges across multiple expressions. It is partially revealed by some comparison to a mustard seed, and additionally revealed in a second comparison to yeast. Its reality, its essence, emerges through adaptation. One sees this same strategy employed throughout the biblical record, and, with it, evidence that one value of an adaptation is the ability of each new expression to reposition the details of some earlier account in a new way.

Those who discuss cinematic adaptations of biblical stories rarely understand this point. A survey of the reviews given Darren Aronofsky's *Noah* (2014) demonstrates as much. Almost every review of *Noah* measured the extent to which Aronofsky and co-screenwriter Ari Handel remained true to the story in *Genesis*. For most, no matter how much equivalence there might be, there is not enough to call Aronofsky's film a faithful adaptation. James Berardinelli, for example, begins his review with the admission: "It's been a number of years since I read the story of Noah in *Genesis*, but I'm reasonably certain there are some discrepancies between the canonical account and the one related by director Darren Aronofsky." Matt Zoller Seitz registers the same caution to his readers: Aronofsky "made a few changes," writes Seitz. "Okay, more than a few. *Way* more" (Seitz). Seitz insinuates that Aronofsky somehow left his source text to produce his own story of Noah, and that such a move betrays something sacred. Seitz even suggests that Aronofsky honors the contemporary action genre formula more than the biblical record. Seitz explains that Aronofsky's *Noah* feels as much like another entry in the "the latest Marvel Comics epic," or something "along the lines of *Star Wars* or *The Matrix*," as it does a biblical epic (web). Ann Hornaday argues something similar when she writes that "the most distracting of Aronofsky's creations … the Watchers—fallen angels who roam the broken world like mournful, stiff-jointed behemoth," move like something at home in the *Transformers* franchise rather than in a biblical adaptation. Hornaday offers that Aronofsky's addition is sure to "give some literalists exegetical fits" (Hornaday). The frequency of some mention of fidelity is enough to question the extent to which contemporary audiences have abandoned some desire for textual conformity. The evidence would suggest they have not. Walter Metz's assessment might still be right: fidelity as it is conceived "in the general reader's sense, may be the life blood of the contemporary globalized Hollywood film industry" (211).

One could contend that some desire for fidelity is a problem of adaptation, but Robert Alter and Frank Kermode explain how it might just as well be a problem of how one approaches the biblical text. Alter and Kermode express regret for the way "our secularized times has opened a gulf between [the Bible] and our general literature" (2–3). They work to fill this gap by satisfying what they deemed at the time of their writing to be a new willingness to interpret the biblical texts "as they actually exist," rather than to analyze them through ancient and distant cultures and forms (4). Alter and Kermode's guide means to "attune" readers to a text that had been lost to them (6). Alter describes in *The World of Biblical Literature* a number of obstacles that modern readers need to overcome to be able to do this, most notably, a willingness to respond to authorless texts. Alter admits that most readers base their reading of a literary work on some notion of authorship, and that this tradition goes back as far as "the constructed authorial figure of Homer" (2). The authored text assumption does not hold for the Bible, though, in part, because "the biblical tradition itself went to great lengths to hide the tracks of the individual author … the writer disappears into *the* tradition" (2–3, emphasis mine). In more recent times, *the* tradition has become *a* tradition, which has only further buried the idea of the authored text. One might more properly consider the Bible "a still being authored text," which is to a say a text still coming into form. The fact that the Bible is a translated text would further support this idea. Every translation is but *a* translation that sits among other translations. As such, its form is being reimagined as often as it is being revered. Alter admits, "Scripture no longer speaks in one clearly prescriptive voice, but its resonances still carry into the recesses of spiritual and political imagination" (210). The text invites a literary imagination, too, one that adopts what Thomas Leitch describes as an active and "writerly" process that permits the opportunity "to become active producers of the text[s] they might otherwise be content to simply read" (18). Such a view should allow the Bible to reassert its literary sense, but other forces sometimes keep that from happening.

Remarkably, filmmakers might be one such limiting force. Those who turn to the Bible have done so with assurances that their films are faithful recreations of their source text. Richard Walsh explains why they had to do so: "many moviegoers considered the portrayal of religious subjects as irreverent in the early days of film"; filmmakers had to overcome this feeling by assuring audiences that their treatments were "authentic and reverent in manner" (2). Adele Reinhartz reminds readers of some of the more direct assurances of historical accuracy found in biblical films. Cecil B. DeMille, for instance, begins *King of Kings* (1927) with the declaration "The events portrayed by this picture occurred in Palestine nineteen centuries ago, when the Jews were under the complete subjection of Rome…" (1). Roberto Rossellini asserts the same level of historical accuracy in his *The Messiah* (1975): "I do not want to invent, or interpret, the Old and New Testaments—but just to present it in 'quotes.' I attempt to reconstruct everything accurately … *The Messiah* will thus present the historical Jesus as portrayed in the Four Gospels through an accurate development of the principle events of his life" (1–2). Reinhartz notes the impossibility of this standard, and the ways those who propose this standard refuse to live by it. "Almost all films," says Reinhartz, "invent speeches for Jesus, and sometimes they even attribute to Jesus … other New Testament personalities" (2). Reinhartz offers *The Greatest Story*

Ever Told (1965) as an example. The film fills the mouth of its cinematic Jesus with the words of the Apostle Paul. The filmmakers must expect those who know the Bible to recognize what they have done, which makes the decision to bill the film as accurate all the more interesting. Reinhartz considers this tendency as evidence that even those who assert exceptional historicity have no desire to deliver it.

What Reinhartz and others underestimate is the extent to which the Judeo-Christian Bible, as a piece of literature, abandons any sense of exceptional historicity. The text is always already looking to reconstitute, to adapt, historical elements. One might even identify this tendency toward adaptation as the essence of the biblical text. From this view, a film based on the Bible that merely reenacts a scene actually violates the biblical record more than those retellings that recombine and repurpose the elements they discover in their source text. One might even set the significance of a biblical adaptation according to its willingness to depart from its source so that something new can be discovered. To return to Walsh for moment, this is just the performance the most meaningful Jesus films perform. The most rewarding Jesus films from Walsh's point of view open space for interpretive acts that distinguish the Jesus on the screen from the audiences' "own ideologies, from orthodox Christianity, from historical Jesus research, and from the Gospels" (13). Walsh contends that today's pluralist and postmodern society demands such a Jesus be put on screen. Such films ask audiences not to accept or reject this Christ, but to "interpret" him, to participate in the ongoing story he occupies himself (14). A close look at the biblical record reveals that the Bible is already doing the very thing that Walsh champions: the Gospels are above all a laying alongside, a marking of the difference between imaginative adaptation and faithful exposition.

Interestingly, these are the kinds of adaptations of secular texts that tend to fare best at the box office. Deborah Cartmell and Imelda Whelehan describe the importance of additions to a source text, claiming, "It is the additions, not the deletions that are largely responsible for an adaptation's box-office success and critical success" (73). The authors cite the relative shortcomings of the first two Harry Potter films as an example of their claim. *Harry Potter and the Sorcerer's Stone* (2001) and *The Chamber of Secrets* (2002) failed to realize the financial or critical success of the later films, in part because they were too faithful to the corresponding books. In short, the films "tried too hard to *be* the book" (75). Emma French finds Shakespearean adaptations released in the 1990s meeting the same fate. Those that remained too faithful to their source, films like Michael Hoffman's *A Midsummer Night's Dream* (1999), failed to generate the critical or commercial success that those like Kenneth Branagh's *Much Ado About Nothing* (1993) or Baz Luhrmann's *William Shakespeare's Romeo+Juliet* (1996) achieved. French concludes that

Shakespearean adaptations rose or fell to the extent that they were at once Shakespeare's version of the story and not Shakespeare's version. A willingness to revere and depart from a canonical text created a "negative" space that allowed audiences to "make their own active reading" (19). One could, of course, create such space without the help of the adaptor. The point French makes, and, to some extent Cartmell and Whelehan, is that the most successful cinematic adaptations of beloved texts tend to insert this space into their narrative. The biblical text is just this sort of text. It offers readers and would-be-adaptors space for new ways of reading to emerge.

The Judeo-Christian Bible presents a group of texts that are endlessly adaptable, in part, because the narrative developed across the biblical text refuses to exist in any one place. It emerges in the space between varied expressions. A "faithful" adaptation of a biblical story, it would follow, must be as unfaithful to its source as it is loyal to it if the adaptation is to honor the spirit of ongoing adaption realized across the biblical narrative. This is just the sort of adaptive work one sees at play in the first two chapters of Genesis, the first book of the Bible. Genesis 1 begins with a story of creation. God sees some void and fills it. He speaks into existence light and darkness, the waters and the sky, the plants and the animals, and, ultimately, human beings. The account is orderly and it appears authoritative until the reader reaches the second chapter and encounters another version of creation. Genesis 2 covers the same acts, but creation unfolds more causally. The Lord God moves among creation and supplies what it needs when it needs it. The account tolerates a kind of intimacy not delivered in the first version. The second story does not deny any part of the first, but it does move in a different direction. Chapter two provides an alternate account, an adaptation.

Biblical scholars attribute the two versions of creation to the presence of two competing sources. Genesis 1.1–2.4a has, as Iain Provan reminds readers, been identified with source P; Genesis 2.4b–25 has been identified with source J. The different sources supposedly explain the different temperaments of each version: "P is liturgical in style, describing seven days of orderly development, whereas J gives us a much more straightforward narrative ... P portrays a transcendent God, one step removed from his creation and creating through words, whereas in J God is "hands on" in creation, fashioning much like a potter, or a smith, or a farmer" (59).

Source-based biblical scholars might be content to let these two versions sit alongside each other as evidence of competing sources. Such a view, though, would stifle the spirit of adaptation the presence of two stories can create. An adaptation scholar would work differently. The two versions would begin to read on each other in the way all adaptations read on each other. In keeping with Andre Bazin's discussion of the literary critic of the future looking back at a dramatic and cinematic adaptation of Steinbeck's *of Mice and*

Men, the adaptation theorist would not see in Genesis 1 and 2 two competing sources, but "rather a single [act] reflected" in two different expressions (26). Bazin further explains, "The chronological precedence of one part over another would not be an aesthetic criterion any more than the chronological precedence of one twin over another is a genealogical one" (26). The most gripping story would be the story between the two versions. Any subsequent adaptation of the story of creation would work as imaginatively as these two versions work with no one version trying to recreate the other. The value of an ensuing adaptation would be its ability to approximate the essence of the story that sits between all creation accounts.

The same spirit of adaptation continues to appear throughout the biblical record. John Goldingay claims that the narrative in Genesis–Exodus exists as a series of stories that are incomplete on their own. Rather than exist as self-contained accounts of historical facts, the individual stories operate "like the episodes in a mini-series, each [part of the "narrative extending from Genesis itself to the end of 2 Kings"] has a degree of completeness and closure … the parts are in some respects self-contained, but they also look beyond themselves" (10–11). As such, each part can be viewed as an adaptation, at least thematically, of some other part. For Goldingay, the primary interest of the story told across Genesis–Exodus is the development of the God character, which assumes different attributes as the story develops. Genesis 1 shows a character "in complete control"; Genesis 2–3 reveals a character that can also act "impulsively, experimentally, and collaboratively" (12). The same expansion continues across the whole of Genesis and Exodus: Genesis 4 uncovers a whimsical side to the God character; Genesis 12–50 assign new names to this character, which further develop an identity; Exodus 1–18 portray God as a warrior; Exodus 19–40 render the same character "a rule-maker" (12–15). From this view, the details of the narrative are important only to the extent that they reconsider earlier dimensions or propose new ones. Each mini-narrative becomes an extension, if not an adaptation of another. The discursive aim of Genesis and Exodus becomes one thing, namely, to develop the character of God. This character can only be viewed completely when the whole of the narrative is also in view. No one revelation reveals the whole story.

One can set The Psalms in the same understanding: no one psalm delivers the essence of what it describes; the whole of any one expression arises across similarly related expressions. This is the view Walter Brueggemann presents. Brueggemann believes that a proper study of The Psalms "need not … consider every single psalm on its own … [nor] … treat each psalm as an isolated entity to be interpreted as though it stood by itself" (17). Each psalm settles into one of three orientations, the psalms of orientation, of disorientation, and of new orientation. Together, and only really together, the three categories reflect "the realities of human experience" (20). These realities can be denoted "seasons of well-being," which accounts for the psalms of orientation, "seasons of hurt, alienation, suffering and death," which accounts for the psalms of disorientation, and times when "joy breaks through despair," which accounts for psalms of new orientation (19). Much of Brueggemann's study is a discussion of individual psalms against the reality he says they reveal. Psalms 8, 33, 112 and 133 serve as psalms of orientation. Psalms 13, 74, 86 and 137 serve as psalms of disorientation. Psalms 40, 65, 96 and 138 serve as Psalms of new orientation.

Two aspects of Brueggemann's study deserve particular mention as they relate to the argument this chapter makes. The first has already been acknowledged: the significance of any one psalm is realized in its relation to another, its participation in some larger framework. This is the same interdependent relationship the Judeo-Christian Bible accepts from beginning to end. Just as importantly, no one psalm inherently belongs to one category. The same psalm may fit in any one of the three categories "depending on the context and intention of the speaker," and, presumably, the reader (22). By way of example, Brueggemann traces the way in which Psalm 30 fits in all three categories. Verses 6 and 7 sing of orientation: "as for me, I said in my prosperity, 'I shall never be moved.' By your favor, O Lord, you had established me as a strong mountain" (NRSV). The next several verses, 7b–10, sing of disorientation: "You hid your face; I was dismayed. To you, O Lord, I cried, and to the Lord I made supplication: What profit is there in my death, if I go down to the Pit? Will the dust praise you? Will it tell of your faithfulness? Hear, O Lord, and be gracious to me! O Lord, be my helper." The last two verses, 10–11, of the Psalm 30 demonstrate new orientation: "You have turned my mourning into dancing; you have taken off my sackcloth and clothed me with joy, so that my soul may praise you and not be silent. O Lord my God, I will give thanks to you forever." Psalm 30 can be read from all three orientations. Its essence emerges between the various ways it can be read. Those who articulate each alternate expression move closest to the story's sense of ultimate significance, a significance one expression can never ever fully capture on its own. In other words, every reading of Psalm 30 depends on every other version for any meaningful sense of essence to emerge, just in the way every psalm depends on every other psalm for any sense of meaningful orientation to emerge.

This same interdependence exists in the four Gospels that constitute the thematic and structural center of the Judeo-Christian Bible. No one gospel captures the whole of the story on its own. The essence of the Christ in each gospel arises from the pairing of stories delivered across the four. This is an idea already recognized in biblical scholarship. Richard A Burridge, for instance, defines the gospels as "a form of ancient biography ... [able to provide] ... an ancient portrait gallery" (8). The notion of a gallery is particularly important to Burridge. No one portrait captures the whole of the subject portrayed in the depiction. The fullness of the subject emerges from the collection of diverse representations. Burridge explains: "when we put several different portraits of the same person together, we can see immediately both the diversity and continuity ... what we do *not* do is to superimpose the images one on the other, or seek to harmonize them into one single photograph, or reduce them to some simple lowest common denominator" (3). As Burridge's analogy relates to the Gospels, the scholar contends that each gospel assumes one of the faces of the four living creatures contained in Ezekiel's vision of God in the first chapter of Ezekiel 1:10: "St. Matthew has a human face, St. Mark the head of a roaring lion, St. Luke a patient-looking ox and St. John a sharp-beaked eagle" (25). The idea is that each gospel has its own existence, its own persona, but each gospel also depends in a canonical sense on the others. No one gospel is complete on its own.

While artists and scholars have tried to synthesize the four Gospel stories into one, Mel Gibson's *The Passion of Christ* is but one example, the impulse to synthesize the stories seems to contradict the significance of canonizing four different Gospel accounts. Francis Watson identifies some of the problems with this push toward synthesis. To begin with, the synthesis would only further close rather than open important aspects of the narrative of the life of Jesus that can exist. The four canonical gospels are but a small set of the number of gospels over the life of Jesus "in circulation during the first two centuries," and almost none of these were circulated as canonical texts (3). The decision to canonize the four gospels that were eventually canonized occurred after the fact so to speak, and only as a continuation of a reality that was even more exaggerated before canonization. More importantly, Watson insists "canonical status is a matter not for authors but for readers; it arises not from composition but from usage" (3). Readers decide what to "read and reread" (3). That decision assigns or denies canonical status. Whatever choices are ultimately made, the final set will tolerate an "irreducible plurality," which is to admit some "contradiction or tension" (4). The differences brought to the set by each version privilege a unique portrayal of the subject. One can identify a "Markan Jesus, a Mattean Jesus, a Lukan Jesus, and a Johannine Jesus, coexisting disharmoniously" (4). Opposition to this plurality, Watson reasons, resists the spirit of the four gospels, which develops through a contest of stories and the adaptive work such a contest assumes will take place.

The Judeo-Christian Bible as a whole creates a similar contest. No one story delivers any definitive essence. Any sense of essence to emerge does so across a contest of stories, and, again, it only holds for a moment. The anthology shows the ways in which every adaptation can relocate the essence of the text being adapted. The adaptation pulls the essence from a text (that might never have had an essence anyway) and moves it to some space between the two versions. The idea of the original and the copy are erased in a play that only knows approximation and estimation. Every adaptation opens a space where the essence of a story can be considered again, where an imaginative retelling can replace faithful exposition. It is in this space that the value of an adaptation is most chiefly realized, as it is in this space that the process of adaptation starts anew, and where all things are made new again.

WORKS CITED

Alter, Robert. *The World of Biblical Literature*. New York: Basic Books, 1992. Print.
_____, and Frank Kermode, eds. *The Literary Guide to the Bible*. Cambridge: Belknap Press of Harvard University, 1987. Print.
Bazin, Andre. "Adaptation, or the Digest of Cinema." *Film Adaptation*. Ed. James Naremore. 19–27. New Brunswick: Rutgers University Press, 2000. Print.
Berardinelli, James. "Noah: A Movie Review." *Reelviews Movie Reviews*, 28 Mar. 2014. Web. 20 Dec. 2016.
The Bible. The New Oxford Annotated Bible: New Revised Standard Version. Ed. Bruce M. Metzger and Roland E. Murphy. Oxford: Oxford University Press, 1991. Print.
Brueggemann, Walter. *The Message of the Psalms: A Theological Commentary*. Augsburg: Fortress Press, 1984. Print.
Bruns, Gerald L. "Midrash and Allegory: The Beginnings of Scriptural Interpretation." *The Literary Guide to the Bible*. Ed. Robert Alter and Frank Kermode. 625–46. Cambridge: Belknap Press of Harvard University, 1987. Print.
Burridge, Richard A. *Four Gospels, One Jesus?* 2nd ed. New York: Eerdmans, 2005. Print.
Cartmell, Deborah, and Imelda Whelehan. *Screen Adaptation: Impure Cinema*. Basingstoke: Palgrave Macmillan, 2010. Print.
Corley, Kathleen E., and Robert L. Webb, eds. *Jesus and Mel Gibson's* The Passion of the Christ: *The Film, the Gospels and the Claims of History*. New York: Continuum, 2004. Print.
Fredriksen, Paula. *On* The Passion of the Christ: *Exploring the Issues Raised by the Controversial Movie*. Berkeley: University of California Press, 2006. Print.
French, Emma. *Selling Shakespeare to Hollywood: The Marketing of Filmed Shakespeare Adaptations from 1989 into the New Millennium*. Hatfield: University of Hertfordshire Press, 2006. Print.
Garber, Zev, ed. *Mel Gibson's* Passion: *The Film, the Controversy, Its Implications*. West Lafayette: Purdue University Press, 2006. Print.
Goldingay, John. "Introduction to Genesis and Exodus." *Genesis and Exodus*. Ed. John W. Rogerson, R.W.L. Moberly, and William Johnstone. 9–34. Sheffield: Sheffield Academic Press, 2001, Print.
The Greatest Story Ever Told. Dir. George Stevens et al. Perf. Max von Sydow, Carroll Baker, Van Hefflin. George Stevens Productions, 1965. Film.
Harry Potter and the Chamber of Secrets. Dir. Chris Columbus. Perf. Daniel Radcliffe, Rupert Grint, Emma Watson. 1492 Pictures, 2002. Film.
Harry Potter and the Sorcerers' Stone. Dir. Chris Columbus. Perf. Daniel Radcliffe, Rupert Grint, Emma Watson. Warner Bros., 2001. Film.
Hornaday, Ann. "'Noah' Movie Review: Russell Crowe in a Slightly Different Take on the Biblical Story." *Washington Post* 27 Mar. 2014. Web. 2 Jan. 2017.
King of Kings. Dir. Cecil B. DeMille. Perf. H.B. Warner, Dorothy Cumming, Ernest Torrence. DeMille Pictures, 1927. Film.
Kranz, David L., and Nancy C. Mellerski, eds. *In/Fidelity: Essays on Film Adaptation*. Newcastle-upon-Tyne: Cambridge Scholars, 2008. Print.

Leitch, Thomas. *Adaptations and Its Discontents: From* Gone with the Wind *to* The Passion of the Christ. Baltimore: John Hopkins University Press, 2007. Print.

The Matrix. Dir. The Warchowski Brothers. Perf. Keanu Reeves, Laurence Fishburne, Carrie-Anne Moss. Warner Bros., 1999. Film.

Il Mesia [*The Messiah*]. Dir. Roberto Rossellini. Perf. Pier Maria Rossi, Mita Ungaro, Carlos de Carvalho. Orizonte, 2000, 1975. Film.

Metz, Walter. "A Tale of Two Potters." *In/Fidelity: Essays on Film Adaptation.* Ed. David L. Kranz and Nancy C. Mellerski. 9–12. Newcastle-upon-Tyne: Cambridge Scholars, 2008. Print.

A Midsummer Night's Dream. Dir. Michael Hoffman. Perf, Kevin Kline, Michele Pfeiffer, Rupert Everett. Fox Searchlight, 1999. Film,

Much Ado about Nothing. Dir. Kenneth Branagh. Perf. Branagh, Emma Thompson, Keanu Reeves. Renaissance Films, 1998. Film.

Naremore, James, ed. *Film Adaptation.* New Brunswick: Rutgers University Press, 2000. Print.

Noah. Dir. Darren Aronofsky. Perf. Russell Crowe, Jennifer Connelly, Anthony Hopkins. Paramount, 2014. Film.

Of Mice and Men. Dir. Gary Sinise. Perf. John Malkovich, Gary Sinise, Ray Walston. MGM, 1992. Film.

The Passion of the Christ. Dir. Mel Gibson, Perf, Jim Caviezel. Icon Productions, 2004. Film.

Provan, Iain. *Discovering Genesis: Content, Interpretation, Reception.* New York: Eerdmans, 2016. Print.

Reinhartz, Adele. *Scripture on the Silver Screen.* Louisville: Westminster John Knox Press, 2006. Print.

Rogerson, John W., R.W.L. Moberly, and William Johnstone, eds. *Genesis and Exodus.* Sheffield: Sheffield Academic Press, 2001. Print.

Romeo+Juliet. Dir. Baz Luhrmann. Perf. Leonardo DiCaprio, Claire Danes, Pete Postlethwaite. Twentieth Century-Fox, 1996. Film.

Scott, A.O. "Rain, Heavy at Times: Russell Crowe Confronts Life's Nasty Weather in 'Noah.' *New York Times,* 27 Mar. 2014. Web. 2 Jan. 2017.

Seitz, Matt Zoller. "Noah Movie Review & Film Summary." RogerEbertwww, 28 Mar. 2014. Web. 20 Dec. 2016.

Stam, Robert. "Introduction: The Theory and Practice of Adaptation." *Literature and Film: A Guide to Theory and Practice of Film Adaptation.* Ed. Stam and Alessandra Raengo. 1–52. Malden, MA: Blackwell, 2000. Print.

_____, and Alessandra Raengo, eds. *Literature and Film: A Guide to Theory and Practice of Film Adaptation.* Malden, MA: Blackwell, 2000. Print.

Star Wars. Dir. George Lucas. Perf. Mark Hamill, Carrie Fisher, Alec Guinness. Twentieth-Century Fox, 1977. Film.

Walsh, Richard. *Reading the Gospels in the Dark: Portrayals of Jesus in Film.* New York: Trinity Press International, 2003. Print.

Watson, Francis. *Gospel Writing: A Canonical Perspective.* New York: Eerdmans, 2013. Print.

Origin-Ality

Sources and Adaptations
of Francophone Voices

Rebecca M. Pauly

French-language literature and film now reflect in France and around the world a complex postcolonial diaspora of cultural diversity that invites exploration of ethnic, gender and aesthetic issues as well as the linguistic interface between standard French and the semantic and syntactical structures, the poetry and poetics, of indigenous languages. Francophone texts can be grouped and approached in a wide variety of categories. We are dealing with several levels of relationship between the sources and adaptations in play: first is lived experience involving valuable traditions of family, village, religion. The second involves movement away from the source, into an alien environment and often problematic encounters with French language and text. Sometimes it's a matter of discovering one's own value system in such an alien environment. Third is the critical response to the western culture imposed on individuals, and fourth involves a theoretical response to the confrontation between these alien value systems and those of the writer's origins and identities.

The next issue in play is the perspective of the writer, from the outside or the inside of the situation, including differences of nationality, race, sex, setting, social, economic and political circumstances. The author as authority and the writer's concomitant narrative voice thus align inside or outside the boundaries of a particular Francophone culture. The questions of difference, alienation, and foreignness including lack of cultural competence arise here.

Most Francophone voices are political, most revolutionary, from the "négritude" of Césaire, Damas, and Senghor in 1930s Paris to the globalizing theories of cultural identity posited by Glissant and Chamoiseau in this century. Many of these voices are caught between two or more cultural, ethnic or religious value systems. The displacement of the writer from the dialect and oral identity of a small indigenous patriarchal world to the progressively urban and sophisticated milieux of academia, a product of these writers' obvious natural creative and linguistic talents, results in a form of exile in the endless confrontation of self and other, present and absent, past and future. The most classic version of this dissection of identity is Cheick Hamidou Kane's *L'Aventure Ambiguë* (1961).

The Francophone writer's first adaptation, intransitive, is inevitably to that of the literary models that acquire the most value in the academic context. The subtle invasion of the creative self by constant exposure to canonic French literature and Eurocentric texts results in projects like Maryse Condé's Guadeloupean 1995 pastiche adaptation, transitive, of *Wuthering Heights*: *La Migration des Coeurs*, which could have also been inspired by the 1992 Kosminsky film with Juliette Binoche of Emily Brontë's 1847 *Les Hauts de Hurlevent*. Once the Francophone writer is immersed in the French language and culture, the next step is to negotiate the academic system (and not always literary); several famous Francophone writers completed engineering or medical school. The line is drawn between self and other with the decision to write in French. A primary source of value is to beat the dominant masters at their own game, and Francophone works are full of examples of indigenous protagonists besting the system, autobiographical narratives of triumph over adversity, especially through creative written expression and extraordinary linguistic aptitude.

At this point the paths diverge. The first response for many Francophone writers is poetic expression, the personal, individual, often ludic working of the French language, not just fabled surrealist poets like Césaire, Damas, and Senghor, but numerous other Francophone writers like Glissant (better known for their later prose works). The poetic voice presents a paradox, even an enigma, and Césaire upon his death in 2008 did not escape criticism for the impenetrable cosmic imagery in his 1939 *Cahier d'un retour au pays natal* (*Notebook of a Return to the Native Land*) which has an introduction by André Breton. These mainly Marxist critics claimed that Césaire's poetic expression is valueless on account of not being transparent enough to send his message to the world; its limiting the message to blackness denies the true world order of the working class. Furthermore, Césaire was criticized for lacking originality, for being swept up by the European surrealists of the day. Yes, he was in Paris, and yes, he knew Breton as well as other young black surrealist poets like Senghor and Damas. In fact, the sheer force and power of expression of these black poets foregrounds both their individual and collective mandate: to spread to the world their origins, their essence, their *négritude*, their

Antilles, their America, or their Africa, and to become a voice *of* their people and *for* their people.

Another valuable adaptation has been the reworking of the *griot* oral tales and fables in French by writers like Diop and Senghor or Kamanda. These texts have an archival value as translated accounts of ancient oral traditions in languages that often have no written form. (This essay does not attempt to address any relationship between modern French and the complex written texts of the great Mali Empire or written works of other ancient cultures in Africa.) Adaptations of oral tales to written French texts represent a reversal of the classic text-to-film adaptation, which moves from the written to the oral media. Animist dialect and characterizations pepper these French texts, which offer equivalencies to the narrative structures and indigenous lexicons, but no definitive translation. The African writer invades and dominates French in a reverse process of colonization, establishing the priorities of an indigenous ethos and diegesis, thereby adapting the French language to the writer's intrinsic needs. The affirmations of originality are multiple; nomination of native flora and fauna, customs and rituals, and proper names all resist adaptation into French and constitute a lexicon of authenticity in the text. These substantive markers stand as sentinels or lighthouses of autochtonic authenticity, markers of both indigenous identity and appurtenance to a native topos. Each culture has its surviving, if phonetically transcribed, semantic and lexical fields which resist the erosion of translation and thereby constitute a linguistic Monument Valley, a referential topography that enlivens the text. The vividly peopled world of the collective animist *griot* imagination generates echoes for the Western reader of other fabled constructs such as the works of Aesop or La Fontaine, but ultimately resists adaptive assimilation.

Of the many male coming-of-age rites of passage autobiographical narratives that distinguish black Francophone literature (including works by Dadié, Laye, Oyono, Kane, Zobel, and Chamoiseau), the motivation to recount one's experiences in a world language partially compensates for the impossible distance and sense of loss the writer feels. It is not just translation but any textual adaptation of the authentic self-in-the-world, in play, at risk. Dadié's persona in his 1959 *Un Nègre à Paris (A Negro in Paris)* offers an intriguing outsider's perspective on Paris and the French which falls into the great satirical tradition of works like Montesquieu's 1721 *Lettres Persanes*, and represents the reverse of the viewpoint that Defoe's 1719 *Robinson Crusoe* proposes. Not all these black autobiographic narrators triumph in their separation from their origins; Kane's Samba Diallo is torn apart in his *Ambiguous Adventure* (1961) of passing from his village Islamic Coranic school in the bush to university circles in Paris; Laye in *L'Enfant noir* (1954) never supersedes the anguish of abandoning his matriarchal heritage; Oyono's Toundi in *Une vie de boy* (1956) perishes as punishment for satirizing the white colonial society; Zobel's José in *Rue Cases-nègres (Sugarcane Alley)* (1974) must adapt to the white *békés'* world without his mentors or family. Stepping out on one's own and challenging linguistic and cultural hegemonies has its advantages but its pitfalls as well.

Films made from these rites of passage autobiographical texts reverse the move from lived experience to written account by reconstructing those scenes with actors for the camera. The films of Zobel's and Laye's novels return to their origins in a number of ways, first using creole and other indigenous dialects in their dialogue, and secondly enacting a thematic of return to the source in the selection of the actors, particularly in *Rue Cases-nègres* (1983), with Douta Seck and Darling Legitimus, both Senegalese actors, in lead roles. The 1995 film of Laye's *L'Enfant noir (The Dark Child)* is particularly intriguing as a restitution of sources that takes the adaptation process full circle. When Laurent Chevallier set out to make the film some forty years after the 1953 publication of the novel, he was directed to Kouroussa, Laye's village, where he found life virtually unchanged from the descriptions in the text. And moreover, the Camara family would go before the camera to reenact the privileged adventure of this first-born of seven brothers, the only one to have left, become educated and learned French. So a nameless inexperienced village child became a perfectly transparent Baba for the film. In fact all the lead roles are interpreted by actors with the same names as the characters from the book which appeared when Laye was 25 years old, but which was set fifteen years before that when he was just ten. This remarkable return to the source with the film version creates a unique juxtaposition of authenticity and adaptation, closing the gap, yet forcing the family as actors to relive the exile and anguish of the original group.

In many of these texts, the adaptation aspect remains at the level of mastering the foreign language, its grammar, syntax, pronunciation. In the film of *Sugarcane Alley* (aka *Black Shack Alley*) José (Gerry Cadenat) distinguishes himself with his intuitively poetic expression in French, while the grown ambitious Carmen (Joël Palcy) struggles with entry-level writing. Like most of the people in these works, he is illiterate, a result of the lack of educational opportunities, but also as a participant in the oral traditions from African griot to New World creole.

Conversely, Francophone expression offers liberation and a voice of freedom to many writers, especially Islamic female voices. The journey into otherness away from the source offers expression of the writer's origin-ality, while at the same time threatening the integrity and authenticity of lived experience in a triple adaptation: from life to text, from mother tongue to learned linguistic system, from original space to successive displacements. The outcry against the brain-drain of the intellectual elite of an indigenous

culture is often justified; many of these talented writers leave, drawn to cos-
mopolitan centers in France and elsewhere, and few return; in fact they create
in their displacement in time and space an impossibility of re-integration
into the cultures of their birth. For some who have escaped multiple forms
of humiliation and injustice, familial and societal, there is simply no question
of return. Others have used their fame and power to become political activists
and legendary figures: Césaire as mayor of Fort-de-France and then deputy
from Martinique to France's Assemblée Nationale; Senghor as the first President of the newly independent Senegal; Diop as his ambassador to Tunisia;
the black martinican Frantz Fanon as a major player in the Algerian war.
Women as well have become not just internationally acclaimed writers and
professors; Aminata Sow Fall for example has been for decades a shaping
force in the educational and cultural ministries of the government of Senegal.

Most emphatically the Islamic female voices address the world in adapting to freedom unheard of in their places of origin; even the brilliant and relatively liberated daughters of French-speaking schoolteachers take up the
cause of the oppressed women of Islam, veiled, confined, illiterate, impover-
ished, silenced, beaten, abandoned for new wives. The spirit of change has
been expressed across dozens of texts, largely novels, where the narrative
becomes the voice of rebellion. Beginning with Mariama Ba's *Une si longue
lettre* (*So Long a Letter*) (1979) from Ramatoulaye to Assiatou, their different
fates are essentially a composite of her own story. This chorus continues
through Djebar, Sebbar, and up to Marjane Satrapi, who experienced her own
lived adaptations, first to revolution, then exile, freedom, and a return to
Iran. The experiences were adapted in the 2003 graphic novel *Persepolis*.

Not only women writers have taken up the cause of disseminating these
Islamic stories in French to the world; both male Moroccan novelists Driss
Chraibi and Tahar Ben Jelloun have demonstrated in many of their works an
incredible sensitivity and empathy in response to the experiences of women
in their culture, in texts ranging from slapstick hilarity to detailed depictions
of gut-wrenching suffering and humiliation. Two of Ben Jelloun's novels,
L'Enfant de sable (*The Child of Sand*) (1985) and *La Nuit sacrée* (*The Sacred
Night*) (1987), not only adapt a Moroccan Islamic tale to the French language,
but they offer complex irony; in the first book the story features a woman
forced to masquerade as a man to please her lunatic father, thus imprisoned
in her male freedom; and in the second volume her suffering and destruction
become inevitable when she finally espouses her authentic female identity,
both internally and externally, and freedom becomes vulnerability.

Perhaps it is Assia Djebar (a carefully chosen pseudonym meaning
"accompanying observer of Mohamet's intransigence") who sums up the many
narratives chronicling the reaction of so many countries to colonial domi-

nance and exploitation, and the formulation of new narratives in their place. A scene in *L'Amour, la fantasia* (1992) depicts the city of Algiers lying in the morning light in 1830 like a beautiful woman reclining, awaiting the inevitable advances, penetration, and dominance of the French armed forces lying just off shore in the harbor. One senses that at that moment the world tilted on its axis forever, and we are still living the consequences. The presumption on the part of the colonial powers of submission and servitude exists alongside colonialism's benefit: it brought to millions of people around the globe access to a dominant world language. The elite of the indigenous writers who mastered it and sent it back to the world constitutes an alternative system of values and a new kind of dominance.

In closing I would like to mention the reverse perspective of adaptation of several Francophone writers, including two Nobel Laureates, who although enshrined in white European canonic literature have come to represent for the world not just peripatetic cultural diversity but extraordinary sensibilities and perspectives on the human condition. Camus, Duras, and Le Clézio all foreground in their works consciousness-raising experiences of difference, exclusion, exile and alienation, and the esthetic and philosophical consequences of their cultural pluralism. These are in fact the same issues of alienation and exclusion that preoccupy minority writers in European French cultures, the voices of "Afrique sur Seine." This last group in fact suffers a painful duality intrinsic to their origins, for they are not the immigrant observers of France that previous generations produced; they are French citizens born on European French soil, a step closer to the heart of their irreducible difference than any French citizen. In a work like Abdel Kechiche's film *L'Esquive* (2003) we witness the adaptation of classic French theater, Marivaux's 1730 *Le Jeu de l'amour et du hasard* (*The Game of Love and Chance*), into the largely beur Maghreb classroom of the Paris *banlieue*. The irony is in the reverse *mise en abyme* as the students in turn adapt the classic French text into their world, rehearsing in the open, staying in character and even in costume, as they in turn become the play-within-the-play.

Finally, there is a mirror doubling of global ethnicities and identities in the world corpus of Francophone literature, as texts decontextualize lived experience and offer a new landscape of centers and peripheries, as Glissant and Chamoiseau call them in *Quand les murs tombent* (Editions Galaade, 2007), within the referentiality of language, to be reconstructed by each reader. Ironically most of the readers of these texts are not the characters within, nor do they know the settings of these writers' origins. But since difference is meaning, as the Franco-Syrian linguist Emile Benveniste stated long ago in *Problèmes de linguistique générale* (1966), these texts constitute a project of cultural and linguistic adaptation to discover new value systems that would seem to be inexhaustible, especially as it confronts not just the inevitability of adapting the self to globalization, but the necessity at the same time of affirming the authenticity and relevance of one's origin-ality.

WORKS CITED

Ba, Mariama. *Une si longue lettre*. Paris: Le Serpent à Plumes, 1979. Print.
Ben Jelloun, Tahar. *L'Enfant de sable*. Paris: Seuil, 1985. Print.
____. *La Nuit sacrée*. Paris: Seuil, 1987. Print.
Benveniste, Emile. *Problèmes de linguistique générale*. Paris: Hachette, 1966. Print.
Brontë, Emily. *Les Hauts de Hurlevent* [*Wuthering Heights*]. Trans. Frédéric Delebecque. 1847. Ebooksgratuitswww, 2006. Web. 9 Mar. 2017.
Césaire, Aimé. *Cahier d'un retour au pays natal*. Paris: Présence africaine, 1956. Print.
Chamoiseau, Patrick, and Edouard Glissant, *Quand les murs tombent*. Galaade, 2007. Print.
Condé, Maryse. *La Migration des cœurs*. Paris: Robert Laffont, 1995. Print.
Dadié, Bernard. *Un nègre à Paris*. Paris: Présence Africaine, 1959. Print.
Djebar, Assia. *L'Amour, la fantasia*. Casablanca: EDDIF, 1992. Print.
L'Enfant Noir. Dir. Laurent Chevalier. Perf. Baba Camara, Madou Camara, Kouda Camara. ONACIG, 1995. Film.
L'Esquive (aka *Game of Love and Chance*). Dir. Abdel Kachiche. Perf. Osman Elkharraz, Sara Frestier, Sabrina Quazani. Lola Films, 2003, Film.
Kane, Cheikh Hamidou. *L'Aventure ambiguë* [*The Ambiguous Adventure*]. Paris: Julliard, 1961. Print.
Laye, Camara. *L'Enfant noir*. Paris: Pocket, 1953. Print.
Marivaux, André. *Le Jeu de L'Amour et du Hasard* [*Games of Love and Chance*]. 1730. Paris: Hachette, 2016. Print.
Montesquieu, Charles de. *Lettres Persanes, 1721*, Paris: Larousse, 2011. Print.
Persepolis. Dir. Vincent Paronnaud, Marjane Satrapi. Perf. Chiao Mastrioanni, Danielle Darrieux, Cathérine Deneuve. 2.4.7. Films, 2007. Film.
Satrapi, Marjane. *Persepolis*. Paris: L'Association, 2000–2003. Print.
Sugarcane Alley (aka *Black Shack Alley*). Dir. Euzhan Paley. Perf. Garry Cadenat, Darling Legitimus. Neff Diffusion, 1983. Film.
Wuthering Heights. Dir. Peter Kosminsky. Perf. Juliette Binoche, Ralph Fiennes, Janet McTeer, Paramount, 1992. Film.
Zobel, Joseph. *La Rue Cases-Nègres*. Paris: Présence Africaine, 1974. Print.

"No one ever sees the Angel"

Adapting The Phantom of the Opera

LESLIE MCMURTRY

There are many ways that interpretations of *The Phantom of the Opera* (1910)[1] lend themselves to the Gothic mode. The plethora of adaptations over the past century,[2] with varying degrees of similarity to the source text, have taken on a life of their own. Criticism of *POTO* is still relatively underdeveloped; as Ann C. Hall notes, while the novel has been critiqued through its associations (mainly its links to Gothic fiction and its Freudian and Jungian interpretations), these readings tend to "diminish" author Gaston Leroux's skill and readers' enjoyment (Hall 2).

This chapter will not focus on Freudian or Jungian readings, but instead I hope to explore an element of the Leroux novel and the adaptations that has been overlooked, and in so doing, give some suggestions as to what qualities have contributed to making this story so enduring. Is Cormac Newark right when he argues that *POTO* resists adaptation as well as definition (75)? One might start this exploration with the Phantom of the title himself, Erik. Part of Erik's giftedness as Leonard Wolf refers to it is his musical acumen as represented and interpreted through his voice, whereas his monstrosity is expressed through his physical repulsiveness (2). One particularly powerful axis in *POTO* is between the hideous, decayed appearance of Erik and his astonishingly beautiful, ethereal voice. Ann C. Hall brings this disjunction beyond just the character of Erik and suggests that the novel and adaptations "require ... a kind of double vision," or indeed, an engagement with two senses that do not always harmonize (3). Erik's physical ugliness is horrible, but he can use his vocal/musical beauty/genius for good or for evil.

"Everything is divided; everyone is tortured" in *POTO* (Hall 4). As we define *POTO*'s and Erik's Gothic engagement with the senses of sight and sound that do not always harmonize, we underline a defining theme of Gaston Leroux's fiction—that appearances can never be relied upon. Why is *POTO* so attractive and so successful across media and time? Those who undervalue the source text and target texts would argue that it is neither, a mere "spectral palimpsest of textual phantoms" (Shah "No Ordinary Skeleton" 9). Such criticism ignores its longevity and its ability to cross and re-cross different strands of media. Some critics do not see any specific or special "value" in the text, likening it more to a fad or a fluke or regarding it as unworthy of its longstanding popular appeal, much less any critical analysis. I would argue that there are a number of dynamics in the core of the *POTO* story that emerge from the source text, the 1910 Leroux novel, but are continually reinvented in the subsequent adaptations, which make it unique and help explain its endurance.

Firstly, I would point to the characters of *POTO*, particularly the three principals (Erik the Phantom, Christine Daaé, and Raoul de Chagny), though also characters like the Daroga and Madame Giry. The ambiguity of these characters sets them apart from their counterparts in Leroux's contemporary writing in the traditions of both French *romans populaires* and English-language Gothic horror/melodrama. While not ciphers, these characters lend themselves to shades of grey in interpretation. Is Christine a fainting damsel in distress or a feminist? Is Raoul a hero, a chauvinist bully, or an inexperienced young man? Is the Phantom a Romantic anti-hero or an unredeemable freak, whose "soul [is where] the true distortion lies" (Hart and Stilgoe)? All of these interpretations can easily be inferred from Leroux's text and are refracted in varieties of re-combination in target texts. While the principals themselves are echoes of the broader theme (or Ur-text) of Beauty and the Beast (Åarne-Thompson folktale type 425C), they have enough individuality to make *POTO* its own recognizable story without drifting away into the realm of myth.

Secondly, the theatricality of the setting of *POTO*—within the Paris Opéra—is exceptionally suited to Leroux's determination to expose the layer below the surface of society's masks. It is also wholly appropriate for creating *mise en scène* and plays-within-plays in audio-visual adaptations such as those on stage, on television, and on film, and represents a unique challenge for media like audio drama. The centrality of music to the core themes also makes most adaptations eminently performable. The theatrical setting of *POTO* also gives license for the story to exhibit larger-than-life emotions and present higher stakes than stories outside of "melodrama." Indeed, while a "high drama of uncommonly beautiful people histrionically acting out a familiar tale of passion, corruption and revenge" (McCabe and Akass 5) could describe *POTO*, the fact that it actually describes the typical *telenovela* plot underlines how vastly appealing *POTO*'s "basal feelings" (Lippert 88) might be.

With this in mind, we will examine the different strategies employed in a sample of the many adaptations that have followed in the wake of *POTO*'s publication in 1910: the 1925 Universal silent film, the long-running Andrew Lloyd Webber musical (1986–) (and its 2004 film), and the audio drama adaptation (2007) from Big Finish Audio Productions. Although sound drama is frequently marginalized as "television without pictures," audio drama is an excellent mode of adaptation due to its inherent conduit directly into the mind, imagery, and emotion. The value that Leroux saw in his tale—beyond that of entertainment—was in highlighting duality while presenting ambiguous characters caught up in grand spectacle framed by music that was, to him and his original audience, familiar. Gauging this through how the adaptations represent the duality of the Phantom himself (sight vs. sound) and how they interpret characters' ambiguity, I present three strategies adaptors have used. If we follow Hazette's formulation of adaptation as "an ideologically charged journey during which archetypal structures and figures are dynamically translated and surreptitiously transmitted," we recognize that *POTO*'s unique attractions create great room for innovation (59). Through this lens, I acknowledge Newark's notion of resistance to adaptation while presenting the many successes achieved by the adaptations.

Sight versus Sound in Leroux

POTO's author, Gaston Leroux (1868–1927), is principally known in France for creating detective Joseph Rouletabille in *The Mystery of the Yellow Room* (1908), though Leroux wrote an immense amount of journalistic copy, dozens of novels that crossed genre boundaries, and stage plays. Despite a general belief in visuality as the supreme sense of the Gothic, sound is frequently evoked by Gothic of many kinds. "Ghosts are eminently audible in Gothic" for "sound without source suggests spectrality" (van Elferen 429, 430). Leroux, like many celebrated writers of the Gothic, was essentially middle class in his beliefs and politics, yet, as Renée Faubion notes, the text is unusually good at ridiculing, at failing to tip its hand. This seems to be underlined by a strategy of disconnect between the evidence of sight and the evidence of hearing.

Duality defined Leroux. Robert de Flers wrote in *Figaro* in his review of Leroux's 1911 stage play (by far his most successful), *L'Homme qui a vu le diable:* "How can M. Gaston Leroux, who is one of the cuddliest and jolliest men I know, be so cruel as to create such nightmares?" (Lamy 55). If Leroux was aware of the dualities in life, he also understood the importance of using sound in his works. Crucially, in *POTO*, Erik is heard by many, but almost never seen. "Exactly!" exclaims the young dancer Meg Giry, "You don't see him, the ghost! My mama has never seen the ghost, but she has heard him" (Leroux[3] 22). "All things considered, who had seen him? After all, the opera was full of men in black evening dress who weren't ghosts. But this particular set of dress clothes had a characteristic feature: it was a skeleton" (15). Much of the humor of the novel is derived from Madame Giry, the concierge of Erik's special box, and her adventures with the invisible but charmingly polite ghost, infuriating the opera's managers. Giry, like Christine, emphasizes that Erik's voice is both emphatically that of a man but also that it sounds "sweet": "'He has the voice of a man, oh! A sweet-sounding man's voice!'" (Leroux 59).

In all versions of the story, Erik and Christine connect first through sound not sight. The Angel of Music, as described by Christine's father, is an aural being only: "No one ever sees the Angel; but he is heard by those who are meant to hear him" (Bair 48). Raoul notes, "I understood all when I learned that Christine had not yet seen him" (Bair 199). Erik is not the only one for whom sound may paint an entirely different picture than sight. From Raoul's perspective, "Christine's angelic and soulful voice might be hiding the heart of a whore" (Hall 23) through the first half of the book—a salient example of interpretations of this character, who may be condemned as a chauvinist for his double standards or merely understood as a jealous, ardent lover. Sound and its perception transforms the callow Raoul into an eavesdropper, something he shamefully admits later (Leroux 35).

In Poe's "The Facts of the Case of M. Valdemar" (1845), "the body does not decay but it, or something, can speak, uttering the impossible words 'I am dead'" (Botting 122). Leroux's Erik responds in similar ways, with his costume at the Shrovetide masked ball declaring, "Don't touch me! I am Red Death stalking abroad!" (Leroux 123) Erik's physical form represents skeletal decay, yellowing flesh, the absence of eyes, nose, and lips, all of which he tries to correct with masks and smart evening clothes. He is described many times as having a "death's-head," "and *the absence* of the nose was a horrible thing *to see*" (Leroux 16, emphasis original). Erik's eyes are "two great black holes like those in skulls" and his hands smell of death (ibid). When he makes a surprise appearance at an opera gala night, astonishing all who see him, "each person [who saw him] thought that if the dead might someday return to sit at the table of the living, they could not have shown a more macabre visage" (Leroux 41). Erik's bizarre "living death" appearance recalls syphilis, porphyria, and exhibited freaks (such as John William Coffey, the Living Skeleton Dude).

Almost immediately after publication, depictions of *POTO* began to emphasize Erik's ugliness over his beautiful voice. Edmond Claris, a friend of Leroux's, advertised his newest novel, "*Un nouveau roman tout plein de cette délicieuse inquiétude qui fait frisonner le lecteur et qui évoque l'image effrayante, spirituelle et doulouresement humaine"* (quoted in Shah "Publication" 13). The first image of the Phantom, the cover by Adolphe Cossard of the 1910 publication, which directly inspired Marcel Allain's *Fantomas* (1911), is both hideous and droll, depicting a grinning skull with wispy hair. Cossard's illustration might reference the "frightening image" suggested by Claris but not the "spiritual and bittersweetly human" aspect he described. Thus, almost from the beginning, a dual vision/hearing was needed to interpret the Phantom, with the visual receiving more emphasis. How would Erik fare in target texts?

The Phantom of the Opera
and Adaptation Studies

The Phantom of the Opera could really be said to "live" in its adaptations. Sevgi Şahin and Laurence Raw suggest that students can benefit from creating their own adaptations in a pedagogical context because they "learn how their subjectivities are inscribed" and that "the art of textual rewriting can help" us understand how experiences are constructed (72). I would argue the many adaptations of *POTO* over the past century provide a window into contemporary subjectivities and social, moral, and political constructions of identity.

It is also worth noting that all of the adaptations examined here are in English (as is much of current scholarship) rather than French, implying another level of (linguistic) translation. Translation "is not only a linguistic process; it involves more formal operations" (Şahin and Raw 74). Given the multitude of adaptations of *POTO*, I have selected four target texts whose way of responding to Erik in depicting him with regard to sound and sight reveal much about their approaches. As stated earlier, critics sometimes dismiss *POTO* as an extension of the Beauty and the Beast fairy tale/myth, with Christine standing in for Beauty and Erik for the Beast. While *POTO* does share some similarities, the story as written by Jeanne-Marie Leprince de Beaumont in the eighteenth century differs substantially from Leroux's novel. For example, in Beaumont, we may wonder whether Beauty will fulfill her promise to the Beast to return and see him after he releases her, as we wonder whether Christine will return to see Erik after having surreptitiously gotten engaged to Raoul. However, in Beaumont's moral instructional tale, Beauty's task is to look past the superficial ugliness of the Beast to see that his kindness, goodness, virtue, and sweetness are more important than any other possible qualities in a husband (Murphy 240). Erik differs from the dim-witted, ugly but virtuous Beast in that his qualities of kindness, goodness, virtue, and sweetness are debatable, and Christine differs from Beauty in that she is not looking for a husband but wants to be a singer and continue her career.

Unorthodox approaches to adaptation studies as evinced by Bruhn and Ingvarsson might be of use regarding the value of adaptations of *POTO*. Bruhn suggests that "any rewriting or adaptation of a text is always influencing the original work," with the most obvious way that a target text changes the source text through changes in readers' perceptions (70). It is undeniable that the source text of *POTO*, the 1910 novel, has been "re-written" in relation to the globally popular stage adaptation by Andrew Lloyd Webber (1986) and its subsequent "re-make" as a film (2004). A similar target-to-source text relationship is at work to that of H.G. Wells' 1898 novel *The War of the Worlds* and the much more famous and influential 1938 radio drama adaptation by Orson Welles. As Ingvarsson notes, even though it is obvious Wells' purpose in 1898 was not to produce an adaptation of a 1938 radio drama, "the radio play nevertheless exerts an intertextual influence on the novel" (266). The other adaptations discussed here do so as well, to a lesser extent.

Strategy I: No Sound—Phantom of the Opera *(1925)*

The 1925 Universal film is the first surviving filmic adaptation of *POTO* that we have.[4] In it, Erik was portrayed in what remains the most iconic performance of the role by Lon Chaney, Sr. Interestingly, Chaney was no stranger to filmic adaptations of novels, his break-out role considered to have been in *The Penalty* (1920), a filmic adaptation of Gouverneur Morris' Gilded Age source text. There are obvious parallels between the anti-hero of *The Penalty*, maimed gangster Blizzard, and Erik the Phantom. As is well known, Chaney was the child of deaf and mute parents and learned early "to use his body much as a dancer would, to create not only situation but also mood" (Anderson 15). Thus, while Chaney began his show-business career in vaudeville, he was particularly well suited to the world of silent films. While he did have a strong and adept voice,[5] as proved by his one and only talkie, the remake of *The Unholy Three* (1930), he was not a trained singer, and "the springs, clamps, and disks that distorted" his face while playing Erik "would certainly have rendered articulate speech all but impossible" (Prawer 218).

Thus the strategy for this adaptation was enforced by technology; how to portray the tender and human side of Erik without the ability to depict his voice? The film had to rely on intertitles, the vicissitudes of musical accompaniment or soundtracks dictated by where it was being shown,[6] and Chaney's performance. While the musical accompaniment would have been different depending on where the film was shown, it is interesting to note that while in Leroux's original novel, Erik plays the organ and sings, the silent film permits only his visually arresting organ playing. "The immensity of the sound of a pipe organ seems well-suited to a horror film's sense of monumentality" post–*Phantom of the Opera* (Brown 5). Clearly, the filmmakers believed the *action* of playing the pipe organ, especially in the crucial unmasking scene, was powerful and important enough to retain in the silent adaptation. Moreover, this early filmic adaptation of the source text enforced the now-iconic *image* of the Phantom playing the pipe organ over and above any other scenes from the novel of his music-making.

Chaney was extraordinarily well placed to depict Erik's pathos and perhaps even the beauty of his voice through visual performance alone. Chaney "remained one of the most consistent box office attractions of the 1920s specifically by playing freaks," creatures like Erik and Quasimodo who "defy anatomical description" (Blyn 37). Though makeup became Chaney's gimmick, he never relied entirely on it—as his multiple "straight" roles attest— "but used it only as the framework within which the character existed. He considered the mental and emotional aspects as well to give credence and depth to the whole" (Anderson 32). Chaney's famous ability to disappear into a crowd (as himself) echoes Erik's desire for bourgeois convention. To date, in no filmic adaptation has Erik ever expressed a desire to drive in the Bois de Boulogne with his wife as a reference to the very ordinariness of it, yet such sentiment is manifest in many interpretations of the role.

Chaney had to use his body and face to depict both the horror of Erik's deformity and the beauty of his ethereal voice; at the very least, the pathos that was the reflection of the bodily horror. As described in Leroux, Chaney's Erik "wore evening clothes all day long, as if he were always ready to take his seat in the 'haunted' box" (Babilas 148). Chaney had trained as a dancer, and despite the generally rigid carriage he brings to the role, he also lends to Erik a certain gracefulness, including "the unmistakable use of his expressive hands," (Anderson 70) which Michael Blake explicitly compares to music (quoted in *Lon Chaney: A Thousand Faces*). While David J. Skal among others has suggested a sexual/Freudian element to Chaney's rigid carriage as Erik, it perhaps also links back to the body horror described by Leroux; horror, Botting maintains, normally happens when a character has a physical encounter with death like touching a corpse: "It freezes human faculties, rendering the mind passive and immobilizing the body" (75).

There is no doubt that Chaney shocked and frightened through his facial makeup depiction of Erik, and this depiction remains the most similar audiovisual example of the source text's "death's-head." Although the startling made-up appearance vaguely evokes a corpse, it is not the face seen by Christine in Leroux. Nevertheless, as Skal has noted, horror films made after the First World War are inevitably influenced by veterans' disfigurement. Leroux wrote his Erik before the widespread reality of *mutilés de guerre*, but Chaney's Erik recalls their "smashed features, missing noses, and mouths full of broken teeth" (Skal 66). Hence, unmistakably, the target text reworks ugliness and pathos based on real-world events that occurred between the writing of the source text and the filmic adaptation.

The 1925 film is the only surviving adaptation made in Leroux's lifetime. Leroux was interested in film; he even wrote in a "para-text" to accompany the film's release, "*Il me semble en avoir donné dans mon ouvrage suffisamment les prevues et j'en reste, pour mon compte, entièrement persuadé*" [It seems to have given my work sufficient credibility and, I remain, for my part, entirely persuaded], a rather coy pronouncement giving little indication of how he perceived Chaney's performance (quoted in Shah "No Ordinary Skeleton" 4). When sound came to the movies, the film was re-released with voices added in (Mary Philbin's and Norman Kerry's), while the Phantom remained silent (due at least in part to Chaney's untimely death of throat cancer in 1930).

Strategy II: A Preeminent Voice, a Sensual Exterior—The Andrew Lloyd Webber Musical (1986–)

Multiple filmic adaptations followed in the wake of the 1925 version, all interesting in their approaches, but by far the most influential target text was the 1986 musical written by Andrew Lloyd Webber, with lyrics by Richard Stilgoe and Charles Hart, directed by Hal Prince, originally starring Michael Crawford and Sarah Brightman. Isabelle Husson-Casta suggests that *POTO* is best achieved in the dark of the theatre or the cinema (5), and the stage musical has proven this to be abundantly clear, now in its 30th year in the West End and remaining the longest running Broadway musical. In a reverse of the 1925 silent film, in which the visual horror of Erik threatened to over-power any notion of his ethereal voice, in the musical, the Phantom has the most eloquent and beautiful voice of any of the male characters. The Phantom in this version, Hall maintains, is "difficult to ignore or dismiss, given this music and these lyrics" (122).

Familiar with the 1984 Ken Hill production,[7] Lloyd Webber was never-theless persuaded to write his own score with talented young lyricist Charles Hart. The casting of the Phantom was originally a gamble, but Michael Craw-ford remains the definitive Phantom vocally because his light, high tenor most closely resembles "the voice of the man" as described by Leroux. Craw-ford's "tender and hypnotic singing voice" (Perry 32) is at its most Leroussian during "The Mirror" and in the graveyard scene.

Wildgen argues that Erik "wishes to be heard, acknowledged, even more than he wishes to be loved" (163). The Lloyd Webber musical, Hall maintains, "relies on the songs to communicate the reasons behind Christine's fascination with Erik" (122). However, the Lloyd Webber musical introduces a new element into adaptations of *POTO*; the Phantom *looks* so suave and so sexy Christine and the audience are visually fascinated by him. The Phantom captivates so consummately through both angelic song and sensual appearance— a far cry from the skeletal figure and hands that smelt of death from the novel. Some of this is likely due to designer Maria Björnson's "complete, thought-through vision" (Lee n.p.). Björnson kept the Phantom in evening clothes but made them sleek and Valentino-esque, complete with the Phantom's liquid black wig. Christopher Tucker designed the Phantom's make up and iconic mask, which was made into a half mask to give the audience more facial and eye contact with the actor. This approach to the mask worked in tandem with Crawford's voice; voice combined with "physical agility" which facilitated expression (Perry 32).

If the musical's Phantom's voice could soar and he was divested of the skeletal, repulsive body of Leroux's Erik, how could he justify the deformity that is key to the character? Lloyd Webber takes credit for introducing the element of the public unmasking as a vehicle for stage rather than the close-up that film offers, at the end of the performance of the Phantom's opera, *Don Juan Triumphant* in the musical number "The Point of No Return." The Phantom's facial deformity is shocking but dissimilar to Leroux's "death's-head," designed to be seen from the furthest seat in the theatre. Interestingly, the unmasking scene from the 1925 film is still considered the most emblematic. However, the Lloyd Webber Phantom appears to have gotten the best deal of all, with his gorgeous voice true to Leroux and his sensual physical movements at least as visually appealing as those of his rival Raoul.

Andrew Lloyd Webber Again (2004)

The scale was tipped even further when the film of the musical was made in 2004. When Hall argues that "with the visual and the aural opposed to one another, distortion, chaos, confusion results when the two attempt to become one" (27), one wonders how far the filmmakers felt they could take their vision of a less-deformed Phantom in order to present an "appealing" anti-hero. The film's interpretation of the Phantom pushes to extremes the ambiguity of the character from the source text.

A film version of Lloyd Webber's musical had been discussed as early as 1988, revived during 2004, with Joel Schumacher as the director, insisting on a young, beautiful cast. Indeed, even the Phantom, as played by Gerard Butler, is beautiful. With the setting of the film moved from 1881 to 1870, impinging on historical fact (given that in 1870 Paris was in the middle of the Franco-Prussian War), the costume and character of the Phantom are also moved to High Romanticism, in common with mid-century Victorian Gothic. "The disturbing and demonic villain" (in this case, the Phantom) retains a "darkly attractive, if ambivalent allure as a defiant rebel against the constraints of social mores" (Botting 92). The film Phantom has also become a moral vigilante, killing Buquet not only to protect himself but because the scene-shifter is a lecher. The film Phantom protects innocent *ballets rats*; he is muscular rather than corpse-like; his deformity is smaller and less severe than in the stage musical; his underground lair seethes with High Romanticism; he nearly bests Raoul in a daring sword fight in a graveyard.

"The vocal balance between the Phantom and Raoul was pivotal to the audiences' understanding of the characters," Lloyd Webber reflected: "When they see the film they think, 'I get it, I know why Christine really fancies the Phantom—I know because he's the right side of danger'" (Lloyd Webber 9). This is a very different rendering of Erik's assimilation of bourgeois values in Leroux, not to mention Christine's attraction to "the Voice." Indeed, the script of the film suggests that Christine is "mesmerized and hypnotized by this *stunning, sexual* master" (script 86, my emphasis). Although the script refers to the Phantom's "rotting face" (91) and "horrifying skull" (188), the actual extent of his deformity has been derisively referred to as no worse than a sunburn.

The film version of the stage musical is interesting for the new scenes and music that it adds, which are comparatively few. One scene that was added for the film was "The Fairground," which is hinted at in the stage musical but was represented scenically in the film. Sometime in the 1830s, a young Madame Giry visits a fairground in which she sees freaks and performers, including a child who will become the Phantom, who is caged, beaten, and degraded for tawdry entertainment. Diane Lake discusses "the integral moment" of film adaptation that is so important, "to leave it out of a film … would be an unthinkable choice" (410). While such a scene as "The Fairground" is nowhere available in the Leroux text, arguably for the 2004 Phantom's character, it *would* be unthinkable to leave out this scene. Crucially, however, for our notion of sight vs. sound in the character of the Phantom, he is *silent* in this scene. He has agency in action—in righteous murder, in fact—but Madame Giry does not feel sympathy with him because of his voice, only because he is mistreated. In arguing for a new approach to "theater film" adaptation, Milan Pribisic suggests that bringing together three media such as film, novel, and stage, "the novel tells the story, while stage and film show and tell" (155). The 2004 film, despite its emphasis on music, seems most concerned with *telling*.

This $95 million film divided phandom, and critics were ambivalent. Schumacher claims part of his motivation for making the film was to bring it to those who couldn't afford tickets or the show didn't play where they lived. This view may have some validity; Alexis Weedon found in a study of paratexts influencing readers and viewers that half surveyed bought a book because of watching the film (121). Hall suggests that Lloyd Webber deliberately created a weak film so the musical could go on playing (126). Fred Botting may have complained that "the new frame [*Francis Ford Coppola's Bram Stoker's Dracula* (1993)] turns Gothic horror into a sentimental romance"; similar accusations could be made against the film of the *POTO* musical, lacking much of the "bite" of the original story (178). Nevertheless, it can be argued that the stage musical subsequently took on elements of the film, particularly in its depiction of the Phantom. For example, the actor chosen to portray the Phantom in the 25th anniversary spectacular at the Royal Albert Hall in 2011 was Ramin Karimloo. Although he had played both Raoul and the Phantom many times on stage, he had also played Christine's father in the film[8] and continued the role of the Phantom in *Love Never Dies* (2010). While a strong vocalist, it could not escape notice that Karimloo's muscular physique and attractiveness channeled more of the film of the musical than the Leroux novel. This has very much proven Bruhn's contention that adaptation "(be it from novel to film or between other media) ought to be regarded as a two-way process instead of a form of one-way transport" (73).

Strategy III: Different Registers— Big Finish Classics (2007)

Several versions of *POTO* challenge the belief in the text's intractability by interpreting Erik's visual/aural duality literally. If such a man as Erik cannot exist in reality but only in prose fiction, such versions address this head-on and cast one actor for his speaking voice and another for his singing voice. As regards Leroux's interest in sound, it is worth noting that the writer kept up to date with the newest fiction and was evidently interested in science and new technology. It is therefore appropriate that the historical incident that catalyzes the discovery of Erik's bones and "inspires" Leroux to write *POTO* is the 1907 burial of *les voix vivantes,* a collection of phonographic recordings in the Opéra's cellars during an "eerily funereal" ceremony (Shah "No Ordinary Skeleton" 2). The "living voices" competing with a dead body corresponds to the way sound recording was approached at the end of the nineteenth century. Jonathan Sterne and Mitchell Akiyama question the desire for the "sonification" of ever-older recordings, especially when such desires manifest in the creation of a digital sound file in 2008 for "the world's oldest recording," a phono-autogram from 1860, which was nevertheless never intended to be played back—the phono-autograph was intended as a device to make the aural visual (555). Despite the many ways *POTO* is rooted in the past (the 1880s), the voices appeal to contemporary technology (1909) to "haunt" the present. Barnaby Edwards' audio drama production is haunted by all previous adaptations to the point that he stresses its closeness in spirit and detail to the 1910 source text.

As argued above, audio drama is a strong contender for realizing the unperformable not only in *POTO* but in Gothic due to its inherent conduit directly into the mind, imagery, and emotion. "A close look at the history and development of radio drama and radio drama adaptation provides a focus for a discussion about the subject on a metalevel," though very little work on this has been done (Huwiler 137–38). Oddly, unlike other contemporary genre fiction, *POTO* has resisted being adapted for audio. Its audio adaptations are few, including a 1943 *Lux Radio Theater* dramatization of the film starring Claude Rains and a CBS *Radio Mystery Theatre* (1975) adaptation starring Gordon Gould and adapted by Himan Brown. The novel, with its rich auditory soundtrack, characters who frequently burst into song or hear things long before they ever see them, would seem like a natural choice for audio adaptation. In 2007, successful audio drama CD subscription service, Big Finish Productions, produced its *POTO*. The adaptation uses the musical sound-map described in Leroux's prose to a literal extent that is unknown in all other adaptations. As Hall points out, Leroux's original readership would have had a running soundtrack of the operas as they read the book (18), including pieces by Gounod, Reyer, Saint-Saëns, Massenet, Guiraud, and Delibes. "How carefully composed Leroux's own soundtrack is" (Newark 69). Newark further notes that in the novel, the sung words of the featured operas are woven into the plot (68).

Perhaps it is in fact the disjunction between sight and sound, this "double vision," that has intimidated would-be audio dramatists with *POTO*. Richard J. Hand suggests that "by the twenty-first century, some people have learnt to be listeners," that is, despite the ubiquity of visual forms, an aural story can still be told well (197). The potentially interactive audio drama of the twenty-first century "demanded a new level of required skills: to listen and physically engage, to take control and even some responsibility in shaping the unfurling narrative" (Hand 197). While we accept that *POTO* is a ghost story with the machinery of the Gothic being revealed as completely human in origin, still, for the ghostly suspense to work, it links with the sound tropes of the Gothic: voices are heard but their origins are not seen. Nevertheless, *POTO* lacks many of the auditory cues we expect from horror: no howling dogs or seaside storms, for example. It is evident how traditional and contemporary theatre and screen culture has assimilated the visual with the auditory for practical, technical, and aesthetic reasons, but sound is a highly significant component in horror fiction (Hand 14). Edwards may well be adhering to the quality Constantidinides cites here, that although "Dracula and Frankenstein's origins are literary, their continuous journeys through the diverse landscape of cinema have detached them from their creators' written portraits, thus demythologizing their authorship and filmic presence" (91). It is, in fact, potentially a failing of the Big Finish adaptation that it adheres *too* closely to the source text. Even Leroux changed lyrics or opera facts to fit his narrative, as Newark points out (72). Hajnal has noted that the late nineteenth century novelistic obsession with ekphrasis has been difficult to bring across in filmic adaptations. While ekphrasis has generally been a visual process, it has been noted in musical composition (for example, Mussorsky's *Pictures at an Exhibition*). However, there does not seem to be a term for a piece of aural drama in which one medium of art (the aural drama) tries to relate to another medium (in this case, the musical compositions described and adapted by Leroux in the 1910 novel) by defining and describing its essence and form. Perhaps this is an explanation for Newark's "resistance" to adaptation?

The Big Finish adaptation features an accomplished cast. Peter Guinness provides Erik's speaking voice, and Matthew Hargreaves his singing voice. This adaptation is notable for allowing Erik to sing the full range of music given to him in the novel, from *Faust* to *Otello* (and while he plays *Don Juan Triumphant* on the pipe organ, he never sings it). Guinness makes Erik "a child of the night" (Husson-Casta x), gravelly and sinister, and distinctive, though his tone hardly suggests soft and gentle. Furthermore, Hargreaves' operatic voice, while encompassing and rich, does not reproduce the whispery, sweet quality of Erik's singing voice in the novel.

Guinness' casting and indeed his performance stems from the way character is created in audio drama. Although we are able to recognize and remember visually up to 10,000 faces, we do not seem to have the same ability to voices unlinked with faces (Beck 97). Nevertheless, "the ear is tremendously sensitive to distortion and levels of semantic implication" (Truax 34). Beck suggests that the audio drama actor must work much more quickly in establishing character:

> Your first lines tell the listener of your character's dialect ... and identity. This information could be later adjusted or confirmed, but you have to be sure of these signals when recording because you stick by them. The difference with radio is that the revealing of character must be gradual and progressive, whatever the signalling you do with your first lines. Stage and screen give a complete display of body, costume, and face [111].

Indeed, the characters in the Big Finish adaptation must *tell* us what Erik looks like; we must accept their word that he is hideous, for we have no way of seeing it ourselves. For example, Madame Giry helps us see "'horror, horror!' Those were Christine's words upon glimpsing the face of the Opera Ghost. And who can blame her? Picture it: a living skull with four black holes where the eyes, nose, and mouth should be…. The face of Death." The only other way to convey Erik's hideousness or perhaps his sinister qualities is through the timbre of his voice, which Guinness accomplishes to good effect.

The "Resurrection of Lazarus" scene from the graveyard in Perros-Guirec where Christine (and a lurking Raoul) hear the violin playing seemingly out of a pile of bones is another representative example. Is it Christine's father's ghost playing? Is it Erik? How can we see? How can we tell? The corporeal quality of characters in audio drama who do not speak has always represented an epistemological challenge. Husson-Casta would argue that Erik's voice "subsumes his body" (32). His voice "continues to grow in silence, in the secret place of our own musical imagination" (34). Indeed, director Barnaby Edwards chooses to represent this theme from Raoul's point of view in the manner of a serial cliffhanger. We understand only the rudiments of Erik's form as he ceases to be the Angel of Music or the spirit of Christine's father and only "see" him when Raoul does.

> RAOUL: Christine, whoever this angel is, he is not your father! Your father lies buried beneath this tomb and there he will remain until Judgment Day.
> CHRISTINE: How—how could you, Raoul? You've destroyed everything!
> [*She runs away sobbing*].
> RAOUL: Christine! Christine!
> [*SFX: Footsteps*]
> RAOUL: Who's there? Show yourself.
> ERIK: You wish to look upon me?
> RAOUL: Step forward into the moonlight if you would.
> [*SFX: Footsteps*]
> RAOUL: I take it I have the pleasure of addressing the Angel of Music? Will you not take off your mask, Monsieur?
> ERIK: Very well.
> [*SFX: Cracking noises*]
> ERIK: Very well. Behold: the face of Death!
> [*SFX: The non-diegetic music builds to a crescendo*]
> RAOUL: No! No! Noooooooooooooo! (Edwards).

In the influential *In/Fidelity* collection from 2008, Thomas Leitch wrote: "Adultery is good; it's productive. I mean it's not good for the family, but it's great for the novelist. It can open up all these productive, newfound possibilities for writing fiction that we never had before. So instead of saying fidelity is good, infidelity is bad, why don't we say fidelity is maybe not so good and infidelity is better" (qtd. in Hazette 45). Edwards' interest in dramatizing *POTO* in aural form was in order to include the music described in the source text and, perhaps, to interrogate the ambiguity of its three main characters (and, by including the Daroga in the adaptation, a character frequently left out, Edwards makes obvious the very absence of the character in previous target texts). Indeed, absences and presences "haunt" the Big Finish adaptation: it retains a narrator, Madame Giry, but dispenses with the mysterious omniscience of the novel's narrator and framing device from the "editor," Gaston Leroux. The characters of Raoul and Christine retain shading that is consistent with their ambiguous portrayal in the novel, with Raoul portrayed by James D'Arcy, a young, handsome actor with a low-pitched, commanding voice who has played both villains and heroes, and who blends Raoul's petulance with bravery and sincerity. Helen Goldwyn's Christine retains a bittersweet innocence while remaining independent from either Raoul's or Erik's demands.

As noted earlier, one strategy the 2004 *POTO* film undertakes to create a sympathetic edge to the Phantom is through the "Fairground" flashback. While Peter Guinness' vocal tone often gives his aural Erik empathy-inducing pathos, this Phantom is always kept at arm's length from the audience. While this is consistent with the source text's approach, in light of Bruhn's assertion that the target text changes the source text through changes in readers' perceptions, the audio drama adaptation has the scope for medium-specific intimacy that is not fulfilled in the Big Finish adaptation. Radio drama and latterly audio drama can and should take full advantage of what Kip Allen calls "fostering the illusion of intimacy." Audio drama possesses a conduit directly into the mind, imagery, and emotion.[9] While quite literally, Erik's singing voice (as performed by Matthew Hargreaves) is beautiful, this aural target text never seems to bring our ear to Erik's soul.

Conclusion

Husson-Casta represents the centrality of sound in *Phantom of the Opera* and its appeal: "*Le style leroussien (en)chante*" (34). The "double vision" (or an engagement with two senses that do not always harmonize) as suggested by Hall is linked with Leroux's career-long interest in justice; as a writer, Leroux was insistent on never letting ourselves being seduced by mere appearances (Lamy 75). The durability of the story as demonstrated by its plethora of audio-visual adaptations seems to suggest this is a popular message, personified, literally, in the person of Erik, whose hideous face and body is held up against his beautiful, otherworldly voice. To this end, some would argue that *POTO* can never be satisfactorily dramatized; there is no human alive who can give us Erik's sinister, commanding speaking voice, physique that is both athletic and skeletal, and a singing voice that could convince us it comes directly from Heaven. It is true, too, that prose cannot achieve the different timbres of sound that the voices have that Leroux describes. *Don Juan Triumphant*, argues Newark, "tempts but exceeds dramatic representation" (75).

I would argue, then, that the most satisfying target text of *Phantom of the Opera* will continue to be the Lloyd Webber stage musical, which embraces the faux-Gothic machinery in its theatricality and allows Erik to be both visually ugly and attractive at the same time while giving in to the supremacy of his voice, seducing everyone with his lyrics, music, and vocals. Paradoxically, by stressing the Phantom's visual appeal almost over and above his sonic musicality, the 2004 film reverses the appeal of not only the character, but the story itself. To an extent, the 2004 film Phantom loses his poignancy when he loses the severity of his deformity. He may seduce, but he risks losing the inherent quality of his "nature" that has given the character such longevity.

Raj Shah suggests that *Phantom of the Opera* is "now poised on the brink of cultural ascendancy" even as it moves further from its source text ("No Ordinary Skeleton" 2). Wolf also argues for understanding *POTO* as "a multidimensional allegory" (Wolf 4). This chimes with Hazette's definition of adaptation that includes archetypes, dynamic change, translation, and transmission. *POTO* has survived where its many Gothic contemporaries have faded from the picture due to the strength and malleability of its main characters and its insistence of the play-within-the-play, which creates a never-ending fun-house mirror of interpretations. In target texts as diverse as silent film, stage musical, and audio drama, *POTO* demonstrates very well that the source text can indeed be "re-written" in relation to its target texts without diminishing either.

NOTES

1. The novel was written in 1908 and published, following its serialization in *Le Gaulois*, in volume form in March 1910.
2. The first known adaptation was in 1916, *Das Phantom der Oper* (Matray).
3. Quotations from Leroux are my translations.
4. As Cormac Newark points out, the 1916 German adaptation is lost.
5. His voice "was deep and virile, quite appropriate to his personality, and it was flexible" according to Anderson (95).
6. It has been accepted for about a decade that there is no such thing as a silent film; "from ambient noise to programme music, the moving image has always been accompanied by sound" (Bell vii).
7. Ken Hill, an accomplished British popular stage producer, debuted his stage musical of *POTO* in 1976. It was revived in 1984 and went on tour in the UK and U.S.
8. The script notes, "Fixed to the plaque is a daguerreotype of her [Christine's] FATHER. There is a sculpted violin in front. (NB. Her FATHER should very vaguely resemble the PHANTOM when disguised)" (78).
9. Accumulated literature confirms that audio dramatization causes listeners to generate many and vivid images. Cf. McMurtry, "Imagination and Narrative, Young People's Experiences," *The Journal of Audio and Radio Media*, 2017.

WORKS CITED

Alfu. *Gaston Leroux: Parcours d'une oeuvre*. Amiens: Encrage, 1996. Print.
Allen, Kip. Personal interview. 29 Apr. 2013.
Anderson, Robert G. *Faces, Forms, Films: The Artistry of Lon Chaney*. New York: A.S. Barnes, 1971. Print.

Babilas, Dorota. "Tod Browning's *Dracula* (1931): The Vampire Wears a Dress Coat." *Dracula and the Gothic in Literature, Pop Culture, and the Arts*. Ed. Isabel Ermida. 137–56. Leiden: Rodopi, 2015, Print.
Beck, Alan. *Radio Acting*. London: A & C Black, 1997. Print.
Behind the Mask: The Story of The Phantom of the Opera. Dir. James Crighton, Perf. Paul Hickey, Jonathan Allen, Michael Coveney. Really Useful Films, 2005. Film.
Bell, Will. "Introduction." *Dramatic Notes: Foregrounding Music in the Dramatic Experience*. 3–24. Luton: University of Luton Press, 1998. Print.
Blyn, Robin. *The Freak-Garde: Extraordinary Bodies and Revolutionary Art in America*. Minneapolis: University of Minnesota Press, 2013. Print.
Botting, Fred. *Gothic*. New York: Routledge, 1996. Print.
Brown, Julie. "*Carnival of Souls* and the Organs of Horror." *Music in the Horror Film: Listening to Fear*. Ed. Neil Lerner. 1–20. Abingdon: Routledge, 2010, Print.
Constandinides, Costas. *From Film Adaptation to Post-Celluloid Adaptation*. New York: Continuum, 2010. Print.
Faubion, Renée. "Notes on Phantom of the Opera." Personal correspondence, 2006.
Hall, Ann C. *Phantom Variations: The Adaptation of Gaston Leroux's* Phantom of the Opera, *1925 to the Present*. Jefferson, NC: McFarland, 2009. Print.
Hand, Richard J. *Listen in Terror: British Horror Radio from the Advent of Broadcasting to the Digital Age*. Manchester: Manchester University Press, 2014. Print.
Hazette, Valérie V. *Wuthering Heights on Film and Television: A Journey Across Time and Cultures*. Bristol: Intellect, 2015. Print.
Husson-Casta, Isabelle. *Le Travail de l' "obscure clarté" dans le Fantôme de l'Opéra de Gaston Leroux*. Paris: Lettres-Modernes, 1997. Print.
Huwiler, Elke. "Engaging the Ear: Teaching Radio Drama Adaptations." *Redefining Adaptation Studies*. Ed. Dennis Cutchins, Laurence Raw, and James M. Welsh. 134–36. Lanham: Scarecrow Press, 2010. Print.
Ingvarsson, Jonas. "Literature through Radio: Distance and Silence in *The War of the Worlds*, 1938/1898." *Adaptation Studies: New Challenges, New Directions*. Ed. Jørgen Bruhn, Anne Gjelsvik, and Eirik Frisvold Hanssen. 265–86. London: Bloomsbury, 2013. Print.
Király, Hajnal. "The Medium Strikes Back: 'Impossible Adaptation' Revisited." *Adaptation Studies: New Challenges, New Directions*. Ed. Jørgen Bruhn, Anne Gjelsvik, and Eirik Frisvold Hanssen. 179–202. London: Bloomsbury, 2013. Print.
Lake, Diane. "Adapting the Unadaptable: The Screenwriter's Perspective." *A Companion to Literature, Film, and Adaptation*. Ed. Deborah Cartmell. 408–15. Malden, MA: Wiley-Blackwell, 2012. Print.
Lamy, Jean-Claude, and Pierre Lépine. *Gaston Leroux ou Le Vrai Rouletabille*. Paris: Éditions du Rocher, 2003. Print.
Lee, Michael. "Maria Björnson." *The Phantom of the Opera at the Royal Albert Hall Souvenir Programme Highlights*, 2011. Print.
Leitch, Thomas. "Adaptation and Intertextuality, or, What isn't an Adaptation, and What Does it Matter?" *A Companion to Literature, Film, and Adaptation*. Ed. Deborah Cartmell. 87–104. Malden, MA: Wiley-Blackwell, 2012. Print.
Leroux, Gaston. *Le Fantôme de l'Opéra*. Paris: Livre du Poche, 2004. Print.
_____. *The Phantom of the Opera*. Trans. Lowell Bair. New York: Bantam Classics, 1990. Print.
Lippert, Bianca. "Betty and Lisa: Alternating Between Sameness and Uniqueness." *TV's Betty Goes Global: From Telenovela to International Brand*. Ed. Janet McCabe and Kim Akass. 83–98. London: I.B. Tauris, 2013. Print.
Lon Chaney: A Thousand Faces. Dir. Kevin Brownlow. Perf. Kenneth Branagh. Turner Classic Movies, 2000. Film.
Mackintosh, Cameron. "The Phantom's Trail." 2015. *The Phantom of the Opera Souvenir Booklet*, n.p. London: The Really Useful Company, 2016. Print.
McCabe, Janet, and Kim Akass. "Introduction." *TV's Betty Goes Global: From Telenovela to International Brand*. 3–30. London: I.B. Tauris, 2013. Print.
McMurtry, Leslie. "Imagination and Narrative, Young People's Experiences." *The Journal of Audio and Radio Media*. Forthcoming.

Murphy, Terence Patrick. *The Fairytale Plot and Structure*. Basingstoke: Palgrave Macmillan, 2015. Print.

Newark, Cormac. "'Vous Qui Faites l'Endormie': The Phantom and the Buried Voices of the Paris Opéra." *19th Century Music* 33.1 (2009): 62–77. Print.

Pednaud, J. Tithonus. "John Coffey: The Living Skeleton Dude." *The Human Marvels*, 2012. Web. 18 Dec. 2016.

Perry, George. "The Phantom." *Andrew Lloyd Webber's The Phantom of the Opera Companion*. 25–45. London: Pavilion Books, 2004, Print.

The Penalty. Dir. Wallace Worsley. Perf. Lon Chaney, Claire Adams, Ethel Grey Terry. Goldwyn Pictures, 1920. Film.

The Phantom of the Opera. Dir. Rupert Julian. Perf. Lon Chaney, Mary Philbin, Norman Kerry. Universal, 1925. Film.

_____. Dir. Trevor Nunn. Perf. Michael Crawford. Her Majesty's Theatre, London, 12 Oct. 1986. The Really Useful Group. Theater Performance.

_____. Dir. Joel Schumacher. Perf. Gerard Butler, Emmy Rossum, Patrick Wilson. Warner Bros., 2004. Film.

_____. Dir. Barnaby Edwards. Perf. Peter Guinness, Helen Goldwyn, Anna Massey, James D'Arcy. Big Finish, 2007. Radio.

Prawer, S.S. *Caligari's Children: The Film as Tale of Terror*. Oxford: Oxford University Press, 1980. Print.

Pribisic, Milan. "The Pleasures of 'Theater Film': Stage to Film Adaptation." *Redefining Adaptation Studies*. Ed. Dennis Cutchins, Laurence Raw, and James M. Welsh. 147–59. Lanham: Scarecrow Press, 2010. Print.

Şahin, Sevgi, and Laurence Raw. "Toward a Pedagogy for Adaptation Studies." *Redefining Adaptation Studies*. Ed. Dennis Cutchins, Laurence Raw, and James M. Welsh. 71–84. Lanham: Scarecrow Press, 2010. Print.

Shah, Raj. "No Ordinary Skeleton: Unmasking the Secret Source of Gaston Leroux's *Le Fantome de l'Opéra*." *Forum of Modern Language Studies* (2013): 1–14. Print.

_____. "The Publication and Initial French Reception of Gaston Leroux's *Le Fantôme de l'Opéra*." *French Studies Bulletin* 138.1 (2016): 13–16. Print.

Skal, David J. *The Monster Show: A Cultural History of Horror*. London: Plexus, 1993. Print.

Sterne, Jonathan, and Mitchell Akiyama. "The Recording That Never Wanted to Be Heard and Other Stories of Sonification." *The Oxford Handbook of Sound Studies*. Ed. Trevor Pinch and Karin Bijstervild. 554–60. Oxford: Oxford University Press, 2012. Print.

Truax, Barry. *Acoustic Communications*, 2nd ed. Westport, CT: Ablex, 2001. Print.

The Unholy Three. Dir. Jack Conway. Perf. Chaney, Harry Earles, Lila Lee, Elliott Nugent. MGM, 1930. Film.

Van Elferen, Isabella. "Sonic Gothic." *The Gothic World*. Ed. Glennie Byron and Dale Townshend. 429–40. London: Routledge, 2014, Print.

Webber, Andrew Lloyd. *Andrew Lloyd Webber's The Phantom of the Opera Companion*. 8–9. London: Pavilion Books, 2004. Print.

Weedon, Alexis. "The Numbers Game: Quantifying the Audience." *Redefining Adaptation Studies*. Ed. Dennis Cutchins, Laurence Raw, and James M. Welsh. 111–32. Lanham, MD: Scarecrow Press, 2010. Print.

Wildgen, K.E. "Making the Shadow Conscious: The Enduring Legacy of Gaston Leroux." *Symposium* 55.3 (2001): 155–167. Print.

Wolf, Leonard. "Introduction." *The Essential Phantom of the Opera: the Definitive, Annotated Edition of Gaston Leroux's Classic Novel*. Ed. and trans. Wolf. 1–15. New York: Plume, 1996. Print.

Fingersmith or Handmaiden

Adaptations from the Neo-Victorian Era to Contemporary Asia

Ela İpek Gündüz

The urge of contemporary writers and producers to adapt older literary products and genres is not an inclination belonging to the 20th and 21st centuries. Adapting other texts as well as from text to film is an ongoing practice which requires the changing of a source text into something different and perceived in different ways by both adapters and audiences. Yet there is sometimes an adversely critical attitude towards the adapted product because of its perceived lack of originality. This has historically been one of the principal determinants of adaptation's value. Because of its inherent "belatedness" when compared to the source text, the target text is often unjustifiably devalued. It is inevitable, however, that, despite this re-usage, the target text is a new entity.

Perhaps all literary products are adaptations, due to their being inspired by their predecessors. Walter Benjamin's idea that "storytelling is always the art of repeating stories" (90) supports this idea by emphasizing the fact that re-use of some older texts is inevitable. It is an unavoidable urge: even writers of classic works remember and re-focus aspects of previous literary products. As Edward Said asserts, "The writer thinks less of writing originally, and more of rewriting" (135). From this perspective, when movie adaptations of canonical works are taken into consideration, they may be regarded as new presentations of source texts through the eyes of directors and screenwriters, filtered through different foci—the camera, the screenplay, actors' performances and so on. This new entity deserves to be approached on its own terms, as a work involving "the movement into a new generic form or context" (Sanders 2).[1] T. S. Eliot claims that works incorporating memories of older texts are no less valuable when compared to the source text: "No poet, no artist, of any art, has his complete meaning alone" (qtd. in Sanders 38). In adaptations you should not imitate all aspects of the text, but add some changes through your interpretation. In this way, Eliot adds a historical dimension to adaptation: through the interrelation of source and target texts, alternative conclusions can be drawn. Adaptations, in that sense, are "rewrites" that "invariably transcend … mere imitation," rather maintaining the purpose of becoming "incremental literature" (Zabus 4). In other words, adaptations benefit from the transition of source texts to new contexts. Their value depends on how the finished product is consumed by audiences. Cultural specificities become intertwined with hybridity of genres, styles or context. This article will try to illuminate such notions of cultural value through a comparison of the BBC adaptation (2005) and the Korean version (2016) of Sarah Waters' novel *Fingersmith* (2015).

The novel *Fingersmith* makes use of an array of elements that depend on our specialized knowledge of the Victorian era and how it remains important in the contemporary world:

> Film adapters build on a hypercorrect historical material realism to usher in a host of anachronistic ideological "corrections" of novels. Quite inconsistently, while adaptations pursue a hyperfidelity to nineteenth-century material culture, they reject and correct Victorian psychology, ethics, and politics. When filmmakers set modern politically correct views against historically correct backdrops, the effect is to authorize these modern ideologies as historically authentic [Elliott 177].

This technique leads to a hybrid of ancient and modern. The BBC adaptation starts with scenes of poverty in Victorian London slums, reflected in the grimy set and costume design. The cruelty of society is reinforced by the narrator's (Sally Hawkins) description of a scaffold from her window. The audience understands the Victorian psyche through the setting, costumes and the actors' performances. Especially the depiction of Lant Street with its smoky atmosphere provides the necessary means for us to empathize with the inhabitants. Those familiar with Waters' novels know that a Victorian story filtered through a contemporary perspective will soon follow.

Fingersmith is about two young women, Sue Trinder and Maud Lilly, whose pasts are inextricably intertwined. Both the novel and the adaptation begin by telling the details of the miserable life of Sue (Sally Hawkins), a poor girl who makes a living through her hands (hence the term "fingersmith") and Maud (Elaine Cassidy), who is rich but dominated by her uncle (Charles Dance).[2] Maud has been brought up by her uncle as a secretary and has remained isolated from the outside world. The girls' socio-economic circumstances are juxtaposed through contrasting images of their abodes–Lant Street and Briar Court. The intrigues begin with Sue's adoptive mother Mrs. Sucksby (Imelda Staunton) and Richard Rivers—known as "Gentleman" (Rupert

Evans) persuade Sue to participate in a plan to rob Maud. Gentleman needs Sue to act as Maud's handmaid to convince Maud to go out with him.

Up until now, the adaptation's narrative proceeds according to Waters' source text, by portraying women of all social classes as subordinate and believing as a result that there is no alternative. Things begin to change, however, when Maud and Sue develop a close relationship; the adaptation traces its development through symmetrical sequences showing their faces, hands, dresses, and dances. When Sue teaches Maud how to kiss Gentleman, and Maud responds in kind, the relationship begins in earnest. The closer they become, the more we realize the adaptation's determination to transcend televisual Victorian convention and impose a modern perspective on the material. Sue's efforts to continue helping Gentleman and Maud becomes complicated. Gentleman teaches Sue painting, saying as he does so, "You have got a talent that your fellow creatures do not have; you also lack a free mind."

Despite the contemporaneity of the material, the adaptation follows convention by remaining largely faithful to the source-test, while constructing the narrative in leisurely fashion, allowing viewers to understand the characters and their relationships to one another. We identify with Sue and Maud as their love affair develops, culminating in physical intimacy. It is at this point we understand the adaptation's neo–Victorian focus, combining history with contemporary issues. The adaptation builds upon the novel's suggestion that marital bliss is impossible for most young women, and the only way for them to find solace is through same-sex relationships.

The second episode of the adaptation attempts to keep the affair under wraps; but director Aisling Walsh makes it obvious that, despite her marriage to Gentleman, Maud's feelings for Sue remain undimmed. When left alone, they exchange long, fervent kisses. When Maud actively demands to make love to Sue, and Gentleman watches them secretly behind the door, we understand the shocking nature of the material, in the Victorian period, especially, when the events are retold through Maud's narration that proves beyond doubt that women of that era were not as innocent as was generally believed. The adaptation of Waters' novel explicitly raises questions about the "Victorian-ness" of the television version. Maud offers positive alternatives for women, many of whom were doomed to become objects for male sexual lust. The lovers' freedom from such conventions is depicted in another sequence where Maud reads pornographic texts without being affected by them. The lesbian couple benefit from their marginalized status by allowing their sexual passions to flourish. It would seem at this point that the value of the adaptation lies in its suggestion of new constructions of femaleness that break free of Victorian stereotypes while offering new possibilities in the contemporary era.

Predictably this idealistic affair does not last. As in the source text Mrs. Sucksby plays an important role in its destruction. Her power to manipulate people, poor and rich alike, reveals the Victorian obsession with power, irrespective of social status. She pretends to kill Gentleman while making the girls' affair public. Although being hanged as a result, she has assumed the initiative that she takes to the grave. This is emphasized in a sequence where Sue watches the hanging from her window with a melancholy expression, as if understanding that she has few future possibilities, either personal or professional. Yet this is only a temporary emotion; in the adaptation's final episode Sue and Maud confess directly about their love for each other when Maud says, "These papers say how I want you, how I love you," and in the last shot on the right side of the frame they kiss each other. Sunlight shines from the window on the left, offering a hopeful future for both girls. These are the points that acquire the value of this adaptation.

The adaptation is an innovative one insofar as it uses its neo–Victorian structure to offer a counter-history of femininity in Britain. Some might argue as to its inauthenticity, but one of the benefits of neo–Victorianism is its refusal to observe the conventions of historical accuracy. As discussed, this BBC adaptation of *Fingersmith* is a neo–Victorian adaptation instead of having a close trace of the Victorian due to its source text's being the representation of the Victorian from a lesbian counter history context. Still, the delusion on the side of the binary between "truth" and "fiction." Rather it suggests the presence of alternative histories that might be presented in fictional form, but in doing so tell us a lot about the secret lives of Victorian women; the kind of material that was seldom referred to in official histories of the period. Past and present are combined in a structure that speaks to both eras, offering alternative perspectives on history while commenting on present-day notions of sexuality. Marginalized groups are given a voice through an adaptation that does not shy away from depicting the benefits as well as the pitfalls of alternative sexualities.

The Korean version of the novel, re-titled *The Handmaiden* for western audiences (*Ah-ga-ssi* in Korean) preserves the basic plot while altering the relationships between male and female characters. The action is transposed from Victorian London to 1930s Korea, occupied by the Japanese. Sarah Waters was intrigued: "it's interesting for me because unlike the other adaptations I've had, this was all done at a bit of a distance from me" (qtd. in Sullivan 1). The story is transmuted into a poor girl's experience of discrimination under Japanese colonialism. The lesbian scenes are more explicit, as compared to the BBC version, while director Park Chan-wook makes extensive use of symbols such as mirrors, gloves (that change their meaning in this version), pools, and lollipops, all designed to emphasize women's subordinate status.

Fingersmith's main attraction lies in the way it compares the past to the present. Waters' source text inserts lesbian figures into the nineteenth century as an important issue, while proving the truth of Gutleben's claim that "the fascination with Victorianism seems inevitably to come with a temptation to denounce the injustice towards some of its ill-used or forgotten representatives such as women, the lower classes or homosexuals" (10). In *The Handmaiden*, by transposing the lesbian couple's story to 1930s Korea, Park Chanwook closely traces the impact of neo–Victorianism on the Korean past. Especially in the beginning scene of the movie, the Japanese invasion reveals the effects of colonialism on women and children at first, and showing that the effects of marginalization gives rise to the lesbian affair. This time the couple comprises a Japanese heiress Lady Hideko (Min-hee Kim) and a Korean handmaiden (Tae-ri Kim). This strategy explores the possibility of relationships being able to transcend politics and class.

The Handmaiden maintains the novel's three-part structure to tell the story from three different views of Japanese Lady Hideko, Sook-hee (Kim Tae-ri), and trickster Fujiwara (Ha Jung-woo). The first part is the one that resembles the original most, is narrated by the future handmaiden Nam Sook-hee who is an orphan brought up as a pickpocket. A Korean cheat (Fujiwara) takes her from the slums to seduce Hideko—the Japanese lady with her Korean uncle Kouzuki (Jin-woong Jo). Fujiwara has the same plan as Gentleman in the BBC adaptation, which is to elope with Hideko, and then put Sook-hee to an asylum to reach her inherited wealth.

Such parallels are rare as *The Handmaiden* follows its own trajectory. The rising voice of the rain, the soldiers' steps are heard and the life of the miserable Korean people is depicted in a gray *mise en scène* dominated by the sight of crying babies on women's laps. Under these circumstances, it is inevitable that Nan-sook Hee should want to escape. When she arrives, she is educated by Kouzuki in courtly behavior, a task accomplished so successfully that she becomes mistress of the household, working closely "the snake" (the Japanese pejorative description of Kouzuki). Eventually Kouzuki resolves to marry her, despite his strange ways. His office is full of pornographic material that he uses to stimulate himself.

As in *Fingersmith*, the trip to Lady Hideko's house is through the green fields signifying hope. As Sook-hee enters the mansion her expression of curiosity indicates her entrance into a different world, one of horror and suspense summed up in Hideko's nightmares, the darkness of the landscape outside and the tree that is used to hang people. These situations, reminiscent of a horror film, form backdrop to the central love-affair that I depicted sensuously, with the camera lovingly focusing on the two women in the bathing scene, as they splash about, suck lollipops and look for Hideko's false teeth which have been lost amid the soap suds. The contrast between interior and exterior scenes suggests the secrecy of the love affair as well as strength; despite the exigencies of the weather outside, the two women focus solely on one another. The effect is to create a more intense ambience completely different from the BBC adaptation. The value of this sequence lies in the possibilities it suggests for women, if they are prepared to cast aside their inhibitions and let their passions go. Once again we are made aware of the arbitrariness of class and national divisions if love is involved.

On the other hand it might be argued that the love scenes in *The Handmaiden* are presented for the male gaze, as the camera focuses lovingly on the actors' naked bodies while emphasizing their fondness for role-play as they rapidly change dresses. Park makes an effort to deflect attention away from the women by having Kouzuki and Fujiwara appear nude as they try to seduce the women. Fujiwara lugubriously eats a peach, sucking in his cheeks as he does so, emphasizing his lustful desires as well as his latent desire for power.

Such sequences seem a long way from neo–Victorianism. But perhaps not: the basic themes of power and patriarchy still pervade the action. Readers of Waters' novel would still be able to recognize the basic scenario, even if it takes place in another country during another historical period. This is of neo–Victorianism's basic qualities—its transhistoricity, even though it might have his origins in a very specific historical moment.

Yet the film refuses to embrace the courage of its convictions, as it depicts male power reasserting itself. The third part looks at Fujiwara's fate, despite the fact that the girls' Sapphic desire has been explicitly satisfied, Hideko is beaten by her uncle, and consigned to her bedroom. We are invited into a secret cellar that is full of cut sexual organs, a way of emphasizing the extent of patriarchal power—any enemies of the Japanese (especially Koreans) are immediately deprived of their manhood. Male sexuality is exaggerated when compared to the eroticism reflected by the women of the film. The males' grotesque behavior carries bestial overtones: at one point Sook-Hee is forced to read pornographic texts for the benefit of a male audience. The film cannot escape the belief that women are always submissive role models.

In the end, despite all the hardships, the two girls are shown together in symmetrical *mise en scène* portraying both the intimacy and the equality between them. Their nakedness is shown with their passionate kisses reflected through the mirrors and the music changes when the spectators see the waves and the moon, suggesting their kinship with nature. Again the film's ambiguity is evident: we are not sure that the female protagonists will have a future in a society so obsessed with male power and sexual perversion. As spectators we remain unsure whether the love-making sequences are not designed to appeal to the male spectator's scopophilic desires, rather than suggesting any form of sexual liberation. *The Handmaiden* does not provide a satisfactory ending: we are left in a state of confusion as to Park's ideological and political take on his material.

When Park thought to produce a nineteenth century film, he found that the BBC had shot it. Then he decided to have a Korean version of it set in 1930s (during the Japanese invasion), but also to get rid of some of the romantic elements of the book, and adapt it to local conditions. Through these changes, he is able "to not only get the element of different classes, servants and aristocrats, but … [to] get the added layer of the backdrop of a society being under colonial rule" (Thompson 1). Yet, as in the case of the BBC version, it does not focus on the minute details of the historical facts of 1930s Korea, instead the appealing pornographic story of a lesbian couple is retold from the Korean perspective. Park explains this interest towards sexuality in Korea as "in Korea the depiction of sexuality isn't any more strictly compared with European countries…. It will earn you a higher age rating. Rather than getting immersed into the seriousness of the moment, sometimes I would rather keep a certain distance and infuse elements of humour into the situation. That is the more adult way to handle situations of sexuality or violence" (Thompson 1).

This aspect is another attraction of the neo–Victorianism that uses sexuality as a tool to bring the once-marginalized lives into the forefront. The Korean version grants the possibility to a subordinated Korean woman to have a relationship with a Japanese woman (which was impossible both because of the Japanese-Korean enmity and the impossibility of lesbianism in those times). Park takes the bare facts of the novel's story and recasts it according to his desire to combine the past and the present: In the uncle's mansion, where the women wear traditional dress, any sense of the era is lost in a timeless world.

In conclusion, the *Fingersmith* movie is a neo–Victorian screen adaptation that transgresses the fictional boundaries of Sarah Waters' novel *Fingersmith* through its voyeuristic positioning of the lesbian identities in a fake Victorian world. *The Handmaiden* as the Korean version of the novel carries the subject matter one step further by transcoding the English cultural material into a Korean pornographic entity. In one way or another, both adaptations are inspired from a Victorian world that hypocritically buries the secret sexualities of lesbians and by explicitly exhibiting these obscene scenes; they attract the attention of the contemporary audience. Inevitably, there are no absolute constructions of value, and each version of a text brings new insights that tell us about the source texts as well as the cultures that produce the adaptation. In both adaptations, through the cinematic conventions, the voyeuristic appetite of the contemporary audience is satisfied by the pornographically designed lesbian love scenes actually foreground what was really happening behind the closed doors of the harsh rules governing the lives of the so-called prudent men. What they contribute to the contemporary cultural entity via neo–Victorianism is: they burst out the unknown ignorance of the modern men into their faces.

The value of neo–Victorian works in transcending past and present stems from its position of being in-between: it is neither totally conventional nor contemporary. The appeal of the neo–Victorian adaptations to contemporary audiences stems from the fact that they criticize the Victorian world while claiming that they are no longer Victorian in their preoccupation with society's injustices. These neo–Victorian movies are a form of post-adaptation that transcends the source/target text binary to make a comment on the value of Victorian times in the present, while commenting on the past. Post-adaptation also inspires the Korean version in handling their own historical material. Both adaptations enhance the historical significance of hitherto marginalized existences through a fusion of past with present.

NOTES

1. As Sanders also asserts: "A limited of foreclosed sense of 'the belatedness' of adaptive literature would restrict the capacity of the appropriation to function as a textual force in its own right. A more positive approach is … [a]cknowledging the 'perpetual belatedness' [of the new versions as] … 'affirmative, productive, inaugural'" (159).

2. "Fingersmith" also connotes a sexual meaning referring to female masturbation.

WORKS CITED

Benjamin, Walter. "The Task of the Translator." *Theories of Translation.* Ed. Rainer Schulte and John Biguenet. 71–92. Chicago: University of Chicago Press, 1992. Print.
Elliott, Kamilla. *Rethinking the Novel/Film Debate.* Cambridge: Cambridge University Press, 2003. Print.
Fingersmith. Dir. Aisling Walsh. Perf. Sally Hawkins, Imelda Staunton, Rupert Evans. Sally Head Productions/BBC, 2015. Film.
Gutleben, Christian. *Nostalgic Postmodernism: The Victorian Tradition and the Contemporary British Novel.* Amsterdam: Rodopi, 2001. Print.
The Handmaiden. Dir. Park Chan Wook. Perf. Min-hee Kim, Tae-ri Kim, Jung-woo Ha. Moho Film, Yong Film, 2016. DVD.
Said, Edward W. "On Originality." *The World, the Text, and the Critic.* Cambridge: Harvard University Press, 1983. 126–139. Print.
Sanders, Julie. *Adaptation and Appropriation.* London: Routledge, 2006. Print.
Sullivan, Kevin P. "*The Handmaiden:* How a Victorian-Set Novel became the Korea-Set Film." *Entertainment,* 9 Nov. 2016. Web. 19 Jan. 2017.
Thompson, Anne. "How Park Chan-Wook's 'The Handmaiden' Reveals His Ongoing Passion for Strong Women." *Indiewire,* 11 Oct. 2016. Web. 24 Jan. 2017.
Waters, Sarah. *Fingersmith.* London: Virago, 2002. Print.
Zabus, Jack. *Breaking the Magic Spell: Radical Theories of Folk and Fairy Tales.* London: Heinemann, 1979. Print.

Reshaping Gloriana

Representations of the British Queens
in Victoria *(2016) and* The Crown *(2016)*

DOROTA BABILAS

Adapting Royal Biographies
for Mass Audiences

The British monarchy is, in popular perception, one of the things that make the United Kingdom distinctive. As David Cannadine has observed in his influential essay on "the invention of tradition," no head of state has been surrounded by more popular ritual than the British sovereign, "with the possible exception of the papacy" (102). Particularly the moments in history when the throne was occupied by a female monarch appear to catch viewers' imagination, imbuing the monarchy with notions of maternity, domesticity and charity associated with femininity (Campbell Orr 76). "The English like queens," commented the Duchess of Saxe-Coburg-Saalfeld in 1819, on the birth of her granddaughter, the future Queen Victoria (Lee 11). The sentiment still rings true two hundred years later, when Victoria's record of the longest reign in the history of the United Kingdom has been broken by her great-great-granddaughter, Elizabeth II. The same sense of infinite value is shared by many people around the globe for whom the British monarchy remains the "truest" in the world. It is therefore understandable why televisual biographies of British queens continue to attract mass audiences. Lavish television spectacles, such as the recently concluded first seasons of *Victoria* (ITV) and *The Crown* (Netflix) offer reassuring and culturally valuable visions of "continuity, tradition, history and pageantry" (Richards 258) while allowing— carefully constructed—glimpses on the private lives of the royals.

In the early days of the cinema, depictions of Queen Victoria were subject to official approval by the Lord Chamberlain and the president of the British Board of Film Censors—as witnessed, for example, on the hundredth anniversary of the queen's accession in June 1937 (Chapman 67). Since then, as I have argued elsewhere (Babilas 12), Victoria has been the subject of a great number of films and TV series, ranging in their portrayals from nearly hagiographical, like *Victoria the Great* (1937) and *Sixty Glorious Years* (1938), both directed by Herbert Wilcox, to highly critical and derogatory, e.g., in ITV's *Edward the Seventh* (1975).

In recent years, there have been several attempts to bring the stereotypically "unamused" monarch back to the audience's attention. In 1996, a little-known romantic episode in the later life of Queen Victoria (played by Judi Dench) was rediscovered in John Madden's *Her Majesty, Mrs. Brown*—presenting the queen's friendship with her Scottish servant, John Brown (Billy Connolly). As Elizabeth A. Ford and Deborah C. Mitchell notice, "More than any other Victoria biopic, *Mrs. Brown* focuses on the tension between public and private worlds" (171), playing out power struggles in different configurations among the government (represented by Prime Minister Disraeli [Antony Sher]), the royal household (with private secretary Sir Henry Ponsonby [Geoffrey Palmer]), the children of the queen, and the solitary widowed sovereign herself, supported by the only man (Brown) who seems to understand her. The value of the film consists of its representation of Victoria's stoicism as she resists the blandishments of her politicians.

A further wave of popular interest in Queen Victoria was occasioned by the hundredth anniversary of her death in 2001. The centenary was marked by numerous museum exhibitions, television documentaries—such as *Queen Victoria's Empire* (PBS), *The Victorians Uncovered* (Channel 4), or *What the Victorians Did for Us* (Channel 4)—and a two-part BBC movie *Victoria and Albert* (dir. John Erman) concentrating on the married life of the queen and the prince consort. Framed by the recollections of the elderly and infirm monarch, the movie presents the relationship between Victoria (Victoria Hamilton) and Prince Albert (Jonathan Firth) as turbulent, with Albert constantly trying to "tame" his free-spirited and temperamental wife. Still, Albert's influence frees Victoria from the power of egoistical advisors and relatives including her mother, the Duchess of Kent (Penelope Wilton), and her bullying companion, Sir John Conroy (Patrick Malahide); her uncle, King Leopold of the Belgians (Jonathan Pryce); her governess, Baroness Lehzen (Diana Rigg), and the prime minister, Lord Melbourne (Nigel Hawthorne) who all think only of their particular interests in relation to her. As soon as Victoria submits to her "natural" role of wife and mother, she regains composure and dignity that help make her a better Queen (Babilas 192–96). As summed up onscreen by the great Duke of Wellington (John Wood): "Monarchy's got to be respectable" if it is to survive at all. The program offers a valuable pointer as to the continuing influence of the monarchy in contemporary British cultures.

Later, *The Young Victoria* (2009, dir. Jean-Marc Vallée) offered a portrayal of the Queen (Emily Blunt) as a spirited teenager struggling with family troubles, conflicting loyalties and excessive expectations of people around her. As Cele C. Otnes and Pauline Maclaran note, Victoria is shown to be—like many fictional and historical princesses, especially Diana—"a victim of tradition" (158). As she observes bitterly at the beginning of the film, "Even a palace can be a prison." Vallée's film might be seen as an attempt to publicize Victoria's biography among a new, younger audience who might sympathize with her determination to break free from this confinement. However, it might also serve a traditionalist ideological agenda, promoting Victorian class and gender divisions as natural and admirable. This proposition sounds especially plausible in view of the fact that the screenwriter of the movie, Julian Fellowes (being also a Conservative member of the House of Lords) is the man responsible for the multiple award-winning ITV series *Downton Abbey* (2010–15)—which projects a reactionary view of Britain and its social class system dating back to the early 20th century. We are projected into the world of nostalgia where the past is perceived as being superior to the present.

As far as the biography of the current British monarch is concerned, there were few if any efforts to portray it on screen, save for the documentary about her coronation as well as officially-sponsored works such as *Royal Family* in 1969, which was watched by 68 percent of the British population (Richards 260). She was always confined to the background, whether as a figure of satire, like in German alternative history *Willi und die Windzors* (1996, dir. Hape Kerkeling), or nostalgia, such as in New Zealand family movie *Her Majesty* (2001, dir. Mark J. Gordon). The first film featuring Elizabeth II as the protagonist was Stephen Frears' *The Queen* (2006) with Helen Mirren in the title role. It told the story of the public crisis after the death of Diana, Princess of Wales, on 31 August 1997. The princess' death in a car crash in Paris was a significant influence on the popular perception of the British monarchy as an institution and the members of the royal family as human beings. The film focused on the tensions between the public functions of the queen and her private feelings, showing her in a sympathetic light, as a hostage of outdated court protocol, wary of a media-dominated world. She might have been reclusive and overly reserved, but she was not heartless. The film proved that the monarchy—including the queen herself—could be effectively re-enacted on screen to emphasize the emotional bits, speculations and indiscretions that the viewers looked for the most. The lives of the Windsor family proved to be a valuable source of inspiration for the film industry, which released several more titles on similar subjects, from the critically acclaimed *King's Speech* (2010, dir. Tom Hooper) to less successful productions, such as royal love story *W.E.* (2011, dir. Madonna) about Edward VIII and Mrs. Simpson or an exploitation of the Princess of Wales' fame in *Diana* (2013, dir. Oliver Hirschbiegel). None of them feature Queen Elizabeth II as a principal role.

A different approach was taken by director Julian Jarrold (one of the directors of *The Crown*) in his romantic comedy-drama *A Royal Night Out* (2015), which shows an apocryphal story of young princesses Elizabeth (Sarah Gadon) and Margaret (Bel Powley) sneaking out of the palace on V.E. Day in 1945 to mingle with the crowd in celebration. The movie follows in the tradition of many royal "escape stories," such as William Wyler's *Roman Holiday* (1953) with Audrey Hepburn as a princess of an unspecified country getting lost in Rome or a completely fictional escapade to Dover attributed to Queen Victoria (Romy Schneider) in *Mädchenjahre einer Königin* (1954, dir. Ernst Marischka). In Jarrold's movie, the future Queen Elizabeth II enjoys a night of adventure and (innocent) romance with a Royal Air Force soldier Jack Hodges (Jack Reynor) as they try to catch up with the rebellious runaway Margaret whose chance encounter with a naval officer takes her to several gambling dens and shady nightclubs in London.

In terms of the construction of the narrative, *The Queen* follows the example of *Her Majesty, Mrs. Brown* in that it shows an older monarch struggling with political pressures building around the choices made in her private life—losing a beloved husband or a rather problematic daughter-in-law. Similarly, *A Royal Night Out* employed familiarization techniques resembling those used earlier in *The Young Victoria*. Both films moved back to the early years of the queens now remembered mostly as stern and matronly, to show them as energetic teenagers trying to balance their royal obligations with a natural youthful need for freedom and friendship. Royal history seems to repeat itself endlessly—the way *The King's Speech* recalled an earlier tale of a monarch overcoming an unmentionable affliction with the help of an unconventional doctor in *The Madness of King George* (1994)—every time proving remarkable qualities of character in members of the Royal Family. The use of such familiar tropes suggests the desire to foreground a value aspect of the royal character—their stoicism in the face of adversity.

Both *Victoria* and *The Crown* were created against a backdrop of discussion regarding royal representations on film. Not much has changed since Jeffrey Richards detected the dual forces of "mythologization accompanied by humanization" (274) of current and historical monarchs alike. Sovereigns, and especially queens, have to balance the responsibilities of their official functions with the demands of their private lives, yet they "all rise above the pressures triumphantly to do their duty and serve the nation, confirming that they are remarkable individuals" (278). In that sense, royal films have something of a cheerleading function, encouraging viewers to follow the protagonists' example.

What might be changing, however, are underlying conceptions of value among the viewing public towards royal history. The reassuring and nostalgic vision of a stable Britain has been challenged by a wave of productions in neo–Victorian style, which aimed at "(re)interpretation, (re)discovery and (re)vision" of the nineteenth century and its ideological legacy (Heilmann and Llewellyn 4). Elements of such work are visible especially in the *Victoria* series (Kinzler 50–57).

Presumed Historical Accuracy

Ostensibly, the most important concern of any historical biography is factual accuracy, and purists are notoriously hard to please. Rather predictably, some press reviewers objected to the liberties taken with both Victoria and Elizabeth II. This seems inevitable in any costume drama—it has been publicized that Queen Elizabeth II herself complained about some inaccuracies concerning military uniforms in *The Young Victoria* (Jamieson). Nevertheless, both recent series have inspired critical press articles concerning possible factual errors (Gibb; Thompson) or questioning the casting choices in terms of the actors' physical similarity to the characters they played (Hawkes).

As far as ITV's *Victoria* is concerned, most objections concentrated on the sensationalism through the sexualization of the narrative. The drama emphasized Victoria's (Jenna Coleman's) physical attractiveness, whereas in reality she was a "short, vulgar-looking child," prone to gaining weight (Gibb). In similar vein, Rufus Sewell was deemed too young, too handsome and too charismatic to play Prime Minister Lord Melbourne, who was in his late 50s at the time of Victoria's coronation, "was overweight and had a tendency to fall asleep and snore loudly in public" (Gibb). There is an added subplot in which Sir John Conroy (Paul Rhys) and the Duchess of Kent (Catherine Flemming) conspire to have the queen declared insane, like her grandfather George III, by scaring her with rats (Ep. 2 "Ladies in Waiting"). Also, one of the queen's uncles, the Duke of Cumberland (Peter Firth), is implicated in a failed assassination attempt (Ep. 8 "Young England"). Most shockingly of all, however, relations between Victoria, Lord Melbourne, and Prince Albert (Tom Hughes) are presented in a manner resembling a love triangle with the queen torn between her feelings for her dashing German cousin and her fascinating mature mentor. The reviewer for *The Spectator*, James Delingpole, complained that the repeated instances of Prince Albert ripping off his shirt and "Lord M." "twinkling with but barely sublimated desire" were cases of irritating

"MillsandBoonification of history" conducted with "brazen shamelessness" to satisfy the most escapist fantasies of the—predominantly female and assumedly unsophisticated—audience (Delingpole). Yet Delingpole's judgment lacks historical perspective—for all the allegedly salacious elements, this series focuses on Victoria's fortitude in the face of adversity as personified by the elder members of her court. By such means the series rehearses the theme of earlier work focused on the royal family and their strength of character.

The Crown also added little morsels to titillate the viewers. In one of the very first scenes of the first episode, King George VI (Jared Harris) tells a limerick full of sexual innuendo (Ep. 1 "Wolferton Splash"). Later on, a heated argument between the queen (Claire Foy) and her husband, Prince Philip (Matt Smith), during their Australian tour is witnessed by the film crew reporting the royal visit (Ep. 8 "Pride & Joy"). The queen's marriage to the independent-minded and domineering Duke of Edinburgh is largely presented as difficult and frequently stormy, with quarrels, bouts of jealousy and veiled accusations of infidelity on both sides. Shockingly, when the queen passionately asserts her love and faithfulness for her husband, he refuses to reciprocate the declaration and remains ominously silent (Ep. 9 "Assassins").

As observed by Jeffrey Richards with regard to earlier works concerned with private lives of the monarchs, "the implicit assumption behind all these films is that being a king or queen does not make you happy and you should leave the job to those who have been trained for it" (275). In the reality of modern tabloid-based media—especially since the highly publicized marital problems of the children of Queen Elizabeth II in the 1990s, culminating in Princess Diana's death—the royals are depicted as "spectacular victims of conspiracy, betrayal, familial opposition and ill-treatment" (278). Despite all its glamour and associated wealth, wearing the crown clearly adds to, not subtracts from the miseries of life. Sometimes the problems of the sovereigns reflect on the whole family. In The Crown also other female members of the royal family—the queen's sister, Princess Margaret (Vanessa Kirby), her mother (Victoria Hamilton, who had played Queen Victoria in the 2001 miniseries) and grandmother (Eileen Atkins)—have to make personal sacrifices, giving up their preferred choices in love, friendship, and family relations. Margaret must break off her engagement to the man she loves, the widowed queen mother is not allowed to have a friend far from the royal court, and Queen Mary's relationship with her eldest son (Alex Jennings) is strained after his abdication as King Edward VIII—the fact recalled several times in the series as an example of shameful neglect and abandonment of his duties, leading to the monarchy as an institution being disparaged. Yet there is something of a paradox here. Although we see successive members of the royal family enduring personal and social torment, they are determined to undertake their duties without demur. Once again value emerges, even through adversity.

Quality—Value—Virtue

Both series were advertised as achievements in quality television entertainment, boasting of very high budgets—allegedly 11 million euros for *Victoria* (Whiting), and the whole of a hundred million dollars for the first season of *The Crown* (Birnbaum; Mangan). As argued by Otnes and Maclaran, in modern consumer culture, this lavish royal treatment in filmic representations makes it easier for the royal family to "maintain the level of fascination they do for many people around the world" (20). Of course, this interest in watching the royals goes back centuries before the invention of moving pictures, and it formed a subject of interest for political commentators such as Walter Bagehot. In *The English Constitution* (1867) he opined that especially the women comprising "one half the human race at least" (38)—the likely primary target audience of today's royal biopics—"care[d] fifty times more for a marriage [in this case, of the Prince of Wales] than a ministry" (38). Still, as Otnes and Maclaran note, historical film and television are perfect means "to convey the grandeur of royal ritual, the stateliness of tradition, and the potency of war" (144). Furnished with spectacular historical costumes, magnificent heraldry, and glamorous sets, royal historical films—similarly to another film subgenre, the heritage film—provide an opportunity to satisfy the audience with luxury and opulence:

> Consider the electrifying image of Elizabeth I on horseback, dressed in chain mail, an abundance of red hair flowing down her back, as she addresses the English troops before they go into battle against the armada. Or the magnificent splendour of the delicate teenage Victoria, her bejewelled coronation crown encircling her head, golden orb and sceptre in her hands, as she majestically returns the gaze of the crowd that throngs Westminster Abbey. Such momentous media moments reinforce the mystic elements that infuse royalty, while simultaneously asserting pride in national heritage and identity [Otnes and Maclaran 144].

In this respect, television biographies of historical queens (assuming that the early years of Elizabeth II's reign have by now reached a suitably remote status of historical events) affirm Bagehot's deep belief in the power of the royals to influence public opinion (76). They offer a pleasurable vision of the country, which in reality may never have existed (Vidal 7–9). But that question is in a sense unimportant; what royal films perpetuate is a vision of cultural value, as suggested by duty, stoicism and perseverance.

In recent years, the most successful—commercially and artistically—heritage production was the six-season ITV period drama *Downton Abbey,* set in a fictional Edwardian country estate in Yorkshire and depicting the intertwined lives of the members of the aristocratic Crawley family and the crew of their domestic servants in the turbulent years between the sinking of the *Titanic* in 1912 and New Year's Eve 1925. With its roots firmly in similar ITV historical dramas of the Seventies such as *Upstairs Downstairs* (1971–77), *Downton Abbey* combined historical reconstruction with conservative content—the focus on material accuracy of clothes and props was matched with thinly veiled glorification of the world of patriarchy and strict social hierarchies; the times of benevolent masters and the "lower orders" who knew their place.

Both *Victoria* and *The Crown* vie for the title of "the next *Downton Abbey*" (Whiting; Gray; Power). *Victoria* introduces a cast of fictitious "downstairs" characters complementing the historical—or, more precisely, historically-inspired—"upstairs" plot. Young Queen Victoria demonstrates sympathetic interest in the lives of the working classes, from the Chartists to her own household staff whose loyalty and dedication seem to derive straight from the recently finished hit series. The subplot concentrates on the career of Miss Skerrett (Nell Hudson), advancing from a junior maid with a hazy past to the position of the Queen's personal dresser, and her budding romance with the inventive Italian baker, Mr. Francatelli (Ferdinand Kingsley). The vision portrayed here is slightly different from *Downton Abbey*, allowing for greater focus on characters from different socio-economic backgrounds as well as the young queen's interest in worldly affairs.

Some reviewers, however, argue that there are more elements of the neo–Victorian than of the heritage mode in *Victoria* (Franchi; de Bruin-Molé; Eckersley). In neo–Victorian productions—mostly film adaptations of modern novels set in the Victorian era, such as Sarah Waters' *Fingersmith* (2011, BBC) or Michel Faber's *The Crimson Petal and the White* (2011, BBC)—the mood is much darker and the depicted historical reality is usually condemned as hypocritical, prudish and unjust. Undeniably, the construction of the presented world in the *Victoria* series does not have such an industrially minded perspective, but, perhaps unwittingly, follows some of Miriam Elizabeth Burstein's tongue-in-cheek "Rules for Writing Neo-Victorian Novels," listing stereotypes commonly found in neo–Victorian fiction. "There must be at least one Prostitute, who will be an Alcoholic and/or have a Heart of Gold" (Burstein)—she turns out to be Miss Skerrett's sister (Ep. 4 "The Clockwork Prince") who in addition has an illegitimate baby and indeed lives in "a Wretched Slum, … Dirty and Damp" (Burstein), fulfilling the inevitable prerequisite that any story set in the Victorian era must contain something "Dickensian" (Burstein). Likewise, Victoria and Albert are "Instinctively Admired by Members of Oppressed Populations" as "True Egalitarians" disregarding all social differences (Burstein). Yet despite such familiar conventions, the characters remain aware of the political reality of their own epoch. They stand for progress, idealism and compassion, which sets the inequalities of the Victorian period in their true light. Much of the material might be familiar, but the value of such criticism does not diminish, especially in the way it serves to illuminate the characters' behavior.

The treatment of history in *Victoria* is more traditionalist than in a typical neo–Victorian production. There is no direct criticism of either the queen personally or monarchy as an institution. On the contrary, Victoria and (later) Albert represent the optimistic belief in scientific and sociological progress, expressed in their keen interest in all things modern. Their honesty and lack of pretentiousness eventually win over any detractors among their subjects, and likewise are supposed to convince the viewers of the virtues of the monarchy and its value to society's future.

The Crown attempts a more difficult task, as the series lacks the perceived interpretative security provided by its remoteness from the presented facts: many of the principal protagonists are still alive. Nevertheless, some biographers of Queen Elizabeth II allude to her "Queen Victoria Syndrome," that is, "the paradox of a reclusive individual at the centre of social and commercial mechanism" (Lacey 153). The series attempts to bring this withdrawn and mysterious personage back into the spotlight and shed some light on her value to society. As some reviewers notice, *The Crown* "is a well-timed meditation on Britain's decline as world power," especially resonant "in this age of Brexit" (Power). On the other hand, much in the fashion of past royal films, the figure of the monarch retains their stable, conservative image in political as well private lives, even if this requires them to make decisions painful to individual members of the Royal Family. Queen Elizabeth has to intervene to break up the controversial romance between Princess Margaret and the divorced Group Captain Peter Townsend (Ben Miles) in the last episode of Season 1. Margaret is forced to publicly assert her adherence to the rules of the Church of England. There are obvious double standards at work here as many Cabinet members are themselves divorced and remarried (including the new Prime Minister, Anthony Eden, played by Jeremy Northam). The Queen has to go back on her own promise to Margaret and forbid the engagement by resorting to emotional blackmail.

Peter Morgan, creator of *The Crown*, tries to avoid adding fictitious subplots, even though some circumstances and interpersonal relations in the series may have been altered for sensational effect. One of the few exceptions, however, is the appearance of Venetia Scott (Kate Phillips), Winston Churchill's young secretary, whose death during the disastrous great fog in London in spring 1952 makes the then Prime Minister Winston Churchill reconsider his political future in light of the calamity (Ep. 4 "Act of God"). The episode throws the Peter Townsend incident into sharper focus: the Queen is no different from anyone else when it comes to making momentous decisions. Such techniques underline the notion of universality. The struggles—personal as well as constitutional—that the monarchs undergo are shared by viewers. Victoria and Elizabeth both choose strong, alpha-male types for their husbands, even if this entails some power negotiations. They also favor decisive and manly advisors. Within such confines, they have to try and develop their characters. They might make mistakes, but their decisions can be well understood. They might be monarchs in their public lives, but they share some of the problems experienced by ordinary people.

Gloriana Alleluia

In many ways, however, the monarchs lead very different lives. This is denoted by the religious music: the opening sequence of *Victoria* unfolds to the accompaniment of a religious-sounding hymn—composed by Martin Phipps and performed by the all-female musical group Mediæval Bæbes. The lyrics contain just two words repeated several times and then recurring throughout the subsequent episode. According to Dan McCulloch, executive producer of the series, Phipps "loved the character" of the young queen and wanted to compose "something that literally came from the heart" (Dowell). The visuals comprise close-ups of Jenna Coleman as Victoria sporting different hairstyles, from a girlish one with long hair worn loose except for a simple braid crown, to a more mature look with braids coiled on the sides of the head with a central parting and a small jeweled pin. The symbolism of this opening points both to Victoria growing up physically and emotionally as well as undergoing a more significant transition from ordinary mortal to Queen. A similar "alleluia," combined with more ominous lines of the "dies irae" features in *The Virgin Queen*, in the scene when Elizabeth (Anne-Marie Duff) has been notified of her accession at the death of her rival sister Mary.

Although the historical Victoria expressed rather ambivalent feelings towards Elizabeth I, whom she perceived as "immodest" (Dobson and Watson 147), in the series Elizabeth I becomes "something of a favorite" of the young queen, who copies her portrait in her sketchbook and contemplates "following her example and reigning alone" (Ep. 3 "Brocket Hall"). At a fancy dress ball at Buckingham Palace, the yet unmarried Victoria appears dressed as Elizabeth I with Lord Melbourne accompanying her disguised as Robert Dudley, Earl of Leicester—her advisor, closest confidant and rumored lover. "It would be unkind for Elizabeth to refuse her Leicester," Lord M. teases her as they dance (Ep. 3 "Brocket Hall"). In fact, Victoria never made a public appearance in the costume of Elizabeth—the whole scene was fictional, though likely inspired by the historical Plantagenet Ball organized at Buckingham Palace in 1842 where the Queen and her husband Prince Albert donned matching costumes of King Edward III and Queen Philippa (Rappaport 113). Thematically speaking in terms of the television series, the ball has the effect of communicating Victoria's specialness as a person; a monarch born to rule who has to fulfill the responsibilities expected of her, despite her personal inclinations.

The transforming power of the crown on the monarchy underlies the opening sequence of *The Crown*. The opening consists of computer-generated extreme close-ups of the crown, which gradually materializes from "shadowy glints of gold and molten metal curling from the darkness" (Ellis-Petersen) to form a vast jewel half-hidden in the gloom. "When the holy oil touches me, I am transformed. Brought into direct contact with the divine," explains King George VI to his young daughter on the eve of his coronation (Ep. 5 "Smoke and Mirrors"). Elizabeth recalls the scene before her own coronation and she approaches the ceremony with trepidation, clearly believing herself to be spiritually changed by it. "Who wants transparency, when you can have magic?" asks the Duke of Windsor watching the television broadcast with his wife and friends (Ep. 5 "Smoke and Mirrors"). Like Walter Bagehot before him, the former Edward VIII shares the conviction that the coronation can transform "an ordinary young woman of modest ability and little imagination" into a virtual "goddess" (Ep. 5 "Smoke and Mirrors"). The viewers are invited to participate in this sentiment.

Elizabeth's life is linked to that of her illustrious predecessor through the name Gloriana, coined by Edmund Spenser in his *Faerie Queene* of 1596 (cf. Dobson and Watson 43). The name also implicitly crops up in the last scene of the final episode of Season 1 of *The Crown*, when the Queen poses for an official photographic portrait. Elizabeth II assumes the royal pose, the voice of the photographer from behind the scenes quoting Spenser's *Faerie Queene*, among other works: "All hail sage Lady whom a grateful Isle hath blessed. Not moving, not breathing. Our very own goddess. Glorious Gloriana. Forgetting Elizabeth Windsor now. Now only Elizabeth Regina" (Ep. 10 "Gloriana"). In the last second the Queen's face lightens with composure and majesty.

Both *Victoria* and *The Crown* make use of the idea of "the two bodies" of the monarch, brought to public attention by the seminal book by Ernst Kantorowicz (1957). At moments of royal pageantry, the "body politic" eclipses the "body physical" which the monarch shares with other mortals. Elevated by the ceremony above the ordinary crowd, the Queens embody the splendor of the monarchy, even despite the fact that their real power has been rapidly shrinking in the passing centuries. Yet both works are careful to suggest that despite the monarchs' elevated status their lives remain valuable to viewers. The "body physical" determines their fate as women, whose lives are socially expected to center on family, marriage and children. Most of us can identify with traditional family values associated with femininity.

"No more housewives, but queens"

Marriage and maternity are presented as inseparable phenomena for both queens. At the end of Season 1, Elizabeth II already has two of her four children (Billy Jenkins, Yolanda Kettle), and Victoria gives birth to her eldest daughter (also named Victoria) with eight more offspring still to arrive. However, whereas for Elizabeth childbearing is a matter of happenstance not given a second thought (children just start appearing on family film reels soon after the wedding), the young monarch in *Victoria* tries her best to avoid pregnancy, resorting to ineffective and sometimes rather eccentric methods of contraception, such as jumping up and down on a sofa following intercourse (Ep. 6 "The Queen's Husband"). Victoria has an understandable fear of death in childbirth (the fate of her older cousin, Princess Charlotte) despite her well-known dislike of small children (Babilas 255–257). *Victoria* tackles the problem of royal childbirth differently, and more sympathetically, than earlier depictions of Queen Victoria. In the first episode of *Edward the Seventh* (1975, ATV) the action opens with a hysterical outburst of the queen (Annette Crosbie) who discovers that she is pregnant for the second time.

Compared with Victoria, Elizabeth II seems to be characterized by a deeper sense of obligation and responsibility. Ever since her childhood she has come across as a very serious girl—especially compared to her sister—aware of the burden that awaits her and ready to do her duty. She seems to rely willingly on tradition as a source of stability in life and support in times of doubt. Eventually, both Elizabeth and Victoria regard marriage and family as crucial aspects of their lives, at least as important as any official regal functions—but it is Elizabeth who appears to be more settled in her reactions.

In this construction of femininity and female social roles, the Queens are once again made more emotionally accessible to a large proportion of the series' intended viewers. It is assumed that even if most female spectators cannot relate personally to the pressures of monarchy, they can easily identify with the pleasures and pains of family obligations—childbearing and childcare, running a house, marital squabbles, etc. This paradox in itself is Victorian in its root and can be traced back to John Ruskin's essay "Of Queen's Gardens" (1864), in which he stated that a submissive wife in her home is, by God's decree, a monarch. Hers is the "power to heal, to redeem, to guide, and to guard.... Will you [the onlookers] not covet such power as this, and seek such throne as this, and be no more housewives, but queens?" (Ruskin).

Recent royal biographies continue to serve the dual purpose of mythologization and popularization of the monarchy. They address an escapist desire of the public to glimpse a life of opulence and luxury, albeit a luxury tinged with the knowledge that it has to be maintained, mostly by women. From a political perspective they attest to the royal family's continued value in contemporary British cultures by arguing that the monarchs are indeed special people, having earned their elevated status through extraordinary dedication and personal sacrifice. In a time of increasing political uncertainty in the aftermath of the Brexit vote, they represent a continuing source of stability. On the other hand, despite the extraordinary nature of their lives, they appear quite normal in their reactions, especially in the way they cope with the traditional divisions of social roles based on gender and class. Especially by emphasizing the private roles of the queens as daughters, sisters, wives and mothers, the films encourage us to revaluate these roles in our own lives.

WORKS CITED

Babilas, Dorota. *Wiktoria znaczy Zwycięstwo. Kulturowe oblicza brytyjskiej królowej.* Warsaw: Wydawnictwa Uniwersytetu Warszawskiego, 2012. Print.

Bagehot, Walter. *The English Constitution.* 1867. London: Routledge, 1894. Print.

Birnbaum, Debra. "Taking *The Crown*: Inside the Royal Treatment of Netflix's New Series." *Variety* 26 Oct. 2016. Web. 30 Nov. 2016.

Blain, Neil, and Hugh O'Donnell. *Media, Monarchy and Power.* Bristol: Intellect, 2003. Print.

Bruin-Mole, Megen de. "ITV's Victoria is Neo-Victorian Fiction at Its Purest." *Angels and Apes* 21 Sept. 2016. Web. 17 Nov. 2016.

Burstein, Miriam Elizabeth. "Rules for Writing Neo-Victorian Novels." *The Little Professor* blog 15 Mar. 2006. Web. 8 Nov. 1016.

Campbell Orr, Clarissa. "The Feminization of the Monarchy 1780–1910: Royal Masculinity and Female Empowerment." *The Monarchy and the British Nation, 1780 to the Present.* Ed. Andrzej Olechnowicz. 76–107. Cambridge: Cambridge University Press, 2007. Print.

Cannadine, David. "The Context, Performance and Meaning of Ritual: The British Monarchy and the 'Invention of Tradition' c. 1820–1977." *The Invention of Tradition.* Ed. Eric Hobsbawm and Terence Ranger. 101–64. Cambridge: Cambridge University Press, 1983. Print.

Chapman, James. *Past and Present: National Identity and the British Historical Film.* London: I.B. Tauris, 2005. Print.

The Crimson Petal and the White. Dir. Marc Munden. Perf. Romola Garai, Chris O'Dowd, Amanda Hale. Orion Pictures/Cité-Amérique/BBC, 2011. Television.

The Crown. Dir. Stephen Daldry et al. Perf. Claire Foy, Matt Smith, Vanessa Kirby. Netflix, 2016. Television.

Delingpole, James. "ITV's *Victoria* Is Silly, Facile and Irresponsible—I Blame the Feminization of Culture." *The Spectator* 26 Sept. 2016. Web. 4 Dec. 2016.

Diana. Dir. Oliver Hirschbiegel. Perf. Naomi Watts, Cas Anyar, Charles Edwards. Ècosse Films/Le Pacte Film, 2013. Film.

Dobson, Michael, and Nicola J. Watson. *England's Elizabeth: An Afterlife in Fame and Fantasy.* Oxford: Oxford University Press, 2002. Print.

Dowell, Ben. "The story behind the Victoria theme tune." *Radio Times* 25 Sept. 2016. Web. 4 Dec. 2016.

Downton Abbey. Dir. Brian Percival et al. Perf. Hugh Bonneville, Jessica Brown Findlay, Michelle Dockery, Carnival Film and Television/Masterpiece Theatre 2010–15. Television.

Eckersley, Holly. "Neo-Victorian Review—Re-Historicising the Victorians: ITV's *Victoria*,' Love Triangles and Notions of Taste." *The Victorianist* 21 Oct. 2016. Web. 9 Dec. 2016.

Edward the Seventh. Dir. John Gorrie. Perf. Timothy West, Annette Crosbie, Robert Hardy. ATV, 1975. Television.

Ellis-Petersen, Hannah. "New drama *The Crown* launches with a title sequence fit for a Queen." *The Guardian* 11 Nov. 2016. Web. 6 Dec. 2016.

Fingersmith. Dir. Aisling Walsh. Perf. Sally Hawkins, Elaine Cassidy, Imelda Staunton. Sally Head Productions. BBC, 2005. Television.

Ford, Elizabeth A., and Deborah C. Mitchell. *Royal Portraits in Hollywood. Filming the Lives of Queens*. Lexington: University Press of Kentucky, 2009. Print.

Franchi, Barbara. "Consuming Victoria: History as Neo-Victorian Fiction?" *The Victorianist* 19 Sept. 2016. Web. 9 Dec. 2016.

Gibb, Bill. "How accurate is ITV's royal drama Victoria?" *Sunday Post* 26 Sept. 2016. Web. 8 Dec. 2016.

Gray, Ellen. "Is *The Crown* your new *Downton Abbey*?" *Philly* 29 Oct. 2016. Web. 6 Dec. 2016.

Hawkes, Rebecca. "Jenna Coleman: I'm not too pretty to play Queen Victoria." *The Telegraph* 1 Sept. 2016. Web. 6 Dec. 2016.

Heilmann, Ann, and Mark Llewellyn. *Neo-Victorianism: The Victorians in the Twenty-First Century 1999–2009*. Basingstoke: Palgrave Macmillan, 2010. Print.

Her Majesty. Dir. Mark J. Gordon. Perf. Sally Andrews, Anna Sheridan, Mark Clare. Silicon Valley Film Fund, 2001. Film.

Her Majesty Mrs. Brown (aka *Mrs. Brown*). Dir. John Madden. Perf. Judi Dench, Billy Connolly, Geoffrey Palmer. BBC Scotland/Écosse Films, 1997. Film.

Homans, Margaret. *Royal Representations: Queen Victoria and British Culture 1837–1876*. Chicago: University of Chicago Press, 1998. Print.

Jamieson, Alastair. "Queen not amused by 'inaccuracies' in The Young Victoria film." *The Telegraph* 15 Mar. 2009. Web. 6 Dec. 2016.

Kantorowicz, Ernst H. *The King's Two Bodies. A Study in Mediaeval Political Theology*. 1955. Princeton: Princeton University Press, 1957. Print.

The King's Speech. Dir. Tom Hooper. Perf. Colin Firth, Geoffrey Rush, Derek Jacobi. SeeSaw Films/Weinstein Company, 2010. Film.

Kinzler, Julia. "Visualising Victoria: Gender, Genre and History in *The Young Victoria* (2009)." *Neo-Victorian Studies* 4.2 (2011): 49–65. Print.

Lacey, Robert. *Monarch: The Life and Reign of Elizabeth II*. New York: Free Press 2002. Print.

Lee, Sidney. *Queen Victoria, a Biography*. London: John Murray, 1904. Print.

The Madness of King George. Dir. Nicholas Hytner. Perf. Nigel Hawthorne, Helen Mirren, Rupert Graves. Samuel Goldwyn Company/Channel 4 Films, 1994. Film.

Mädchenjahre einer Königin. Dir. Erich Engel. Perf. Jenny Jugo, Olga Limburg, Renée Stobawa. Klagemann-Film GmbH, 1936. Film.

Mangan, Lucy. "*The Crown* Review—the £100m gamble on the Queen pays off royally." *The Guardian* 4 Nov. 2016. Web. 7 Dec. 2016.

Otnes, Cele C., and Pauline Maclaran. *Royal Fever: The British Monarchy in Consumer Culture*. Berkeley: University of California Press, 2015. Print.

Power, Ed. "Is *The Crown* the new *Downton Abbey*? 7 Reasons to watch the Epic Netflix drama." *The Independent* 4 Nov. 2016. Web. 6 Dec. 2016.

The Queen. Dir. Stephen Frears. Perf. Helen Mirren, Michael Sheen, James Cromwell. Pathé Pictures, 2006. Film.

Queen Victoria's Empire. Perf. Lawrence James, Donald Sutherland, Frances McDevitt. Brian Lapping Productions/History Channel, 2001. Television.

Rappaport, Helen. *Queen Victoria: A Biographical Companion*. New York: ABC-CLIO, 2003. Print.

Richards, Jeremy. "The Monarchy and Film 1900–2000." *The Monarchy and the British Nation, 1780 to the Present*. Ed. Andrzej Olechnowicz. 256–79. Cambridge: Cambridge University Press, 2007. Print.

Roman Holiday. Dir. William Wyler. Perf. Gregory Peck, Audrey Hepburn, Eddie Albert. Paramount, 1953. Film.

Royal Family. Dir. Richard Cawston. Perf. Michael Flanders, HRH Queen Elizabeth II, HRH Prince Philip. BBC/ITV, 1969. Television.

A Royal Night Out. Dir. Julian Jarrold. Perf. Sarah Gadon, Bel Powley, Jack Reynor. Ecosse Films, 2015. Film.

Ruskin, John. *Sesame and Lilies: Lecture II—Of Queen's Gardens.* 1864. Web. 6 Dec. 2016.

Sixty Glorious Years (aka *Queen of Destiny*), Dir. Herbert Wilcox. Perf. Anna Neagle, Anton Walbrook, C. Aubrey Smith. Herbert Wilcox Productions, 1938. Film.

Spenser, Edmund. *The Faerie Queene.* 1590. Oxford: Oxford University Press, 1977. Print.

Thompson, Rachel. "How accurate is Netflix's *The Crown*?" *Mashable* 12 Nov. 2016. Web. 6 Dec. 2016.

Trowbridge, Serena. "Victoria, the Victorians and us." *Birmingham City University Blog* 6 Sept. 2016. Web. 6 Dec. 2016.

Upstairs Downstairs. Dir. Bill Bain et al. Perf. Gordon Jackson, Angela Baddeley, David Langton. London Weekend Television, 1971–77. Television.

Victoria. Dir. Daisy Goodwin et al. Perf. Jenna Coleman, Tom Hughes, Rufus Sewell. Mammoth Productions, 2016. Television.

Victoria and Albert. Dir. John Eman. Perf. Victoria Hamilton, Jonathan Firth, Patrick Malahide. A&E/BBC, 2001. Television.

Victoria the Great. Dir. Herbert Wilcox. Perf. Anna Neagle, Anton Walbrook, Walter Rilla. Herbert Wilcox Productions, 1937. Film.

The Victorians Uncovered. Perf. Michele Bunyan. United Film and Television Productions, 2001. Television.

Vidal, Belén. *Heritage Film: Nation, Genre, and Representation.* New York: Columbia University Press, 2012. Print.

The Virgin Queen. Dir. Coky Giedroyc. Perf. Anne-Marie Duff, Tom Hardy, Hans Matheson. BBC, 2005. Television.

W.E. Dir. Madonna. Perf. Abby Cornish, Andrea Riseborough, James D'Arcy. Semtex Films. IM Globe, 2011. Film.

What the Victorians Did for Us. Perf. Adam Hart-Davis. BBC, 2001. Television.

Whiting, Kate. "Eight reasons why new £11million drama Victoria is the next *Downton Abbey*." *Independent* 24 Aug. 2016. Web. 6 Dec. 2016.

Will und die Windzors. Dir. Hape Kerkeling. Perf. Kerkeling, Brigitte Mira, Irn Hermann. Hanover Film/Norddeutscher Rundfunk, 1996. Film.

Wordsworth, William. *The Sonnets of William Wordsworth: Collected in One Volume with a Few Additional Ones, Now First Published.* London: Edward Morton, Dover Street, 1838. Print.

The Young Victoria. Dir. Jean-Marc Vallee. Perf. Emily Blunt, Robert Friend, Miranda Richardson. Momentum Pictures, 2009. Film.

Shakespearean Adaptation as Challenge[1]

Edward Bond's Lear

ÖZLEM ÖZMEN

"I take it we are all agreed, we shattered ones who have seen Bond's *Lear*, that it is an imposing and disturbing piece of work."—Holmstrom 42

The concept of value in literary works is a subjective and a political phenomenon as it shapes the ways in which texts are regarded in relation to each other and to certain ideologies. For instance, the construction of the canon is a consequence of value judgment among literary critics. Whether a literary work is esteemed of high value because it is canonical or it is canonized because it is considered valuable may not be clear; however, it is evident that these concepts are interrelated in the construction of literary and cultural hierarchies among texts. The idea that value in literature is a subjective; hence an unreliable concept is offered by Beardsley: "even if there is such a thing as aesthetic value, it cannot be a property of literary works, for since they have no existence apart from the experiences of readers … there is nothing objective in which value can be located" (238). The reader is central in the process of value attribution to literary texts, hence value is not a universal concept agreed upon by every reader as each person has different viewpoints about certain texts. Additionally, the idea that supports the role of politics of value in the construction of literary hierarchies is provided by a definition of the term "value" that also includes its "ability to serve a specified purpose or cause a particular effect" (Meyer-Lee 335). This indicates that the value of a given work of art is determined in terms of its function for the formation or preservation of certain ideological concerns.

It is no wonder, then, that it is mostly the canonical art forms that are highly acclaimed as valuable since the canon is determined by ideological formations. Specifically, Shakespeare, as the writer situated in the center of the western canon (Bloom 75), has widely and mostly mistakenly been considered "eloquent of values both commercial and cultural; simultaneously expressive of both material and ideological power" (Holderness xiii). The view that situates Shakespeare above all prominent writers for reasons such as his status as a timeless writer with an exceptional potential to speak to all ages attributes a highly philosophical essence to his works and perpetuates perceptions about him "as a regulative standard or mystified icon of value" (Lanier 31). Although the claim for cultural and literary iconicity on his part has secured an important place for Shakespeare in the literary canon, it needs to be noted that various intermedial and interideological adaptations (Laera 7) of his works substantially subvert such accepted and unchallenged norms about him and unearth underdeveloped or neglected ideas in his texts with regard to certain ideologies they are used to serve.

Adaptation and appropriation of canonical literary works are the most compelling practices that make it possible to rethink about the idea of value in relation to these texts. Adaptation's role in reconsidering the politics of value in literary works is similar to the function of deconstruction. In relation to deconstruction as a way of revaluing literary texts, Schiralli, in his "Reconstructing Literary Value," suggests that "deconstructionists typically view literary texts as incapable of bearing any fixed meaning, durable reference, or distinctive value" (115). Some scholars embrace preconceptions about the uniqueness and originality of a given source text: if reshaped, its fundamental value is affected. In spite of the abundance of negative arguments about the revisions of Shakespeare's works, there have been various adaptations of them that have challenged their superior status by providing alternative views and proving that they are not stable objects. Charles Marowitz supports this practice as such: "It is this high-varnish approach to Shakespeare which is his chiefest foe—the detestable conservative notion that all one ever needs to do with 'classics' is preserve them" (3). Adaptation is a regenerative as well as a subversive practice, offering alternative versions of classic texts that challenge viewer preconceptions. In response to the conservative approach that supports preserving the integrity of Shakespeare's texts, Marowitz highlights the disadvantage of accepting these works as beyond adaptation: "[T]he stronger and more obsessive the Shakespeare Establishment becomes, the more it will hold back the flow of new dramatic possibilities which transcend what we call, with a deplorable anal-retentiveness, the canon" (10). Unless obsession with canonicity as an idea and a practice can be set aside, the value of a classical work cannot be reassessed due to lack of appropriate alternatives. That belief might extinguish the whole purpose of stage performance, as Marjorie

Garber observes: "[Shakespeare's plays] are living works of art that grow and change over time, not museum pieces that must only be preserved in some imagined state of purity" (652).

A significant Shakespeare adaptation in contemporary British drama is Edward Bond's *Lear* (1971). The play illustrates that rewriting is actually a useful practice and it is also possible to produce valuable works of adaptation. Although it has been more than four decades since the premiere of the play, it is still worth studying in order to discuss the value of adaptation itself and its function on the reconsideration of the concept of value. Kevin J. Wetmore claims that "[a]daptation is ... an 'original' work, in and of itself, especially if its audience has no referent to which to compare it for fidelity" (626). In the case of Edward Bond's *Lear*, there is a very strong referential point as the play was criticized for failing to remain loyal to Shakespeare's source. The challenge of adaptation in terms of value when compared to the source text is aptly put forward by Thomas Leitch: "Even if the adaptations are remakes in the same medium, their most conscientious attempts to replicate the original will betray their differences, and thus their inferiority" (161). The major reason why Bond's *Lear* was considered inferior to Shakespeare's *King Lear* is the play's loose association with the source text, in addition to its excessive display of violence. Considering the criticism of Bond's *Lear* in terms of "the anxiety of inauthenticity," which is more precisely defined as "the fear that any derivative of Shakespeare ... must necessarily lose the 'aura' of the original" (Rothwell 82), the play was basically regarded as a cheapening of a canonical work. This can be observed in the reviews following the play's initial production at the Royal Court Theatre, London, in 1971. The *Today's Cinema* critic opined that "*Lear* by Edward Bond ... takes some of the basic ingredients of Shakespeare's play, but only a handful of the characters, and spends three hours pursuing violence and unrelenting horror" ("Pursuit of Violence" par. 1). Neil Stevens of the Birmingham *Evening Mail* voiced his opinion more bluntly: "When it comes to Shakespeare I'll take the Bard rather than the Bond any day" (par. 12). Stephen Purcell believes that such negative reviews about the adaptations of Shakespeare's texts inevitably reinforce the preconceptions about the superiority of the source text: "[A]s long as the majority of dominant voices in theatre reviewing see the Shakespearean text as fixed and primary rather than open to contestation through performance, there will be more than an element of monument-building about the whole enterprise" (369).

Edward Bond proposes his own ideas about the creation of a work of art that is, obviously, different from Shakespeare's own. According to Bond, the value of a literary work needs to be judged by its relevance to its socio-economic background, and the writer's responsibility to their readers in terms of providing appreciable messages. In response to claims for an exceptional relevance of *King Lear* to all periods, as Jan Kott claims "above all others the Shakespearean play of our time" (162), Bond only agrees that Shakespeare provides valuable instances of issues such as "human cruelty and misery ... goodness, devotion, loyalty and self-sacrifice" (Foakes 1). However, the problem with Shakespeare's play lies in his uncritical treatment of these concepts as Bond argues: "[A]s a society we use the play in a wrong way. And it is for that reason I would like to rewrite it so that we now have to use the play for ourselves" (qtd. in Hay and Roberts *Bond: A Study* 105–06). Shakespeare did not intend to talk about the social, economic and political problems of his age, and this fault has not been detected in subsequent performances over the last four centuries. On this view, Bond believes he is investing *Lear* with added value by transforming the narrative elements of the host text. In his play, Lear is no longer the same man, Cordelia is not his daughter, the other daughters are named differently, and there is no Gloucester subplot. Bond justifies the necessity of such transformations in his version by arguing that Lear and his coterie have normally been represented as "Renaissance figures [who don't] impinge on our society" (qtd. in Scharine 183). Hitherto Lear has been overwhelmingly represented as a victim, "more sinned against than sinning" (*King Lear* III, ii, 267), rather than a responsible mature man. Conversely, Bond illustrates Lear's stubbornness in demanding absolute power and unquestionable loyalty from his daughters as the root of ensuing troubles throughout the play.

Bond actually questions the value of Shakespeare's play as he thinks that "[i]n a play, the value of an idea isn't in its literal sense but in the relation a character bearing the responsibility of having such an idea" (qtd. in Hay and Roberts *Edward Bond* 45). In light of this opinion, the representation of Lear as a man aloof from the consequences of his wrong decisions with only a touch of regret is not a sufficient way to get the message across to audiences if Shakespeare had intended to give a political message at all. In *King Lear*, Lear utters words of repentance; however, fails to act on his feeling of regret. Bond presents Lear as a man more aware of his faults, as a suffering character imprisoned by his daughters (*Lear* II, i, 48) and tortured later on. Upon realization of his past mistakes, he expresses his shortcomings more convincingly through the metaphor of a bird as he looks at himself in the mirror: "No, that's not the king.... This is a little cage of bars with an animal in it" (*Lear* II, i, 49).

Edward Bond expresses his reason for transforming Lear thus: "Lear, who has seen himself on postage stamps, ... on monuments as a hero and father, sees himself for the first time as he really is—as a bad father and a bad king" (qtd. in Hay and Roberts *Bond: A Study* 127). He makes a point about the dangers of obsession with power. Ultimately, his death is far from tragic; on the contrary Bond presents Lear remembering how many lives he has ended (*Lear* II, vii, 80), which shows that he actually recognizes his mistakes as a prelude to paying the ultimate price by dying on the wall. In many ways the play can be seen as a riposte to romantic revivals of the Shakespearean text that revive the play as the tragedy of a single person. Such transformations in the play display that the act of ennobling an irresponsible authority figure as in Shakespeare's play proves how societies accept corruption and shows their inability to eradicate violence and inequality.

This form of representation extends to the subsidiary characters that are either already corrupt figures themselves or eventually turn out to be vengeful and violent beings. In Warrington's case, for instance, a loyal and honest person is transformed into a malevolent figure through the vile treatment meted out to him by Lear's daughters. Likewise, Bond alters the characterization of Cordelia and the relationship she has to her father. At the beginning of the play, she is an innocent ordinary woman, the wife of the Gravedigger's Boy. Later on she turns out to be the most destructive tyrant. As the wronged daughter of Lear, she cannot be a benevolent figure as she has been excluded from the mainstream of society: even in the Shakespearean text Bond identifies her as "an absolute menace … a very dangerous type of person" ("Drama and the Dialectics" 8). Appropriately, she is presented as a vile figure, which is a more suitable characterization considering the corrupt society in Bond's text that does not readily accept innocent characters.

The ending of *Lear* also substantially alters that of the source text. By avoiding the reconciliation of Cordelia and Lear, and by casting Cordelia as a successive oppressor, Bond does not let revolution take place at the end and thereby suggests that corruption still exists. With the final stage image of an old man trying to dig up the wall, Bond suggests that the only way Lear can expiate his sins is to recognize his mistake with a small deed. Lear has understood he is the cause of chaos in his society; hence his attempt to destroy the wall is a symbolic challenge to the establishment he created in the first place. Evidently, Bond regenerates his philosophy of art "as a guide to practical activity" (*Selections* 146): the play offers a new beginning rather than a nihilistic conclusion. Bond intends to emphasize the necessity of action in order to stop corruption.

Apart from being seen as a daring attempt to subvert the narrative elements of Shakespeare's *King Lear* with transformations of characters and the plot structure of the source, Bond's play was also severely criticized for being excessively violent when it first appeared. It has widely been considered that Bond was inconsiderate to portray gory images on the stage, and he has been criticized for "lacking in common humanity" (Wardle 23) for this. It is reported that, in the play's initial production, there were people who literally fainted at the performance of violence on the stage ("Not for the Faint Hearted"). However, the violence in Bond's play should not be seen only in terms of performance ethics as he argues the amount of violence in the play is for the purposes of giving social message to the audiences concerning the endemic nature of violence in real society. Bond believes that it is a violent society in which people have to live, and nobody really does anything credible for the elimination of the disease. The representation of violence in Bond's play needs to be considered in relation to his aspiration to blend emotional integrity with reasoning faculty through art practices. Bond supports the idea that "[w]hen emotion and reason cannot be reconciled in a work of art ... the work of art does not serve society or ourselves; alienation makes audiences ineffectual" (Bradley 133). Therefore, as Bond transgresses the standards of epic theater that is based on reason and alienation set by Brecht by requiring the audiences to engage with the social message of the play both through their senses and minds, he succeeds in introducing a different kind of theatrical production that he calls "rational theatre" (Cohn 93) or "Theatre of Humanism" (Bond "Bond's *Lear*"). As Christopher Innes suggests, "Bond sees outraging the audience emotionally as a sort of shock therapy designed to galvanize their consciousness into life and provoke them into viewing society 'objectively' and 'rationally'" (93). For this purpose, the violence in *Lear* should not be considered only in terms of its effects on the audience emotionally but the intended function of this effect needs to be valued. Therefore, the value of the text should not be limited to its influence on the spectator's emotions but extended to its powerful representation of the possible consequences of loss of humanity in real society.

In terms of value, *Lear* offers a modern take on Shakespeare's play that, while invoking the source text, reworks it to make a comment on the consequences of living in a society where only the fittest can survive. Contrary to what the original theater reviewers might have observed in 1971, *Lear* deserves to be approached on its own terms as a representation of life at that time. Earlier productions of Shakespeare's *King Lear*, such as the famous Peter Brook production of the mid–60s, inspired by Jan Kott, might have made similar points, but Bond consciously aims for an alternative form of discourse and characterization. This is also evident in the way he deals with violence, which is represented in the form of "aggro-effects" peculiar to Edward Bond's plays, possibly the most striking and memorable example of which is the stoning scene in *Saved* (1965).

The violence Bond portrays in his adaptation is actually an extension of the violence mentioned in Shakespeare's play. Warrington's torturing scene in *Lear*, for instance, resembles Gloucester's fate in Shakespeare. An example that displays Bond's critical attitude towards the idea of violence ironically with his explicit portrayal of it is Fontanelle's autopsy scene. The scene where Fontanelle, now dead, has her organs and viscera removed has been inspired by the Shakespearean line "Let them anatomize Regan; see what breeds about her heart" (*King Lear* III, vi, 292). In this particular instance, Bond draws our attention once more to the contagion of corruption and vileness in human beings, especially as Lear mentions his own contribution to the degeneration in Fontanelle's character: "Did I make this—and destroy it?" (*Lear* II, vi, 73). This elaborates a point made in the preface to the play that the daughters' characters have apparently been "formed by his [Lear's] activity, they were children of his state, and he was totally responsible for them" (qtd. in Scharine 218). Bond suggests the idea that if we follow Lear's malevolent example, "we become tense, nervous and aggressive, and these characteristics are fed back into our young" ("Author's Preface" 8).

The violence in the play is also closely related to economic social hierarchies. Continuous violence in the context of the play gives the idea that in unequal social structures violence is endemic: "an unjust society must be violent" (Bond "Author's Preface" 9). Servants, frightened for their future at the hands of their ruthless masters, commit violent acts in the hope of survival such as the Fourth Prisoner who removes Lear's eyes, and Soldier A who tortures Warrington to please Bodice and Fontanelle. Another social criticism revealed in the display of violence in the play is against technology. For instance, in Lear's blinding scene, the act of violence is carried out quite calmly to demonstrate the devaluation of humanity in favor of technology, which proves the truth of Bond's observation: "I can see a continuity of technology but not of culture" (qtd. in Buckley par. 4). Apparently, he illustrates that what is valued in social life may actually be at the expense of cultural reformation that is essential for the elimination of violence and corruption.

Despite the amount of violence, Bond considers *Lear* an optimistic work. Referring to the last two workers on the stage who look at Lear's dead body a second time, Bond suggests "[t]hey are the really important people in the play—they represent for me a new possibility for change in society. They are my equivalent of Fortinbras" (qtd. in Hay and Roberts *Bond: A Study* 137). Bond's theory of art suggests that art needs to inquire, and try to provide solutions. As a result, his play is not only a valuable work in its own right, a comment on contemporary western cultures, but also one that offers answers—if we are prepared to heed them. The ending of the play suggests that "[h]umanity will continue to exist as long as one person remembers its existence" (Scharine 215). Considering the transformations in *Lear* in light of such philosophical ideas Bond intended to relay renders the adaptation more meaningful both socially and artistically.

I find Bond's play valuable not only as an adaptation but as a play in itself particularly because it is concerned with social problems and tries to offer solutions for the betterment of society. Behind the representation of all violent and inhumane acts in the play, as a writer who believes in the transformative power of art, Bond criticizes the current establishment and attempts to incite change in his audiences in order to make the world a more equal place. Hay and Roberts refer to the importance of Edward Bond's *Lear* as his "first play in which Bond argues that direct action is imperative" (*Bond: A Study* 104). Attributing a social and moral function to art (Bond "The Rational Theatre" xiii), Bond does not see theater as isolated from society, but as a valuable catalyst for social change. He explains himself thus: "I think art must have a social function because I think art is the confrontation of justice with law and order, and as justice is always the good thing and law and order is not, then art in that sense is always creative, always evolutional" (qtd. in Hay and Roberts *Edward Bond* 27). Appropriately, the value of Bond's adaptation needs to be considered in terms of its contribution to the creation of a just and enlightened society.

NOTE

1. This essay is a revised version of a part of the first chapter of my doctoral dissertation titled *Re-writing Shakespeare in the Twentieth Century: Edward Bond's* Lear, *Arnold Wesker's* The Merchant *and Howard Barker's* Gertrude—The Cry *in Socio-Historical Context*.

WORKS CITED

Beardsley, Monroe C. "Aesthetic Value in Literature." *Comparative Literature Studies* 18.3 (Sept. 1981): 238–47. Print.
Bloom, Harold. *The Western Canon: The Books and School of the Ages*. New York: Harcourt Brace, 1994. Print.
Bond, Edward. "Author's Preface." *Plays Two: Lear*. 3–12. London: Methuen, 1972. Print.
_____. "Bond's *Lear*." *The Humanist* (Mar. 1972). Print.
_____. "Drama and the Dialectics of Violence." Interview by Roger Hudson, et al. *Theatre Quarterly* 2.5 (1972): 4–15. Print.
_____. *Plays Two: Lear*. London: Methuen, 1972. Print.
_____. "The Rational Theatre." *Plays Two: Lear*. ix–xviii. London: Methuen, 1972, Print.
_____. *Selections from the Notebooks of Edward Bond: Volume One: 1959 to 1980*. Ed. Ian Stuart. Vol. 1. London: Methuen, 2000. Print.
Bradley, Lynne. *Adapting King Lear for the Stage*. Farnham: Ashgate, 2010. Print.
Buckley, Leonard. "Media." *TLS*. Print.
Cohn, Ruby. "Bond, Edward." *Contemporary British Dramatists*. Ed. K.A. Berney. 90–3. New York: St. James Press, 1994. Print.
Foakes, R.A. "Introduction." *King Lear*. The Arden Shakespeare 3rd Series. 1–151. London: Bloomsbury, 1997. Print.
Garber, Marjorie B. *Shakespeare After All*. New York: Pantheon Books, 2004. Print.
Hay, Malcolm, and Philip Roberts. *Bond: A Study of His Plays*. London: Methuen, 1980. Print.
_____. *Edward Bond: A Companion to the Plays*. London: TQ, 1978. Print.
Holderness, Graham. "Preface: 'All This.'" *The Shakespeare Myth*. Ed. Holderness. xi–xvi. Manchester: University Press, 1988. Print.
Holmstrom, John. "Royal Court *Lear*." *Plays and Players* (Nov. 1971): 42–53. Print.
Innes, Christopher. *Modern British Drama: The Twentieth Century*. Cambridge: Cambridge University Press, 2002. Print.
King Lear. Dir. Peter Brook. Perf. Paul Scofield, Irene Worth, Alec McCowen. Royal Shakespeare Theatre, 22 Nov. 1962. Theater Performance.
Kott, Jan. *Shakespeare, Our Contemporary*. New York: Doubleday, 1964. Print.
Laera, Margherita. "Introduction: Return, Rewrite, Repeat: The Theatricality of Adaptation." *Theatre and Adaptation: Return, Rewrite, Repeat*. Ed. Laera. 1–19. London: Bloomsbury, 2014. Print.

Lanier, Douglas. "Shakespearean Rhizomatics: Adaptation, Ethics, Value." *Shakespeare and the Ethics of Appropriation*. Edited by Alexa Huang and Elizabeth Rivlin. 21–41. Basingstoke: Palgrave Macmillan, 2014. Print.

Leitch, Thomas M. "Twelve Fallacies in Contemporary Adaptation Theory." *Criticism* 45.2 (2003): 149–171. Print.

Marowitz, Charles. "Reconstructing Shakespeare, or Harlotry in Bardolatry." *Shakespeare Survey*. Ed. Stanley Wells. 1–10. Cambridge: Cambridge University Press, 1988. Print.

Meyer-Lee, Robert J. "Toward a Theory and Practice of Literary Valuing." *New Literary History* 46.2 (2015): 335–55. Print.

"Not for the Faint Hearted." *Chelsea Post*, 1 Oct. 1971. Print.

Purcell, Stephen. "'That's Not Shakespeare': Policing the Boundaries of 'Shakespeare' in Reviews." *Shakespeare* 6.3 (Aug. 2010): 364–70. Print.

"Pursuit of Violence and Horror." *Today's Cinema*, 22 Oct. 1971. Print.

Rothwell, Kenneth S. "How the Twentieth Century Saw the Shakespeare Film: 'Is It Shakespeare?'" *Literature/Film Quarterly* 29.2 (2001): 82–95. Print.

Scharine, Richard G. *The Plays of Edward Bond*. Lewisburg: Bucknell University Press, 1976. Print.

Schiralli, Martin. "Reconstructing Literary Value." *The Journal of Aesthetic Education* 25.4 (1991): 115–19. Print.

Shakespeare, William. *The Arden Shakespeare: King Lear*. Edited by R.A. Foakes. London: Methuen, 1997. Print.

Stevens, Neil. "This Lear Will Give You the Horrors." *Birmingham Evening Mail*, 30 Sept. 1971. Print.

Wardle, Irving. "*Lear*." *The Times*, 30 Sept. 1971. *Bond on File*. Ed. Philip Roberts. 23. London: Methuen, 1985. Print.

Wetmore, Kevin J. "Adaptation." *Theatre Journal* 66.4 (Dec. 2014): 625–34. Print.

Food for Thought
or "mental chewing gum"

Truman Capote's Crime Adaptations
and Cultural Memory Work

SUZANNE DIAMOND

There is an old joke about a clipboard-carrying scientist who studies a leaping frog. "Jump!" says the scientist to the frog; when the amphibian complies, the scientist diligently measures the distance of his leap and scribbles onto his clipboard: "Frog with four legs jumps four feet." He removes one of the frog's legs and issues the same imperative. Measuring the frog's jump again, he records: "Frog with three legs jumps three feet." This leg-reducing and jump-measuring process continues until the scientist finds himself setting a legless frog onto the table. "Jump!" he commands. "Jump!" After a pause, the scientist scrawls onto his clipboard: "Frog with no legs cannot hear." This bit of silliness underscores a point of serious cultural value when it comes to approaching how we process high-profile crime in culture; our preoccupation with habitual and rigid ways of knowing can obstruct what we might otherwise observe.

This precaution is particularly important, as I mean to argue, when it comes to understanding the social value of adaptation analysis as we struggle to understand the co-functioning of crime memory and storytelling. As several commentators within the field of criminology have observed, the study of crime has become narrowly professionalized and restrictively scientific (Wheeldon, *passim* and Currie 176–78). Likewise, media analysts have drawn hasty and dispiriting conclusions about crime knowledge and crime memory, arguably based on the restrictive epistemological tools they have employed. For example, Robert Reiner's analysis dramatizes the kind of limiting stance and consequently reductive conclusions we might enrich by paying closer attention to the dynamic of crime story adaptation. Reiner posits that despite the contemporaneous frenzy that high-profile true crimes tend to generate in the popular imagination, these events do not tend to linger in cultural memory. In the long run, he concludes that high-profile true crimes—sensational for a moment—eventually amount to not much more than "mental chewing gum" (302). Michael Brookes et al. set out to test Reiner's hypothesis empirically, and their testing tools—along with their findings—invite a challenge. Using photographic images of recent high-profile murderers and their victims, along with fill-in-the-blanks tests, Brookes and his team set out to gauge how accurately these figures can be identified by randomly selected members of the British public. Many of those surveyed more or less "fail" Brookes' crime-memory tests, and his team concludes that Reiner is correct. "Despite the fact that we are now living in a media-saturated age, often dominated by images of exceptional crimes such as murder, they claim, 'many high-profile incidents do not linger in the public's collective memory'" (Brookes 12).

In a similarly restrictive vein, crime media analysts often complain that the genre of "true crime" misrepresents the actual crime statistics in contemporary culture. The genre, we are informed, skews inaccurately suburban and white (Murley). According to this second argument, true crime fails as "news." Taken together, these observers imply that when it comes to the topic of murder, we mistake what is happening while it's happening, and then forget what has happened afterwards. Such dismissals are contested, however, by the intense popularity of the true crime genre, especially when we consider those cases with clear and repeated attractions for literary, dramatic and filmic adapters. Some readers have begun to question the positivistic certainty behind pronouncements such as those generated by Reiner and Brookes (cf. Kruse). I, too, have begun to suspect that, like the proverbial legless frog, we popular audiences must not be as deaf as we might appear.

Several theorists have identified a popular knowledge project within contemporaneous true crime processing (Grochowski and Hayward). Frequently-adapted American true murders dramatize something even more striking: that intensely revisited true crimes signal a kind of knowledge production that is far from settled, that crime adaptation can actually be viewed as a sustained popular interrogation of the truth yielded earlier by specific true crime narratives. Viewed this way, the process whereby crime events transmute themselves into one story form and then another can offer a valuable gauge for understanding how audiences respond to the historically and culturally contingent features of crime and justice. To say this differently, by exploring the fidelity of any adapted true crime story—not strictly its adherence to or departure from a prior text but its relationship to the series of iterations that it joins—we stand to gain valuable insights about how a contemporary culture revisits and revises its memory of what happened and why. Such revisions promise greater insight about how high-profile murders are known and recollected, I would argue, than more literalist projects like the one Brookes and his team impose on British citizens. Understanding high-profile murders as food for thought in the popular imagination makes new investigations imaginable; on the contrary, deciding in advance that murder represents failed reporting or "mental chewing gum" makes easy dismissals too pardonable. I am currently engaged in as yet unpublished scholarship that pursues several recursively-adapted high-profile American murders precisely in terms of their function as collective memory projects; this chapter will initiate an examination of one of them. In general, I hope to illustrate that repeatedly reworked high-profile crimes signal a complicated ongoing cultural impulse to get the story right.

One flagrant example of the repeated reworking of a true crime is the 1959 Clutter family massacre in Holcomb, Kansas, by Dick Hickock and Perry Smith. In a literal sense, the perpetrators and victims in this case presented little mystery: the Clutters and the tragic fate they had endured could be unraveled one day after the crime, and shortly afterwards their assailants, Hickock and Smith, were pathetically easy for the authorities to convict. Horrifying as the murders had been, the legal case was of open-and-shut type from a law enforcement perspective. Its facts, if facts are all we are after, are filed away in the cultural archive. We know who did it, and we know to whom it got done. As is so often the case, however, the facts are complicated and they do not seem to be all we are after. The story of the Clutter murders and their aftermath—along with its meaning—remains unsettled, as we witness in the intense and recursive creative attention the murders and the trial have generated over the years. Aspects of this case have resisted what Aleida Assmann would call archival memory (77) and it therefore remains, like a number of other high-profile murders, suspended in what I would call a cultural cold case file. What we do know of this crime—due in large measure to Truman Capote himself—is that much more remains to be learned. Each factual discovery about the crime and its aftermath introduces further unsettlements and necessarily forces the interrogation of the accounts that have preceded it. The narrative unreliability associated with this well-known massacre, after all, begins with co-defendant Perry Smith, who offers two distinct versions of the murders, according to both Truman Capote and KBI investigator, Alvin Dewey.[1]

Besides becoming a media sensation of the type that was once less familiar, this horrifying crime has occasioned multiple reboots. The most famous and complicated, of course—due as much to its author's self-promotional skills as to his literary talent—is Capote's 1966 "nonfiction novel," *In Cold*

Blood. Later treatments of this spree-killing encompass media formats rang-ing from film to television mini-series to graphic fiction. Every adaptive man-ifestation of this crime has amplified wildly different aspects of the contexts that explain the Clutter murders, lending to the crime event itself the socially contested features we generally associate with any foundational mythology. Thus, as I have argued elsewhere, the fidelity studies approach often dismissed by adaptation theorists become not only defensible but invaluable when the topic is true crime (Diamond).

Recently, I formed a relevant insight while teaching Mythology and Lit-erature, a general education course that encourages allegorical and plot analy-ses of myths from various cultures. Many of these tales are new to my learners; with Bible stories, however, many are deeply familiar. As we explored the plots in Genesis one day, a learner's resistance got me ruminating about the stakes involved in crimes with multiple adaptations. "This is not the way I heard the story," he insisted. His demeanor reflected an impulse to guard a prior iteration against revision. Respecting that impulse, I offered what back-ground I could on when and how the Bible had been assembled; on the textual mischief imposed by both linguistic translations and thousands of years of human handling; on the ways ancient stories have endured something resem-bling the children's game of telephone. But this learner's disquiet clearly lin-gered, and I believe that the resistance he gave voice to relates to the way we contest stories about actual crimes. Given their anchors in an inaccessible prehistory, myths challenge their audiences to seek the truth even as they provide a substitute *for* it. My learner was expressing an anxiety for fidelity to some prior iteration of events in the Garden of Eden, for a narrative he had internalized and no doubt unwittingly helped to compose himself, one which must have felt, for him, more comfortable, or useful, or truthful.

Criminal justice narratives, like myths, represent a quest for the truth, but they carry with them an added pressure: since crimes so clearly require retribution, there are high stakes involved in getting at the facts immediately. In the face of murder, it does not do to throw up hands and observe a knowl-edge crisis. Yet the truths underpinning the facts can elude the instruments of law enforcement. The story of an evocative murder, like my learner's inter-nalized Garden of Eden, is co-authored by culture as it percolates over a longer historical period than criminal prosecution could allow. And like the revised version of Genesis against which my learner resisted, true crime adap-tations promise—and threaten—to re-open what had earlier seemed decided matters of justice.

By bringing the tools of adaptation studies to bear on the theoretical investigation of crime, I argue that we might offer a qualitative enrichment to theorists in criminology, media analysis, and psychology, and we might benefit, at the same time, from ways of discussing murder and its demon-

strable fascinations for audiences. Within theoretical criminology, one witnesses a welcome hunger for a better grasp of these less scientific ways of
knowing about crime. Johanna Wheeldon, for example, makes the case for
what she terms a "'constitutive criminology,' a field less invested in statistical
findings and more open to other, more speculative forms of crime knowledge-
making; citing Richard Rorty, she asserts that 'knowledge is what we are justified in believing ... and justification is a social phenomenon rather than a
transaction between a knowing subject and reality'" (400).

Wheeldon suggests that "[p]ragmatism's enduring legacy, is based on a
resistance to the description of new problems using established orthodoxies"
(400). In criminology, particularly, this means adopting what Wheeldon calls
an "ironist" position regarding the production of knowledge. "Ironists," she
posits, "are those who recognize the arbitrary historical conditions of their
own assumptions, thoughts, and beliefs" and who understand that "the
defense of any one vocabulary as final is folly. Old descriptions must give
way to newer, more socially useful ones" (398). Elliot Currie voices a similar
impulse to broaden academic criminology; he is particularly concerned about
the way the field has become sidelined within a wider popular discourse
regarding law enforcement. Like Wheeldon, Currie assails an increasing
obsession with quantification within his field. Whereas Wheeldon objects to
the unilingual exclusivity of a strictly statistics-oriented criminology, Currie
contests how this obsession with numbers has rarified the discipline at the
expense of its own cultural and political relevance. Instead of this hyper-
professionalism, he proposes that we "need to build more 'horizontal' relations among relevant disciplines within the academy itself. The tendency
toward isolation of academic criminology from a broader public is reflected
in a similar isolation of the academic fields from each other.... Done with
energy and commitment, it can wear down the isolation of individual disciplines" (187). Wheeldon suggests that by embracing plausibility instead of
scientific certainty as a discursive goal and by inviting interdisciplinary speculation, those of us who prioritize conversation ahead of zero-sum contests
over "what is" might move beyond our own institutional brands of intolerance. Aiming to emphasize the false comforts of numerical analyses, she
quotes Rorty's suggestion that we should "complete the process of secularization by [thinking] of the desire for non-linguistic access to the real as [a
goal as] hopeless as that for redemption through a beatific vision" (119).

Now, while I applaud this progress narrative on behalf of something
called secularization, I must confess I'm personally losing faith in it. And
while I acknowledge the futility of quests for "non-linguistic access to the
real"—which, for present purposes I might translate as "for actualities beyond
mere stories"—I would observe that even disciplinary reform is inevitably
local. Wheeldon and Currie hope to reform criminological discourse by

broadening their discipline's exclusive reliance on statistics. Those of us engaged in textual and adaptation studies, I suggest, could facilitate our own versions of disciplinary reform precisely by reversing Rorty's formulation and broadening our fetish for texts. That the real is inevitably mediated by some linguistic form or another is a flavor of Kool-Aid that literary and cinematic scholars have been happily drinking for a while (and legitimately so). However, it is at least arguable that the obsession with formalism has insulated our analyses as much as the fetish for numbers has confined criminology. If indeed "knowledge is what we are justified in believing," as Wheeldon posits, and "justification is a social phenomenon" (398), then knowledge itself can be fruitfully acknowledged as something of a faith-based community, one that could benefit mightily from a widened social appeal (cf. Birchall). Mark Seltzer has argued that "modern society resides in that interval between real and fictional reality," a reality which he describes as "bound up, through and through, with the reality of the mass media" (16–17). I suggest that we might pursue the interdisciplinary benefits of "believing" in the elusive real after which true crime and its adaptations are fervently questing. Indulging such a belief holds the promise that we might meet instructive counterparts in criminology and media analysis halfway.

The Clutter murders represent a case study in how true crime narratives steer crime mythology. "What happened" to the Clutter family in November 1959 eludes a settled narration, even for one of the murderers, Perry Smith, who himself wound up telling two versions of the massacre. In turn, Smith's confession possesses scant significance for Capote; the writer aims to reframe not the killers' disclosure but the deed itself, whose fundamental unknowability parallels the murky prehistory from which all myths take root. From this perspective, Smith, no less than Capote, is an adapter of the event, and Bennett Miller's 2005 film *Capote* signals not simply a reworking of a prior text but, more fundamentally, an ethical interrogation of the murky motives at the heart of *In Cold Blood* as a knowledge project. Miller's reformulation of the story examines not Truman Capote's text *per se*, but, instead, the layers upon which Capote's and later stories of the murder are ultimately founded.

In a pivotal scene within Miller's film, we witness Capote (Phillip Seymour Hoffman) in Perry Smith's (Clifton Collins, Jr.) prison cell, shedding all pretense of peripheral interest in the murderer's fate to bare the fact the author's sole reason for visiting is to gain intimate knowledge about the night of the murders. In a downright menacing tone, Capote informs Smith that "there is not a word or a sentence or a concept that you can illuminate for me. There is one singular reason I keep coming here. November 14, 1959. Three years ago. Three years. Hmm? That's all I want to hear from you." This filmic examination of Capote's motives is made intensely ironic in that it follows seamlessly from Capote's saccharine declaration to *New Yorker* editor,

William Shawn (Bob Balaban), that he is "going to miss" Perry. The perfect welding together of Capote's sentimental scene with Shawn, on the one side, and his merciless scene with Smith, on the other, conveys the tantalizing idea that Capote shields even himself from a rigorous inventory of his motives. And this duality is richly suggestive. Ralph F. Voss notes that a narrative "presented or seen as a 'true story' or even as 'based on a true story' has powerful appeal, the fascination of the 'real'—whether it is in fact real or not" and that Capote had a great deal to do with "refining, upgrading, and exemplifying the now very popular true crime genre" (94). Capote, he argues, generated a blueprint for structuring crime narration; I wish to illustrate that Capote's blueprint—viewed retrospectively through the lens of Miller's film—exposes a kind of inclination that mirrors the aggression it purports to merely observe.

Robert Eisenbauer suggests that Capote's book amounts to a modern repurposing of the ghost story, and this should return our attention to the storyteller who enjoys giving fright. In his narration of a horrifying event, Capote resembles Perry Smith, he argues, not least "in his desire to inspire reverence, to make others cower. The monstrous belongs to the aesthetic armamentarium of the modernist," he claims, "putting us back in touch with the insulting essence of things; horror movies and the tabloids inspire a sense of fused or confused religiosity akin to the sublime" (16). If Capote effectively weaponizes Smith and Hickock's harrowing deed, the popularity of his story indicates that audiences, for their part, hunger just as much as the storyteller for the "insulting essence" of murder.

Capote's posture towards Smith, in the scene Miller stages, models a corresponding and equally ambivalent thirst on the part of viewers, one that rationalizes the quest for non-linguistic access to the murder event within a self-deceptively sentimentalized moral or clinical interest in the murderer. In this scene, we are made starkly aware that the author's impulse to eclipse the murderer vies mightily with his desire to understand him. Although this fundamental ambivalence remains muted within Capote's own text and in Richard Brooks' 1967 film—which invents a bland substitute for the book's author in the form of an invented character named simply Jensen (Paul Stewart)—Miller's reframing of the story shines a spotlight on the dark duality within Capote's project that has confused audiences (Capote included) about his "positions" regarding crime and justice.

Smith, Hickock, and even the Clutter family are malleable and dispensable characters in Capote's construction of the crime. One of several suspenseful moments in Capote's *In Cold Blood*, for instance, occurs when the Kansas Bureau of Investigation (KBI) gets its first material lead in the Clutter family murder case. Agent Harold Nye, dispatched at dusk and on his own to the humble Hickock family home, arrives to interview one of the alleged killer's parents. Mr. and Mrs. Hickock are under the illusion, we are informed, that Nye's visit concerns a series of bad checks written by their problematic son, Dick. These parents, concerned and law-abiding people, oblige Agent Nye by speaking candidly about Dick, his personal history, his proclivities as a small-time con man, his recent companions and activities. "Perhaps if they had known the true meaning of the caller's presence," Capote's text observes, "the reception tendered [Nye] would have been less gracious, more guarded" (193). When the Hickock's narrative begins not only to shape a time line compatible with the murders but to name the accomplice proposed by a prison informer, Nye's internal drama becomes most palpable. The trick to making this case, he is sure, is to maintain as cool and offhand a manner as he can manage, and thereby to facilitate as much of this compromising information as he can gather; thus, "Nye, whose normal voice is cuttingly nasal and naturally intimidating, was effecting a subdued temper, a disarming, throwaway style." Regarding Dick's demeanor on the dates in question, he asks, in a tone of voice the reader might reconstruct as wistful: "did anything in his manner strike you as unusual? Different?" (195). Though even a faithful film adaptation must omit a lot of the book that ostensibly inspires it, Brooks' film sees fit to incorporate this interview and the interiorized drama it presents in a whole-cloth manner; the scene features Nye (Gerald S. O'Loughlin) glancing about the Hickock's humble quarters and asking Dick's guileless and ailing father (Jeff Corey) casual questions about the shotgun's most recent use. This scene can be viewed as paradigmatic; it epitomizes not strictly a turning point in this investigation but also, more broadly, possibilities inherent in the cultural inspiration and reconstruction of the "true crime." In both Capote's "nonfiction novel" and the Brooks film, this veiled and disingenuous interrogation enacts a powerful binary tension between the thrill of an advancing prosecution, on the one hand, and the counterbalancing pathos of an unwitting confession, on the other. For one's internal prosecutor, these novelistic and filmic scenes are satisfying "gotcha" moments in the case; for one's internal defense counsel, however, they feel like lapses in the spirit, if not the letter, of due process. But what arguably makes this encounter between Nye and the Hickocks most engaging is the likelihood (based on recently-surfaced KBI records) that it never occurred. The thrill and the threat of discovery have been manufactured.

Recent litigation between Nye's surviving son and the KBI has brought to light a number of investigation documents that, as Kevin Helliker reports, appear to contradict several aspects of Capote's construction of the case, among them this powerful farmhouse scene. According to Helliker, KBI records brought home and stored by Agent Nye senior (who has passed away) and now in the possession of his adult son, indicate that Nye did not visit the Hickocks at dusk or on his own, but, instead, that "four law enforcers— three KBI agents and a local sheriff's deputy—converged midday on the farm.

They found only [Hickock's] mother at home. They made no pretense of pursuing a parole violation. Executing a search, they found the shotgun, took it outside and fired it to collect the empty casing for ballistic purposes. They also confiscated clothing that appeared to be smattered with blood."

Capote's embellishments might seem harmless and even unnecessary, but their sheer number in one scene alone is striking: the agent is accompanied by several lawmen; their arrival time occurs not dusk but, instead, in broad daylight; the ailing parent is not present at all, and the present parent could hardly have been much deluded about the nature of the lawmen's visit. In the narration of this crime, Capote and Brooks have identified an occasion to entertain. Helliker points out that, in addition to these changes, KBI records also force a revised notion of the investigative time line; chief investigator, Alvin Dewey—the quick-moving "hero" of both Capote's and Brooks' *In Cold Blood*—waited five days before pursuing inmate Floyd Wells' tip, because he was initially committed to the concept that the Clutters had known their killers (17). Yet, embroidered or not, few would dispute the visceral intensity—the nagging feeling of veracity—contained by this scene of a stealth interrogation; the question is, why?

According to the testimony of several nonfiction authors, any storytelling grounded in true experience tends to seize upon the drama to which we are treated in Agent Nye's disingenuous farmhouse interview. In an essay intriguingly titled "The Journalist and the Murderer," Janet Malcolm posits that the journalistic interviewing of a criminal subject inevitably involves a process of "seduction and betrayal." The interviewee, she says—invited to take a "narcissist's holiday" by the interviewer's apparently rapt attention—tends to abandon his caution in a "Scheherazade-like" quest to maintain and perhaps utilize the intoxicating attention (72). The journalist, on the other hand, has altogether different motives in mind. In what purports to be an interiorization of Perry Smith's consciousness, Capote's text demonstrates an acute awareness of this dynamic by actually dramatizing the seductive allure of attention as it is experienced by Smith; Smith, we are told, had been drawn back to Kansas City not so much by the score Dick Hickock has in mind as by the prospect of re-engaging his former fellow inmate, Willie-Jay (59). Months earlier, Willie-Jay had energetically analyzed Perry's letters and his character; the prospect of regaining such flattering attention draws Perry like a magnet back to the forbidden state, for "in Willie Jay his vanity had found support, his sensibility shelter, and the four-month exile from this high-carat appreciation had made it more alluring than any dream of buried gold" (59). If the magic of the interview environment amounts to a "narcissist's holiday," Malcolm informs us, the written outcome of this process generally signals the vacation's end as the subject's disclosure becomes reified in the writer's testimony. Viewing the story that results, she explains, an interviewed subject is often "confronted with … [the] mortifying spectacle of himself flunking a test of character he did not know he was taking" (38). This mortification is an inevitable outcome of the struggle for story-management because, while the subject might have believed the purpose of the interview was to record his or her "story," the interview finally serves the journalist's own narcissistic purposes. Malcolm enables us to speculate that writers, like adapters more generally, supplant the supposed "source text" in the act of reworking it.

Some insist that this betrayal of the written-about subject distinguishes investigative journalism from public relations writing and, by extension, interrogation from homage, and these terms alone have implications for the study of adaptation, since Patrick Radden Keefe enables us to see that homage and interrogation are not easily disentangled when the subject is criminal transgression. Granting that journalists often betray the alliance subjects imagine has been implied by an interviewer's high-carat attention, Keefe maintains that "just as often (indeed, probably much more often) the truth of a story is obscured in ways large and small because the journalist elects not to break that implicit compact—but to honor it." "The access-for-depiction dynamic," he suggests, "is at least as prevalent a tendency in journalism as the seduction-and-betrayal routine" (Keefe). I would add to these insights that both the access-for-depiction and the seduction-and-betrayal games involve competitive quests for the upper hand in a manipulative contest between murderer and storyteller.

Helliker helps us to illustrate that an access-for-depiction dynamic permeates *In Cold Blood*, particularly in the relationship between Capote and KBI's lead investigator, Alvin Dewey (Helliker). A clever example of this charge may be found in Keefe's work, which points out that although Capote "never fully copped to his liberties and inventions, insisting that … interview subjects who later disputed his account were either lying or mistaken," the author had been right to suggest that any narrative representation of events inevitably entails a measure of artifice (Keefe). Keefe cites a telling letter—written by Capote on August 16, 1961, and addressed to Marie Dewey—in which Capote prods Marie's memory about when she had first seen pictures of the two suspects in the Clutter case. In this letter, the author explains to Mrs. Dewey that he intends to use her memory to construct a scene depicting the experience she recalls, but he assures her that, should memory fail her or prove vague, he does not mind inventing details. In the resultant scene, Alvin Dewey comes home, having just obtained mug shots of Perry Smith and Dick Hickock. Marie, who remains for the moment unaware of recent developments in the case, "greets him with a recitation of the household emergencies that have occupied her day: the family cat attacked a cocker spaniel; one of their boys fell from a tree" (Keefe). But when her husband silently pours two cups of coffee and extends a manila envelope in her direction, something in his demeanor pries Marie's attention from her own pre-occupations. Capote's text recounts that she dries her wet hands, sits down, takes a sip of the proffered coffee, and opens the envelope. Like the scene involving Agent Nye and Dick Hickock's parents (recounted earlier), this scene is vivid. Keefe suggests persuasively, however, that, while its veracity is not as directly challenged by corroborative documents as the one between Nye and Dick's parents, its artifice is equally strong. "Perhaps Marie Dewey had photographic recall and an exceptional eye for detail," Keefe concedes. "Maybe [upon prompting from Capote's letter,] she remembered that night some eight months earlier as if no time had passed. Perhaps the cat really did claw the cocker spaniel on that particular day. But I doubt it" (Keefe).[2] Again, what we witness in Capote's text is his tendency to use the Clutter family massacre as an occasion to generate a crime drama entirely of his own design.

Carolyn Wells Kraus, like Malcolm, underscores what we might polem-ically describe as the complimentary sociopathies connecting the writer (and, by extension, his audiences) to the murderer. With refreshing starkness, she proposes that "[m]y job consists of sucking people's gut out." That is to say, "I am a journalist" (283). Kraus posits that "journalists have long understood what writers from other disciplines have become self-reflective about in the postmodern climate. Writers are predators" (286). The central feature of a writer's predation, she suggests, is the presumption of proposing to accurately take on the perspectives of other people. Occurring "at the intersection of seemingly opposite sensibilities: the urge to record and the urge to create," nonfiction writers make *use* of people, Kraus observes, claiming for them-selves not only the ability to *know* others thoroughly but also the hubris to claim veracity for their inevitably repurposed constructions (286). This claim, of course, opens itself to larger questions: what might it mean to "know" oth-ers who could have done what Smith and Hickock did to the Clutter family in November of 1959?

Inevitably, a true crime plot must launch itself somewhat from extant templates. Capote's book and Brooks' film, in turn, both inflect familiar para-noid plot lines in which the perpetrator and the cop are merged. As Robert Eisenbauer notes, Capote's book echoes the duality of a Dr. Frankenstein, who seems simultaneously to lament and luxuriate in the sinister deeds of his monster; Capote, he says, "embraces both the traumatizing of the town and the psychology of the murderer, finding the taste savory as chocolate" (9). The murderers are monsters, in the contemporaneous news media as well as in Capote's and Brooks' constructions, but in both of these treatments they are monsters whose interiorized vulnerabilities and traumatic flash-backs—in both literary and filmic formats—also compel audiences to identify with them. As monsters and as humans they stimulate a complex economy wherein awe and revulsion coexist. As Edward J. Ingebretsen argues, the monster "pleasures as well as polices, although we rarely talk about the pleasure. The monster-face is a mask placed on someone whose offense is obliquely desirable to us, however much we disguise that knowing from ourselves or call it something else." Monsters, he claims, "help a community re-define itself" (4). The murderer's predation inspires the storyteller's predation, and the storyteller's predation, in turn, inspires the audience's predation: each, in her manner, quests after unmediated knowledge—both horrible and fascinating—of the events that elude narration from the start, the murders themselves. Each, in her manner, disguises this quest from herself.

Given this fundamental ambivalence, it is not surprising that audiences have wrestled with questions about the exact nature of advocacy within Capote's work and the adaptations that have followed it. To some readers, *In Cold Blood* has resembled an intensely researched police procedural, deeply identified with law enforcement. Clearly this interpretation inspired William Burroughs' famously hostile open letter to the author, which, as Voss and others have observed, reads like a hex in historical hindsight. Burroughs claims to write on behalf of a "department" known as "the reader," and he accuses Capote of having

> placed your services at the disposal of interests who are turning America into a police state by ... deliberately fostering the conditions that give rise to criminality and then demanding increased police powers and the retention of capital punishment to deal with the situation they have created. You have betrayed and sold out the talent that was granted you by this department. That talent is now officially withdrawn. Enjoy your dirty money. You will never have anything else. You will never write another sentence above the level of *In Cold Blood*. As a writer you are finished [Burroughs "Letters of Note"].

In some ways, Capote clearly invited the perception that his storytelling project adhered as closely to the goals of law enforcement as Burroughs assumes. While publicizing his work, he repeatedly insisted that his project coincided with the authorities' pursuit of justice. And although the terminology would not become available until after Capote's death, his impulse to align both police work and his own mission with what we could later call a knowledge project is abundantly clear in hindsight. Jane Howard's interview with the author, for example, notes that Capote "shared the fierce concern of Alvin Dewey, the detective in charge of the case, to learn why, and by whose hand, the Clutters had been slain, and to get to *know* the dead family better than they had *known* themselves" (Howard 70, my emphases). In fact, Capote's research process itself closely resembled the procedures employed by investigators. Like the KBI, Capote insisted on separating those to be interviewed and questioning them individually. Indeed, his goals at certain points so closely mirror those of the investigators' that their respective talking points become indistinguishable. For instance, early on in the case—and in the chapter titled "Persons Unknown"—Capote's story features Dewey exhorting his investigators with the idea that "'we have to keep going until we *know* the Clutters better than they *knew* themselves'" (123). Later in the same chapter, Dewey reports progress on this goal to local attorney, Clifford Hope: "I've come to feel I *know* Herb and the family better than they ever *knew* themselves. I'm haunted by them. I guess I always will be. Until I *know* what happened" (172, my emphasis). Gerald Clarke's biography confirms Capote's ideological alignment with law enforcement imperatives concerning Smith and Hickock; he notes that Capote "did not subscribe to the fashionable view of the sixties that criminals were victims of society" (43).

The broader historical record lends credence to Capote's alliance with state-sanctioned authority, too; as noted in Clarke's biography, testifying in opposition to the Supreme Court's Miranda ruling before a Senate subcommittee, Capote argued that the Miranda rights would unnecessarily confine the police in their work. In these hearings, the author proposes the essentialist theory that "people simply will not accept the fact that there is such a thing as a homicidal mind." He told the senators that "there are people who would kill as easily as they would write a bad check, and that they achieve satisfaction from it as I might from completing a novel or you from seeing a proposal of yours become law" (Clarke 368–69). Here, Capote's analogies are telling: equating the satisfaction achieved through murder with occupational satisfactions an author achieves through writing or a lawmaker achieves through legislation, Capote betrays the writer's shifting and unsettled identifications with the law and with law breaking alike.

To better comprehend the predation in Capote's approach to his criminal subjects, it is necessary to peel back layers of biographical and storytelling mythology. Voss posits that the author suffered after the completion of this text presumably because of an authentic experience of attachment to the murderers, and particularly to Smith. Hence, "Capote's compassion for Perry in the narrative is obvious," Voss notes, "but his own romantic attraction to Perry is less so" (119). Voss anchors this surmise about romantic attachment primarily to Harper Lee's recollection of Capote's first courtroom sighting of Perry, a recollection which has spawned its own mythology: Lee recalls Capote nudging her and whispering excitedly, "'Look, his feet don't touch the floor!'" Her own response to this enthusiasm is "'Oh, oh! This is the beginning of a great love affair'" (Voss 119). But as Clarke himself disclaims (and as Voss acknowledges) "in fact, their relationship was more complicated than a love affair: each looked at the other and saw, *or thought he saw*, the man he might have been" (327). Clarke, like Miller, calls attention to how the crime writer's own inner workings are on display within his work.

However, this reading of Capote and his supposed romantic relationship to the Clutter family's murderers mystifies, oversimplifies and therefore forecloses upon important avenues of thought about Capote's storytelling. It might be cynical to suggest that seduction and romance *never* coincide; at the same time, acknowledging that they do not *always* coincide is just plain sensible. I wish to complicate the oversimplification of "romance" to unearth alternative features in the ambivalence between Capote's project and the killers it enlivens. This ambivalence helps to explain why readers have formed widely disparate interpretations of how and for whom advocacy functions in the book and in Brooks' film. Miller's rereading of Capote's project invites us to subject Capote to examination in precisely the manner Capote used to examine the criminals. When we do this, we can outline the mercurial alliances—shifting stances completely divorced from the pressures of law enforcement—that wrestle within *In Cold Blood*. Much has been made of Capote's affection for Smith, and admittedly there are passages where Capote's text elicits sympathy on Smith's behalf. In one striking moment, wedged between quotes attributed to Smith—and within a text that elsewhere demonstrates a frequent and nimble use of "free indirect" discourse—one encounters what feels like a strangely direct appeal for sympathy towards the murderer: "Look at his family! Look at what had happened there! His mother, an alcoholic, had strangled to death on her own vomit. Of her children, two sons and two daughters, only the younger girl, Barbara, had entered ordinary life, married, begun raising a family" (130). The exclamation points ending the first two sentences seem to anchor this speech in a profoundly emotional identification with Perry's perspective; yet the use of the third-person form and the distancing "there" in the second sentence insist on distance. Additionally, based on Perry's evident rancor towards his sister and his lack of the requisite perspective to define ordinary life, it seems unlikely that he would credit her in any terms, let alone in this almost clinical language, as the only one who had entered it.

Far more predominant in Capote's text, however, are the moments where the author elects to satirize Smith or submit him to coldly ironic send-ups. One such moment occurs when Smith recounts having foolishly confided in Dick Hickock. In a passage redolent of irony, Capote's story recounts that Smith had told Hickock that

> "I've always been an outstanding character detective, otherwise I'd be dead today. Like if I couldn't judge when to trust somebody. You never can much. But I've come to trust you, Dick. You'll see I do, because I'm going to put myself in your power. I'm going to tell you something I never told anybody. Not even Willie-Jay. About the time I fixed a guy." And Perry saw, as he went on, that Dick was interested; he was really listening [131].

This confession reveals what Malcolm would define as a risky "Scheherazade" move on Perry's part, one that anyone who empathized with him would likely advise against. Capote's text, Brooks' film and also Kaplan's two-part television movie all amplify this ill-advised confession and upgrade it from an abject and misguided occasion of trust into a strategy involving implausible foresight and cleverness. In all of these versions of the story, Perry has actually devised a maneuver that will alert him immediately if Hickock winds up selling him out to the police (which, of course, he does). This plot feature constructs the apparently naïve Perry as a schemer just as cunning as his partner in crime, if a bit more loyal; once the two ex-convicts are apprehended, Perry remains stoic until the moment when police relay back to him Dick's admission about the time when Perry had "fixed a guy" (148). For me, as a viewer, this point in the plot calls instantly to mind Brooks' visual punctuation: as Perry the shackled Robert Blake's in a headlight-illuminated and snarling tight shot, as he glances backward into in the police car behind him and growls about "the brass boy" and how easily he told all.

This kind of strategizing does not align smoothly with the Perry Smith Capote conjures elsewhere, in post-publication discussions of his interviews with the murderers, however; contrasting Hickock's memory for detail with Smith's in a 1966 interview with George Plimpton, Capote notes that "Perry ... was very bad at details of that sort, though he was good at remembering conversations and moods" (Plimpton "The Story"). This feature of Smith's strategizing, visually amplified in Brooks' car scene, appears embellished for additional reasons. Records now indicate, for instance, that Perry Smith rode from Las Vegas back to Garden City in the police vehicle *behind*, not in front of, the one in which Hickock was transported. The embroidery, initiated by Capote and sustained in later iterations by Brooks and Kaplan, takes Smith's otherwise foolhardy and pathetic prison cell disclosure and invests it with a creative and cunning foresight. The fiction writer thereby improves on Smith's criminal method.

Far from advocating for Smith, Capote's ironies often operate against him. Smith's immaturity is the material of quiet satire, as we see in his notions about past romances, serious endeavors, or future prospects. First, we find out about Smith's short-lived romance with "Cookie," the nurse who simply cared for him after his motorcycle accident, yet whom, we are told, he insists he "almost married." Cookie facilitates a high-brow snicker about Smith's reading level, too, since "she was a swell kid ... and she had liked him, babied him, inspired him to read 'serious literature'" (116). Smith later undergoes the writer's parodic treatment over the naiveté of his dreams for the future; when the more pragmatic Dick asks Perry how he envisions the two of them making a living in Mexico, the story impersonates Perry's incredulity with mischievous free indirect narration:

> "How?"—what could Dick mean? The question dazed Perry. After all, such a rich assortment of ventures had been discussed. Prospecting for gold, skin-diving for sunken treasure—these were but two of the projects Perry had ardently proposed.

> And there were others. The boat, for instance. They had often talked of a deep-sea fishing boat, which they would buy, man themselves, and rent to vacationers—this though neither had ever skippered a canoe or hooked a guppy [118].

Not content to simply recount this list of absurd pipe dreams, the text indulges a mean kind of fun at Smith's expense, characterizing these arguably sad and unrealizable visions as a "rich assortment" of projects. In each of these instances, satire eclipses sympathy as the painfully obvious begins to dawn on Perry: "Heretofore, Dick had always encouraged him, listened attentively to his talk of maps, tales of treasure, but now—and it had not occurred to him before—he wondered if all along Dick had only been *pretending*, just kidding him" (118). The book's playful treatments of Perry's earnestness add up and they mitigate the customary interpretation of the text as "special pleading" on Perry's behalf.

Interestingly, the book extends a most palpable and under-observed commiseration not to Smith, but instead to Hickock, as the beleaguered and more practical con-man of the pair. In late life interview reported by Helliker, Alvin Dewey recounts that "the treatment people received in Mr. Capote's book depended on whether he liked them. 'I was the luckiest.'" Likewise, his wife, Marie Dewey, tells George Plimpton that Capote "was fond of Perry. He didn't like Hickock" (Plimpton "Capote's" 65). Asked about these likes and dislikes, however, Capote all but confesses that the monsters he traced lived as much inside him as within the two murderers he analyzed. When asked by Howard whether he liked either of the killers, for instance, he narcissistically retorts, "that's like saying 'do you like yourself?'" (Howard 72). Indeed, perhaps it is.

In fact, while several sources have registered Capote's dislike for Hickock—whose more conventional upbringing made for a less engaging backstory than Smith's—the veiled affinities between Capote's narrator and Hickock merit closer attention. For example, in his 1966 interview with Plimpton, Capote credits Dick with a memory that rivals his own, and in which the author took vociferous pride. Generally tight-fisted when it comes to praise for others, Capote admits that

> Dick had an absolutely fantastic memory—one of the greatest memories I have ever come across.... Dick could give me the names and addresses of any hotel or place along the route where they'd spent maybe just half a night. He told me when I got to Miami to take a taxi to such-and-such a place and get out on the boardwalk and it would be southwest of there, number 232, and opposite I'd find two umbrellas in the sand which advertised "Tan with Coppertone." That was how exact he was. He was the one who remembered the little card in the Mexico City hotel room in the corner of the mirror that reads "Your day ends at 2 p.m." He was extraordinary [Plimpton "The Story"].

Features of Hickock's con-man personality are, in fact, reflected in Capote's life story and, much later, in the author's own career-ending miscalculation. The journalist and this murderer seemed to share a fatal under-estimation of other people. Interrogated in the novel by Agent Roy Church about the series of bad checks he has written, for example, Hickock himself registers pride in his exceptional recall: "[t]he prisoner, evidently proud of his one authentic gift, a brilliant memory, recited the names and addresses of twenty Kansas City stores, cafes, and garages, and recalled, accurately, the 'purchase' made at each and the amount of the check passed" (Capote 247). Of course, in this "scene," as in Agent Nye's "scene" with Dick's parents (cited earlier), Church is engaged in the veiled interrogation strategy calculated to maintain the flow of compromising disclosures on the Dick's part. Dick, for his part—as yet unaware that he and Smith have been picked up, not for check-fraud alone, but for murder—reveals momentarily the con man's underlying contempt for others. Capote's book shows Church asking, with, feigned appreciation: "I'm curious, Dick. Why do these people accept your checks? I'd like to know the secret" (Capote 247). It is this vacation from cau-tion the investigator works to prolong. And, like the duped interviewee in Malcolm's model of the journalist and subject, Dick flunks a character test he does not know he's taking by yielding to vanity in answering, "The secret is: people are dumb" (247).

This question and its answer are not probative, regarding either check-fraud or murder, and hence their expansion within the book could seem out of place. But small unguarded disclosures like this reveal both Hickock's atti-tude towards others, on the one hand, and something apparently tangential *about* Hickock that intrigued Capote, on the other. Attitudes like this accu-mulate within any fiction and they become reified in our references to char-acter. Yet whose character Capote's text works to know here remains an open question, since Capote's trajectory as a writer later oddly echoes Dick's crim-inal smugness.

While promoting *In Cold Blood*, Capote often boasted about a future collection he had in the works. During his lifetime, however, what he unwisely wound up publishing instead of this larger work were three roman-à-clef styled chapters that appeared in *Esquire* magazine—"Unspoiled Monsters," "Kate McCloud," and "La Cote Basque"—based on compromising conversa-tions the author claimed to have witnessed among members of the café society into which he had ingratiated himself. Many of Capote's wealthy companions were scandalized to encounter thinly disguised renditions of themselves in these chapters, in connection with embarrassing items of gossip; as a result, and with few exceptions, they dropped and permanently ostracized Capote. It is fair to characterize these three essays as petty in tone, and when they resurfaced posthumously, bound and titled as *Answered Prayers*, Tina Brown dismissed them as a "socio-pornographic *Ragtime* rife with the low cackle of camp" (Brown). *In Cold Blood* had been superior to any of Capote's fiction, she argues, in large part because "the nonfiction constraints of libel, taste and feeling were just what he needed at a time when his internal editor seems to have collapsed."

My point in bringing up this series of events is that the social miscalculation indulged by Capote in publishing these essays bears a striking resemblance to Hickock's rationale for how he got away with passing bad checks. Those closest to Capote, for instance, had instant forebodings about Capote's incendiary chapters and attempted to caution the author against releasing them. Clarke, Capote's biographer, for example—referring to himself as "the friend" in a manner that emulates *In Cold Blood*'s self-effacing narrator— recalls a July afternoon when he discussed "La Cote Basque" with Capote in Gloria Vanderbilt's pool, while its owner was away: "[A]fter the friend had read his manuscript, Truman identified, one by one, the models for his characters. 'But Truman, they're not going to like this,' protested the friend. Floating on his back and looking up at a sky of cloudless serenity, Truman lazily responded, 'Nah, they're too dumb. They won't know who they are'" (Clarke 467). Sadly, they *did* know, and like Hickock—though to a much lighter degree—Capote paid a price for his miscalculation that stung him to the core.

Even the "facts" Capote recounts about Hickock betray a striking competition between disgust, on the one hand, and a grudging identification if not admiration, on the other. The novel relates that Hickock was "rather a bookworm," and that he was mainly interested in "sex, as represented in the novels of Harold Robbins and Irving Wallace" (Capote 360). Reading tastes described this way seem harmless enough, making Smith's castigation of the texts as "degenerate filth for filthy degenerate minds" seem inexplicably prudish and controlling. Elsewhere, however, Capote's recollection of Hickock's reading tastes provokes a wholesale revision of Hickock's psychology and Smith's response. To Howard, Capote recounts that Hickock "'had me combing obscure bookshops for paperbacks on the most lurid sex crimes imaginable'" (71–72). How do we reconcile the reader of Harold Robbins with the reader of lurid sex crimes? How do we account for the writer willing to confuse the two or who saw fit to "comb obscure bookshops" to provide this material to a convicted murderer?

The contrast between these alternative Hickocks challenges any reconciliation, and it opens onto other descriptive infidelities in Capote's characterization of Smith's accomplice. In Capote's book, for instance, Hickock records for an examining psychiatrist, "Dr. Jones," a personal history; in it, Hickock suggests that his main motive for going to the Clutter home on that fateful night involved the prospect of sexually violating Nancy Clutter: "One thing I never told you about the Clutter deal is this. Before I ever went to their house I knew there would be a girl there. I think the main reason I went there was not to rob them but to rape the girl. Because I thought a lot about it. That is one reason why I never wanted to turn back when we started to. Even when I saw there was no safe" (Capote 313). Of course, skepticism is appropriate here and for reasons not merely restricted to questions about Capote's veracity. As defendants, Hickock and Smith were required, we are told, to produce these life histories in connection with the prospect of launching an insanity defense. That Hickock would have gone to such lengths simply to perpetrate a rape stretches plausibility, but not beyond the breaking point. However, compelling information now exists that contradicts Hickock's and/or Capote's account of the rape motive. Plimpton's 1997 interviews include one with the Reverend James Post, the prison chaplain featured in Capote's and Brooks' stories, who refuses to give Willie Jay's address to Smith when the latter calls him from the Kansas City bus terminal. Post, who knew the two inmates and had attended their executions, was later summoned by Hickock's first wife, when one of her sons was having trouble dealing with his father's dark legacy. Taking the boy to his father's grave and counseling him, Post recounts to Plimpton that "I said his dad wasn't the sex fiend that Capote tried to make him out … like trying to rape the Clutter girl before he killed her. It didn't happen. And other things—lies, just to make it a better story" (Plimpton "Capote's" 70).

Repeatedly, one tries to weigh all rhetorical possibilities: Capote has taken several demonstrable liberties with this true crime. Might he have taken such violent liberty with Hickock's criminal propensities? Has Post decided that Hickock's own narrative matters less than the requirement to relieve a grieving son's shame? Did Capote dislike Hickock or simply the con-man he identified/projected within the man? I don't suggest that these questions can be answered in any final way; what I *am* suggesting is that such questions are profoundly important and that "fidelity analyses" can be strategically invaluable in our attempts to understand how they become addressed in narrative and artistic form.

Has Capote himself calculated that the reckless endangerment of two dispensable men's legacies is worth less than his own storytelling prowess? Clarke reports that Capote was opposed to the death penalty—"'institutionalized sadism,' he termed it" (368), and Brooks' film seems to weigh in this way. Outside of the text, however, Capote's own words are more equivocal. Since he relied on this "nonfiction novel" to invent himself as an authority on criminal justice, his declared stances on crime become deeply relevant. Asked in 1966 by George Plimpton about his stance on capital punishment, Capote says, "I feel that capital crimes should all be handled by Federal Courts, and that those convicted should be imprisoned in a special Federal prison where, conceivably, a life-sentence could mean, as it does not in state courts, just that" ("The Story"). Even in his review of the novel's reconstruction of Smith and Hickock's hanging, it is hard not to read an almost ghoulish detachment from the human stakes involved in the spectacle. Discussing his strategy for the hanging "scene," Capote quips: "The whole thing," as he tells Kroll, "was done from Al Dewey's point of view. I didn't find the place as gloomy as he did, and as it was described in the book. After all, what were we there to see, a prizefight?" (60). Such a callous attitude surfaces in his response to a similar question from Howard, who records that "anguishing though he found the spectacle of [Hickock's and Perry's] execution[s], he was not and is not entirely opposed to capital punishment. 'Essentially I'm on the side of the victim, not the murderer,' he says, 'and if the alternative to capital punishment is parole and recidivism, in other words, more murders, then I *am* in favor of it'" (75).

Admittedly, as in his statement to Howard (quoted earlier), Capote reiterates that the best solution would be a Federal prison wherein every life sentence would mean exactly that. But even as he proposes this solution he equivocates: "'There is a lot of sentiment around against capital punishment,' Capote elaborates, 'but murder isn't romantic. There's no mystery about it. Terrible things happen to people, and not just in books either'" (75). This response could be construed in a number of ways, either as an argument for mitigation or as a rationalization for a *laissez-faire* detachment. In interviews, Capote might have demurred about his crime analysis qualifications; he tells Plimpton that, while he had "learned a good deal about crime, and the origins of the homicidal mentality," in his preparation of the book, his qualifications in this area still represent "a layman's knowledge and I don't pretend to anything deeper" ("The Story"). Such humility was fleeting, however, as it apparently did not hamper Capote's ability to predict unquestioned futures for Hickock and Smith, as he does his interview with Howard; "'Dick was a small time punk and crook and might have remained one all his life,'" he announces. And "'Perry would have killed someone, eventually, if not the Clutters'" (Howard 72). Such forecasts—along with essentializing testimony before the Senate subcommittee regarding "the homicidal mind," and his handy but vague solutions such as the Federal prison idea—certainly lay claim to the expert authority Capote demurs about in his interview with Plimpton ("The Story").

And yet, for as fervently as he modeled knowing on Dewey's investigative principles, Capote wished to try on the characters of the murderers, too; his way of knowing them, as I have indicated at the outset of this essay, is to extrapolate from himself. In his interview with Howard, Capote sidesteps her question about whether he liked the killers. As a diversionary response, he offers the tantalizing observation that "'[w]hat mattered was that I *knew* them as well as I know myself'" (72). Indeed, how much or how little "knowledge" Capote claims with this enigmatic answer remains a mystery. But Capote's impulse to substitute knowing for liking is revealing. For among the observations that the selective gaze of *In Cold Blood* finds fit to include are Perry's own shifting ruminations on the relationship—or lack of one— between knowing and *caring*, and thus perhaps, by extension, between the ambivalent "reportage" and advocacy on display in his journalistic project. In Capote's book, Smith confesses in prison—to his visiting Army friend, Dan Cullivan, we are told—that "it's easy to kill—a lot easier than passing a bad check" (326).[3] The main reason, Perry claims, is that he had only known the Clutter family for an hour; "[i]f I'd really *known* them, I guess I'd feel different. I don't think I could live with myself. But the way it was, it was like picking off targets in a shooting gallery" (326–27, emphasis added). Yet perhaps it should come as no surprise that Perry's self-explanations, too, are the rhetoric of a moment and not the clarification of any sustained character trait or ethical principle. For example, after the Clutter massacre, he broods about his one surviving sibling, a sister Capote names "Barbara"—someone Perry clearly *had* known for considerably longer than the requisite hour, and whose only observable misstep seems to have been a chastising letter—and in Capote's book Perry tells Dick that "the only *real* regret I have—I wish the hell my sister had been in that house" (166).

Clearly anyone looking for an overarching criminological or literary theory from Capote—like anyone seeking a guiding rationale for the murders from Smith or Hickock—is barking up the wrong tree; Capote's stances towards the murderers and their deeds—in fact, towards crime in general— are wildly inconsistent. Encountering the author early on in Holcomb, Kansas, during the first days after the murders, for example, Dewey recalls an author more dedicated more to his craft than to anything resembling criminal detection. He recounts an exchange with Capote that becomes amplified in Miller's film. Capote, in Dewey's recollection, "said he came out to write a story and that it made no difference to him whether the crime was solved or not" (Kroll 61).

Miller's *Capote*, drawing inferences from Clarke's biography, delves most deeply into the ambivalence that structures both Capote's literary project and the audience engagement this high-profile crime has clearly sustained. Miller's centralization of the crime writer shifts the focus from the killers to the author who wishes to know them better than they knew themselves. It centralizes Capote's manipulation of Smith and Hickock, of Nelle Lee (Catherine Keener), and the Deweys (Amy Ryan and Chris Cooper) alike in the service of his own literary fame. More than it references a prior "text," this adaptation attempts to get closer to the real conditions beyond the text; in the process, it brings the crime writer's other-eclipsing narcissism into sharp focus. Thus Capote's histrionic performance of concern for the criminals can be weighed alongside his callous abandonment of them.

Like the predatory journalist described by Malcolm, Keefe, and Kraus or the stealth investigator proposed in Agent Nye's visit to the Hickock farmhouse, each adaptation of the Clutter massacre and its aftermath repurposes events as myths are wont to do, here giving prominence to a previously incidental drama, and there erasing or downplaying a once central story attribute. Within a climate of diminishing facts, this high-stakes knowledge project keeps inviting fidelity analysis, not merely for the gratification of some imagined resemblance to earlier texts, but—more fundamentally—for the purpose of establishing continually revised notions of what is true, what is just. If indeed myths can be said to challenge an audience to continue seeking the truth even as they provide a substitute *for* it, those crimes that sanction multiple adaptation surely function as an elusive fund of modern myth-making material. Perhaps completing the process of secularization is a faith we can do without, so long as stories about actual transgressions keep prompting us to examine what we *do* believe and why. By focusing attention on murder events that occasion such brisk storytelling exchange—indeed by acknowledging, for collaborative purposes, that palpably real, if elusive, social objectives are at stake within linguistic reconstructions of crime—we facilitate interdisciplinary quests to better *know* the mnemonic value of multiply-reworked crimes. We insist on the possibility, in other words, that even legless frogs possess perfect pitch.

NOTES

1. See also Plimpton, *Truman Capote*, for a relevant later interview with Dewey. In one version confessed by Smith, he and Hickock each kill two of the victims. In a subsequent version, he revises this account to claim responsibility for all four murders, but the reason is dubious; he says he wishes to spare the feelings of Hickock's mother. Alvin Dewey maintained his belief in the former account, while Truman Capote insisted that he himself believed the latter. The bottom line: we do not know the "truth."

2. At the time of the book's publication, Marie Dewey vehemently denied the kind of arrangement with Capote that would bespeak access for depiction arrangement, but her denials involve some strange equivocations; see Kroll, 61. In response to Kroll's implied question about Capote's possibly cynical "use" of her husband and herself, Marie "indignantly" retorts, "He's far above that. He's something more than any of us." At the same time, however, directly after this denial, Mrs. Dewey communicates clear bedazzlement over having been brought to New York by Capote (albeit after the book's publication) and getting to meet Capote's A-list friends, such as Jackie Kennedy, Barbara Paley, Bennett Cerf, and Arlene Francis. "[T]hey love Truman just as we did," Mrs. Dewey gushed; "[h]e enriched our lives." As Helliker reports, Capote required Columbia Pictures to pay a $10,000 "consulting" fee to Mrs. Dewey in connection with the preparation of Brooks' film (Helliker).

3. As Keefe reports, some conversations—in Capote's book attributed to Smith's former military buddy, Dan Cullivan—actually involve Capote himself, who writes to Cullivan for permission to make the substitution.

WORKS CITED

Assmann, Aleida. "History, Memory, and the Genre of Testimony." *Poetics Today* 27.2 (Summer 2006): 261–73. Print.

Birchall, Clare. *Knowledge Goes Pop: From Conspiracy Theory to Gossip.* Oxford: Berg, 2006. Print.

Brookes, Michael, David Wilson, Elizabeth Yardley, Mohammed Rahman, and Sophie Rowe. "Faceless: High-Profile Murders and Public Recognition." *Crime Media Culture* 11.1 (2015): 61–76. Print.

Brown, Tina. "Goodbye to the Ladies Who Lunch." *New York Times Book Review*, 13 Sept. 1987. Web. 8 Mar. 2017.

Burroughs, William. Letter to Truman Capote (1970). *Letters of Note*. Web. 6 Mar. 2017.

Capote. Dir. Bennett Miller. Perf. Phillip Seymour Hoffman, Catherine Keener, Chris Cooper. Sony Pictures Classics, 2005. Film.

Capote, Truman. *In Cold Blood: A True Account of a Multiple Murder and Its Consequences*. New York: Signet, 1966. Print.

Currie, Elliott. "Against Marginality: Arguments for a Public Criminology." *Theoretical Criminology* 11.2 (2007): 175–190. Print.

Diamond, Suzanne, "Whose Life *Is* it, Anyway? Adaptation, Collective Memory, and (Auto)Biographical Processes." *Redefining Adaptation Studies*. Ed. Dennis Cutchins, Laurence Raw, and James M. Welsh. 95–110. Lanham: Scarecrow, 2010. Print.

Eisenbauer, Robert. *After Romanticism*. New York: Peter Lang, 2008. Print.

Grochowski, Tom. "The 'Tabloid Effect' in the O.J. Simpson Case: *The National Enquirer* and the Production of Crime Knowledge." *International Journal of Cultural Studies* 5.3 (2002): 336–56. Print.

Hayward, Keith J. "Opening the Lens: Cultural Criminology and the Image." *Framing Crime: Cultural Criminology and the Image*. Ed. Hayward and Mike Presdee. 1–16. London: Routledge, 2010. Print.

Helliker, Kevin. "Capote Classic *In Cold Blood* Tainted by Long-Lost Files." *Wall Street Journal*, 8 Feb. 2013. Web. 9 Mar. 2017.

Howard, Jane. "Horror Spawns a Masterpiece: Truman Capote's Bestseller on a Kansas Crime." *Life*, 7 Jan. 1966: 58–76. Print.

In Cold Blood. Dir. Richard Brooks. Perf. Robert Blake, Scott Wilson. Columbia, 1967. Film.

_____. Dir. Jonathan Kaplan. Perf. Anthony Edwards, Eric Roberts. Pacific Motion Pictures, 1996. Film.

Infamous. Dir. Douglas McGrath. Perf. Toby Jones, Daniel Craig. Warner Bros., 2006. Film.

Ingebretsen, Edward J. *At Stake: Monsters and the Rhetoric of Fear in Public Culture*. Chicago: University of Chicago Press, 2001. Print.

Keefe, Patrick Radden, "Capote's Co-Conspirators." *The New Yorker*, 23 Mar. 1989. Web. 7 Mar. 2017.

Kraus, Carolyn Wells. "On Hurting People's Feelings: Journalism, Guilt, and Autobiography." *Biography* 26.2 (2003): 283–97. Print.

Kroll, Jack. "*In Cold Blood* ... An American Tragedy." *Newsweek*, 24 Jan. 1966: 59–63. Print.

Kruse, Corinna. "Producing Absolute Truth: CSI Science as Wishful Thinking." *American Anthropologist* 112.1 (2010): 71–91. Print.

Lee, Harper. *To Kill a Mockingbird*. New York: J.B. Lippincott, 1960. Print.

Malcolm, Janet. "The Journalist and the Murderer: I—The Journalist." *The New Yorker*, 13 Mar. 1989: 38–73. Print.

Murley, Jean, *The Rise of True Crime: 20th Century Murder and American Popular Culture*. Westport, CT: Praeger, 2008. Print.

Plimpton, George. "Capote's Long Ride." *The New Yorker*, 13 Oct. 1997: 62–70. Print.

_____. "The Story Behind a Nonfiction Novel." *New York Times*, 19 Jan. 1966. Web. 6 Mar. 2017

_____. *Truman Capote: In Which Various Friends, Acquaintances and Detractors Recall His Turbulent Career*. New York: Anchor, 1998. Print.

Reiner, Robert. "Media Made Criminality: The Representation of Crime in the Mass Media." *The Oxford Handbook of Criminology*. Ed. Mike Maguire, Rodney Morgan and Robert Reiner. 302–37. Oxford: Oxford University Press, 2007. Print.

Seltzer, Mark. *True Crime: Observations on Violence and Modernity*. New York: Routledge, 2007. Print.

Voss, Ralph F. *Truman Capote and the Legacy of* In Cold Blood. Tuscaloosa: University of
    Alabama Press, 2011. Prin.
Watson, Adam. "Capote's Bias: *In Cold Blood* as an Anti-Death Penalty Argument." *Adam
    Watson*, 7 Mar. 2001. Web. 8 Mar. 2017.
Wheeldon, Johanna. "Ontology, Epistemology, and Irony: Richard Rorty and Re-Imagining
    Pragmatic Criminology." *Theoretical Criminology* 19.3 (2015): 396–415. Print.

Textual Museums
in Edith Wharton
and Orhan Pamuk

HÜLYA YAĞCIOĞLU

Edith Wharton's *The Age of Innocence* (1920) and Orhan Pamuk's *The Museum of Innocence* (2008) are set in highly restricted, upper-class metropolitan societies and portray the love stories of male protagonists who have to choose between their fiancées and the other women they are in love with. As a background of each protagonist's failed love story, the novels explore how material culture shapes and determines human relations. In each text high culture is manifested through material objects, which become fundamental in understanding the deeper social, and personal issues the novels problematize. Both novels depict specific historical periods in the past: *The Age of Innocence*, published in 1920, is set in 1870s New York City; *The Museum of Innocence*, published in 2008, is set in 70s and 80s Istanbul. By describing the societies of their childhood and youth, Wharton and Pamuk not only fictionalize but also adapt history in their texts. Although the authors claim historical veracity in their adaptation of history, their novels are mostly concerned with how they subjectively reconstruct the past in relation to the present and future. I argue that the writers imagine the past periods as innocent and idyllic times to create a myth of the origins of their respective cultures possibly in order to resist the cultural change brought about by modernity. The former novel was set during the heyday of industrial capitalism and its attendant proliferation of consumer goods. The latter was set in the late modern era in a developing nonwestern country experiencing modernity and the consequences of capitalism in a different and arguably belated way: not only the Republic of Turkey experienced modernity belatedly, but 1870s New York is a belated Europeanization of a still un-cultured

New World. In their adapting and constructing specific historical backgrounds, each author fictionalizes the effects of drastic social changes on human lives. The novels question how conceptions of value changed as a result of capitalism, especially with the profusion of consumer products. This essay will examine the idea of preservation of cultural values through material objects, and show how the practices of consumption and collecting in each novel determine its structure.

Preservation of Cultural Values through Objects

Although *The Age of Innocence* takes place in the period of about 30 years between the 1870s and the very early 1900s, Wharton wrote it in 1920, a time when she felt the dramatic effects of World War I and found solace in the past. She wrote to Sara Norton: "I am steeping myself in the nineteenth century ... which is such a blessed refuge from the turmoil and mediocrity of today—like taking sanctuary in a night temple" (Lewis 424). *The Age of Innocence*, above all, is an account of the transience of cultural values and the idea of outliving the material world. Although Wharton criticizes the traditions and conventions of the 1870s New York society through Newland Archer's unfulfilled love for Ellen, the novel is an attempt to collect and preserve the past as it is, even in its imperfect state. All Edith Wharton's texts share the "assumptions that the authentic and the real are in some sense precarious, in need of preservation, and that they reveal their purest meaning in the form of special collections and related kinds of archival representation" (Bentley 58).

By bringing together the fragments of the past, Wharton adapts old New York through archival representation. She posits that "the compact world of [her] youth has receded into a past from which it can only be dug up in bits by the assiduous relic-hunter ... and its smallest fragments begin to be worth collecting and putting together before the last of those who knew the live structure are swept away with it" (*A Backward Glance* 781). Just as the material culture of those times is carefully examined so too the social norms and cultural conditions that shape 1870s New York are preserved as precious relics. The novel is "a retrospective study of a New York subculture, now extinct, an ethnography of a distinctive set of customs and a way of life which no longer exists" (Trumpener and Nyce 162). Since she imagined the novel as a solid historical document of the era, she took great care to represent the details of the 1870s accurately: the mustaches ("not tooth brush ones, but curved & slightly twisted at the ends"), the clothes and buttonhole flowers (violets by day, gardenias by night), the manners and language (no slang)

(Knights 20). Wharton's endeavor becomes more interesting as she imagines the society of old New York as another extinct civilization in human history: "What I could not guess was that this little low-studded rectangular New York ... would fifty years later be as much a vanished city as Atlantis or the lowest layer of Schliemann's Troy, or that the social organization which that prosaic setting had slowly secreted would have been swept to oblivion with the rest" (*A Backward Glance* 55).

The novel represents the city as an ancient tribe, "with the inscrutable totem terrors that had ruled the destinies of [Archer's] forefathers thousands of years ago" (*The Age* 2). Many critics note the anthropological language in the novel, designating upper-class New York society, for example, the farewell dinner party organized for Ellen is a form of ritual of violence, a "tribal rally around a kinswoman about to be eliminated from the tribe" (Wharton *The Age* 234). The author constantly alludes to pharaohs, rites, pyramids, a hiero-glyph world, and so on in order to compare old New York to other vanished civilizations. Despite its pretense of sophistication and progression, as evident in their attending operas and balls, old New Yorkers cannot escape the "totem terrors" of their tribe (*The Age* 4). Their irrational taboos, strict and unbend-able social rules, and conformity to tradition will be incomprehensible to future generations.

Even the title of the novel has anthropological overtones—like earlier ages, such as the Stone Age or Bronze Age, the "age of innocence" is also transitory, and transience points to the relative insignificance of that time in human history (Saunders 95). The novel juxtaposes the past and the present to reveal social change, which is an issue related to modernity as it prob-lematizes the relationship between tradition and the present. Not surprisingly, the end of the novel marks the dramatic effects of modernity in *fin-de-siècle* America, as years later (in 1902), Archer witnesses the social and technolog-ical transformation of New York into "an international networked metropolis" from "a provincial outpost of the 1870s" (Klimasmith 555). The new society is so different from the old, as past restrictions are now transgressed and "all the social atoms spun around on the same plane" (Wharton *The Age* 248). Thus, one need not wait long to compare the cultural background of the novel with the present in order to see the extent of social transformation. Despite concerned reactions to social transformations—for example, Mrs. Archer's laments about social change—the genteel class disappears together with the times as a result of turbulent changes in America at the turn of the twentieth century.

In *The Adaptation of History: Essays of Ways of Telling the Past*, Defne Ersin Tutan and Laurence Raw argue that all historical documents and inter-pretations of the past "should be treated [and welcomed] as adaptations" as there is no other way of coming to terms with the way history is understood

(10). Despite her claims of historical accuracy, what Wharton does here is to adapt history: to engage with the past regardless of being completely truthful to make sense of the present and future. Wharton's "backward glance" at her society is in line with Orhan Pamuk's retrospective look at Istanbul society in *The Museum of Innocence*:

> Many readers and visitors will already understand it only too well, but in the expectation that much later generations—such as those who will visit our museum after 2100—might find the term opaque, let me now lay aside fears of repeating myself and set down a certain number of harsh—in times past, the preferred word would have been "unpalatable"—truths. One thousand nine hundred and seventy-five solar years after the birth of Christ, in the Balkans, the Middle East, and the western and southern shores of the Mediterranean, as in Istanbul, the city that was the capital of this region, virginity was still regarded as a treasure that young girls should protect until the day they married [61].

The passage on virginity above best exemplifies the transience and the gradual loss of hitherto established values, which renders *The Museum of Innocence* a similar attempt to reevaluate the past. Just like Wharton, Pamuk writes about the long-gone world of his childhood and youth with almost anthropological accuracy. In doing that, he cannot help adapting the past to indicate how "it represents different things to different generations" (Raw "Retelling" 65). The novel is a textual museum, preserving the old local material objects accompanied by extinct species of people, manners, and emotions (for example, Kemal's outdated love). One may see the author's attempt to preserve the past through archival representation in his protagonist Kemal, who obsessively collects artifacts related not just to his personal past but also the cultural history of the society he lives in. The "archaic" museum objects in Kemal's collection also frame the background of his "love" for Füsun, which will be viewed as something prehistoric and incomprehensible to future generations.

Both novels are set in periods of cultural transformation. The late nineteenth and early twentieth centuries as the backdrop of *The Age of Innocence* can be described as "the transitional period from a so-called 'productive ethic' to a new 'consumerist ethic' in the wealthy and industrialized Western countries" (Francescato 11). In this new age of consumption, one's existence came to be defined by the possession and display of some luxury goods. Istanbul in the latter quarter of the twentieth century is also an appropriate setting for Pamuk's depiction of the period of transition to Turkish modernism: a time when the nation was on the brink of change as it witnessed an explosion in imported Western products resulting in the integration of The Republic of Turkey into the capitalist world of the West. The novel covers the period that witnessed both the ban on the importation of foreign goods in the name of protecting local Turkish industry and the later liberalization of Turkish trade in the mid–80s. At one point, the protagonist describes the Istanbul bourgeoisie's interest in new foreign commodities thus; they "trampled over one another to be the first to own an electric shaver, a can opener, a carving knife, and any number of strange and frightening inventions, lacerating their hands and faces as they struggled to learn how to use them" (125). Connoting social status and prestige, such foreign inventions along with luxurious Western commodities like the Jenny Colon bag become signifiers of the Turkish upper-class. The growing consumption of such commodities, however, devalues many local products such as Meltem, the Republic of Turkey's so-called first domestically-produced soda, which cannot compete with its Western counterparts. Zaim, Kemal's friend and the owner of the Meltem Soda Company, complain that people "couldn't care less about a Turkish-made drink, even though it's cheaper and healthier" (411).

The novel recounts the love story of the protagonist Kemal, a young and wealthy businessman in Istanbul, for Füsun, a poor distant relative of Kemal. Before meeting Füsun, Kemal buys an expensive Jenny Colon bag for his fiancée Sibel from the Şanzelize Boutique. The rich and bored Westernized housewives of the period would not open art galleries, "but boutiques, and stocked them with trinkets and whose ensembles smuggled in luggage from Paris and Milan, or copies of 'the latest' dresses featured in imported magazines like Elle and Vogue, selling these goods at ridiculously inflated prices to other rich housewives who were as bored as they were" (5). The name of the boutique—Şanzelize—itself is a transliteration of the famous avenue in Paris (Champs-Élysées). So, it appears as a sign of failed modernity—it sounds Western but bears an imitated name and sells "fake" Western bags. Of course, Sibel instantly understands that the bag is not an original Jenny Colon and rejects the gift. Her attitude indicates the manners of contemporary consumer society for which the idea of a thing matters more than its function. Commodities have been "generalized into signs of recognition, they facilitate the reciprocation of status among people" (Baudrillard 19–20). Belonging to a certain social class, Sibel's constructed identity depends on the conspicuous display of authentic and expensive commodities: Wearing a fake bag may endanger her social status and thereby frustrate "the desire to excel in pecuniary standing and so gain the esteem and envy of one's fellowmen" (Veblen 24). Consumption becomes an end in itself, totally unrelated to the use value of objects and the needs of the consumers. For Füsun, on the other hand, the use value of things are more important than their exchange value: "If you ask me, people's dislike of imitations has nothing to do with fake or real, but the fear that others might think they'd 'bought it cheap.' For me, the worst thing is when people care about the brand and not the thing itself" (144). The gap between the real and fake Jenny Colon also presents an allegory of Turkish modernity: the fake Western bag in a way stands for the Westernized Turk—he seems Western at first sight, but one has to look closely to see he is not quite. The text recounts how the members of Istanbul bourgeoisie are still old-fashioned and conservative when it comes to the issues of sexuality, virginity and marriage despite their seemingly modern appearance.

Through his love for Füsun, Kemal's conceptions of value regarding material objects change. He ultimately finds the hidden value of objects that are used and loved and possess an intimate relation to their owners in Füsun's world. Füsun's house is the ultimate antithesis to his consumerist world as it is not a space of discarded commodified objects of consumption, but a realm of "innocent" objects that are essential to the everyday life of an ordinary middle-class family.

The principle underlying Kemal's collection might be to salvage the past through authentic material objects. Pamuk has provided an external representation of such desires through the creation of a physical museum in central Istanbul. It portrays the material world of the pre-capitalist Republic of Turkey that shaped its residents' spiritual world for years. In the novel Kemal's attempt to collect these things might represent some form of protection against the commodities of the West. In these "innocent" objects he finds the glimpses of "the real" *vis-á-vis* the expendable objects of the modern era. Only by preserving such objects can he defy the values of his bourgeois world.

Although Füsun's house primarily contains seemingly local, non–Western objects as such, it is possible to see the signs of the spread of capitalism to middle-class households:

> All these objects—the saltshakers, china dogs, thimbles, pencils, barrettes, ashtrays— had a way of migrating, like the flocks of storks that flew silently over Istanbul twice a year to every part of the world.... What is certain: Someone somewhere had produced the first of these saltshakers, and then others made molds from them for mass production in many other countries, so that over the years, millions of copies had spread out from the southern Mediterranean and the Balkans, to enter the daily lives of untold families.... Another wave of saltshakers would always arrive, the old ones replaced with the new ... and each time people would forget the objects with which they had lived so intimately, never even acknowledging their emotional attachment to them [Pamuk *Museum* 510].

Mass production gives way to exchangeability or the replacement of old objects of everyday life with new ones. Thus, the capitalist mode of production changes the value of object and places it on a different level, where it is easily consumed rather than being kept. As a result, humanity's relation to objects lacks the intimacy and the emotional attachment that was previously found in the old times. Pamuk elsewhere suggests that being in love like his protagonist may help to see how deeply, intimately and emotionally one relates to objects which are otherwise alienated from us as indicated by Marxist theory (*Manzaradan Parçalar* 408). Pamuk's protagonist seems to be a romantic who tries to establish an emotional attachment to material things as a reaction to his alienated and objectified world.

Textual Museums: The Practices of Collecting and Constructions of Value

The practice of collecting emerges as an important focus of both novels. Artifacts, paintings, and bric-a-brac stored in the interiors of *The Age of Innocence* reveal the relationship between connoisseurs and aesthetes. Wharton was immensely interested in nineteenth-century visual arts, especially in the Pre-Raphaelites. Even the title of the novel was inspired by Joshua Reynolds' painting of the same name. Throughout the novel, Ellen Olenska is compared to many famous paintings: She embodies "a kind of restless, Pre-Raphaelite lady-in-waiting," and "a nameless, languid lady in a Monet painting" with a parasol at another scene at Boston Common (*Age* 184). There are some other references to art works throughout the novel: Mr. Beaufort boldly displays Bouguereau's famous nude painting, "Love Victorious," in his drawing room. Mr. Letterblair's house walls are adorned with the prints of famous paintings such as John Singleton Copley's "The Death of Chatham." There seems to be a different inspiration for the practice of art collecting, a prestigious obsession of the upper classes that sought to create imaginary interiors based on "the power of purchase" as the components of the interiors began to be "picked up" rather than "built up" (Agnew 140). The bibelot or object of beauty and rarity, became the metaphor of this new trend of art appreciation, in which art is shifted from museum to living room, and fragmented and reformatted in its minuscule form for display in the bourgeois interior spaces (Watson 23). Throughout *The Age of Innocence* our attention is drawn to the mass produced bronze and steel statuettes situated on the mantelpieces. The drawing rooms are stuffed full of expensive collectibles such as Saxe porcelain, gilt jardinières, Baltimore silverware, velvet puffs, Isabey miniatures. Just like a consumer, collectors remove objects from their original locations and relocate them in a different realm, in fulfillment of a fantasy that they will be transformed into creators (Stewart 158). In his seminal essay "The Work of Art in the Age of Mechanical Reproduction," Benjamin juxtaposes the real work of art, which is "unique" and "permanent," with its "transitory," mass-produced counterpart (221). The main difference, however, lies in the lack of what he calls "aura" in the reproduced art object: "Even the most perfect reproduction of a work of art is lacking in one element: its presence in time and space ... that which withers in the age of mechanical reproduction is the aura of the work of art.... By making many reproductions it substitutes a plurality of copies for a unique existence" (220–21). In the age of consumer collectors, a similar process occurs as objects are removed from their point of origin to museums, from museums to marketplace as reproduced commodities, and from the marketplace to bourgeois interiors. Valuable products lose their basic value as they are transformed into commodities.

Bentley asserts that the museum is a place for "hunting for the real" for Wharton, as it combines a range of customs and objects (56). "[As] Counter-institutions to the factory," they no longer provided "a visible history of the culture itself: that is, a display of objects rich with symbolic, local significance. Instead, they are storage areas for authenticity and uniqueness per se, for objects from any culture or period whatever that were said to be irreplaceable" (qtd. in Bentley 56). The displays might be eclectic, but the institution as a whole offered a valuable insight into human history as well as permitted visitors to contemplate the exhibits, not acquire them. Wharton chooses the Metropolitan Museum as a backdrop to Archer and Ellen's final meeting in *The Age of Innocence*. The Met reflects the 19th-century interest in "lost cities and buried antiques" (Tomkins qtd. in Saunders 96). These antiques, "the recovered fragments of Ilium," consisted of "hardly recognizable domestic utensils, ornaments and personal trifles—made of glass, of clay, of discolored bronze and other time-blurred substances" (312). This description adds another twist to the juxtaposition between authenticity and fakeness in the novel. These "time-blurred" artifacts become living witnesses to the past, with their accumulated stories of lost cultures. Looking at the collection on the glass shelves, Ellen comments: "It seems cruel, ... 'that after a while nothing matters' ... any more than these little things, that used to be necessary and important to forgotten people, and now have to be guessed at under a magnifying glass and labeled: 'Use unknown'" (312). Alpers defines the "museum effect" as the "tendency to isolate something from its world, to offer it up for attentive looking" (27). The everyday artifacts of an ancient tribe become aestheticized museum objects on display. Wharton elsewhere notes that when a "too-highly treasured relic" is "fenced about, restored, and converted into a dry little museum," it loses "all that color and pathos of extreme age" (*A Motor-Flight through France* 89). It is always up to the museum visitor to try to interpret these objects to come up with a narrative about the past. But is that possible in a world dedicated to capitalism and domestic display? The material and cultural conventions that determine Archer's society inhibits judgment; as a result he "ossifies" and becomes "a curious and endearing relic" (Singley 513). The last chapter of *The Age of Innocence* opens at an inaugural reception for some new Metropolitan Museum galleries. Among "the spoils of ages" and "a series of scientifically catalogued treasures," Archer imagines the specter of Ellen in her long seal-skin cloak, walking the museum's old corridors (Wharton *The Age* 347). The building itself becomes a museum of the mind for Archer in which he stores his memories of Ellen. His contemplation of her from a distance suggests that he regards her value as an aesthetic object to be neither possessed nor physically enjoyed. Not belonging to this age and space and unmatched by the objects around her, she is the real exotic "museum object" to be protected against time.

When we look at the narrative of *The Museum of Innocence*, Kemal creates a museum of objects reminiscent of his love for Füsun. Collecting refers to building a private relationship with the world of objects through possession and accumulation, which engenders different dynamics between subject and object. Walter Benjamin describes it as a practice of divesting objects of their use values: liberated from "the drudgery of being useful," collected objects are relocated in a subjective realm to open up infinite possibilities for the collector (*The Arcades Project* 8). The collector positions the objects "into an other space, a utopic or heterotopic space where value, far from being a mystery, is, to the collector, utterly transparent" (Brown 158). It is a realm in which s/he creates a different value system for objects, quite different from their use or exchange values.

There is a different temporality in a collection as it simultaneously halts the progress of history and rejects the passage of time. Displaced from their everyday contexts, atemporal objects are eternalized as proof of the past, frozen in the timelessness of the collection. Baudrillard describes the collector as a neurotic who constructs a "synchronic haven" of objects, the values of which are determined by him alone ("The System of Collecting" 16). The value of objects is primarily emotional and relies on their evocation of treasured sentimental moments of the past. While the display of Füsun's handkerchief serves to remind Kemal of her caresses, a crystal inkwell and pen set denotes "the refinement and the fragile tenderness [they] felt for each other" (Pamuk *The Museum* 30). Kemal also constantly replaces the china dogs on the top of Keskin's television set; only after these bibelots stay there long enough to absorb the memories of the household can they become a part of Kemal's collection.

In Marxist interpretations of commodity fetishism, an object is divested of its production history and use value to have "mere exchange value." According to Benjamin, in collecting, objects are not only "freed from the drudgery of being useful" but also divested of their exchange values (*The Arcades Project* 19). Kemal's collection opens up truly personal realms; not only are objects like the quince grater or Aunt Nesibe's thimble displaced from use values, but also disposable things like empty bottles and cigarette butts, which have neither use nor exchange values, are assigned value. Kemal's hoarding suggests that he has a problem grasping the objects' real value (or lack thereof). "Engaged exactly in a struggle against universal commodification," the collector "confers on objects 'only a fancier's value, rather than use-value'" (Abbas 220).

Commodity fetishism seems to undermine Kemal's museum project, which resists the proliferation of commodities and their easy consumption and disposal. Or perhaps not: Stewart posits that if objects are positioned in "a cycle of self-referential exchange," they acquire renewed value (165). Kemal starts substituting some objects with new and more expensive replacements, and even at times with money. He creates another value system for these (mostly worthless) objects based once again on money. His actions do not suggest a "transcendence of worldly objects in the mystical sense, but preservation of them in a materialistic manner" (Vanwesenbeeck 69). Kemal's museum appears to be shaped by bourgeois values, established by an entrepreneur taking pride in the disappointments in his past and finally coming to terms with his life.

The author Orhan Pamuk opened the real museum of the novel, the first museum in the world based on a work of fiction, in Istanbul in 2012. The Museum of Innocence is made up of cultural artifacts and daily objects used in 70s and 80s Istanbul, which were once, for the author, part and parcel of not only material life but also a spiritual life that evaporated. The author's concern about cultural extinction is echoed in his protagonist, Kemal, who feels sorry that "all these things, saturated with memories of people who had once walked the streets of Istanbul, and lived in its houses, and were now mostly dead, would eventually disappear without ever having been brought together in a museum, or sorted, or set within a frame" (Pamuk *Museum* 506). Pamuk asserts that "a museum should not be flags—signs and symbols of power" but should express "whatever a life is made of, its dreams and disappointments" to take pride in (*A Talk with Orhan Pamuk: Caressing the World with Words*).

In sum, Wharton and Pamuk nostalgically return to the past and evoke cultural and political "ages of innocence" in these novels. The authors "adapt" history by creating an idyllic version of the specific past periods perhaps as a reaction to the loss of cultural values with the advent of capitalism. Although set in different centuries and social contexts, each work portrays how capitalism has wrought radical cultural and social transformations that have changed human beings' conceptions of the value of material objects. In the practices of consumption and collecting in each novel we saw how objects are decontextualized from their use values to be assigned different values. The dichotomy between originality and fakery regarding objects is also important in terms of value. The idea of collecting lends itself to the museum trope, which has both a thematic and a stylistic function in Wharton and Pamuk. Both novels work as historical archives to represent and preserve culture: they are textual museums conserving and displaying a specific time with the drama of people, manners, and material world. And yet, the authors cannot help constructing their own histories and subjectively interpreting the past while selecting, collecting and ordering the relics of yore. Their ways of adapting history and relating it to questions of value may be regarded as a calculated response to the loss of social, cultural, and moral values.

WORKS CITED

Abbas, Ackbar. "Walter Benjamin's Collector: The Fate of Modern Experience." *New Literary History* 20.1 (1988): 217–37. Print.
Agnew, Jean-Christophe. "A House of Fiction: Domestic Interiors and the Commodity Aesthetic." *Consuming Visions Consuming Visions: Accumulation and Display of Goods in America, 1880–1920*. Ed. Simon J. Bronner. 133–57. New York: Norton, 1989. Print.
Alpers, Svetlana. "The Museum as a Way of Seeing." *Exhibiting Cultures. The Poetics and Politics of Museum Display*. Ed. Ivan Karp and Steven D. Lavine. 25–32. London: Smithsonian Institution Press, 1991. Print.
Baudrillard, Jean. "The System of Collecting." *The Cultures of Collecting*. Ed. John Elsner and Roger Cardinal. 7–25. London: Reaktion, 1997. Print.
_____. "The System of Objects." *Jean Baudrillard: Selected Writings*. Ed. Mark Poster. 10–28. Stanford: Stanford University Press, 1988. Print.
Benjamin, Walter. *The Arcades Project*. Trans. Howard Eiland and Kevin McLaughlin. Cambridge: Belknap Press of Harvard Press, 1999. Print.
_____. "The Work of Art in the Age of Mechanical Reproduction." *Illuminations: Essays and Reflections*. Ed. Hannah Arendt. Trans. Harry Zohn. 217–53. New York: Schocken Press, 1969. Print.
_____. "Unpacking My Library: A Talk about Book Collecting." *Illuminations: Essays and Reflections*. Ed. Hannah Arendt. Trans. Harry Zohn. 59–69. New York: Schocken Press, 1969. Print.
Bentley, Nancy. "'Hunting for the Real': Wharton and the Science of Manners." *The Cambridge Companion to Edith Wharton*. Ed. Millicent Bell. 47–67. New York: Cambridge University Press, 1995. Print.
Brown, Bill. *A Sense of Things: The Object Matter of American Literature*. Chicago: University of Chicago Press, 2003. Print.
Ersin Tutan, Defne, and Laurence Raw. *The Adaptation of History: Essays on Ways of Telling the Past*. Jefferson: McFarland, 2013. Print.
Francescato, Simone. *Collecting and Appreciating: Henry James and the Transformation of Aesthetics in the Age of Consumption*. Cultural Interactions: Studies in the Relationship between the Arts. New York: Peter Lang, 2010. Print.
Klimasmith, Betsy. "Salvaging History: Modern Philosophies of Memory and Time in *The Age of Innocence*." *American Literature* 80.3 (Sept. 2008). 555–581.
Knights, Pamela. "Forms of Disembodiment: The Social Subject in *The Age of Innocence*." *The Cambridge Companion to Edith Wharton*. Ed. Millicent Bell. 20–46. New York: Cambridge University Press, 1995. Print.
Lewis, R.W.B. *Edith Wharton: A Biography*. 1975. New York: Fromm, 1993. Print.
Orlando, Emily J. *Edith Wharton and the Visual Arts*. Tuscaloosa: University of Alabama Press, 2007. Print.
Pamuk, Orhan. *Manzaradan Parçalar: Hayat, Sokaklar, Edebiyat. [Pieces from the View: Life, Streets, Literature]*. Istanbul: İletişim, 2010. Print.
_____. *The Museum of Innocence*. Trans. Maureen Freely. New York: Vintage, 2009. Print.
_____. *The Naive and the Sentimental Novelist*. Charles Eliot Norton Lectures. Harvard University Press, 2010. Print.
_____. *Şeylerin Masumiyeti. [The Innocence of Objects]*. Istanbul: İletişim, 2012. Print.
_____. "A Talk with Orhan Pamuk: Caressing the World with Words." Interview by Nathan Gardels. *Huffington Post* 18 Mar. 2010. Web. 4 Mar. 2017.
Raw, Laurence. "Retelling European History on Film: An Essay Review." *Film and History* 41.2 (2011): 64–68. Print.

Saunders, Judith P. "Portrait of the Artist as Anthropologist: Edith Wharton and 'The Age of Innocence.'" *Interdisciplinary Literary Studies* 4.1 (Fall 2002): 86–101. Print.

Singley, Carol J. "Bourdieu, Wharton and Changing Culture in *The Age Of Innocence.*" *Cultural Studies* 17.3/4 (2003): 495–519. Print.

Stewart, Susan. *On Longing: Narratives of the Miniature, the Gigantic, the Souvenir, the Collection.* Durham: Duke University Press, 1993. Print.

Trumpener, Katie, and James M. Nyce. "The Recovered Fragments: Archeological and Anthropological Perspectives in Edith Wharton's *The Age of Innocence.*" *Literary Anthropology: A New Interdisciplinary Approach to People, Signs and Literature.* Ed. Fernando Poyatos. 161–69. Amsterdam: John Benjamins, 1988. Print.

Vanwesenbeeck, İclal. "Poverty, Class, and the Turkish Question in Orhan Pamuk's *The Museum of Innocence.*" *Journal of Turkish Literature* 7, Orhan Pamuk Special Issue (2010): 58–72. Print.

Veblen, Thorstein. *The Theory of the Leisure Class: An Economic Study of Institutions.* 1899. Introd. Stuart Chase. New York: The Modern Library, 1934. Print.

Watson, Janell. *Literature and Material Culture from Balzac to Proust.* Cambridge: Cambridge University Press, 1999. Print.

Wharton, Edith. *The Age of Innocence.* 1920. London: Penguin Classics, 1996. Print.

_____. *A Backward Glance: An Autobiography.* 1933. Introd. Louis Auchincloss. New York: Simon & Schuster, 1998. Print.

_____. "A Little Girl's New York." *Harper's Magazine* 176 (Mar. 1938): 356–64. Print.

_____. *A Motor-Flight through France.* London: Macmillan, 1908. Print.

Caesar Must Die (2012)

Shakespeare in Prison

HUI WU

Since the movies came into being, there have already been many film versions of Julius Caesar's story in ancient Rome, especially based on Shakespeare's famous play with the same title. For example: *Giulio Cesare* by Giovanni Pastrone (1909); *Caesar and Cleopatra* by Gabriel Pascal (1945); *Julius Caesar* by Joseph L. Mankiewicz (1953); *Julius Caesar* by Herbert Wise (1979, BBC); and *Caesar* by Uli Edel (2002).

However, the most innovative and thrilling one appears to be *Caesar Must Die* (original title: *Cesare deve morire*) by the Italian brothers Paolo and Vittorio Taviani. It came out in 2012 and won the Golden Bear as well as the award for Catholic Human Spirit at the 62nd Berlin International Film Festival. It was also nominated for Best Picture, Best Director, Best Editing and the Audience Prize at the 25th European Film Awards. What makes this adaptation so valuable?

The filmmakers search for life's significance by focusing on prisoners as a special social group and on prisons as a neglected corner within society. Looking at history from a prisoner's perspective challenges the audience's preconceptions both of prison life and the capacity of Shakespeare to embody the existence of a frequently marginalized group. Caught by surprise, the spectators reflect on new constructions of art and reality, past and present, crime and punishment.

Presenting Double Tragedies

Julius Caesar by Shakespeare is a typical character tragedy. It is caused by a noble man's misfortune and weakness. Caesar's ambition and conceit

127

lead to his murder. This misdeed later triggers turmoil and war. In contrast, the tragedy of the prisoners in the film has the characteristics of a contemporary tragedy caused by the inner desires and spiritual sufferings of the detainees. The experience of attending rehearsals for six months makes them rethink notions of friendship, betrayal, power and violence both in the drama and in their own lives. For example, when rehearsing the scene of stabbing Caesar (Giovanni Arcuri), they surround his body, whereupon Cassius (Cosimo Rega) and then Brutus (Salvatore Striano) read meaningful lines: "Let's bow down. Let's dip and wash our hands with blood. How many centuries hence will this glorious scene of ours be acted over? In kingdoms not yet born, in language not yet invented. And how many times must Caesar bleed on stage? Like here today, in this prison of ours lying on this stone, no worthier than the dust." This speech refers not only to the tragedy of Caesar; but to the performers' lives, deemed "no worthier than the dust." The prisoners can physically and psychologically experience their own crimes. Art can be powerful—a therapeutic enhancement of the antique concept of catharsis.

The collapsing of past and present creates inter-textuality as well as valuable perspectives on both periods, ancient and modern. The ancient Roman heroes with historical costumes and abundant colors form a strong contrast with the real convicts in gray clothes. We can also empathize with the characters, both the prisoners and the Shakespearean roles they play. Rehearsing *Julius Caesar* lets the prisoners temporarily overcome their loneliness and discover the beauty and freedom of art. Although Caesar features in the title of both play and film, the true protagonist here is Brutus, whose character is very different from the actor playing him. Brutus is honest and cherishes democracy and freedom. Both Brutus and Cassius want to build a republic, but the former one hates tyranny and the later one only hates the tyrant (Bloom and Jaffa 85). Brutus' noble thoughts put him into a moral dilemma: to kill or not to kill Caesar, that is the question. The prisoner who plays Brutus bears the same sufferings: "If only I could tear out Caesar's spirit without cutting open his chest." He had uttered similar words to his friend about an opponent, and as a result, they both were arrested. Can problems only be solved by violence? This question tortures him so much that he cannot continue the rehearsal. Another example: when Decius (Juan Dario Bonetti) comes to lure him to go to the senate, Caesar feels suspicious. In real life, the prisoner who plays Caesar also distrusts his fellow-inmates.

Finally, the contradictions between the two worlds emerge as we are shown the vulnerable side of Caesar. Brutus kills him for justice and liberty, but then kills himself for having violated his democratic ideals. From the prisoner's perspective, the guilt arising from Caesar's assassination, coupled with memories of their own crimes is too much to bear. The prisoner playing

Brutus only secures release after he becomes a real actor after his release. Another prisoner who plays Caesar writes a book named *Free Inside*. To some extent, their crimes and missteps have been redeemed and they can rediscover their humanity. The Tavianis tell an intriguing story and discuss such fundamental questions of society like the purpose of crime and punishment. The film does not show either the confession or the remorse of the prisoners, but we see their characters changing through rehearsal and performance. The film pleads that art has the potential to educate and change people. It lets us rethink Brutus' question: is the best way to answer violence with violence? Does Caesar's death improve the situation? As we know, his abolishment is followed by turmoil and another upheaval. As the Chinese philosopher Wang Yangming (1472–1529) observes, it is easy to eliminate the bandit in the mountains, but hard to eliminate the bandit in the mind. At the end of the film, the prisoner realizes the consequences of his confinement entirely. The effect of enlightenment and redemption is what the artists and the audience really want to see.

Aristotle claimed in his *Poetics* that the function of tragedy is to mold people's emotion by pity and fear (78). Regarding tragedy as an art means to purify people's mind. The end of the film responds to its opening, it repeats the scene when the convicts are sent back to their cells after the successful performance and return to their quotidian roles, even though something is different about them now. The valuable experience of art makes them realize their present condition and reflect on their existence. Can literature provide redemption for their life in prison? After returning to his cell, the inmate who plays Cassius talks to himself: "Ever since I became acquainted with art, this cell turned into a prison." By "dancing with chains," the prisoner becomes aware that the real confinement is not only physical, but also mental. He and his companions start to think about love and hatred, democracy and dictatorship, freedom and confinement, loyalty and betrayal, peace and violence. Inevitably, they are confronted with paradoxes. Self-redemption and transcendence do not automatically lead to clearer understanding, but raise more questions about humanity's position in the world and its future direction.

The purification provided by art is more like a painful nirvana: goodness, truth and beauty emerging from fear and pity. The drama stimulates the will to live, but the prisoners can't implement it, they can only yearn for it. This brings us to the double message of the film: real death and artistic rebirth exist side by side, but the former is no substitute for the latter. This is Shakespeare's clear message in *Julius Caesar*. Like many revolutionary goals in history, Brutus' notion of a republic is perhaps a good idea but can never be achieved, but only leads to tragedy. On the other hand the process of struggle gives meaning and value to his life. As Antony said at his funeral: "All the conspirators save only he / Did that they did in envy of great Caesar. / He only in a general honest thought / And common good to all, made one of them. / His life was gentle, and the elements / So mixed in him that nature might stand up / And say to all the world, 'This was a man'" (*Julius Caesar* V, v, 67–74).

But how to present the noble man through images and how to show the values of this humanistic, but tragic spirit on screen? That is the challenge of this adaptation that not only benefits from a deliberate decision to incorporate parts of the source-test in the screenplay, but also from the directors' creative "tell" and "show." The film actually includes four layers of narration: (1) in the year 44 BC, when Caesar was assassinated with 23 stabbings by the senate headed by Brutus and Cassius. (2) A world suggested through the historical books *Parallel Lives* by Plutarch and *Twelve Emperors' Biography of Rome* by Suetonius, who both reported the story of Caesar, although their writing styles were quite different. (3) Shakespeare's play *Julius Caesar*, written around 1600, based on Plutarch, and focusing on the most thrilling and tragic moment—Caesar's death. (4) The real murderers in prison rehearsing Shakespeare's play and "assassinating" Julius Caesar. The fact they have committed similar crimes in their past lives adds a disturbing authenticity to the performance that no professional actors could achieve.

There are two plot lines in the film: the rehearsal of the play by the prisoners, and their actual performance on stage. According to Simmons, the three "S's" of narrative can be observed: the *surprise* at the beginning (for example the prediction on 15 March and the subtitles to introduce the prisoners on the screen), the *suspense* (for example, the secret preparation of the assassination or the frequent interruptions of the rehearsal) and the *satisfaction* at the end (killing the tyrant, the murderers' suicide and the successful performance) (Simmons). The rehearsal makes the prisoners gain self-respect and discover the significance of individual experience. It is the play-within-the-play structure that combines art with reality to make the film more meaningful and attractive. The narrative unfolds according to two times and spaces: ancient Rome and contemporary Rome (in the prison of Rebibbia). The narratives balance one another: following the rehearsals, we see the prisoners beginning the performance in an atmosphere of celebration at Caesar's return from the battlefield. By the end of the performance however, the mood changes abruptly as the senators conspire to kill him for his ambition. Octavian quells the resultant riot and restores peace. In a similar way, the story of the film starts with an interesting selection of actors and a smooth rehearsal. But then, Caesar's story sparks fierce quarreling among the prisoners about past grievances. As a result, they stop playing. After a process of rethinking and reconciliation, the actors continue their rehearsal and give a successful performance. However, when the curtain falls and the lights go off, the actors become prisoners once again and have to return to their cells silently. The interplay of drama and reality makes the film dynamic and philosophical at the same time.

Two color modes represent the two times and spaces in the film. The rehearsal of Shakespeare's play is shown in black and white. It was filmed six months earlier than the color version. The reality of life in prison is shown in color and takes place in the present. Ironically, it is the black and white rehearsal that gives the prisoners an experience full of vitality and passion, and lets them forget their situation temporarily. On the contrary, the "colorful reality" in prison confronts them with a boring and lonely life without hope. Though the play-within-the-play is a traditional narrative structure, the Tavianis have exercised their inventive minds in *Caesar Must Die*. They not only develop the plot, but also emphasize the value of the film through visual means—for example, the contrast between black-and-white and color.

This is not the first time that non-professional actors have performed in a movie. But it is probably the first performance involving actual prisoners on film. The Tavianis emphasize their achievements through a powerful visual language and straightforward narrative. There are distinct echoes of Italian New Realism—for example, when the actors are selected, each prisoner's performance in front of the camera is actually a public exposure of his essential self. Nowadays, it is quite common to use documentary elements in feature film and fictional elements in documentary film. These hybrids are often called docudramas. The Tavianis film draws on that tradition to make a comment on the enduring role of art in society. They use flashback to create suspense. For example, the first shot of the film is the facial close-up of Brutus with a dignified expression. Then he slowly lifts the dagger hanging over his head, followed by a freeze-frame of the dagger. Actually, that will be the end of the stage performance in the film, but already in the beginning, it exerts a strong visual impact. Later on the successful performance renders the actors highly excited on stage, but then they have to return to their real identities as prisoners. Just within a few minutes, we witness a dramatic change of mood, suggesting the value of art but simultaneously recognizing that it is no alternative to everyday life. The actors have to serve their sentences out.

On the other hand the past has a profound influence over the present, as suggested through the flashback from the present performance to the rehearsal six months ago. The directors use changes of color and background voices to suggest this link. The rehearsal of Act 2, Scene 2 and the dialogue between Caesar and Decius, suddenly switches to a quarrel between two players about their relationship and a conspiracy in the past. Quite often, two stories develop simultaneously. In fact, there is no clear line between the two levels—the dramatic performance and the film's action—because every man plays two roles. They move seamlessly on and off the stage, unifying art and life. Montage creates similar dramatic and thematic effects. After the performance the three prisoners who played Caesar, Brutus and Cassius return to their cells one by one guarded by prison officers.

When the actors are selected, twelve candidates give self-introductions in identical mid-shots. This sequence is followed by five close-up shots of the selected men one after another with music played by an harmonica and subtitles to identify their names, crimes and length of sentences. The counterpoint of sound and picture reflects the inner desires and struggles of the inmates as well as their real situations. At the apex of rehearsals, Caesar is surround by his opponents who want to kill him. There are five shots of five opponents standing up in file and assassinating the dictator together. The function of the montage here is to emphasize the way in which the actors relive the process of murder that landed them in prison. At the last stage performance four actors declaim one after another, "Fight for freedom!"—freedom for both body and soul, for individuals and humanity. Though the lines are not from the play, they are very stirring.

The rehearsal and the performance both have closed endings, just like Shakespeare's play. The death of Caesar is the main climax, the suicide of Brutus another one. The stunning scene that starts the film reappears at the end, but does not serve a repetitive purpose. On the contrary its fundamental value consists of prompting reflection on the consequences of confinement, and how past actions inevitably cast a shadow over the present. The ending is not a happy one, but rather argues for the capacity of art to promote speculation on the consequences of one's life choices. We enjoy a multileveled experience of history and reality through watching the performance. The directors do not tell us much about the prisoners' lives after the performance. Shakespeare's story is finished, but the lives of the prisoners continue. Cosimo Rega, who played Cassius, is the last one to enter his cell. The door is locked behind him. He stands in the room, looking about and then looking straight ahead with complicated and thoughtful expression. The lens slowly focuses on his face half in shadow and half in bright. Finally Cosimo says to himself: "Ever since I became acquainted with art, this cell turned into a prison." Keeping silent for a while, he turns back to fetch the coffee pot and makes himself an espresso. The picture gradually dissolves-out and the music rings. The film ends. The Tavianis continue their never-ending exploration of humanity, with the inconclusive ending suggesting both positive and negative outcomes. The prisoners have become more reflective, but that does not alter the monotony of their day-to-day existence. Like any valuable film, *Caesar Must Die* offers the pleasure of psychological discovery to the audience as well as spiritual satisfaction.

WORKS CITED

Aristotle. *The Poetics.* Trans. Malcolm Heath. New ed. London: Penguin, 1993. Print.

Bloom, Alan, and Harry V. Jaffa. *Shakespeare's Politics.* 1964. Chinese ed., Beijing: Phoenix Publishing Media Group/Jiangsu People Press, 2006. Print.

Caesar and Cleopatra. Dir. Gabriel Pascal. Perf. Claude Rain, Vivien Leigh, Stewart Granger, Flora Robson. Gabriel Pascal Productions and Independent Producers, 1945. Film.

Caesar Must Die. Dir. Paolo Taviani and Vittorio Taviani. Perf. Cosimo Rega, Salvatore Striano, Giovanni Arcuri. Kaos Cinematografica, Stemal Entertainment and Le Talee, 2012. DVD.

Giulio Cesare. Dir. Giovanni Pastrone. Perf. Giovanni Pastrone, Luigi Mele. Italia Films, 1909. Film.

Julius Caesar. Dir. Joseph L. Mankiewicz. Perf. Marlon Brando, James Mason, John Gielgud, Louis Calhern, Edmond O'Brien. MGM, 1953. Film.

_____. *Julius Caesar.* Dir. Herbert Wise. Perf. Richard Pasco, Keith Michell, Charles Gray. BBC/Time-Life Television, 1979. Television.

_____. Dir. Uli Edel. Perf. Jeremy Sisto, Richard Harris, Christopher Walken. De Angelis Group, Degeto Film and Five Mile River Films, 2002. DVD.

Plutarch. *Parallel Lives.* Trans. John Dryden. New York: CreateSpace, 2014. Print.

Shakespeare, William. *Julius Caesar. The Complete Works.* Ed. Stanley Wells and Gary Taylor. 627–55. Oxford: Oxford University Press, 1988. Print.

Simmons, Annette, *The Story Factor: Inspiration, Influence and Persuasion Through the Art of Storytelling.* Cambridge, MA: Perseus 2011. Print.

Suetonius. *On the Lives of the Twelve Caesars.* Trans. James Rives. London: Penguin Classics, 2007. Print.

Pride and Prejudice and Programming

A Stylometric Analysis[1]

AGATA HOŁOBUT and JAN RYBICKI

"A virtual template for a Hollywood romantic comedy" (Cartmell *Pride* 227), Jane Austen's *Pride and Prejudice* (1813) has enthralled film and television audiences for almost eighty years, with the earliest adaptation, an hour-long television film produced by Michael Barry, dating back to 1938. Since that time the book has been regularly brought to the screen with varying degrees of leniency. Classic adaptations include two cinematic versions directed by Robert Z. Leonard (1940) and Joe Wright (2005) and a succession of television miniseries produced by Campbell Logan (1952, 1967), Barbara Burnham (1958), Jonathan Powell (1980) and Sue Birtwistle (1995) for the BBC (Cartmell, *Pride* 228). The filmmakers' belief in the novel's value is not incidental. Screenwriters and critics praise Austen for her logic and love of detail, which are inherently filmic and hence adaptation-friendly (Cartmell, *Jane* 18). Interestingly, filmmakers' attraction to the story coincided with the emergence of talkies. As Deborah Cartmell explains, *Pride and Prejudice* was earlier deemed unfit for the screen, because it seemed relatively uneventful and over-dependent on verbal style, two qualities which were difficult to capture in a silent film (*Jane* 4). It is arguably this signature style that is essential to all straight versions of *Pride and Prejudice*. Reflected in screen dialogue, this style distinguishes them from other classic novel adaptations and period dramas, regardless of their other generic similarities.

A vehicle for verbal style, screen dialogue has attracted relatively little attention among western film and adaptation scholars.[2] Yet it performs an important role in many film and television genres and seems crucial for the adaptation genre, which highlights its own hypertextual status. This genre,

134

as defined by Thomas Leitch, displays such distinctive features as reliance on carefully reconstructed period detail (architecture, interior design, visual art and music evocative of the epoch), a penchant for intertitles and overemphasis on words, books and authors (2008). According to Deborah Cartmell, other genre-specific features include self-referential focus on the media, appeal to a feminine audience and "implicit and explicit tributes to the author" (*Pride* 229–30).

Successfully scripted dialogue offers valuable contributions to several of these genre-specific effects. As a straightforward vehicle for period language it can potentially reflect the author's style of writing, if that is the intention of the filmmakers and television producers. Moreover, it helps create an impression of historical authenticity together with costumes, make-up and set design. Its compatibility with period setting seems to be taken for granted, judging by frustrated remarks of reviewers and filmgoers who have found certain dialogue lines inappropriate for a classic novel adaptation (Harris 48, Cartmell *Jane* 86).

Research Aims and Methodology

Since several adaptations of Jane Austen's *Pride and Prejudice* are considered the pinnacle of the genre and representative of its various traits (Cardwell 99), we decided to apply digital methods known as *computational stylistics* to explore the extent to which filmic speech imitates her authorial style. We extracted dialogue lines from four screen versions of the novel that openly acknowledge their affinity to the literary source. These included two cinematic versions directed by Robert Z. Leonard (1940) and Joe Wright (2005) and two BBC adaptations directed by Cyril Coke (1980) and Simon Langton (1995). These adaptations were authored by acclaimed novelists and screenwriters: Jane Murfin and Aldous Huxley (1940); Fay Weldon (1980); Andrew Davies (1995) and Daborah Moggach (2005), which rendered the textual material rich and stylistically complex. We also compiled an extended comparative corpus of dialogue, composed of looser adaptations: Gurinder Chadha's *Bride and Prejudice* (2004) and Dan Zeff's miniseries *Lost in Austen* (2008), and period dramas set in another epoch.

We subjected the textual material to diverse methods of computational analysis aiming to:

- establish how much of Austen's original writing is transferred verbatim onto the screen, even though literary and film dialogue differ in function and form;
- explore the stylistic and stylometric affinities between Jane Austen's dialogue (and narrative) and the screenwriters' original dialogue;

- measure the stylistic and stylometric affinities between different film and television adaptations of *Pride and Prejudice* to find signals of genre intertextuality and cross-pollination of dialogue conventions;
- verify the stylistic and stylometric value of Austen adaptations when compared to period dramas set in another historical epoch and based on another literary source.

Although our verbocentric approach may strike the reader as mechanistic and fidelity-oriented, it is by no means intended to reduce the study of adaptation to statistically verifiable verbal transfer. It is also not supposed to rival the valuable interdisciplinary approaches, which combine expertise in literature, media and culture to explore the aesthetic and ideological impact of literature on screen.[3] On the contrary, our contribution is intended to complement the existing syncretic approaches, shedding new light on the verbal exponents of intertextual relationships between the novels and their various rewritings. It can also contribute to a better understanding of the adaptation genre in the context of other screen representations of the past. These results can be further explored in an in-depth qualitative analysis.

Verbatim Quotations

At the first stage of our analysis, we employed simple lexical measures to check the number of verbatim quotations in each of the film and television scripts, using WCopyFind plagiarism-detection software (Bloomfield 2011–2016), which compares any two texts searching for identical or quasi-identical word n-grams (clusters of n words). As could be expected, this simple test shows that it is the television productions that transport more of Jane Austen's prose literally onto the screen. In order to perform this analysis, we used full dialogue scripts transcribed from the recordings of the selected film adaptations and full dialogue lifted from Austen's literary original, all of these in electronic form. If we consider identical sequences of five words or more, as much as 29 percent of screen dialogue in both classic television productions: Andrew Davies' *Pride and Prejudice* (1995) and Fay Weldon's *Pride and Prejudice* (1980) comes directly from the book. It is only Fay Weldon, by contrast, who incorporates extensive literal quotations from the narrator (as much as 2 percent of film dialogue); and various female characters are entrusted with most of that—including the celebrated first sentence of the novel. More distant adaptations incorporate less Austenian material, although Deborah Moggach still "borrows" as much as 19 percent of all filmic speech from the author. Quite significantly, a certain overlap can be noticed between adaptations, as demonstrated in Table 1.

Table 1. Word five-grams overlap between texts.

Number of matches and % of text	Texts compared	
435 (0%)	Austen_Pride_N_1813	Austen_Pride_D_1813
205 (1%)	Lost_2008	Austen_Pride_D_1813
1158 (7%)	Pride_1940	Austen_Pride_D_1813
6820 (29%)	**Pride_1980**	**Austen_Pride_D_1813**
629 (2%)	**Pride_1980**	**Austen_Pride_N_1813**
413 (1%)	Pride_1980	Pride_1940
9273 (29%)	**Pride_1995**	**Austen_Pride_D_1813**
284 (0%)	Pride_1995	Austen_Pride_N_1813
134 (0%)	Pride_1995	Lost_2008
711 (2%)	Pride_1995	Pride_1940
2262 (7%)	Pride_1995	Pride_1980
2266 (19%)	**Pride_2005**	**Austen_Pride_D_1813**
435 (3%)	Pride_2005	Pride_1940
8 44 (7%)	Pride_2005	Pride_1980
1182 (10%)	Pride_2005	Pride_1995

If we consider longer stretches of text (identical sequences of at least ten words), 16 percent of Andrew Davis' and 15 percent of Fay Weldon's scripts employed the author's original dialogue. While the numbers become significantly and understandably lower, the length of the sequences studied makes them now go beyond some of the sentence boundaries, suggesting a very Austenian dialogue. On the other hand, no adaptation borrows from the narrative at this point, as shown in Table 2.

Table 2. Word ten-grams overlap between texts.

Number of matches and % of text	Texts compared	
3682 (15%)	Pride_1980	Austen_Pride_D_1813
5086 (16%)	Pride_1995	Austen_Pride_D_1813
814 (2%)	Pride_1995	Pride_1980

Thus the screenwriters' declarations of being "true to the text" find reflection in computational analysis (Cartmell *Jane* 67).

This phenomenon becomes even more significant when the same comparison is applied to another set of a novel and its film adaptations: two different English translations of Henryk Sienkiewicz's *Quo Vadis* made in 1896 (Curtin) and 1897 (Binion and Malevsky), together with two of its many filmic versions: the Hollywood production of 1951 and the international miniseries of 1985. While the use of a translation could be normally seen as introducing an additional (and unwanted) variable, it must be remembered that at least the earlier of the adaptations were made in an English-language country and thus certainly on the basis of one of these translations. The five-word cluster overlap is almost non-existent between individual translations and individual adaptations (at most 1 percent), while that between the two literary translations is 28 percent.

Of course, the percentages of reused dialogue in *Pride and Prejudice* adaptations even in the top cases (ca. 30 and 15 percent, respectively) are a minority in the film or serial scripts. While the bulk of the dialogue aims to convey most of the novel's meanings—or at least to push the plot, in its surface structure, towards an ending more or less consistent with the literary original—the relationship between the two is less evident and needs to be studied with more refined stylometric methods.

Stylometric Analysis

Chief among these methods rely on most-frequent-word frequencies: counting the appearance of the top 100, 200, ..., 1000 words in the frequency rank list has been shown to be a very successful in authorship attribution studies; more importantly, this has been found to produce similarity/difference patterns that are due to other signals, such as chronology, genre, or gender.[4] While this focus on those very frequent function words—instead of the usual literary concentration on meaningful content words—might seem counterintuitive in cultural studies, it must be borne in mind that the sheer number of the former provides much better statistical evidence than the meager participation of latter. Indeed, one of the first stylometric studies to move beyond authorship attribution methods is an analysis of dialogue in Jane Austen, and begins thus (Burrows *Computation* 4–6):

> It is a truth not generally acknowledged that, in most discussions of works of English fiction, we proceed as if a third, two-fifths, a half of our material were not really there. For Jane Austen, that third, two-fifths, or half comprises the twenty, thirty, or fifty most common words of her literary vocabulary.... Eight personal pronouns, six auxiliary verb forms, five prepositions, three conjunctions, two adverbs, the definite and indefinite articles, and four other words ("to," "that," "for," and "all"), each of which serves more than a single main grammatical function, almost always find their place—and usually about the same place—among the thirty most common words of each novel.

It must be said that while empirical evidence is plentiful for the existence of minute yet consistent differences in frequent-word usage between authors, genres, time periods, the exact mechanism is unknown. Attempts to explain it usually go along the following lines (McKenna et al. 152): "The possibility of using such simple evidence for such large purposes rests upon the fact that words do not function as discrete entities. Since they gain their full meaning only through the different sorts of relationship they form with each other, they can be seen as markers of those relationships and, accordingly, of everything that those relationships entail."

Since analysis of this kind usually compares values for hundreds of words, multivariate statistics is performed to establish the degree of difference or distance between all individual texts. The method applied in this study uses the Delta distance measure (Burrows *Delta*) which quantifies the difference between pairs of texts according to the formula

$$\Delta(T,T_1) = \frac{1}{n}\sum_{i=1}^{n}\left|z(f_i(T)) - z(f_i(T_1))\right|,$$

where

$$z(f_x(T)) = \frac{f_x(T) - \mu_x}{\sigma_x},$$

n = number of words,
$f_x(T)$ = raw frequency of word x in text T,
μ_x = mean frequency of word x in a collection of texts,
σ_x = standard deviation of frequency of word x.

To state the same in more descriptive terms: the z-score for a given word in each text is evaluated to produce a better description of its usage than mere arithmetic mean, and this is why its frequency's standard deviation is also used (bottom formula); then the z-scores for a given word are compared in each pair of texts, one is subtracted from another; the result is given in absolute values; and these absolute values for all the very frequent words used in the analysis are summed for each pair of texts, and divided by the number of words; and this produces the Delta distance. The procedure results in a matrix of values for the texts in the studied corpus; cluster analysis is applied to the matrix. The results of cluster analysis are visualized in tree diagrams that put together ("cluster") texts separated by least Delta distance. In the procedure applied in this study, cluster analysis was performed for 100, 200, … 1000 most frequent words; the results were pooled in a consensus tree to show the strongest connections preserved over changing word-list size and/or in network analysis that visualizes both weak and strong connections between the texts. All steps of the analysis were made with the "stylo" stylometric package (Eder et al.) for the statistical programming environment R (R Core Team); network analysis was made with "Gephi" (Bastian et al.). Additional tests were performed with a modified version of the same method:

instead of using single words, the texts were converted to part-of-speech tags using automatic grammatical parsing software, Treetagger (Schmid), and clusters of 5 of these were counted to provide results somewhat above the purely lexical level; indeed, this approach has been described, not pejoratively, as "a cheap surrogate for syntax" (Dipper and Schrader).

Figure 1 shows both a consensus tree (left) and a network analysis (right) for the full text of Austen's *Pride and Prejudice*, and dialogue from various Austenian serials and films. Both show, much like the earlier WCopyFind analysis, that the distance (difference) in most-frequent-word usage is the smallest for the TV serials, while film adaptations or films on Austenian themes retreat to the far side of both graphs. Of the latter, the network analysis additionally highlights a fairly strong similarity to the novel in the 2005 feature film.

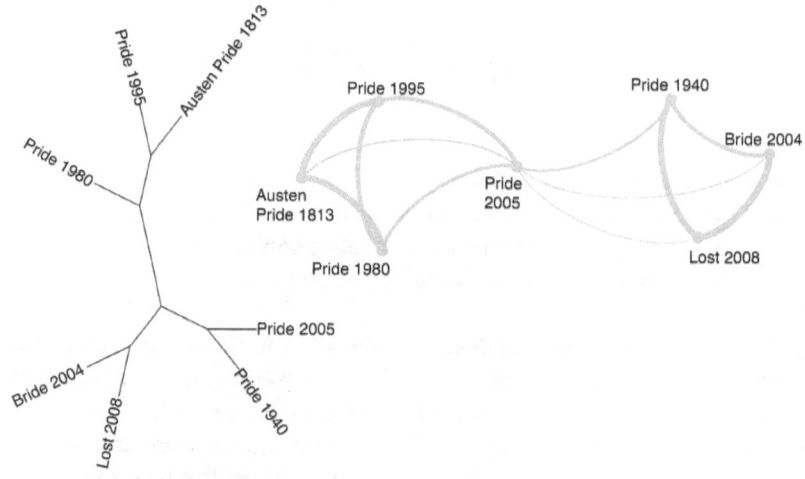

Figure 1. Results of Delta distance analysis for *Pride and Prejudice* the novel and its adaptations in terms of word frequencies.

Obviously, a comparison between the full novel and the dialogue of the adaptations, while necessary, is not enough: a much more precise image of the verbatim affinities between the literary original and its translations into the audio-visual medium can be produced by splitting the novel into dialogue and narrative. Figure 2 presents the network diagram for this set of texts. Quite understandably, the previous graph is all but reproduced here; the only additional feature now is that it is Austen's dialogue that has stronger connections to its adaptations than her narrative; and that her narrative has some similarity to the dialogue in Weldon's 1980 *Pride and Prejudice*. All this is in agreement with the results of the earlier (and independent) analysis by common word n-grams.

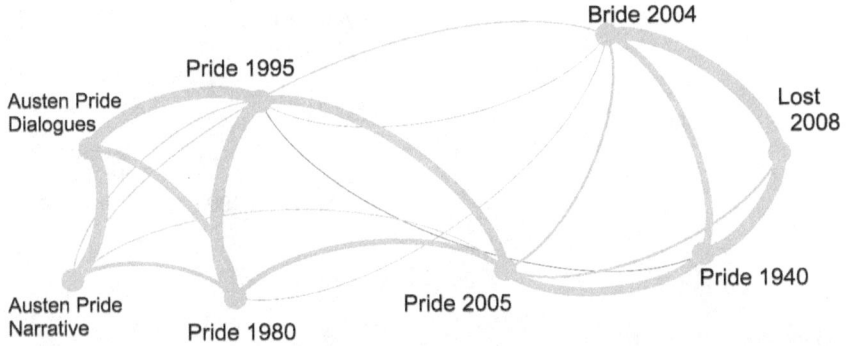

Figure 2. Network analysis of Delta distance for *Pride and Prejudice* the novel (divided into dialogue and narrative) and its adaptations in terms of word frequencies.

When the same set of texts was converted to sequences of consecutive word five-grams, and frequencies of these were counted, the results were slightly different (Figure 3). This "syntax surrogate" method shows a very strong affinity between the dialogue of the novel and that of the BBC serialization of 1995; the literary original's sentence structure seems also to be relatively well-preserved in the 2005 film adaptation. By contrast, Fay Weldon's script, while strongly imitative of Austen's writing at the lexical level, was no longer so at the level of (POS-modeled) syntax.

To place these results in a broader context, a comparison was made again with the *Quo Vadis* corpus as described above, with two more additional texts set in the Roman context: the dialogue in the feature film *Gladiator* (2000) and the TV series *Rome* (2005). Figure 4 presents the diagram for most-frequent words. It shows that, in this perspective, film adaptations are close to their literary originals in both the Austenian and the Sienkiewiczian corpus, which stands in an interesting contrast to the latter set's very different behavior in terms of 5-word-cluster overlap. This diagram also does not seem to answer the question of the identity of the literary original for either of the *Quo Vadis* adaptations, since similarities between them (and between the two translations) are of the same order of magnitude. There is a slightly stronger stylometric affinity between Austen's dialogue and the two television serials (especially that of 1995); once again, the other adaptations recede from the utterances in the novel in a very logical way; in fact, *Bride and Prejudice* is so distant that its most-frequent-word usage bears a much stronger affinity to that in *Rome*.

In Figure 5, the "surrogate syntax" signal is now quite similar in the three novels, suggesting that sentence structures in the original literary dialogue differ from those in film adaptations. Consistently with the other

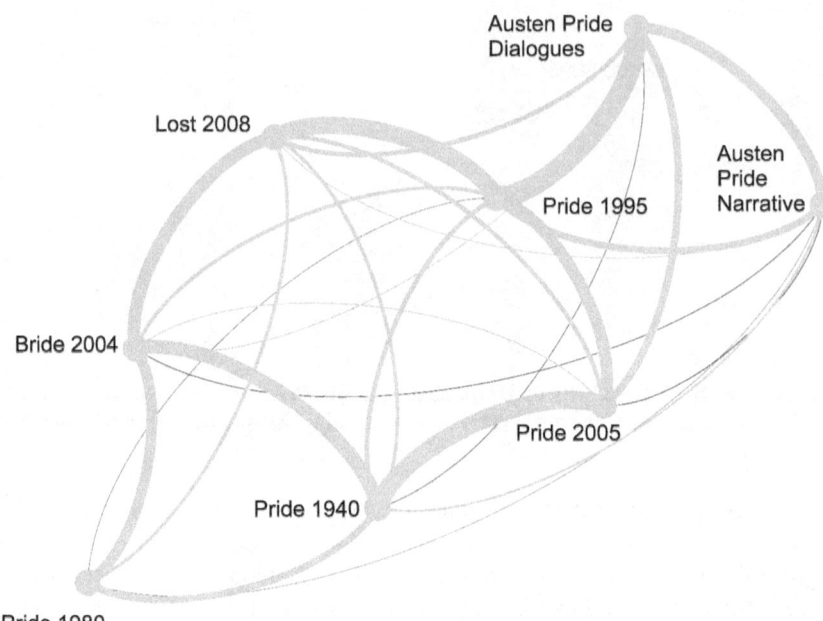

Figure 3. Network analysis of Delta distance for *Pride and Prejudice* the novel (divided into dialogue and narrative) and its adaptations in terms of part-of-speech five-gram frequencies.

results, here, too, some television serials share more stylometric traits with the literary adaptations: this is very true of the 1985 *Quo Vadis* production and the BBC *Pride and Prejudice* of 1995; and quite untrue of the 1980 miniseries (but that has already been seen above). These results call for an indepth qualitative analysis of the dialogue to explain these stylistic mechanisms.

Conclusions

Stylometric analysis offers a panoramic view of intertextual relations that connect different adaptations of *Pride and Prejudice* to the novel itself and to other productions. This bird's-eye-view clearly confirms a marked stylistic and stylometric division into cinema and television genres, with the latter quoting verbatim more of the textual material, but also imitating Jane Austen's verbal style more suggestively than the cinema productions. This confirms critics' remarks that classic television adaptations "endeavour to offer the viewer the closest approximation to reading the novel" (Cartmell

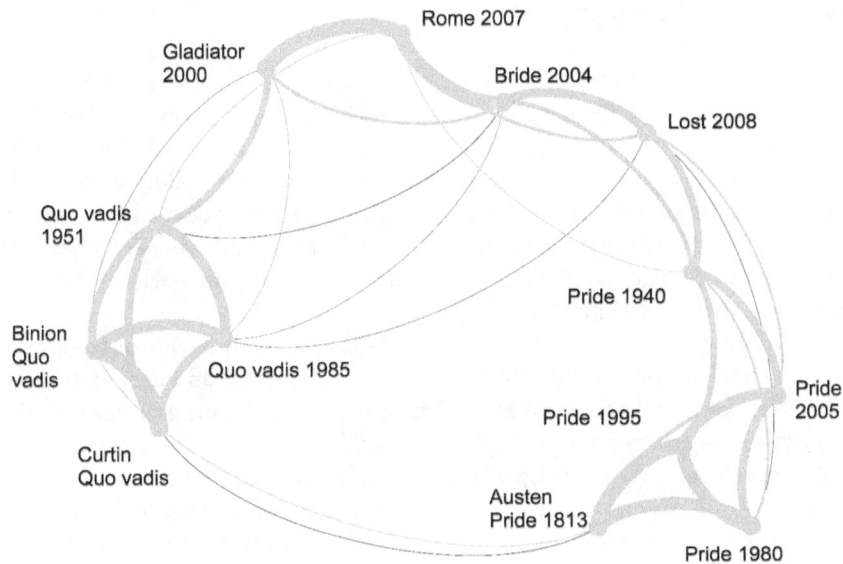

Figure 4. Network analysis of Delta distance for the joint *Pride and Prejudice* and *Quo Vadis* corpora (dialogue in the novels and in their adaptations) in terms of most-frequent-word frequencies.

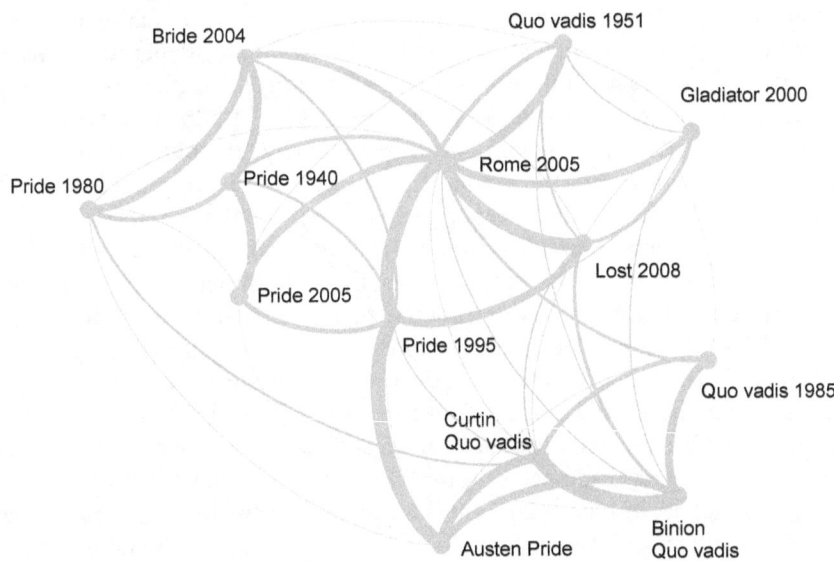

Figure 5. Network analysis of Delta distance for the joint *Pride and Prejudice* and *Quo Vadis* corpora (dialogue in the novels and in their adaptations) in terms of part-of-speech five-gram frequencies.

Jane 22) and that they identify both with literary and televisual traditions, achieving validation from tight connections to literary sources (Cardwell 81). It is also interesting that the highest values for dialogue word cluster overlap—close to 30 percent as observed between the novel's dialogue and those in the two miniseries—is similar to what usually occurs between two literary translations of the same novel into a given language; this has been observed in this study for the two English versions of *Quo Vadis*, but earlier reports of the same also exist (Filipek).

Another interesting result is the stylistic and stylometric consolidation of Austen adaptations in the context of other adaptations and period dramas. This seems to imply that visualizations of *Pride and Prejudice* offer a stylistically homogenous portrayal of their epoch's language, which differs considerably from varied and presumably more random representations of antiquity. Indeed, on the verbal level, Austen film and television productions may constitute a separate genre marked by the writer's authorial fingerprint (Cardwell 134; Troost and Greenfield). Finally, our stylometric mapping has revealed intricate relationships between dialogue in respective adaptations, proving that they inform and cross-pollinate each other. Scholars have often mentioned intertextual links that connect classic novel adaptations to each other and to other filmic counterparts (Cardwell 133). Our graphs demonstrate that these effects can be also traced at the level of film dialogue. At the same time, the overall image is not entirely clear. Some adaptations—again, mostly and understandably, the serial ones—of Austen take large direct fragments of the literary dialogue, and this is consistent with the results obtained in the analysis of most-frequent-word frequencies. Yet when part-of-speech n-grams are compared, the similarity is preserved for only one of the TV miniseries. The *Quo Vadis* corpus seems to behave more consistently: the television production remains close to the original for the POS test. But there is another problem: the two translations of the Polish classic, while sharing almost a third of five-word clusters of the dialogue, are almost entirely unconnected in this respect. It is highly unlikely that the filmmakers used yet another translation as their source: the two used in this study were by far the earliest and the most popular—and the most accessible. True, three more appeared before the making of both productions, but they were quite obscure; of these, at least one seems to have been lost and cannot be dated. More probably, the makers of both adaptations relied less on the literary version than did the adapters of Jane Austen; after all, she is a native of England. Henryk Sienkiewicz was not, and his exceptional burst of American rather than British fame was short-lived and mostly confined to the last few years of the nineteenth, and the first two decades of the twentieth century (Rybicki). This dilemma can only be solved with more experiments on larger corpora of novels and their film adaptations. Only then some general observations can be made on the extent of consistency of the phenomena observed and/or on the frequency and the variety of idiosyncrasies.

NOTES

1. This research has been financed by Poland's National Science Centre as part of the 2013/11/B/HS2/02890 grant, "Film Genre and Audiovisual Translation Strategies. A Case Study in Historical Film."
2. For the discussion of film dialogue and its functionalities, see, for example, *Journal of Screenwriting* published by Intellect; Kozloff; Jaeckle; and Henrykowski.
3. For the discussion of Jane Austen's *Pride and Prejudice*, see, for example, Cardwell; Cartmell; Geraghty, Troost and Greenfield; Giddings and Sheen; Macdonald and Macdonald; Monaghan, Hudelet and Wiltshire; Parrill; Pucci and Thompson; Thompson; and Troost.
4. The usual reading list of the field usually begins with Mosteller and Wallace; Holmes; Burrows; Hoover and Jockers. For a most recent introduction, see Rybicki et al.

WORKS CITED

Austen, Jane. *Pride and Prejudice. The Project Gutenberg E-Book*. 26 Aug. 2008. Web. 10 Sept. 2016.
Aishwarya Rai Bachchan. 2004. ADD Media Entertainment, 2005. DVD.
Bastian, Mathieu, Sebastien Heymann, and Mathieu Jacomy. "Gephi: An Open Source Software for Exploring and Manipulating Networks." *Proceedings of the Third International AAAI Conference on Weblogs and Social Media*. Menlo Park: AAAI Press 2009. Web. 27. Nov. 2016.
Bloomfield, Lou. WCopyFind, *The Plagiarism Resource Site*. 2011–16. www.plagiarism.bloomfieldmedia.com/wordpress/software/wcopyfind. Web. 27 Nov. 2016.
Bride and Prejudice. Dir. Gurinder Chadha. Perf. Martin Henderson,
Burrows, John F. *Computation into Criticism: A Study of Jane Austen's Novels and an Experiment in Method*. Oxford: Clarendon, 1987. Print.
_____. "'Delta': A Measure of Stylistic Difference and a Guide to Likely Authorship." *Literary and Linguistic Computing* 17 (2002): 267–287. Print.
Cardwell, Sarah. *Adaptation Revisited: Television and the Classic Novel*. Manchester: Manchester University Press, 2002. Print.
Cartmell, Deborah. *Jane Austen's* Pride and Prejudice. *The Relationship Between Text and Film*. London: Methuen Drama, 2010. Print.
_____. "*Pride and Prejudice* and the Adaptation Genre." *Journal of Adaptation in Film and Performance* 3.3 (2010): 227–243. Print.
Cartmell, Deborah, and Imelda Whelehan. "A Practical Understanding of Literature on Screen: Two Conversations with Andrew Davies." *The Cambridge Companion to Literature on Screen*. Ed. Cartmell and Whelehan. 239–50. Cambridge: Cambridge University Press, 2007. Print.
Dipper, Stefanie, and Bettina Schrader. "Computing Distance and Relatedness of Medieval Text Variants in German." *Text Resources and Lexical Knowledge: Selected Papers from the 9th Conference on Natural Language Processing KONVENS 2008*. Ed. Angelika Storrer, Alexander Geyken, Alexander Siebert, Kay-Michael Würzner. 29–51. Berlin: de Gruyter 2008. Print.
Eder, Maciej, Jan Rybicki, and Mike Kestemont. "Stylometry with R: A Package for Computational Text Analysis." *R Journal* 8.1 (2016): 107–121. Print.
Filipek, Anna. "*Pan Tadeusz*, or Translating the Untranslatable: An Analysis of English Translations." MA thesis. Kraków: Uniwersytet Jagielloński, 2014.
Geraghty, Christine. *Now a Major Motion Picture: Film Adaptations of Literature and Drama*. Lanham: Rowman & Littlefield, 2008. Print.
Giddings, Robert, and Erica Sheen, eds. *The Classic Novel: From Page to Screen*. Manchester: Manchester University Press, 2000. Print.

Gladiator. Dir. Ridley Scott. Perf. Russell Crowe, Oliver Reed, Joaquin Phoenix. 2000. Universal Pictures, 2004. DVD.

Harris, Jocelyn. *"Such a Transformation!* Translation, Imitation and Intertextuality in Jane Austen on Screen." *Jane Austen on Screen.* Ed. Gina Macdonald and Andrew F. Macdonald. 44–67. Cambridge: Cambridge University Press, 2003. Print.

Hendrykowski, Marek. *Słowo w filmie: historia, teoria, interpretacja.* Warszawa: PWN, 1982. Print.

Holmes, David. "Vocabulary Richness and the Book of Mormon: A Stylometric Analysis of Mormon Scripture." *Research in Humanities Computing* 3 (1994): 18–31. Print.

Hoover, David L. "Corpus Stylistics, Stylometry, and the Styles of Henry James." *Style* 41 (2007): 174–203. Print.

Jaeckle, Jeff, ed. *Film Dialogue.* London: Wallflower Press, 2013. Print.

Jockers, Matthew. *Macroanalysis: Digital Methods and Literary History.* Urbana: University of Illinois Press, 2013. Print.

Kozloff, Sarah. *Overhearing Film Dialogue.* Berkeley: University of California Press, 2000. Print.

Leitch, Thomas. "Adaptation, the Genre." *Adaptation* 1.2 (2008): 106–120. Print.

Lost in Austen. Dir. Dan Zeff. Perf. Jemima Rooper, Elliot Cowan. 2008. Epelpol Entertainment, 2009. DVD.

McDonald, Gina, and Andrew F. McDonald, eds. *Jane Austen on Screen.* Cambridge: Cambridge University Press, 2003. Print.

McKenna, Wayne, John F. Burrows, and Alexis Antonia. "Beckett's Trilogy: Computational Stylistics and the Nature of Translation." *Revue informatique et statistique dans les sciences humaines* 35.1–4 (1999): 151–171. Print.

Monaghan, David, Ariane Hudelet, and John Wiltshire, eds. *The Cinematic Jane Austen: Essays on the Filmic Sensibility of the Novels.* Jefferson, NC: McFarland, 2009. Print.

Mosteller, Frederick, and David L. Wallace. *Inference and Disputed Authorship: The Federalist Papers.* Reading, MA: Addison-Wesley, 1964. Print.

Parrill, Sue. *Jane Austen on Screen and Television. A Critical Study of the Adaptations.* Jefferson, NC: McFarland 2002. Print.

Pride and Prejudice. Dir. Michael Barry. Perf. Curigwen Lewis, Andrew Osborn. 1938. BBC. Television.

_____. Dir. Robert Z. Leonard. Perf. Greer Garson, Laurence Olivier. 1940. Warner Home Video, 2006. DVD.

_____. Dir. Campbell Logan. Perf. Daphne Slater, Peter Cushing. 1952. BBC. Television.

_____. Prod. Barbara Burnham. Perf. Jane Downs, Alan Badel. 1958. BBC. Television.

_____. Dir. Joan Craft. Perf. Celia Bannerman, Lewis Fiander. 1967. BBC. Television.

_____. Dir. Cyril Coke. Perf. Elizabeth Garvie, David Rintoul. 1980. BBC Video, 2004. DVD.

_____. Dir. Simon Langton. Perf. Jennifer Ehle, Colin Firth. 1995. BBC Video, 2000. DVD.

_____. Dir. Joe Wright. Perf. Keira Knightley, Matthew Macfadyen. 2005. Universal Studios Home Entertainment, 2006. DVD.

Pucci, Suzanne R., and James Thompson, eds. *Jane Austen and Co. Remaking the Past in Contemporary Culture.* Albany: State University of New York Press, 2003. Print.

Quo Vadis. Dir. Mervyn LeRoy. Perf. Robert Taylor, Deborah Kerr, Peter Ustinov. 1951. Galapagos, 2016. DVD.

_____. Dir. Franco Rossi. Perf. Klaus Maria Brandauer. 1985. Koch Media, 2016. DVD.

R Core Team. *The R Project for Statistical Computing.* R Foundation for Statistical Computing, 2014, www. R-project.org. Web. 27 Nov. 2016.

Rome. Creat. Bruno Heller, William J. MacDonald, John Milius. Perf. Kevin McKidd. 2005. HBO, 2006. DVD.

Rybicki, Jan. "Sienkiewicz po angielsku." *Przekładaniec* 15 (2006): 101–126. Print.

Rybicki, Jan, Maciej Eder and David L. Hoover. "Computational Stylistics and Text Analysis." *Doing Digital Humanities: Practice, Training, Research.* Ed. Constance Crompton, Richard J. Lane and Ray Siemens. 123–44. Abingdon: Routledge, 2016. Print.

Schmid, Helmut. "Probabilistic Part-of-Speech Tagging Using Decision Trees." *Proceedings of International Conference on New Methods in Language Processing*. Manchester, 1994. Web. 27 Nov. 2016.

Sienkiewicz, Henryk. *Quo Vadis?* Trans. Samuel A. Binion and S. Malevsky. Philadelphia: Altemus, 1897. Print.

_____. *Quo Vadis: A Narrative of the Time of Nero*. Trans. Jeremiah Curtin. Boston: Little, Brown, 1896. Print.

Thompson, James. "How to Do Things with Austen." *Jane Austen and Co. Remaking the Past in Contemporary Culture*. Ed. Suzanne R. Pucci and James Thompson. 13–30. Albany: State University of New York Press, 2003. Print.

Troost, Linda V. "The Nineteenth-Century Novel on Film: Jane Austen." *The Cambridge Companion to Literature on Screen*. Ed. Deborah Cartmell and Imelda Whelehan. 75–89. Cambridge: Cambridge University Press, 2007. Print.

Troost, Linda V., and Sayre Greenfield, eds. *Jane Austen in Hollywood*. Lexington: University Press of Kentucky, 1998. Print.

Aki Kaurismäki's "outrageously improvisatory" Adaptations of Four Familiar Literary Source Texts

DENNIS ROTHERMEL

It's not the note you play that's the wrong note—
it's the note you play afterwards that makes it right or wrong
—Miles Davis

The wrong note is not quite accidental, nor completely intended. It is fortuitous, as if fated, though not foreseen. The wrong note leads to unanticipated exploration, to reveal what had not been conceived beforehand. It arises in practice or performance, and stays there until another wrong note relieves it. It shifts the scale, alters the chord, and there is meaning to that shifting. It is meaning that retains what had been the frame of harmony in its augmentation. Aki Kaurismäki cherishes the wrong note. His film adaptations indulge improvisation upon the known frame of story and meaning inherent to the source. The purpose and value of the Kaurismäkian adaptation is not in how it is truthful to the source, but in how it is not.

Hamlet Goes Business (1987)

Hamlet's father's ghost calls him stupid. Hamlet (Pirkka-Pekka Petelius) hesitates to kill Klaus (that is, Claudius) (Esko Salminen) not because he finds the man in a state of grace, praying, but because Hamlet is discovered standing there next to him, armed and ready to murder (Shakespeare, *Hamlet*

III.iii.73–96). There is no soliloquy about the meaning of life dependent upon taking courageous action (III.i.1–89). It's all just about the passionless intrigues of doing business. In the contemporary setting, Klaus plots to sell off the family business interests in paper milling and shipbuilding in order to corner the Scandinavian market for manufacturing rubber ducks. Ofelia (Kati Outinen) has one of those rubber ducks floating next to her when she drowns herself, in the bathtub, rather than bedecked with garlands and weeds, as her clothes bore her up mermaid-like in the flowing stream (IV.vii.165–182). Rubber ducks versus ocean ships—the equivalence replicates the proverbial widgets of putative products in business-school textbooks and schoolbook algebra problems. More deliberately ridiculous than the abstract product-value place holder, rubber ducks as bankable investment gloriously underscore that the actual business product is not just dramatically but also philosophically immaterial. What's at stake in terms of what a business entity produces is thus generally irrelevant to genuine human purposes.

There is a concluding twist in the plot that is anticipated by a puzzling detail in the first scene. Hamlet is complicit in the murder of his father, with whom he never got along. Hamlet is undone not by treachery by his nemesis, but, like the soldiers in Kurosawa's adaptation of *Macbeth* who attack him spontaneously before Birnam wood can make its oft-forewarned march to Dunsinane, the hero's demise is different in Kaurismäki's rendition (Shakespeare *Macbeth* IV.i.106; V.iii.2; V.iii.74; V.v.50–51; V.viii.35). Instead of Horatio extolling the virtues of the dying prince and wishing him adieu in the company of angels, Hamlet is summarily dispatched by the leader of the workers (Matti Pelonpää) who would suffer most if he were to survive (*Hamlet* V.ii.364–365). The leader of the workers has a convivial dog at his side. Polonius" (Esko Nikkari's) speech to Lauri (that is, Laertes) (Kari Väänänn)—Shakespeare's oft unacknowledged satirical lampoon of pompous self-aggrandizing wisdom—is distilled to its self-centered essence: don't lend lest you lose both money and friend, and don't pay back what you borrow any sooner than you have to (I.iii.58–81). Lauri's ultimate confrontation with Hamlet results in Hamlet smashing a large radio console onto Lauri's head—and he staggers around that way for a few steps with a radio for a head.

Hamlet Goes Business is all about the preternatural dour selfishness that is the normative rule for behavior and attitude in business, particularly in large corporation leadership. Hamlet exemplifies what that culture will freely tolerate: narcissist, vindictive, conniving, manipulative, rapacious, predatory, and not necessarily exceptionally intelligent. Woe betide the nation that lives under the rule of a leader of that ilk! There is no tragedy, nor sympathy for the title character or any character, save the dog. On the contrary, it is a hoot—from start to finish, outlandishly, gloriously excessive in taking liberties with Shakespeare's most famous play. There is, however, one segment of the screenplay that retains an unaltered segment from the source text, which otherwise is willfully truncated and distorted. Hamlet carefully reviews acting style with the hired actors prior to the staging of the play that he conceives to test Klaus' reaction upon seeing his presumably secret deed played out in mime in front of him. Though condensed, in this case the sentiment of the Shakespearean text is retained. Shakespeare invests his title character with a keen appreciation for the subtleties of the theater, which serves as a confession of the playwright more than it provides necessary character construction for the playwright's mouthpiece: "Speak the speech, I pray you, as I pronounced it to you, trippingly on the tongue; but if you mouth it as many of your players do, I had as lief the town-crier spoke my lines. Nor do not saw the air too much with your hand, thus, but use all gently" (III.ii.1–5).

And—what do you know!—this advice precisely fits the manner of acting one finds implicitly according to the filmmaker's discretion in the film, much as obtains in many Kaurismäki films. That nearly-deadpan delivery of dialogue, nearly-neutral emotiveness, along with the loose editing that renders continuity of space and time stilted, the bland distancing of major characters, and the sustained residual defiance of plausibility—these are all traces of the traits that Gilles Deleuze uses to distinguish crystalline from organic cinema (126–33). Crystalline cinema indulges playing outlandishly with falsity, undermining sympathy and admiration of a hero protagonist, defiance of diegetic coherence, and willfully inventive distortion of reference to a non-virtual world, including source texts. There isn't a formula for the crystalline, which, rather, designates the open-ended entrée into playful creativity by dispensing with all aspects of the verisimilitude that defines mainstream cinema. One can sum it up by saying that, among other aspects, crystalline cinema amounts to *documentary* footage of actors playing out roles in scenes, with no effort in their performance nor intention in the script to make it seem ordinary and realistic. If you don't see the understated power of the sly irreverence, then you just don't get the humor of it. To call it satire doesn't quite get it—the comic hyperbole and absurd interjections undermine the potential underlying critical message of a satire. But this film's absurdities distance the narrative from any claim to realism, even more than its distance from its literary source, however tempered that could be by just satire. Kaurismäki delights in simply playing around with the text, and telling an entirely different story.

Kaurismäki claimed not to know or what to know anything more about the Shakespearean text than from having once seen Laurence Olivier's movie version (1948) (Toiviainan 34). One shouldn't take from that off-hand dismissal acknowledgment of inspiration that Olivier's rendering may have had upon Kaurismäki's film, and least of all an intention to contribute an new treatment to the canon of film adaptation of *Hamlet*. *Hamlet Goes Business*, rather, is a concerto of wrong notes. Each sly step away from the source elicits humor in the recognition. Theorists of comedy tend to focus reductively upon what makes us laugh, and particularly upon the sudden incongruity that gets the laugh (Morreal 9–15). But—if one can excuse the paraphrase— "there are more things in humor and mirth, Horatio, than dreamt of in your theories" (I.v.167–68). The humor of *Hamlet Goes Business* is that of *I see what you're doing and it's good fun*. One smiles wryly rather than laughs, and the smile endures unspent in the emotive release, growing cumulatively with every new wrong-note instance. It is an intellectual humor.

Juha *(1999)*

The temporal setting for Juhani Aho's spare novel, *Juha*, is overtly vague, which the author assiduously defended in a satirical pseudo-academic essay (Vähämäki ix). The story is meant to be timeless—not about any specific historical cultural setting. Juha, a woodsman, and his wife Marja have sunk into emotional indifference. Juha rescues a wayfarer, Shemeikka from being accosted by a gang of thieves. Shemeikka encourages Marja to believe she is doomed to age without ever having been truly loved. Juha is unsuspecting and taken with the stranger, getting himself drunk sharing conversation. Shemeikka wins her over. She throws herself in the boat that he's taking down river. Shemeikka's attraction to her wanes after he seduces her. Marja learns once he brings her to his home that she's only this year's conquest. The following summer, Shemeikka finds a new lover, younger and potentially his bride. Marja suffers from the deception and the neglect, and she gives birth to a baby boy.

Juha seeks help to regain his wife—but nobody comes forward. He goes looking for Shemeikka, hoping to find Marja. But she hides from him when he appears there. She eventually decides to leave and find her way home, leaving her child behind. Her maid is happy to see her, but not so the mother-in-law. She lets Juha believe that she was abducted, and says nothing about the child. She pines for the child, and for the child's father. Juha stews in his doubts about her. Marja finally confesses to having a child. They leave together to confront Shemeikka and to retrieve the child. Juha strikes Shemeikka with a stool, breaking his arm, and then again, breaking his leg. Shemeikka is insistent that Marja had come with him willingly, which Marja isn't able to contradict. When they arrive home, Juha leaves Marja and the child on the shore and quietly pushes the boat away, discarding the pole. He is wracked with guilt for having crippled Shemeikka, who was innocent of having abducted Marja forcefully and demoralized learning for certain that Marja had left him willingly. He lets the boat drift away towards the dangerous river rapids, where he will perish.

That's how it unfolds in Juhani Aho's novel. It is thoroughly altered in the adaptation. Kaurismäki chose to make the fourth Finnish film adaptation of a popular novel by a revered early 20th-century Finnish author a silent film—replacing the novel's intricate dialogue and tormented emotional interior monologues with the blunt, understated, gesticulated communications of silent-film pantomime. Much of the figurative imagery, particularly connections with the river, are lost. A rubber duck shows up in the film, among the things that Marja (Kati Outinen) packs into her suitcase when she leaves Juha (Sakari Kuosmanen).

A cryptic reference to Sam Fuller ("Arrest this man") shows up, written in English in chalk on the blackboard on the wall in the police station as Juha learns that there is no case of Marja having been kidnapped if it's clear that she left him willingly:

But, arrest whom? Juha? Shemeikka? (André Wilms) Marja? The police detective? Or perhaps it's Aki Kaurismäki's self-deprecating joke, a graffito left on the wall by the one person on the set with a purpose in sharing the reference. There is no ambiguity about Marja's departure in the film—though the married couple is depicted as blissfully happy at the outset, which contrasts sharply with the mutual estrangement evident at the beginning of the novel. They farm their cabbage patch and sell the produce at market, travelling back and forth on Juha's motorcycle and side car. She cares for their sheep. When she leaves Juha, she leaves him a note declaring her love for Shemeikka, who first appears driving his classic American sports car, a 60s-era Corvette, on the road near where Juha plows a field on a tractor. The sports car overheats, and Shemeikka solicits Juha's assistance. Juha hops down from the tractor, grabbing a crescent wrench as big and long as his arm, which had rested in a scabbard affixed to the side of the tractor. Juha opens up the hood to the car and goes to work on it with his absurdly gigantic wrench. In place of the chrome letters, "Corvette," attached to the tip of the engine hood, the car is designated "Sierck," which is taken as homage to Douglas Sirk, née Dietlef Sierck. (Nestingen *The Cinema of Aki Kaurismäki* 34; Toiviainan 42; Werner 68)

Later, Juha sleeps with the wrench by his side, drunk, and alone, Marja is relegated to sleeping on the floor rolled up in a rug. Juha had supplied Shemeikka with home-made liquor, which Shemeikka surreptitiously dumps into a planter, while maintaining eyes for Marja. Juha shows Shemeikka the five pistons he's extracted from the sports car, which is famous for its over-powered V8 engine, which, of course, has eight pistons. He explains that he'll need to order parts to complete the repair. At first, Marja resists Shemeikka's advances and talk, but begins to warm up when she overhears Juha's crass explanation to Shemeikka that he had married Marja in spite of the fact that she was beneath him socially. Marja becomes gradually attentive to Shemeikka's entreaties, especially in light of her youth and Juha's age. Her attention to Juha wanes quickly—she lets him eat packaged food heated in the microwave, while she practices putting on makeup and browses glamour magazines.

Marja leaves with Shemeikka when he returns to fetch his repaired car. He seduces her on the way to Helsinki. Once there he deposits her in a nightclub with women in residence who are employed to entertain gentlemen clients. Shemeikka wants her to join in that duty, but she refuses, and is hence relegated to washing floors. Juha takes the bus into the city, with an axe packed away in his knapsack. He shows up at Shemeikka's night club, pushes the body guards out of the way, and confronts Shemeikka, wielding his axe. Shemeikka has a pistol and shoots Juha twice when the big man comes at him. Juha is strong enough not to succumb immediately. Shemeikka discards his weapon, ashamed for what he has done with it. Still as single-mindedly determined as he was before Shemeikka shot him, Juha backs Shemeikka into a walk-in freezer. When he re-emerges, his axe is bloody. He liberates Marja and takes her to the train station. The ending is thus all turned around— with the sly iconic invocation of Juha's fatal descent over a waterfall in the novel. Instead, Juha lies dying from the gunshot wounds in a trash dump. A mighty steam roller approaches; the pointed treads protruding from its large, turning, steel wheels visually approximate a steady but lethal river rapids waterfall. There is no maid servant, nor a mother-in-law, but there is a lovingly loyal dog, Laika, who runs after the bus when Juha entrusts the dog to a neighbor before leaving for the confrontation in the city. An assistant for Laika is identified in the end credits.

The soundtrack is filled from start to finish with situationally underscoring emotive music, in the manner of film scores composed for newer releases and performances of silent-era films, including leitmotifs for the three major characters. Occasionally a noise associated with what happens on the screen slips into the soundtrack, such as the ding the microwave makes when Marja casually prepares Juha's dinner. There are two musical episodes, and the music we hear is noticeably not quite exactly synchronous with what we can see the musicians and singers perform—so the soundscape comes asymptotically close to mirroring the visual action but while ostensibly not quite uniting with the visuals. This slight but noticeable separation of the visuals from the soundscape provides an additional wedge to distance the film from ordinary film conventions. A singer sings a nineteenth-century French ballade, "*Le temps de cerises*," celebrating the lure and dangers of falling in love with a pretty woman in the time of cherry blossoms, which is sung in French by a Finnish actress (Elina Salo), with lyrics in translation following in the intertitles after the verse. Kaurismäki revives—in camp fashion—silent-cinema conventions of intertitles following characters visibly speaking, and obtrusive detail shots and close-ups to let clues and reactions cement in our understanding of the story. The violent confrontations in the final scene are discretely pantomimed in fake gestures or off-camera. Kaurismäki regulars Kati Outinen and André Wilms portray Marja and Shemeikka respectively. Shooting the film as silent allowed for casting the French-speaking Wilms in a lead role, though depriving Outinen the opportunity to deliver dialogue in her native tongue.

The only vaguely identifiably temporal artifacts of an American sports car, a microwave oven, and the combination of accordion and electric guitar in the musical numbers all contribute to the film having retained Juhani Aho's intentional temporal vagueness. Appropriation of silent-film *mise en scène* underscores that intention even more, though while stripping away the convoluted dramatic and emotive nuances of the novel. That transformation opens up the intrusion of the same sort of absurd intrusions that one sees in *Hamlet Goes Business*: the rubber duck, the enormous crescent wrench, the French song, a wilting cactus in a pot on a shelf on the wall in the room that Marja is consigned to in Shemeikka's bordello, and the abstruse reference to Sam Fuller. These aspects all distance the narrative from more than just a temporally determinant setting. Kaurismäki goofs around with elements of the narrative that would otherwise cement its verisimilitude. The film is thus variously threaded with Kaurismäki's conceits and inventions, which, whether perceived or not, neither laden the film with symbolically suggestive intimations of meaning, nor obscuring the narrative. One understands both the diegesis and the narrative as refracted through Kaurismäki's prismatic constructions. There is homage to Sirk and Fuller, and yet the film doesn't itself resurrect the style or substance of either. The story as translated to film becomes mutedly melodramatic, and without being a cautionary tale, as evidenced by how drastically Kaurismaki converts the conclusion: Juha is mortally wounded from Shemeikka's gun, yet kills him with an axe before dying himself. In the novel, Juha cripples Shemeikka viciously, and Juha commits suicide when his conscience reveals to him how wrong that was. In the film, it is Schemeikka who shows a pang of conscience, when he discards his pistol disgustedly. Kaurismäki demonstrates, especially for a Finnish audience familiar with the novel, how melodrama intertwines several characters tortuously, and also how the altered tonalities of character and deeds render it no longer as ostensibly melodramatic, but no less emotively convoluted. One of the principles of musical *serialism* is how the inherent melodic drive of a twelve-tone series changes emotively with application of retrograde and inversion, while retaining the power of its complexity (Perle 3–10). And this applies well to Kaurismaki's transformation of *Juha*, which we can see again as a series of wrong notes. Douglas Sirk could conceivably have done a film version of *Juha*, but we have hardly an invocation of Sirkian cinema in the replacement of "Corvette" with "Sierck" as the nameplate for a fast automobile. There is no more Sirkian in the film than there is Fulleresque by virtue of the equally inexplicable passing nod to Sam Fuller, nor in the evocation of the Chaplinesque in the ridiculously large wrench. There is the rubber duck, which gives us the hint: these are all instances of Kaurismäkian play with loose ends, playful red herrings.

La vie de Bohème *(1992)*

In his Preface to *Scènes de la vie de bohème* (*The Bohemians of the Latin Quarter*), Henri Murger rejects the importance of the context of the story: "The class of Bohemians referred to in this book are not a race of today; they have existed in all climes and ages, and can claim an illustrious descent" (5). Murger then hints that the first known Bohemian was Homer, "who lived from hand to mouth round the fertile country of Ionia, eating the bread of charity, and halting in the evening to tune beside some hospitable hearth the harmonious lyre that had sung the loves of Helen and the fall of Troy" (5). Murger's 1851 text consists of fragmentary episodes connecting a steady set of main characters. The loose structure of the novel reflects its origins in short stories that the author published in 1845–49 (Samuels vii). The story spans several years. The locale is Paris at some overtly indeterminate time in the 1840s: "184–" (Murger 138, 234). Associations of Murger's Bohemians—the painter Marcel, the musician and painter Schaunard, the philosopher Colline, and the sculptor Jacques—with relatively unknown contemporary figures have been made, along with the assumption that Rodolphe, a poet, is Murger himself (Samuels ix–x).

So the locale and the time frame are somewhat vague, and associations with historical personages loose. Giuseppe Giacosa and Luigi Illica exploited the lassitude of definition of time and place, and the looseness of story line, in their libretto for Giacomo Puccini's *La Bohème*, which premiered in Turin in 1896. Their version drew vaguely from some of the content of the source text, but invented much, including a well-defined story arc concluding in poignant tragedy. Though not indicated in the text of the libretto, the opera's setting has come to be determined as "about 1830" in Paris (Melnitz 173–175). The libretto is in Italian, with the consequence of Murger's poet, Rodolphe, and painter, Marcel, becoming Rodolpho and Marcello. Schaunard and Colline are retained, as are Mimi and Musette, Rodolpho's and Marcello's lovers respectively. The sculptor, Jacques, is discarded, as is Schaunard's inamorata, Phemie.

Puccini's opera is perhaps far better known than Murger's novel. One can see, however, how Kaurismäki's adaptation takes Murger's advice about the life of the Bohemian being non-specific to time and place as a point of departure, much more extensively than Puccini's opera. The time frame in Kaurismäki's film is contemporary—Nineties Paris—but without specification more precisely than *printemps* and *automne*. Slow pans at rooftop level, and a couple of scenes in cars traveling the Champs Élysées identify the locale as Paris, with incidental indication of the suburban commune of Malakoff. The dramatic action, however, takes place at scenes that could be anywhere in the city's neighborhoods away from identifiable landmarks. The first of the roof-top sweeping views begins the film, and then descends below to the street, evoking the opening of René Clair's *Sous les Toits de Paris*. What persists in both opera and film, but more prominently in vacillation in the film, is the precariousness of the lives of artists struggling to make a go of it, such as Murger sees as essential to Bohemians everywhere: "Those who compose [the real Bohemia] are really amongst those called by art, and have the chance of being also amongst its elect. This Bohemia, like the others, bristles with perils, two abysses on either side—poverty and doubt" (16). Though poverty seems inevitable even after the unforeseeable windfalls of proceeds from their craft, Kaurismäki's Bohemian heroes are never far from energetic self-confidence, always in the game of trading ironies. Likewise, their romantic outlooks are elusive or ephemeral. It is an unquenchable delight in impish, irreverent, literary repartee that they exercise with each other and particularly to take advantage of those not able to match their wit, the landlord in particular. There is exercise of the genius underlying their art just in the matter of managing to survive. This element Kaurismäki particularly realizes from Murger's general depiction of Bohemian life: "Their daily existence is a work of genius, a daily problem which they always succeed in solving by the aid of audacious mathematics" (17). Audacious inventiveness becomes the theme unifying every scene in the film. From the beginning of the story, it is landlords, cops, and other personages in position of authority who are the usual targets of their machinations (Murger 19–21).

Kaurismäki often uses actors again in subsequent films. As he has made films in Finland with Finnish dialogue and in France with French dialogue, his casting of actors both native French- and Finnish-speaking in the same film impose changes to the material. That he chose to do *Juha* as a silent film allowed casting André Wilms as Shemeikka. For *La vie de bohème*, with dialogue in French, casting Wilms as Marcel but the Finnish actors Matti Pellonpää and Kari Väänänen as Rodolpho and Schaunard respectively meant Pellonpää's stilted declamatory and very brief expressions in ostensibly carefully rehearsed French could no longer pass as the language of the poet of the Bohemians as Murger had it. So, Rodolpho rather than Marcel becomes the painter, Albanian but raised in Barcelona, which suffices to explain his accent and limited expression. And "Rodolpho" rather than "Rodolphe" makes sense for that heritage. Marcel becomes the writer. Schaunard is still the musician/composer and artist. Marcel rather than Schaunard begins the story, and this shift to the literary focus leads to changing Schaunard's first utterance of the novel—"By Jove!"—to Marcel's "*Merde*" (Murger 19). Väänänen's more felicitous but still foreign accent is understandable by his being Irish. Colline, the philosopher in the novel and also the opera, is omitted entirely. Marcel thus inherits Colline's line that he finds Shakespeare to have been "a great philosopher" (Murger 352).

Kaurismäki's version of the opening scenes introduce Marcel, Rodolpho and Schaunard to each other, but in different order than the novel. Marcel (rather than Schaunard) reads the eviction notice on the wall of his apartment. He then sequesters his typewriter outside the window, stuffs some clothes in a satchel, and descends to the entrance, where he pretends surprise that the landlord awaits him there. Maintaining his suave composure, he offers to go immediately to his bank to get the past due rent. The landlord insists that his muscled but dullard young assistant, Hugo, accompany. Outside the entrance to the bank, Marcel tells a passing policeman that Hugo has been casing the bank for weeks, and that his accomplice is to be found in a parked car around the corner, holding a copy of *Le Monde* upside down. The policeman buys it and walks off frame with the uncomprehending Hugo in tow, and Marcel quickly walks off in the opposite direction. The improbability of such an antic working lies at the heart of the humor of the bit, which is amplified by the stagey *mise en scène*. Marcel and Hugo walk into the medium-long static shot from the left, closely set against the background of the bank storefront behind them. The policeman walks in from the right, and then leaves opposite from his entrance, as does Marcel. As the scene vacates, the shot lingers a moment, typically Kaurismäkian, but this time to reveal a peace symbol painted on the bank window as the actors depart. The entirety of the bit with Hugo sent along by the landlord and then fobbed off on the cop is Kaurismäki's emendation of the scene.

Completely broke, Marcel enters a restaurant, takes a seat at a table where Rodolpho (rather than Colline in the novel) is finishing his soup course, and then orders two half servings of trout (rather than rabbit stew), explaining to his table-mate and new acquaintance that a combination of two half-orders usually results in more fish than one whole trout. But the last order of trout has been promised to Rodolpho, and when it arrives, as one two-headed fish, Rodolpho insists on sharing it. They enjoy the meal and each other's company, over much wine.

Marcel had sent the landlord a formal letter, from the Ministry of War, explaining in elaborate erudite detail how his belongings in the apartment the landlord was obliged to keep for one year, during which time Marcel could retrieve them upon payment of rent due. This momentarily stymies the landlord who has already rented the apartment to Schaunard (rather than Marcel), who arrives with his piano loaded in a truck. So when Marcel arrives with Rodolpho (rather than Schaunard with Colline and Rodolphe) in tow that evening, Schaunard is already inside, playing piano, which Marcel identifies as violin-playing. Schaunard and Marcel debate who has rights to what, which Rodolpho finally interrupts with the suggestion of "irrigating" their explanations with three bottles of wine that he produces, inheriting that line from the novel where it is assigned to Colline. And they do interrupt the debate for the sake of the wine.

Rodolpho is still matched with Mimi, and Marcel with Musette. How Marcel and Musette first meet in the novel is transferred to how Rodolpho first meets Mimi, including the explanation upon that first encounter that he will offer her a place to stay in his apartment alone, because the couch is too hard to sleep on, and he is much too hot-blooded and she is beautiful. Oh, and also because the dog, Baudelaire (played by Kaurismäki's own canine companion, Laika), has nightmares and makes noise during the night. Rodolpho tells her he will sleep in a friend's apartment, but he spends the night in the cemetery, where he absconds with a bouquet of flowers to bring back to Mimi the next morning, but she is already gone, leaving behind a friendly note about looking for a place to live and finding a job. There is no dog in the novel. Rodolpho's dog is named after the poet who was active, and Bohemian, in Paris during the period that Murger's novel addresses (Samuels ix). Kaurismäki's dog is named after the dog launched into orbit by Russian space exploration in 1957, the first passenger on a Sputnik capsule. And Kaurismäki's production company for this film is named Sputnik.

Aside from becoming the writer among the Bohemians in the film, Marcel also gains a surname: Marx. André Wilms will play a character by that name again, and not so different in character from his role in *La vie de bohème*, 20 years later in Kaurismaki's *Le Havre*. There are two ways how that fuller name, Marcel Marx, makes oblique sense. First, the historical setting of the novel, Paris in the 1840s, includes the years 1843–45 that Karl Marx lived in Paris, composing essays, editing a radical political journal, becoming acquainted with Friedrich Engels, and also composing the first attempts of the much larger project of a critique of capitalism that would emerge some twenty years later, *Das Kapital* (Berlin 76–111). And we see Marcel Marx as sympathetic to a Marxist outlook in both films.

A second oblique association, though, tantalizes. In a scene closely replicated in the film, Marcel has gained an opportunity for commissions for his painting, but he needs a better coat than the one he has at hand. A man, a pompous but obtuse bourgeois from Nantes, just then comes to the door, looking for the painter recommended to him for portraits. Schaunard poses as the painter, and suggests the man pose for him sitting down but without his coat, which Marcel offers to hang up for him but then puts it on and sneaks out. Negotiations for a price take into account whether hands are included in the rendering, and the seasonal cost of paints. Schaunard prolongs the sitting, suggesting they order dinner delivered. Marcel returns just in time later to give the coat back.

In this scene in the film, Marcel has an appointment with a magazine publisher, to interview as the editor of a fashion magazine, and Rodolpho is at his easel when the hapless businessman, Blancheron, appears (Jean-Pierre Léaud, doing his best dead-pan cluelessness). Rodolpho is standing next to an ostensibly completed self-portrait, with his easily recognizable distinctive masculine face and mustache reflected in the mirror in between and captured exactly in the portrait. Presented with this tripled image of the painter, Blancheron asks who the subject is. "Ma mère," is Rodolpho's matter-of-fact response. When Rodolpho completes the portrait that evening, Blancheron wants to have his coat back. Rodolpho stands there without reacting and pauses a bit longer than comfortably, but then just in time for Marcel to return with the coat, explaining that since it had been dusty, he had it cleaned, citing the charge, which will be added to the bill for the painting and supper. It's a jolly scene, showing the Bohemians putting on an elaborate but practically inspired hoax, on the fly instinctually cooperatively. One thinks about how the brothers bamboozle a policeman set upon arresting them by removing furniture from a room and then posing as an elderly woman in a rocking chair. One set of three jolly friends rampaging fearlessly through a marginal existence with ingenious little scams, guaranteeing absurdist mayhem whenever the three of them occupy the scene together, compare well with a different set, who happen to be played by brothers.

Marcel, Rodolpho, and Schaunard discuss the artists they think to have best leveled the constraining influence of traditional style: Kazimir Malevich (1878–1935), particularly his "Black Square," Arnold Schoenberg (1874–1951), Alban Berg (1885–1935), Anton Webern (1883–1945), and Arthur Rimbaud (1854–1891). As radical as their influence may have been, these are all figures in painting, music, and poetry from an earlier generation *vis à vis* the Bohemians in the film but a subsequent generation vis a vis the novel. As sincere as their avant-garde aspirations are, Marcel, Rodolpho, and Schaunard are equally adept at frittering away the sums they realize from their work, while all the while justifying frivolous expenditures as aspects of strict economizing. Blancheron finds Rodolpho later to purchase his masterpiece, "The Crossing of the Red Sea," a complex surrealist composition featuring Rodolpho holding a small canvas with an abstract figure on it, and three wine bottles in a basket below. When Rodolpho is ready to sell Blancheron his remaining paintings to help fund Mimi's hospital stay, he's asked about the painter, whom he claims is Becker, that is, Paula Modersohn-Becker, a nineteenth century artist with a recognizable style very much like Rodolpho's paintings that we see in the film—representative and realistic renditions of their subjects, though with flattened perspective and moderately cubist flat surfaces fitting together geometrically. The paintings in the film are credited to Paula Oinonen, who also gets listed separately in the end credits as an executive producer and "*coach de Mme Laika*." Blancheron opens up a gallery, with "The Crossing of the Red Sea" featured prominently in the window, for a much larger price, and the abstract figure in the small painting within the painting replaced with *sucre* (sugar), which is Blancheron's business source of wealth. "*La voix du peuple est la voix de dieu*," Rodolpho mutters in the clipped, uninflected delivery that accompanies all of his expressions whether sincere, factual, or ironic.

Marcel has taken the enormously thick manuscript for his play in 21 acts, *The Avenger*, to publishers in town without finding any interest in it. Once he secures the editorship for the fashion magazine, he persuades the publisher to include serializing the works of Baudelaire (the poet, not the dog) in the magazine. Instead, he serializes the 21-act play. The publisher fires him and demands the return of the large advance he had paid out. Sam Fuller shows up this time in person, portraying the gruff literary journal publisher. Fuller carefully steps through a few lines of dialogue in French, ostensibly repeating phonetically what he's just then been instructed to enunciate. He puffs on a big fat cigar and is more than sufficiently gruff for the part even without speaking. His parting shot to Marcel, pronounced slowly, with the same deliberate cadence of his brief phonetic recitations in French, and while leaning out of the back seat window of the big, long American limousine, "you son of a bitch!"

Mimi and Musette had attended a performance of Mozart's *Marriage of Figaro*—the tickets were part of the sale of Rodolpho's "Crossing the Red Sea." They sit seriously attentive and then amused during Figaro's teasing Cherubino ("*Non piú andrai*") regarding the dreadful change in his life coming down the road. The two women listen again stone-faced and catching each other's severe looks during Schaunard's (Kari Väänänen'a) performance of his masterwork for piano—"The Influence of Blue on the Arts," a cacophonous, rebellious, but uninspired composition entailing much banging on the piano, ranting against the police, making siren noises with a kazoo, and dissonant repetitive motifs. The two women notice in particular how Rodolpho and Marcel seem absorbed in Schaunard's performance. Later, in a café together, they talk about needing to leave their feckless Bohemian lovers. Musette knows of a well-off farmer in Alsace who would welcome her, and she invites Mimi to join her there later.

As Mimi sees Musette off at the train station, a continuous silhouette of passengers sitting in train windows passes along projected onto the wall behind them. When Musette leaves, her shadow follows her, melding into the train silhouette, and then a cloud of steam blows in from the right. It's a charming and blatantly contrived effect, and presumably much easier and less expensive than arranging the scene actually at a train station with a departing train involved. Here and generally, Kaurismäki's *mise en scène* gravitates to that composition of the two figures next to a flat background, in medium-long view. It is stagey, but without histrionics. The shot lingers for a moment after the dialogue concludes, thus not to propel the dramatic action headlong into the next scene. The projection of shadows from a light source behind the unseen structures behind the camera view that imbues a transparently faux depth. Alternatively, when the flat-wall background is a restaurant or store window, it is the silhouette images on the translucent surface that serve that same purpose of shadow-constructed depth. Low background street noise similarly injects implied depth of situational context beyond the visual image. The combination of these effects creates an intimation of depth—both beyond the background of the image and behind the camera view. It is a creation of spatial depth that is neither atmospheric nor geometrical perspective in that the composition does not place objects at different distances relative to the camera. The imagery of the black-and-white film are consistently complexly composed, without heavily interpretative formal expression. The chiaroscuro nevertheless contains the full range of blacks and grays, from pure white to pure black, as if adhering to Ansel Adams' zone system (Adams). The shot of Rodolpho in the overnight jail, sitting against the wall along with others in the jail, evokes the dramatic contrast chiaroscuro composition of Caravaggio's *The Calling of St. Matthew*.

Louis Malle has a cameo as the gentlemen at the next table when Rodolpho embarrassingly is missing his wallet full of money from the proceeds of sale of his masterpiece. He had purchased the wallet new, just for holding the cash, and it was promptly stolen on the Métro. The police were about to arrest him, so the gentleman's offer would have saved the day, but then Rodolpho's passport reveals his having been in the country three years without a visa, residence permit, or work permit. His apprehension by the police thus results in his deportation back to Albania.

Baudelaire (the dog) rejoices vociferously when Rodolfo sneaks back into the country months later. More subdued but just as fervent is Rodolfo's reunion with Mimi. At a picnic in the countryside, Mimi and Rodolpho share gently intimate moments under a tree by the bank of a river, along which swim a pair of swans—who, of course, mate for life. But Mimi will leave him, asserting that she will always love him, but that life is difficult.

Mimi tells Rodolpho that he is as handsome as the Italian film star, Lino Ventura. The actor, Jean-Paul Wenzel, who portrays Francis, Mimi's boyfriend, the two times she and Rodolpho are separated, resembles Ventura remarkably. Francis drives a big American car, which, in combination with Gassot's (Sam Fuller's) limousine, adds up to two big American cars. When Mimi, following her conversation with Musette, leaves Rodolpho, he retires to a bar, where he downs a long series of drinks, while the radio next to him plays a song, "*Je bois systematique pour oublier les amis de ma femme*" (Goraguer). Later, he finds her with Francis, and simply stands outside for her to see him. She leaves Francis without saying a word, and we hear "You Better Leave My Kitten Alone" in the soundtrack (John, Turner and McDougall).

Rodolpho stands transfixed next to the hospital bed where Mimi lies dying. He leaves to bring her a bouquet of wildflowers, daisies as it turns out, which are violets in the novel (Murger 399). When he returns, she has expired, and he drops the flowers to the floor, which recapitulates an image from earlier in the film, when the flowers he retrieves from the cemetery where he spent the night that first time he met Mimi eventually dry out and get dumped on the floor before she appears again. When she points it out, Rodolpho allows that had he known it would be so long before he saw her again, he would have found plastic flowers. When he leaves Mimi's death bed, he walks away alone, followed by Baudelaire, and another dog, as we hear a somber ballade about lost youth, in Japanese (Nakata).

Even with Mimi's death, the emotiveness of the acting is tempered, the montage is deliberate and stagey, and the temporal transitions abrupt. Appropriate to the dramatis personae, Kaurismäki takes a place among the Bohemians, having as much fun in the music composition of the film as Schaunard does with his "The Effect of Blue on the Arts," with the cinematographic composition as does Rodolpho with his "Crossing of the Red Sea," and the narrative as does Marcel with his peripatetic conversations with everyone.

What Kaurismäki attempts is not a new telling or re-telling of the story of Munger's Bohemians. The novel provides not the basis for the film but its instigation. There aren't techniques of adaptation so much as instances of rendering the source falsely. Kaurismäki follows his wrong notes, inverts or reverses the tonalities of the original, and this time with the passing homage to the twentieth century serialists—Webern, Berg, and Schoenberg. The loose ends abound, and the sly jokes as well. In the way that serialism is purely intellectual but hardly unemotive music, so the film's humor is intellectual, but hardly dull-witted.

Crime and Punishment *(1983)*

There is no dog in Kaurismaki's adaptation of Dostoevsky's *Crime and Punishment*, but the opening scene features a beetle crawling slowly across a wooden surface, until it's smashed in two by a falling axe. Rahikainen (that is, Raskolnikov) (Marku Toikka) is the one who wields the axe—an accouterment of his job working in an abattoir. He jokes about using an axe later to the detective, but just to taunt him. He murders instead with a pistol, which changes hands and imbues its present owner each time with the urge to kill. Music segues from seemingly non-diegetic to diegetic and back again to non-diegetic. Fragments from Shostakovich's *Fifth Symphony* arise periodically, with accents aligning with significant dramatic point—no more than a few bars at a time, but all from the long, slow build-up of complex harmonic tension that finds release only in the falsely celebratory finale, which does not arise in the film's soundscape. Popular reception of the symphony in Russia in 1937 understood it as a profoundly and relentlessly biting musical critique of Stalinism (Maes 35–45, Volkov 183). Rahikainan's critique of social conscience is as biting. He shows no signs of suffering from guilt. He toys with the police, who are sure he's the culprit and who are also sure that his conscience will eventually compel him to confess. He does confess, but still without pangs of conscience—it's one last step in his endeavor to execute a principle. At one point, when the police are sure to have discovered the telling piece of evidence among the many that he has planted for them to find, he eludes them by attending a performance of Mozart's *Marriage of Figaro*. He leaves at the end of Act II (*"Voi signor, che giusto siete ci dovete ascoltar"*), when it becomes clear that Figaro's machinations are undone and he is cornered to marry against his desire.

But there is no marriage in this story, either. No more than does the facetious resolution of Shostakovich's harmonies resonate in the soundscape, does the dystopian lack of conscience of Rahikainan ever subside, nor in those who handle the gun. Contrary to Dostoevsky's protagonist, Rahikainan finds neither guilt nor reconciliation (Toiviainan 31). His confrontations with Inspector Pennanen Kaurismäki (Esko Nikkari) accomplishes in ostentatious shot-reverse-shot, but from straight on, pointed directly at the actor from each side, rather than normal over-the-shoulder views. The principle of existential isolation and moral indifference that Rahikainan *probes conscientiously* is what he shares with Pennanen. Pennanen believes Rahikainan ultimately wants to confess, needs to confess, and his conscience will irresistibly force him to confess. Professionally, he has that inclination as a matter of experience dealing with crime. But morally, he, too, is indifferent. It's just about doing his job, which intermittently involves coping with a heinous crime. Rahikainan and Pennanen are on equal ground intellectually and morally. As had Rahikainan's encounter with Eeva (Aino Seppo), who witnesses his initial confession at the crime scene but denies it to the police, and the man who takes Rahikainan's gun from her—the mere handling of an instrument of lethal force abrogates ordinary moral dispositions. The police inspector will be the first to experience that from a career coping with witnessing the unconscionable. Ultimately, Rahikainan confesses as his ultimate taunting of Pennanen, showing him up for the lack of authenticity about his own conscience.

The interlinking elements of the dog, Laika, Sam Fuller, rubber ducks, Mozart's *Marriage of Figaro*, the convenience casting of actors indifferent to language barriers, a pistol never wielded with consummate skill, an axe, in addition to a personally preferred style of unhurried, non-perfect montage, and gracefully stilted acting and delivery—these all remind us that it is Aki Kaurismäki who presides over the goofiness. Kaurismäki's adaptation of source texts in these four films revels in the instigation for taking immodest liberties with a well-known text. Any aspect that shows simplistic fidelity to the source text would signal failure to do something interesting. Moreover, all four adaptations easily elicit knowledge of the particulars of the source texts among at least a significant element of the audience who will see the film—*Juha* for Finland, *La vie de Bohème* (either the novel or the Puccini opera) for France (and elsewhere), and *Hamlet* and *Crime and Punishment* internationally. The liberties taken with Juhani and Murger texts are more intricate, in part likely inspired by the author's published encouragement in both cases not to fix upon a clear temporal setting. The delight that the films elicit arises in the framework of that cognizance and in appreciation of the outlandish liberties taken therewith. The targeted audience already knows the source texts sufficiently well to discern Kaurismäki's willful variance, and the wry humor that variance elicits. These films are laced with running gags, loose strings, homages to filmmakers Kaurismäki esteems, but without imitation, and obscure allusions, which not every viewer will get. There are no particular consistencies in these element of construction. Kaurismaki's proliferation of disparate elements and borrowings elicits the perception of a pastiche style (Nestingen 19). Better, though is how each film comprises a particular assemblage of compatible elements which, though, defy unity in the whole. The set of elements of cinematic style is different for each of these four adaptations. Musical selections draw from different traditions, generally not indigenous to the diegetic context, but at times ambiguously diegetic or non-diegetic. But in each case the choice for musical content is specific to the narrative, and not gratuitous. Least of all does it arise that particular musical styles engender a consistent affect (Barkemeyer 21–27). If not from a radio, phonograph, juke box, etc., diegetic music in these films is performed by musicians in front of the camera. What aids the choice of Kari Väänänen as Schaunard in *La vie de bohème* is that he plays piano, as we can see in the two scenes where Schaunard performs at the keyboard. The choices for the entire construction follows what makes sense relative to the adaptation, and not in the least appropriate to the source text.

There are films and filmmakers to offer similar examples, but the best correlate for these four Kaurismäki films lies perhaps in John Coltrane's appropriation of a Rogers and Hammerstein tune, "My Favorite Things." As is expected with jazz, the transformation of the tune into an opportunity for improvisation effectively invents a fabulous cultural setting into which it is launched, its recognizable origin heard turned over a dozen ways and gaining what wasn't there in so much as a trace in the original. And good jazz always makes you smile—as do these four films. It is a warm, engaging, intelligent humor, and completely goofy.

In these and his other films, Kaurismäki wanders off into the possibilities for cinema in Deleuze's crystalline realm. In a related context, Deleuze explicates the creative venture of stuttering for a writer: "When stuttering no longer affects preexisting words, but itself introduces the words it affects ... these words no longer exist independently of the stutter, which selects and links them together through itself" (Deleuze "He Stuttered" 107). For every single moment Kaurismäki's film jars loose expectations of conventional cinematic drama, montage, *mise en scène*, characterizations, use of non-diegetic music, lighting, etc., this is a moment of stuttering. The shot-reverse-shot in *Crime and Punishment* owes nothing to its ubiquitous but nearly invisible affect in conventional scene construction. The indiscernibility between earnest expression and irony in every one of Rodolpho's speeches jars the affect loose in the same way. The snippets of Shostakovich's Fifth Symphony are jarring in every instance. Juha's ridiculously large wrench is jarring, as is the rubber duck that Marja packs into her suitcase. The ever-so-close but separate alignment of soundtrack and image in musical sequences in *Juha* is jarring. The transparently phony rendering of Hamet's father's ghost in faded superimposition is jarring. The construction of faux depth in *La Vie de Bohème* is jarring. Laika is jarring in every appearance for simply not ever being necessary to the scene or narrative. Coltrane's very first intonation of the familiar melody already jars, because already there is something entirely different from the original, which sets us ready to hear the continuous variations that arise in the improvisations that follow. There is creativity in jarring loose, in stuttering, such as Marcel, Rodolpho, and Schaunard admired in those greats of their arts who leveled the traditions that they inherited: "Creative stuttering is what makes language grow from the middle, like grass; it is what makes language a rhizome instead of a tree, what puts language in perpetual disequilibrium" (111).

A film critic, self-identifying as a native New Yorker, and commenting on Cher's performance in *Moonstruck* (1987), recently explained an aversion to an actor not being able to effect a reasonably passable regional/ethnic accent (New York Italian-American, in the case in question), with this analogy: "[It's not] the equivalent of a movie's using a 1948 model car in a movie set in 1946. It was more like having everyone travel by horse and buggy in 1946. It was so wrong as to be a distortion of the movie's world" (Lasalle).

Yes, precisely. It's precisely where that distortion prevails where Kaurismäki dwells.

WORKS CITED

Adams, Ansel. *The Negative. The New Ansel Adams Basic Photography Series/Book 2.* Ed. Robert Baker. New York: New York Graphic Society, 1981. Print.

Aho, Juhani. *Juha.* Trans. Richard A. Impola. New York: Aspasia Books, 2005. Print.

Barkemeyer, Jörn. *Filmmusik bei Aki Kaurismäki: Eine Analyse der Musik und ihrer Verwendung as dramaturgishes Gestaltiungsmittel.* Saarbrücken: Verlag Dr. Müller, 2011. Print.

Berlin, Isaiah. *Karl Marx: Thoroughly Revised Fifth Edition.* Ed. Henry Hardy. Princeton: Princeton University Press, 2013. Print.

Coltrane, John. *My Favorite Things.* New York: Atlantic Records, 1961. Song.

Crime and Punishment. Dir. Aki Kaurismäki. Perf. Markku Toikka, Aino Seppo, Esko Nikkari. Helsinki: Villealfa Filmproduction Oy, 1983. Film.

Deleuze, Gilles. *Cinema 2: The Time-Image.* Trans. Hugh Tomlinson and Robert Galeta. Minneapolis: University of Minnesota Press, 1989. Print.

_____. "He Stuttered." *Essays Critical and Clinical.* Trans. Daniel W. Smith and Michael A. Greco. 107–14. Minneapolis: University of Minnesota Press, 1997, Print.

Dostoevsky, Fyodor. *Crime and Punishment: A Novel in Six Parts with Epilogue.* 1866. Trans. and ann. Richard Pevear and Larissa Volokhonsky. New York: Vintage, 2007. Print.

Goraguer, Alain, composer. *Je bois.* Lyrics by Boris Vian. Song.

Hamlet. Dir. Laurence Olivier. Perf. Olivier, Eileen Herlie, Basil Sydney. Two Cities, 1948. Film.

Hamlet Goes Business (Hamlet liikemaailmassa). Dir. Aki Kaurismäki. Perf. Pirkka-Pekka Petelius, Esko Salminen, Kati Outinen. Helsinki: Villealfa Filmproduction Oy, Finland. 1987. Film.

John, Little Willie, Titus Turner, and James McDougall, songwriters. *Leave My Kitten Alone,* 1959. Song.

Juha. Dir. Aki Kaurismäki, Perf. Sakari Kuosmanen, Kati Outinen (Marja), André Wilms. Sputnik, Finland, 1999. Film.

Lasalle, Mick. "Ask Mick Lasalle." *The San Francisco Chronicle,* 9 Oct. 2016. Web. 20 Mar. 2017.

La Vie de Bohème. Dir. Aki Kaurismäki. Perf. Matti Pellonpää, Evelyne Didi, André Wilms. Paris: Pyramide Productions, Films A2, Pandora Filmproduktion, Svenska Fiminstitutet, 1992. Film.

Le Havre. Dir. Aki Kaurismäki. Sputnik, Pyramide Productions, Pandora Filmproduktion, 2011. Film.

Maes, Francis. *A History of Russian Music: From Kamarinskaya to Babi Yar.* Trans. Arnold J. Pomerans and Erica Pomerans. Berkeley: University of California Press, 2002. Print.

Melnitz, Leo. *The Opera Goer's Complete Guide.* Trans. Richard Salinger. New York: Mead, 1913. Print.

Moonstruck. Dir. Norman Jewison. Perf. Cher, Nicolas Cage. MGM, 1987. Film.

Morreal, John. *Comic Relief: A Comprehensive Philosophy of Humor.* Malden, MA: Wiley-Blackwell, 2009. Print.

Mozart, Wolfgang Amadeus, composer. *Le nozze di Figaro.* Libretto by Lorenzo da Ponte, based on a stage comedy by Pierre Beaumarchais. 1785. Opera.

Murger, Henri. *The Bohemians of the Latin Quarter* [*Scènes de la vie de bohème*]. 1888. Minneapolis: Filiquarian, 2007. Print.

Nakata, Yoshinao, composer. "In the snowing town, only my memories are passing by…" *Yuki no furu machi wo.* Lyrics by Naoya Uchimura, arranged by Toshitake Shinohara, performed by Toshitake Shinohara. Lyricstranslatewww. Web. 10 Jan. 2017.

Nestingen, Andrew K. *The Cinema of Aki Kaurismäki: Contrarian Stories.* Chicago: Wallflower Press, 2014. Print.

_____, ed. *In Search of Aki Kaurismäki: Aesthetics and Contexts.* Special issue *Journal of Finnish Studies.* Dec. 2004. Print.

Puccini, Giacomo, composer. *La bohème*, opera in four acts, 1896, libretto by Giuseppe Giacosa and Luigi Illica, English translation by William Fense Weaver. Opera.

Renard, Antoine, composer; Jean-Baptiste Clement, lyrics, "*Le temps de cerises*," 1866. Song.

Rodgers, Richard, composer, and Oscar Hammerstein, II, lyricist. "My Favorite Things." *The Sound of Music*, 1959. Song.

Samuels, Maurice. "Introduction: Henri Murger, *The Bohemians of the Latin Quarter* [*Scènes de la vie de bohème*]." Trans. Ellen Marriage and John Selwyn. 1–11. Philadelphia: University of Pennsylvania Press, 2003. Print.

Shakespeare, William. *Hamlet*. Ed. Harold Jenkins. Boston: Thomson Learning, 2003. Print.

_____. *Macbeth*. Ed. Sandra Clark and Pamela Mason. 3rd ed. London: Routledge, 2015. Print.

Shostakovich, Dmitri. *Symphony No. 5 in D Minor*, Op. 47, premiered in Leningrad, 1937. Music.

Sous les toits de Paris. Dir. René Clair. Perf. Albert Préjean, Pola Illéry, Edmund T. Gréville. Films Sonores Tobis, 1930. Film.

Throne of Blood (*Kumonosu-jô*). Dir. Akira Kurosawa. Perf. Toshirô Mifune, Isuzu Yamada, Takashi Shimura. Toho Company, Japan, 1957. Film.

Toiviainan, Sakari. "The Kaurismäki Phenomenon." *Journal of Finnish Studies* (Dec. 2004): 20–45. Print.

Vähämäki, Börje." Introduction." *Juha* by Juhani Aho. 8–22. New York: CreateSpace, 2013. Print.

Volkov, Solomon. *Testimony: The Memoirs of Dmitri Shostakovich*. https://en.wikipedia.org/wiki/Solomon_VolkovTrans. Antonina W. Bouis. New York: Harper & Row, 1979. Print.

Werner, Jochen. "Talking Without Words: Aki Kaurismäki's Rediscovery of the Virtues of Cinema." *Journal of Finnish Studies* (Dec. 2004): 69–76. Print.

"This is how I lied about coming up with the idea for writing about *The Brothers Grimm* [2005]"

Incoherent Narration in Terry Gilliam's Adaptation

Wickham Clayton

In the DVD commentary for *The Brothers Grimm*, director Terry Gilliam makes an observation regarding editing a work to cater to a specific audience, which he then unwittingly links to the concept of adaptation:

> One thing that was interesting is, Rapunzel, the girl in the tower, Rapunzel, noticed at one point her ... her clothes had grown too tight around her belly—it's clear, in the original stories that she'd been impregnated by the prince who was crawling up her hair every other day. And the brothers Grimm actually bowdlerized that story in their later editions even though it was in the first edition. They trimmed that story down so the implication that she was pregnant was removed because it would not frighten off the middle-class audience they were appealing to, so I was a bit more for-giving of what Disney had done to the Grimms' fairy tales realizing they had already started that process long before Disney was born.[1]

This reminiscence demonstrates, if not exactly explicates, a significant (though not universal) tendency of viewers knowingly attending a movie adaptation: There is additional pleasure, and even forgiveness, granted to the adaptation that arises from the understanding of its source text.

Maria Tatar expresses the adaptive value and flexibility of fairy-tales: "Beginning in the 1960s, writers with many different agendas rediscovered fairy tales, and they soon recognized that the stories were not written in granite. They were so elastic, malleable, and resilient that they could be stretched and molded into quirky new shapes without losing their narrative mass" (xvi). Gilliam continues this tendency in *The Brothers Grimm* by not only reimagining and reinventing the stories, but also by proving that the origin of these tales differs from the Grimm sources in his own version of adaptation.

Adapting the Legends

The screenplay for *The Brothers Grimm* was originally written by Ehren Kruger, and eventually presented to Gilliam, which he accepted as he needed a project; His attempt at adapting Miguel de Cervantes' *Don Quixote* tragically collapsed as documented in the film *Lost in La Mancha* (2002). According to Gilliam: "[The producer] Chuck [Roven] had been on top of me, obviously pushing me to do 'Grimms' and so I said, 'Okay, I've got to do something.' And reading it I saw I could make an interesting world and maybe if I could rewrite the thing I could make a better film" (qtd. in McCabe 23, emphasis mine). As Gilliam's other potential projects fell through, he continued with *The Brothers Grimm* in spite of his reservations, largely because he felt the material had the potential to match his sensibilities, and he needed to stay in work (McCabe 3–23).

Gilliam's oeuvre up to that point demonstrated that he not only had an aptitude for folklore and adapting fiction,[2] but could freely and loosely use legends and folk stories to add detail to a narrative, whether essential or not. In *Time Bandits* (1981), Gilliam's young protagonist, Kevin (Craig Warnock), encounters historical figures such as Napoleon (Ian Holm) as well as folk tale renderings of historical figures such as Robin Hood (John Cleese) and King Agamemnon (Sean Connery) as well as perhaps the most significant figure in folklore: The Supreme Being (Ralph Richardson). In *The Adventures of Baron Munchausen* (1988), the protagonists encounter such mythical figures as the King and Queen of the Moon (Robin Williams under the pseudonym Ray D. Tutto, Valentina Cortese), the Roman God Vulcan (Oliver Reed), and the Goddess Venus (Uma Thurman). Additionally, in *The Fisher King* (1991), the character of Parry (Robin Williams), a vagrant in New York, conceives himself as a knight in search of the Holy Grail, directly influenced by the legend of King Arthur. The utilization of such myths, legends, and folklore, frequently appear in Gilliam's films. According to Ofir Haivry: "Story-narratives and their preservation are important in all of Gilliam's movies, especially so in *The Brothers Grimm*" (114).

Gilliam's initial reservations regarding the script show an immediate concern for the extent to which the Grimms' stories were included and rendered in the film. Gilliam said: "I thought it was two-dimensional characters chasing a narrative, trying to keep up with a narrative and the stuff just seemed not to be coming from the heart of the piece, which was fairytales and a lot of the things that happen in it were nothing to do with Grimm's fairytales" (qtd. in McCabe 23). These concerns were also stressed by the initial director of photography, Nicola Pecorini[3] who wrote: "I had read the script a little while before and in all truth I fell about laughing. The problem was that it was shallow. It was a well-conceived series of gags but it completely missed the point, and Terry's works are fantastic simply because of the incredible depth (or height) that he manages to reach" (qtd. in McCabe 20). However, Pecorini's diary also reveals the initial approach to the adaptation of these stories: "Spent the day with Terry: went through a lot of 'visual references' mostly romantic, strong lights where you need to see, black on black for the rest" (qtd. in McCabe 29).

It therefore becomes apparent that Gilliam demonstrates significant commitment to the source material, not necessarily in a reverential sense, but by revering the fairy tales as integral to any story about the Grimms. However, his methods do not necessarily incorporate these specific adaptations as separate from the narrative; the decision to use Robin Hood and the Goddess Venus could have been altered to accommodate other prominent mythological figures. However, their relevance exists inasmuch as they provide material for rich fantastical detail, and illuminate Gilliam's preoccupation with legendary forms. His approach, particularly with *The Brothers Grimm*, becomes one of referencing these tales. In closely analyzing the film itself, we can see how this was realized in practice.

Todd Berliner once described the experience of Terry Gilliam's *Brazil* (1985), as Gilliam "grabbing you by the ear and saying 'let's go for a walk.'"[4] I mention this as I feel it is descriptive of Gilliam's oeuvre—his films are quite narratively dense and complex, and elude simple, high-concept summarizing. With that in mind, I will assess the value of Gilliam's adaptive methods as succinctly as possible.

Jacob "Jake" and Wilhelm "Will" Grimm (Heath Ledger, Matt Damon) are brothers who run a unique confidence scam. Jake, a bookish academic, has heavily researched local folklore, and is keeping a notebook of what he learns and finds. With this knowledge, he and Will, the confident mouthpiece of the brothers, find out about local superstitions, and stage performances whereby they claim to rid the area of whatever supernatural threat frightens them. However, the invading French army discover their scam and threaten their lives. Local French representative, General Delatombe (Jonathan Pryce) and his highest-ranking subordinate, Cavaldi (Peter Stormare), threaten them, but agree to let them go if they will solve the mystery of young girls disappearing from a local village. Jake becomes convinced that the folk tale that this problem appears to be based upon is actually rooted in the supernatural. They must then figure out how to save the girls and the village, destroy the threat, and evade the retribution of Delatombe.

Peppered throughout the narrative, there are references to a myriad of folk tales, Grimm stories, and well-known adaptations thereof. Of the more recognizable stories referenced, viewers are treated to references to and renderings of "Little Red Riding Hood" (Grimm and Grimm 146–55); "Hansel and Gretel" (Grimm and Grimm 72–85) (called Hans and Greta in the film); "Snow White" (Grimm and Grimm 246–61); "Cinderella" (Grimm and Grimm 119–33); "Rapunzel" (Grimm and Grimm 54–62); and "The Gingerbread Man." Some of these were recorded by the Grimms, and others are part of our own contemporary folklore, but altogether they provide a mosaic of familiarity that can tap into the viewers' collective childhood. This can be evinced through Gilliam's *mise en scène*: at one point, an old lady in a black cloak (Fero Velecky) knocks on the door of a hut, and offers the person who opens it a bright red apple. Although the intent and context of this is not provided, it conjures precise visual and narrative details from *Snow White and the Seven Dwarfs* (1937). Of this, Gilliam says: "This, the old crone coming to the door, was just something I threw in at the last moment with a red apple, because I knew all the children, the minute they saw, they would say: '[gasps] It's … it's Snow White!' There's a… there's a bit of that in the film, putting characters or little moments in that kids would recognize from all the Disney films that they saw" (qtd. in *The Brothers Grimm* DVD commentary). Gilliam reinforces Pecorini's earlier statement: the film can not only be seen as a palimpsest of adaptations of stories by the Brothers Grimm, but also an adaptation of adaptations of these stories.

However, unlike this brief reference that occurs before the scene proper begins, many of the other references are included in significant portions of the narrative. The actual supernatural threat is rife with selected segments of various fairy tales. A Thuringian queen (Monica Bellucci), centuries ago, used black magic to attain eternal life. However, the spell she used did not result in her retention of youth and beauty, but for a reflection in a mirror. The Mirror Queen, as she is also known, is secured in a high tower. In order to regain her youth and beauty, she must drink the blood of twelve young girls. It is the disappearance of girls from the local village that provides the impetus for Will's and Jake's investigation. Helping in her quest is a huntsman (Tomás Hanák) who is also a lycanthrope, to whom she demonstrates romantic favor, yet has mystified to elicit devotion. Her power apparently lies in the mirror which retains the semblance of her beauty, and only by destruction of her mirror is she vanquished.

The Mirror Queen becomes a distinct reference to the wicked queen in 'Snow White' who frequently looks at her reflection in a magic mirror. In the story, the queen asks, "Mirror, mirror, on the wall, / Who's the fairest one of all?" (Grimm and Grimm 250).[5] The mirror, for a time tells the Queen she is, until Snow White surpasses her in fairness. It is therefore relevant that the mirror in *The Brothers Grimm* reflects the youth and beauty of the queen. In the story, the Queen asks a huntsman to kill Snow White, yet the huntsman can't bring himself to perform the act, letting Snow White go. This then is manifested in the film by the werewolf hunter who aids the Queen.

Additionally, the Mirror Queen's residence in an isolated tower is an explicit reference to the story of Rapunzel. In this story, a princess is locked in a tall tower, and is visited by her true love, a prince. The princess, Rapunzel, grows her hair out so long that the prince is able to use it to climb up the tower to visit her. In the film, the Mirror Queen, over the centuries, has grown her hair incredibly long, and it is implied that the hunter uses this to climb up into the tower to visit the Queen, and in a darkly comic sequence, Jacob attempts a quick escape by using the hair impulsively to support himself as he jumps out the window. Unfortunately, the hair rips, and while his fall is softened, Jake becomes covered in a long stream of hair upon landing.

Two stories that have not been attributed to the Brothers Grimm are also integral to the narrative: "Jack and the Beanstalk" and "The Gingerbread Man." In the former, a young boy, Jack, sells the family's cow for magic beans, which initially seems to be a scam that could leave the family destitute. However, the beans grow a giant beanstalk, which Jack climbs to discover a rich giant who he can steal from to support his family. "The Gingerbread Man" is the story of, conveniently, a gingerbread man who attains sentience and must elude those who want to eat him. In *The Brothers Grimm*, the gingerbread man is a magic creature made from mud in a well, who manages to consume a young girl from the village in disguise as a boy, and deliver her to the Queen, providing the eleventh young girl needed by the Queen to attain her youth and beauty; the final being Anjelika (Lena Headey), the local hunter and tracker enlisted to help the Grimms and later revealed to be the daughter of the hunter/werewolf. The story of "Jack and the Beanstalk" is the first reference introduced in the film, as young Jake uses money intended for the purchase of medicine for their ailing sister for "magic beans," and act which young Will viciously berates him for. This is apparent as a mistake as opposed to mystical intervention as it is later revealed their sister died. This event significantly informs the relationship between the brothers, and often becomes a point of resurfaced tension, with the practically-minded Will continually challenging Jake on his lingering idealistic belief in the fantastic, and the veracity of elements of the folklore he researches.

The Grimm short stories are adapted into the film in a manner that is integral and inextricably linked to the overall narrative. This provides a challenging level of narrative complexity, whereby elements traditionally used for style, flavor, or amusement are intricately bound to the story itself—viewers dismiss these references at their own peril. However, many more elements from these and other stories are referenced and adapted within the film in less significant ways. Even so, they manage to establish and create a strong sense of this universe where the folklore contains a certain amount of veracity, if not wholly accurate.

Much of this centers around the supernatural problem that the Grimms are attempting to solve. The first kidnapping that is shown in the film is of a little girl in a red cape and hood (Alena Jakobová), picking food in the forest before being chased and captured just before she can reach the village. This strongly alludes to "Little Red Riding Hood," which is later shown in Jake's notebook, as he writes "Little Red Riding Cape." The next kidnapping shown as two children are shown in the forest, leaving bread crumbs in an attempt to prevent getting lost. The girl refers to the boy as "Hans" (Martin Svetlik), and the boy calls the girl "Greta" (Denisa Vokurkova)—an obvious reference to "Hansel and Gretel."

In addition to the shot containing the witch with the red apple, other elements of "Snow White," appear throughout the film. For instance, The Mirror Queen uses blackbirds such as crows and ravens as familiars, which is more precisely linked to *Snow White and the Seven Dwarfs*. References to "Cinderella" make an appearance, once when Cavaldi refers to the brothers, while they are cleaning, as "little Cinderellas," and in a sequence where the hunter lays Sasha's body in the ground and makes glass slippers appear on her feet as part of the ceremonial burial he provides for them. The hunter's lycanthropy creates a link to the Grimm story "Little Red Riding Hood," wherein the young girl in the red cloak is pursued by a wolf, an event which is, of a fashion, rendered in the first shown kidnapping sequence. The fact that the wolf turns into the hunter, whose weapon of choice is an axe echoes the same story whereby the wolf is dispatched by a hunter with a hatchet. Like both "Sleeping Beauty" (not a Grimm story) and "Snow White," Anjelika is brought back to consciousness from a kiss by Jake, and in turn, Will is brought back to life by a kiss from Anjelika. For guidance into and out of the forest which is constantly changing, and therefore unreliable for travelling by landmarks, Anjelika, and later Will, ask a frog for directions, and in order to get the frog to comply, they must lick it, being a direct reference to "The Frog King, or Iron Heinrich" (Grimm and Grimm 3–13).

The queen's need to drink the blood of the girls to regain her youth is suggestive of the story of Countess Elizabeth Bathory, a 16th- and 17th-century Hungarian countess who it is believed, with the help of others, killed hundreds of young girls. Folk tales have utilized her story, and it has been frequently rendered in modern culture such as in the film *Countess Dracula* (1971), and the novel *Dracula, the Un-Dead*. (Stoker and Holt)[6] In folk tales as well as in modern retellings, the Countess bathed in and/or drank the blood of the young girls to either retain or regain her youth and beauty. Although this is not based on a Grimm story, this further demonstrates the range of folk tales, legends, and myths adapted within the film.

But Is It "Adaptation"?

Hitherto I have used the terms "reference" and "adapt" almost interchangeably. I hereby posit that, within the parameters of *The Brothers Grimm*, the references to fairy tales, folk stories, myths, and legends, whether addressed by the (real) Grimms or not, can be conceived of as forms of adaptation. There is work and research to support this position, and, based on my own analysis of the film, is essential to understanding the value of narrative explication as well as the cyclical relationship between the source, the adaptation, and the imagined sources of adaptation.

Thomas Leitch provides a useful starting-point in discerning whether Gilliam's renderings of these fairy tales can be regarded as adaptations. He creates a scale consisting of ten "strategies" (123) of appropriation, which he describes as "between adaptation and allusion" (92) in an attempt "to develop a more detailed grammar that would either break down adaptation into non-evaluative modes ... or at least provide a stronger rationale for the difference between intertextual and hypertextual relations." (95) I will draw on Leitch's ideas in my analysis of *The Brothers Grimm*, thereby creating an understanding of the adaptive processes which Gilliam undertakes.

The first strategy which can be applied is termed *revisions* (106). Leitch writes: "Unlike adaptations that aim to be faithful to the spirit rather than the letter of the text, however, revisions seek to alter the spirit as well" (106–07). Gilliam utilizes this strategy with most of the fairy tales that are integral to the narrative or explored in depth. The Queen from "Snow White,"; the composite wolf from "Little Red Riding Hood" and hunter from "Snow White"; the magic beans from "Jack and the Beanstalk" as well as the frog from "The Frog Prince"; and the eponymous Gingerbread Man"—all have been revised to accommodate specific points in the narrative while utilizing a substantial number of elements from the source texts. Despite their brevity, I would also include the references to "Rapunzel" and the Báthory legend as they inform both the efforts of the protagonists as well as the motivations of the antagonists.

On the far end of Leitch's spectrum, there is *allusion*, which he perceives as "quotations from or references to any earlier text" (121). The strategy overtly applies to the passing shot of the "crone" with the red apple, and Will's initial proposition to play "Who's the Fairest of them All" with the twin village girls before the queen is introduced. This extends to the inclusion of the glass slippers from "Cinderella," and can even be arguably applied to the inclusion of the girl from "Little Red Riding Hood" running from apparent danger, and the children from "Hansel and Gretel." Leitch's framing of allusion as opposite to adaptation, in terms of textual engagement, problematizes my claim of references as forms of adaptation. Leitch does not wholly dismiss allusion as adaptation, but appears to deem it adaptation of a minimal nature. Linda Hutcheon addresses this manner of text quotation when she poses the question "What is *not* an adaptation?" (170). She answers this question by invoking the following conditions: "[D]efining an adaptation as an extended, deliberate, announced revisitation of a particular work of art does manage to provide some limits: short intertextual allusions to other works or bits of sampled music would not be included" (ibid.). I would argue that, if we take Hutcheon's definition, *The Brothers Grimm* retains some plausibility as an adaptation or even a series and/or collection of adaptations. The title creates the expectation that, even without knowing the narrative, there will be references throughout to the tales they have written. This, therefore, makes the various references both announced and deliberate. What's more, they are subject to variation from the source texts. Hutcheon speculates that "perhaps the real comfort [in engaging with an adaptation] lies in the simple act of almost but not quite repeating, in the revisiting of a theme with variations" (115).

Furthermore, some of these references fall firmly within the realm of parody. Hutcheon asserts that "what we might, by analogy, call the adaptive faculty is the ability to repeat without copying, to embed difference in similarity" (174). The stories are consistently altered as part of a cyclical method of variance and fabrication. This cycle moves from the events in the film, to the familiarity with the stories themselves, and returning to the events as invented by the director. This, then, leads me to address one of Leitch's systems of textual engagement which provides a significant overall framework for how *The Brothers Grimm* is founded structurally upon other texts.

Holding the multiplicity of adaptations and allusions to the (real) Grimms' fairy tales together is an underlying sub-narrative about the research the Brothers have undertaken for their folk stories. This, in many ways, falls in with what Leitch calls "*(meta)commentary and deconstruction*" (111). This constitutes the framework of the film: Jake researches and takes notes on folk tales, recording them in a notebook which is framed as narratively significant. At one point, the film emotionally engages viewers by leading them to believe that the notebook has been destroyed in a forest fire. Although Will uses this knowledge for monetary gain and self-preservation, these schemes are not linked to stories with which the viewer would be familiar. Jake outright claims familiarity with some of the folk stories that much of the supernatural events are based upon. This knowledge will eventually, once the credits roll, manifest itself in the form of the stories we are now familiar with. It is this knowledge that renders all textual allusions in *The Brothers Grimm* important—although they may seem narratively superfluous, they assume a metafictional significance, as they result in the fairy tales that viewers are familiar with. It is here that we experience an adaptational form of electronic feedback: viewers experience a uniquely cyclical adaptive process, whereby they watch an adaptation of fairy tales that the characters have adapted for the viewers. The fictional source of adaptation is actually the adaptation of the stories with which the viewer is already familiar. Lars Elleström delineates two different kinds of representation: "Representations of media may be marginal and brief, but they may also be crucial and elaborate or anything in between. I call the former representations 'simple,' the latter 'complex.'"(120) As "anything in between" can succinctly describe the range of representation, it would be safe to say that, based on Elleström's definition, *The Brothers Grimm* comprises a complex representation of a body of fairy tale texts, and the complexity is compounded by this unusual dynamic between the source texts, the on-screen events, and the implied off-screen events.

Jamie Sherry writes of a type of adaptation that consists of "the usurping of source material through palimpsestic rewriting, in which the subsequent adaptation either gains status and cultural value over the original text, or significantly infiltrates readings of it" (375). An element of this exists in *The Brothers Grimm*, but in a regressive form. Instead of overwriting the adaptation or even an adaptation of the process of adapting Grimm's fairy tales, Gilliam seems to palimpsestically rewrite the concept of the source text. The film's representation of the early stages of adaptation is, in fact, the adaptation. And while the argument could be made that what is represented is an actualized rendition of the stories the Grimms already researched in the film, I am arguing that, ultimately, what we see is the actual source of those folk tales.

At the same time, *The Brothers Grimm* sits uneasily with the concept of the (meta)commentary or deconstruction. No actual attempts at adaptation occur onscreen. However, everything that occurs is part of the process of adaptation: we witness Jake researching folk stories, rereading and writing notes, and observing the mystical occurrences in the story. The viewer's knowledge of the existence of the Grimms' stories, whether they know the Grimms wrote them or not, leads the viewer to realize that this will lead to the recording of the story in written fairy tale form. The film, though, ends before the process of writing actually occurs, and therefore claiming it is a story about the process of adaptation is uncomfortable. Therefore, the narrative excludes a representation of the actual writing of the tales, while leaving the film relating uneasily to the strategy of (meta)commentary or deconstruction. This creates a vast amount of ambiguity as to whether Jake and/or Will recorded and published the versions of the original tales they heard or radically altered their own experiences prior to publication. The suggestion that they had not yet published the tales is supported by the fact that the notebook, which is saved at the end, only contains the notes pertaining to the tales they would later write. This redaction, between the events that the viewer witnesses onscreen and the real-life existence of the stories, along with the implication that Jake will be the one to write the stories, is significant. It is this element of the narration which demonstrates Gilliam's unique approach to this unusual system of (meta)commentary or deconstruction. It is also this elliptical exclusion of the process of adaptation that informs the extent to Gilliam's control of the narration, and the innovative manner in which the film functions on a cognitive level.

Coherence through Incoherent Narration

In looking at how this approach to adaptation works both narratively and cognitively, it would be useful to look at a theory put forward by Regina Schober. She writes: "I propose a view of intermediality that emphasizes the dynamic, reciprocal and relational nature of media adaptations as opposed to traditional approaches built on the presupposition of clear-cut medial borders and unidirectional cause and effect relationships." (91) Alex Symons describes "intermediality" thus: "In concise terms, I define an intermedial text as a text produced in one medium that includes content appropriated from another medium, and that exhibits characteristics of both" (32). A very close relationship exists between Schober's and Symons' definitions; in translating stories, information, and ideas across media, the resultant text bears strong imprints from the media of its source. However, Schober's definition breaks down clear lines surrounding these media as well as the media of related sources and texts. While traditional definitions of adaptation are often rooted in the literary, the work of Hutcheon and Leitch manage to open up this discussion to include an array of different media. However, these definitions of adaptation, aren't as centrally modeled on the blurring of the lines between media as the way intermediality is presented here.

Schober's described model is that of networking, utilizing comparisons with information technology and linked electronic informational resources. "Following this network logic," Schober writes, "effects cannot be clearly allocated to particular causes because action occurs in the collaboration and interaction of different agents" (104). Gilliam appears to be reliant upon an additional aspect that Schober implicitly suggests: the manner in which the information that the viewer has going in to the film informs the way in which the narrative itself is constructed. I argue that fundamentally *The Brothers Grimm* is a thoroughly incoherent text, which only manages to seem coherent due to viewer involvement.

Todd Berliner, in his work on narration in Seventies Hollywood movies, primarily addresses incoherence, not in its common metaphoric sense of irrationality or meaninglessness "but rather in the literal sense to mean a lack of connectedness or integration among different elements" (25). Many "seventies films frustrate straightforward narration and avoid fulfilling narrative promises in conventionally satisfying ways" (53). This is precisely the type of incoherence present within *The Brothers Grimm*. Most precisely, significant narrative information seems either absent, or explained much later on, or not explained at all. While it is admittedly a challenge to keep up with this narrative, it doesn't feel disjointed, because significant narrative links are reliant upon viewer familiarity with the fairy-tales.

At the opening of the film, where Jake produces the "magic beans," in an allusion to "Jack and the Beanstalk," the sequence appears as a silly and unusual act. To decode it Gilliam places extreme reliance on the viewers' familiarity with this tale, so that he can use the incident, within the first few minutes of the film, to explain the difference in the brothers' personalities.

Gilliam relies on similar knowledge, even though explanations appear later on. The sequence where Little Red Riding Hood is chased by the werewolf/hunter, only makes complete sense retrospectively—the assumption on the part of the viewer that the girl is being chased by a wolf is developed through sound design. When we later see the hunter lose his lycanthropic disguise, it demonstrates to the characters that they are facing something supernatural, and that the creature who is attacking the girls possesses human sentience, even if it is being mesmerically influenced.

Significant plot points appear to lack motivation. Cavaldi encourages Jake to revive the seemingly dead Anjelika with a kiss, and she in turn brings Will to life in the same way. Again Gilliam does not utilize screen time on plot-points which could appear narratively stilted and unnecessary, but relies on the viewers' familiarity with stories such as "Snow White" and "Sleeping Beauty" to act as a facilitator so that the ending provides a natural, and even expected, solution to the problem of two major characters being killed. Terry Gilliam has stated that he wanted to place many references to the fairy tales throughout *The Brothers Grimm*, as a source of pleasure for the viewers. My argument here is that much of Gilliam's use of references could be considered allusions as they are wholly integral to the overarching narrative effect of the film, though this occurs on a very basic, foundational level. This particular text is valuable for study as it creates a significant and distinctive conceptualization surrounding the use and relevance of adapting fairy tales, and how this process of adaptation can be used as a narrative tool. Familiarity with these stories does not preclude clear anticipation of the mode of adaptation, and Gilliam, thinking around this process within his depiction of it, creates a complex film, and creates a re-conception—a fanciful one, at that—of where these stories originated. Also, that these stories are commonly known is utilized to create sense and meaning out of a narrative that is largely incoherent, and therein lies the value of the myriad adaptations in *The Brothers Grimm*. The adaptations themselves, and even (sometimes especially) the allusions bear the significant narrative function of linking and connecting the seemingly disparate and incoherent elements of narrative.

NOTES

1. This is verified by Tatar (60, note 11).
2. See *Jabberwocky* (1977).
3. Pecorini was a regular Gilliam collaborator who was fired from the project by executive producers Bob and Harvey Weinstein of Miramax/Dimension.
4. This is paraphrased, as this occurred in 2001 and my precise memory may not be what it once was. However, I believe it is very close, and it is well within the spirit of the comment. The lecture was delivered as part of an undergraduate Film Studies course at the University of North Carolina–Wilmington.
5. This line is directly referenced in the film, as Will, a philanderer, meets two village girls, twin sisters, at a celebration following their staged destruction of a witch. Jake declines the opportunity to woo the girl of his choice, and Will turns with one arm around each, saying, "Let's play a game: it's called 'Who's the Fairest of Them All?'"
6. To see how both fact and myth are difficult to delineate with regards to Báthory, see Thomas, "The Secret," 38–43.

WORKS CITED

The Adventures of Baron Munchausen. Dir. Terry Gilliam. Perf. John Neville, Eric Idle, Sarah Bailey. 1988. Sony Pictures Home Entertainment (USA), 2005. DVD.
Berliner, Todd. *Hollywood Incoherent: Narration in Seventies Cinema.* Austin: University of Texas Press, 2010. Print.
Brazil. Dir. Terry Gilliam. Perf. Jonathan Pryce, Kım Greist, Robert de Niro. Embassy International, 1985. Film.
The Brothers Grimm. Dir. Terry Gilliam. Perf. Matt Damon, Heath Ledger. 2005. Dimension Home Video (USA), 2005. DVD.
Cervantes, Miguel de. *The Adventures of Don Quixote.* Trans. J.M. Cohen. Harmondsworth: Penguin, 1963. Print.
Countess Dracula. Dir. Peter Sasdy. Perf. Ingrid Pitt, Nigel Green, Sandor Elès. 1971. Network Home Entertainment (UK), 2006. DVD.
Elleström, Lars. "Adaptation within the Field of Media Transformations." *Adaptation Studies: New Challenges, New Directions.* Ed. Jørgen Bruhn, Anne Gjelsvik, and Eirik Frisvold Hanssen. 113–32. London: Bloomsbury. 2013. Print.
The Fisher King. Dir. Terry Gilliam. Perf. Robin Williams, Jeff Bridges, Adam Bryant. 1991. Sony Pictures Home Entertainment, 1999. DVD.
Grimm, Jacob, and Wilhelm Grimm. *The Annotated Brothers Grimm: The Bicentennial Edition.* Ed. and trans. Maria Tatar. New York: Norton, 2012. Print.
Haivry, Ofir. "'It shall be a nation': Terry Gilliam's Exploration of National Identity, Between Rationalism and Imagination." *It's a Mad World: The Cinema of Terry Gilliam.* Ed. Jeff Birkenstein, Anna Froula, and Karen Randell. 104–17. London: Wallflower, 2013. Print.
Hutcheon, Linda. *A Theory of Adaptation.* Abingdon: Routledge. 2006. Print.
Jabberwocky, Dir. Terry Gilliam. Perf. Mıchael Palin, Harry H. Corbett. John le Mesurier. 1977. Sony Pictures Home Entertainment (UK), 2003. DVD.
Leitch, Thomas. *Film Adaptation and its Discontents: From 'Gone with the Wind' to 'The Passion of the Christ.'* Baltimore: Johns Hopkins University Press, 2007. Print.
Lost in La Mancha. Dir. Keith Fulton and Louis Pepe. Perf. Terry Gilliam, Johnny Depp, Jeff Bridges. 2002. Optimum Releasing (UK), 2003. DVD.

McCabe, Bob. *Dreams and Nightmares: Terry Gilliam, The Brothers Grimm, and Other Cautionary Tales of Hollywood*. London: HarperCollins, 2005. Print.

Schober, Regina. "Adaptation as Connection: Transmediality Reconsidered." *Adaptation Studies: New Challenges, New Directions*. Ed. Jørgen Bruhn, Anne Gjelsvik, and Eirik Frisvold Hanssen. 99–112. London: Bloomsbury, 2013. Print.

Sherry, Jamie. "Paratextual Adaptation: *Heart of Darkness* as *Hearts of Darkness* via *Apocalypse Now*." *A Companion to Literature, Film, and Adaptation*. 374–90. Ed. Deborah Cartmell. Malden, MA: Wiley-Blackwell, 2012. Print.

Short, Sue. *Fairy Tale and Film: Old Tales with a New Spin*. Basingstoke: Palgrave Macmillan, 2015. Print.

Snow White and the Seven Dwarfs. Dir. William Cottrell, David Hand, Wilfred Jackson, Larry Morey, Perce Pearce, Ben Sharpsteen. 1937. Walt Disney Studios Home Entertainment, 2009. DVD.

Stoker, Dacre and Ian Holt. *Dracula the Un-Dead*. London: HarperCollins, 2009. Print.

Symons, Alex. *Mel Brooks in the Cultural Industries: Survival and Prolonged Adaptation*. Edinburgh: Edinburgh University Press, 2012. Print.

Tatar, Maria. "Preface: Magical and Mythical—Two Hundred Years of the Brothers Grimm." In Jacob Grimm and Wilhelm Grimm, *The Annotated Brothers Grimm: The Bicentennial Edition*. Ed and Trans. Maria Tatar. xv–xxi. New York: Norton, 2012. Print.

Thomas, Sean. "Bathory Redux." *Thetoffeewomble*. Oct. 2009. Web. 27 Nov. 2013.

_____. "The Secret of the Bloody Countess." *Fortean Times* 223 (June 2007): 38–43. Print.

Time Bandits. Dir. Terry Gilliam. Perf. Sean Connery, Shelley Duvall, John Cleese. 1981. The Criterion Collection (USA), 1999. DVD.

Towards a Method
for Negotiating
Adaptation versus Allusion

CHRISTOPHER WYDLER

Historically, intertextuality has been the basis for determining the difference between an allusion and adaptation. In *Film Adaptation and its Discontents* (2007), Thomas Leitch demands the field of adaptation to reevaluate the negotiation between the two. Leitch presents ten strategies that use intertexts to categorize and construct a "logical progression from faithful adaptation to allusion" (123). Yet Leitch also notes these strategies are "embarrassingly fluid" (123). Given the variety of allusions in popular texts, a more sustained method of categorizing adaptations might be needed. For example, the television show *Gotham* (2014) knowingly draws its authority from the comic book character Batman, as acknowledged in every episode from the credit line "Based on characters created by Bob Kane and Bill Finger." Yet, the episode entitled "Lovecraft," offers a paratextual link to the horror writer H. P. Lovecraft. On the surface, this can be read as an allusion; however, a more sustained analysis of the episode that follows suggests the Lovecraft reference assumes more value than just an allusion. Readers of *Gotham* would do well to consider the television show as adaptations that operate in a narrative dichotomy. Though *Gotham* is based on characters published by Detective Comics (DC), the competing Lovecraft narrative blurs the line between adaptation and allusion. This dichotomy in *Gotham* presents a suitable case study to challenge how we categorize or identify allusions within an adaptive text. The Lovecraft narrative in *Gotham* is consciously suppressed in favor of the associations to the Batman material. Therefore, I argue that different ideologies regarding allusions versus adaptation dictate how we assign value to an adaptive text. I argue at length that the "Lovecraft" narrative presented in *Gotham* aligns itself to Lovecraft's "Herbert West-Reanimator." I use this example to try and distinguish the different values attributed to allusion and adaptation.

It is no surprise that *Gotham* is an adaptation of the famed Caped Crusader and Dark Knight Batman. *Gotham* opened its pilot episode with the dramatic scene of Bruce Wayne's parents (Grayson McCouch and Brette Taylor) being murdered in a dark alley, arguably the quintessential piece of narrative retelling for any adaptation. Only *Gotham* does not focus on Bruce (David Mazouz) and his *alter ego* as the main protagonist. Instead, the narrative concentrates on Jim Gordon (Ben McKenzie) the future commissioner of Gotham Police Department. While the adaptation does not solely focus on Batman, it highlights the white knight aspects of Gordon's character. For example, in the first siting of Gordon we see creates an inherent juxtaposition to the more familiar Dark Knight. The camera adopts a tilted angle, capturing Gordon as a quasi-saint sent from heaven to save Gotham. Gordon wearing white reinforces this reading and a fantasy sequence comprised of a medium long shot where light eddies through a window above Gordon's head, resembling a halo. *Batman* readers are witnessing a more innocent and liberal Jim Gordon reminiscent of the comic *Year One* (1987).[1] Nonetheless, Gordon's character is completely differentiated from that of Bruce. When the detectives Gordon and Harvey Bullock (Donal Logue) initially arrive on the Waynes' murder scene, light reflects off an alley wall above Gordon as if he is surrounded by a halo. In contrast, light is absent in close up shots of Bruce foreshadowing the transformation of the boy into the Dark Knight. The lighting in this scene reflects a clash of personalities between Bruce and Gordon that recalls the plot lines of the comics.

The Batman mythos has engaged with Lovecraft texts since "Batman #258" (1974) through the location of Arkham Asylum. The term "Arkham" is a Lovecraft creation. Arkham is a fictional town in New England featured in Lovecraft's *Cthulhu Mythos*. In Lovecraft's shared fiction universe, Arkham is also the home to the Miskatonic University. Herbert West studies at Miskatonic and engages in many of his experiments there in "Reanimator." In DC comics, the insane asylum Arkham derives its name from Lovecraft's creation. The inception of Arkham came about during the Bronze Age[2] of comics where narratives became more socially relevant and took darker turns. Arkham Asylum can be considered a staple of the Batman mythos. By Batman mythos, I am referring to the comic titles associated with the Batman family and Gotham City.[3] In the Batman mythos, Arkham is a fictional psychiatric hospital that has housed Batman's rogue's gallery including the Joker, Harley Quinn, Killer Croc, Mr. Freeze, the Mad Hatter, "Two-Face" Harvey Dent, the Riddler, and the Scarecrow. Lovecraft serves two surface purposes in *Gotham*: a title of the tenth episode of the first season and the character Dick

Lovecraft (Al Sapienza). While the presence of Lovecraft and Arkham are evident in *Gotham*, it should be understood it is more than a coincidence. In the foreword to *The Dark Age* (2006), a now-defunct publication from DC, editor Jack C. Harris confirms Lovecraft's Arkham as the source of the Arkham Asylum (5). Likewise, in "The Madness of Arkham Asylum" (2008), Paul Lytle also confirms "Arkham was named after H. P. Lovecraft's infamous city, which Lovecraft himself described as 'with-cursed' and legend-haunted" (111). Not only is Arkham a mystifying place, but it is also considered to be a site of change in reaction to the traditionalist movements in comics of the Eighties. For example, in *Super-History: Comic Book Superheroes and American Society* (2012), comic book scholar Jeffery Johnson argues that Arkham Asylum was perceived as an alternative to the conservative heroes and signals "the willingness to embrace new ideas and understandings" (153). Many of the new ideas Johnson is referring to are themes explored in Bronze Age Batman narratives including the psyche of Batman in Miller's *Year One* and Grant Morrison's *Batman: Arkham Asylum* (1989). Morrison's *Arkham Asylum* treated Batman's villains as mirrored versions of the cape-crusader. In *Gotham*, the second half of the first season makes a similar narrative change by shifting from setting to the characters. The episode "Lovecraft" initiates a paratext that prompts us to acknowledge H. P. Lovecraft's influence in the adaptation. It is the narratives outside the Batman mythos that are most compelling to the study of adaptation, in light of the fact that *Gotham* may be borrowing more from Lovecraft than simply the name of the famed Asylum.

It is the competing narratives at work in *Gotham* that are most valuable. The dichotomy in *Gotham* generates a contrast between composite Batman narratives and "Herbert West—Reanimator." Using these texts as a guide, we will try and understand the different values attributed to adaptation and allusion. In *A Theory of Adaptation* (2006), Linda Hutcheon argues adaptations are multifaceted and operate in various dimensions. By design, an adaptation's connection to multiple works postulates the identity of the adaptive text. Hutcheon asserts that: "in all cases, the engagements with these other works in adaptations are extended ones, not passing allusions" (21). By comparison, Leitch questions the validity of attempting to categorize adaptations through an exclusive intertextual lens. Leitch maintains that intertextuality is a problematic tool in classifying or categorizing adaptations because intertexts do not "adequately demarcate the frontiers of adaptation, the places it shades off into allusion" (94). While Hutcheon maintains the adaptive text engages all intertexts, Leitch argues that "categorical discussions of adaptation ignore these problems entirely by privileging a small number of intertextual relations as exemplary of all adaptation and passing over others in silence" (95). In other words, an intertextual reading of adaptations may overlook some references in a text while favoring others. Reading adaptations through intertexts can be pleasurable, but also frustrating, depending on the readers' experience with the competing narratives at play. Where Hutcheon and Leitch differ in their theories of reading adaptations through intertexts is in their assumption of a knowledgeable reader. Distinguishing allusion from adaptation becomes a matter of subjectivity and reader recognition.

Given the frequency of allusions in popular texts, a more sustainable method of distinguishing between adaptation and allusion is required. Conventionally speaking the allusion is of scant value; it refers mostly to past references in literary texts. Then there are conventional allusions; references that spring to readers' mind even before they are mentioned in texts. Robert Stam *et al* define an allusion as "taking form of a verbal or visual evocation of another film, hopefully as an expressive means of commenting of the fictional world of the alluding film" (*New Vocabularies* 211). Whether comprehended by readers or not, the allusion is basically an inference, often taken for granted by readers. The problem with this definition of allusion is that it overlooks the allusion's relation to an adaptation. If one allusion is followed by another allusion in a text, then the allusions might be redefined as intertexts. An adaptation on the other hand resides in a narrative, the whole of a text, and hence assumed a superior status. Nonetheless Robert Stam's scholarship on adaptation and intertextual dialogism only complicates the relationship between adaptation and allusion. According to Stam, intertextual dialogism exists in the conception of the adaptation as "every text forms an intersection of textual surfaces" ("Beyond Fidelity" 64). Intertextual dialogism is open-ended and can generate an infinite number of readings. While the concept of intertextual dialogism has been instrumental in reshaping the study of fidelity in adaptations, the concept is problematic in practice. Leitch finds contention in the concept because intertextual dialogism is too much associated with allusions; in other words, the meaning is dependent on the readers' experiences. Although I agree with Leitch that intertextual dialogism can be problematic, I would argue for a model that takes into account the multifaceted nature of the cinema and television aesthetic. I propose a model that considers three essential rules that could guide the reading of an adaptation and determine the value distinction between adaptation and allusion.

The model I propose relies on a comparative analysis of plot and stylistic language between texts. The parameters of this model I am suggesting take into account derivation of plot, the replication of textual identifiers, and a proliferation of stylistic identifiers translated in the adaptive aesthetic. Adaptation scholars agree that an adaptation is layered whether the text is visual or written. Film and television is ideal for my proposition because of the multifaceted construction of the medium. Plot shares similar characteristics with narrative. In *Narrative Discourse* (1980), Gérard Genette argues there are four contributors to narrative: order, duration, speed, and frequency (35).

These four contributors of narrative make up what Genette identifies as *pseudo-time*; in other words, a false sense of time that influences the consumption of a text. However, this notion of narrative time conflicts with George Bluestone's claim that the "formative principle in the novel is time [and] the formative principle in the film is space" (61). Marie-Laure Ryan, on the other hand, constructs a more functional definition of narrative as "situating stories within a class of related entities" (26). When a reader consumes a text, the act of consumption is predicated on the relevance of events to the reader's existence in the plot. Categorizing the plot in terms of its source or sources would condense any variety of response. This phenomenon also affects the way we perceive allusions and adaptations; the allusion assumes its customary function of being a means to aid comprehension. An adaptation is a far more complicated act, requiring us to see the text in full and make a value judgment thereafter.

The second notion, the replication of textual identifiers, requires us to perform an intertextual mapping of allusions that occur. A single allusion does not qualify as an intertext if that allusion is empty; in other words, an allusion that would not detract from the plot of an adaptation. According to Liam Burke, author of *The Comic Book Film Adaptation* (2015), textual identifiers often surface in comic book adaptations to pay homage to iconic moments in comic book narratives. It is up to us to perform an intertextual mapping of such allusions to make sense of them. For example, Burke argues that the explicit use of architextuality in the title shots of Robert Rodriguez and Frank Miller's film *Sin City* (2005) "enables loose borrowings to suggest fidelity to the knowing member of the audience ... [and] these borrowings also regularly cite specific elements from the books" (161). Textual allusions are common in comic book adaptations. Spider-Man film adaptations, from Sam Raimi's *Spider-Man* (2001) to Marc Webb's *The Amazing Spider-Man* (2012), borrow iconic moments of Stan Lee and Steve Ditko's Spider-Man character. For example, both Raimi's *Spider-Man* and Webb's *The Amazing Spider-Man* depict the death of Uncle Ben. Uncle Ben's death serves more than a narrative device to service the characterization of Spider-Man but also seeks value in remaining faithful to its source. However, it is only one instance of the directors using allusion to pay homage to their sources. One such allusion can be viewed as homage to a source. A series of linked textual identifiers, on the other hand, constitutes a pattern of plot replication in which the allusions assume more significance. In that sense they acquire more value compared to the single allusion.

By default an adaptation conceives its own language modes dictated by the reader. Therefore, the difference between adaptation and allusion signifies recognizing the distinction between semantics and syntax in an adaptive text. In *The Comic Book Film Adaptation*, Burke fails to clarify this discrepancy between the semantic and syntactic qualities of an adaptation. According to Burke, "recent comic book adaptations have displayed previously unseen levels of faithfulness to their source texts and the wider tenets of the medium" (130). Burke associates this phenomenon with what Colin MacCabe terms the grammar of value. MacCabe argues that the grammar of value for texts establish how accessible a text is in the context of predetermined circumstances. Specifically, MacCabe claims the grammar of value is "always in play in allocations of resources that determine the questions of access: what shall be preserved in this archive or library, what should be placed on a national curriculum or individual syllabus" (9). The concept of grammar of value is evaluative in nature and serves as an important model to consider when reading adaptations. Burke applies the grammar of the value model to comic book adaptation because the proliferation of the genre in recent years has commanded unforeseen homage to source material. The emphasis of the hypotext can be discriminatory to the unknowledgeable spectator. In other words, the distinction between allusion and adaptation becomes transparent. For this reason, I take issue with the term "grammar of value" because it implies there is no difference between the semantics or syntax of an adaptation. More to the point, Burke's usage of the grammar of value treats a passing allusion as equal to a rooted adapted narrative. If readers assign value in adaptations by engaging with a multitude of intertexts, then the passing allusion only serves as a construct of the genre of comic book adaptations. Hence the sematic of a narrative constitute an adapted text whereas the syntax governs the presence of allusions. Together, the sematic and syntactic qualities of a text establish adaptive semiotics to provide a basis for distinguishing how value is assigned to adaptations versus the allusions that may arise in that text.

Adaptive semiotics is not easily identifiable but constitute stylistic transference of medium specific discourses. Christian Metz theorizes that the "specific nature of film is defined by the presence of a *langue* tending toward language" (59). Stam et al. argue that intertextual dialogism functions "within all cultural production, whether literate or non-literate, verbal or non-verbal, highbrow or lowbrow." Hence adaptive semiotics are not limited to specific language codes whether artistic, cinematic, or printed prose (*New Vocabularies* 210). Stylistic identifiers in the adaptive aesthetic function within a duality of language. Recognizing adaptive semiotics is dependent on a knowledgeable spectator, and therefore requires a different level of competence from simply identifying allusions. A range of knowledgeable spectators generates tiers of spectatorship that increases and extends our understanding of an adaptation. Stylistic identifiers can appear to the knowing spectator in multiple forms including genre, tone, and/or framing principles. If an adaptation requires more value than allusion, it can be attributed to the sophistication involved in decoding an adaptation.

For the remainder of this work, I want to put this model to practice by analyzing the episode "Rogue's Gallery" of *Gotham*. For both "Rogue's Gallery" and "Reanimator." Lovecraft's tale "Herbert West—Reanimator" is a zombie allusion to the strange experiments of Dr. Herbert West. *Gotham's* "Rogue's Gallery" concerns the investigation of a patient in Arkham Asylum who is experimenting on other patients with the intentions of controlling them. In "Reanimator," West can be read as the monster while the unnamed narrator, West's assistant, is the hero. The narrative is a first person account of the horrors of Dr. West and the narrator can be considered the hero because he escapes West's demise. By comparison, Gruber (Christopher Heyerdahl) is the monster in "Rogue's Gallery" and the hero is Jim Gordon who eventually slays Gruber. Gruber's character also goes by the alias the Electrocutioner. The Electrocutioner first appeared in "Electric City: Part 1 #644" (1992) created by Chuck Dixon. The villain went by the name Lester Buchinsky who took the Electrocutioner mantle after his brother dies. The original Buchinsky is closer in age to Batman compared to his counterpart in *Gotham*. *Gotham's* Electrocutioner is Jack Gruber, and alias of a Jack Buchinsky who is much older than the comic book character. More to the point, Gruber's rise as a villain is incited through electrotherapy experiments on patients in Arkham Asylum. Gruber shares intense ambitions with West in using scientific means to control and enslave individuals. In other words, *Gotham's* Electrocutioner takes a swift departure from its comic book counter part considering how closely aligned this character is with Herbert West. Similarly, the title of the episode "Rogue's Gallery" functions as an allusion. The phrase "Rogue's Gallery" is a reference to the comic book colloquial that depicts a group of villains associated with a hero. The phrase also references the term used to describe a police collection of criminals. For example, Batman's rogue's gallery consists of the villains Joker, Catwoman, Scarecrow, Two-Face, Riddler, Poison Ivy, Bane, etc.[4] The reference has no barring on the plot of the episode besides the passing reference that a Batman villain will be introduced. This is a pivotal moment we can distinguish the difference between the sematic quality and syntactic quality of an adaptation. The syntax of the episode title primarily serves as an allusion to Batman's villains. Beyond the passing allusion, the reference contains no meaning or value that services the narrative. Consequently, the sematic quality of the text privileges "Herbert West." The ending of this episode also pays homage to the narrative style of "Herbert West," in that, the episode ends with an epistolary narration that calls attention to Lovecraft's writing style of "Herbert West." Comparing plots or plot points, as previously stated, is only an initial point of comparison that warrants further analysis. This first rule can be commonly identified between adaptive text and source text. Comparing plot points can be a simple and derivative task. In theory, the comparison of plots between texts offers a basis to engage in a more sustainable analysis of intertexts between the narratives in question. Comparing plots of two different narratives serves as an appropriate entry point to further assess the next two rules.

"Rogue's Gallery" follows a similar narrative progression supported by a hypertextual consistency with Lovecraft's "Reanimator." Articulating the textual identifiers proposed in rule two calls for a comparative analysis of cross-textual consistencies that arise in *Gotham* as a hypertext of "Reanimator." Stam defines hypertextuality as a text that is a former entity to an "anterior text that transforms, modifies, elaborates, or extends" (66). The hypertext is embedded with the anterior text. In this sense, *Gotham's* anterior text is a composite of the Batman and Lovecraft mythos. The authority of *Gotham* derives from Batman sources while Lovecraft is the anterior text. On the surface, *Gotham's* mid-season finale titled "Lovecraft" can be considered an allusion because the episode lacks a substantial connection to the author Lovecraft beyond homage. However, it is the episodes that follow the mid-season premiere in which the Lovecraft mythos drives the plot. For example, Arkham Asylum, the staple of the Batman mythos inspired by Lovecraft's works, is the main setting for "Rogue's Gallery." As a textual aspect of the show alone, one could consider the setting an allusion. However, the antagonist Jack Gruber connects "Rogue's Gallery" to Lovecraft's "Reanimator" in appearance and medical malpractice. In the "Reanimator," the antagonist Dr. Herbert West is described as a slim man with "yellow hair, pale blues eyes, and a soft voice" (228). The onscreen comparison in Gruber is nearly an exact match to Lovecraft's West. In the viewer's first look at Gruber, Gruber is disguised as Prospero from *The Tempest*. The second appearance of the character, however, captures the character full frame as a soft-spoken, pale white male with grey-blond hair thus aligning with West and Gruber.

However, it is the medical malpractice consistent with West that is most intriguing and supports the hypertextual mapping. In "Reanimator," West scientifically attempts to reanimate newly deceased individuals on multiple occasions. West becomes closer to reanimation every time, with the final experiment resulting in the loss of his own life as the zombie reanimated and killed West similar to the novel it is parodying, namely Mary Shelley's *Frankenstein* (1818). In the episode "Rogue's Gallery," Gruber perfects his experiments on mental patients in an effort to create the perfect specimen to control and do his bidding. Without the audience knowing at the moment Gruber is evil, Gruber describes his first victim as "a man already dead." In other words, Gruber's first experiment is done on a man figuratively dead and Gruber is trying to repurpose that body. This act of experimentation is reminiscent of the pulp zombie popular during Lovecraft's time. The zombie has a rich history in American literature. In contemporary literature and film, the modern zombie is often depicted as a demonic, flesh eating, reanimated person. The modern zombie was popularized with George Romero's film *Night of the Living Dead* (1968) and in Robert Kirkland's adapted television series from a comic series of the same name *The Walking Dead* (2010). However, the pulp zombie is the first zombie introduced to Western culture that was influenced by Haitian voodoo practices. The pulp zombie often found its place in horror-associated fictional publications. In "The Ways and Nature of the Zombi," Hans Ackermann and Jeanine Gauthier trace the origins of the zombie back to religious practices in Africa that would partake in resurrecting the souls of individuals. In the west, zombie traditions became acts used to gain control. Ackermann and Gauthier claim that one motive for "zombification [can be] profit through exploitation of slave labor" (475). Reading the zombie as a disenfranchised agent is an embedded connection between *Gotham* and "Reanimator." However, there is a point of difference that provokes a different reading between the two as a reaction to the hypertext being a modified narrative of the anterior text. West's experiment turning against him provokes a reading that privileges agents and anti-establishment beliefs. On the contrary, Gruber retains an authority on his subjects. Both readings subject viewers to differing social commentaries inherent in a zombie narrative.

The third rule toward a model for negotiating adaptation versus allusion and the procreation of stylistic identifiers translated in the adaptive aesthetic can be assessed in a number of different ways. Fortunately, film and television offer a textual aesthetic unique to the medium. For this particular study, I will focus solely on the adaptation of genre taking into account that there are stylistic entities of certain genres inherent to cinema and television. Lovecraft based all of his tales in horror, a genre fairly untouched in the Batman mythos. Instead, contemporary Batman adaptations opt to root the narrative stylistically in film noir, most notably Tim Burton's *Batman* and *Batman Returns* (1989/1992) and Christopher Nolan's *Batman Begins* (2005). Past Batman adaptations are flooded with crane and aerial shots, establishing shots, and expressionism inherent of film noir. To some degree, *Gotham* remained faithful to the film noir genre during the pilot premiere. For example, *Gotham* opens its pilot with an aerial shot of Gotham City as well as an establishing shot of the alley before the Wayne murder. However, at the start of the mid-season premiere, *Gotham* foregoes its ties to the film noir convention to adapt the horror genre in "Rogue's Gallery." When the insane patients of Arkham are chasing Dr. Leslie Thompkins (Morena Baccarin), there is a tracking shot followed by a close-up that reveals her expression of terror. Likewise, while running down a hallway of Arkham, the scene cuts and the camera is positioned at a tilt giving the impression the point of view is from a victim. The composition of shots changes the dynamic of the narrative. Instead of a story that poises mystery, we receive a tale of fear. These stylistic traits inherent of the horror genre are transferred to a narrative that would be otherwise absent if *Gotham* was only faithful to the Batman mythos.

For the sake of space, I limit this analysis to the "Rogue's Gallery" episode of *Gotham*. However, it should be noted that the "Herbert West" narrative expands to varying degrees through the second half of the season. The episode that follows "Rogue's Gallery," "What the Little Bird Told Him," screens Gruber and his victims searching for the criminals that put him in Arkham. At the end of Lovecraft's short story "Herbert West," West's reanimates search out for him as well. The shift in focus from Gruber's villainy to his victimization expands the adaptation from translation to commentary. Likewise, the narrative arc of Fish Mooney (Jada Pinkett Smith) is also narratively parallel to the events of "Herbert West." For example, in the season finale, "All Happy Families are Alike," an augmented and experimented on Mooney makes her way back to Gotham City to face her *creator*, or her Herbert West. The theme of reanimation situated in zombie narratives also becomes a cornerstone of the second season of *Gotham*.

The model proposed here towards a negotiation between adaptation and allusion warrants further analysis; nevertheless, I am hopeful that the model proposed here will sustain an intelligent debate when put to practice in other multi-modal adaptations. While comic book adaptations would benefit from this model greatly, I am confident this model would be just as valuable in a range of adaptive texts. The first rule of categorizing plot may be simple but does provide a great entry point for a more complicated analysis. The next two rules comprising this model, however, may warrant more concerns in some instances. For example, when configuring the rule of isolating a web of textual identifiers, one concern might be the question of how many textual identifiers constituted a web? In most cases, the most faithful of adaptations would presuppose much parallel continuity between the adaptive text and its source. Loose adaptations though, would be less interconnected. Likewise, the third rule can also be problematic. In this study, I restricted my analysis to comparing genre between unalike works. While the former is adequate for this study considering the competing narratives of *Gotham* and "Reanimator," transferring a narrative to a different genre is not a new phenomenon in western adaptation. This model has potential for many adaptation scholars to relieve the complication of distinguishing textual allusions from adaptation. Nevertheless, this model has limitations.

Adaptation scholars have debated about the usefulness of intertextuality as a basis for determining adaptation from allusion. This model could have the potential to generate new understandings of how influential a source could be on the adaptation. Take *Pretty Woman* (1990) for example. The film is arguably a modern take on *Cinderella*. While the protagonist Vivian Ward (Julia Roberts) goes to the opera with Edward (Richard Gere), Vivian does not leave a token behind before midnight. However, Vivian does leave Edward for a short period of time after exclaiming, "this is not the fairy tale she wanted." Compared to Cinderella, the intertexts of *Pretty Woman* are inverted to some degree and I would think this model could entangle the allusions present in the film. This study of *Gotham* presented here could also be expanded to include the intertexts of *The Tempest* and Shelley's *Frankenstein*. Although this may be a work in progress, the model presented here could have the potential to answer the pain staking question often asked, "Fidelity to what?"

NOTES

1. *Year One*, later retitled *Batman: Year One*, is written by Frank Miller and illustrated by David Mazzucchelli. This narrative arc was originally published as in the ongoing *Batman* series #404–407. The story recounts Bruce Wayne's first year as a crime fighter while also examining Jim Gordon's life as a police officer. The narrative arc ends with Batman and Gordon's partnership.

2. The Bronze Age of comics is an informal name given to the comics published between the years 1970 and 1985. While many characters and plot lines continued from the Silver Age (1956–1970), the narratives of the Bronze Age were considered darker and socially relevant because these comics engaged with issues of poverty, drug use, alcoholism, environmentalism, racism, and politics. The Golden Age of comics is from 1938 to 1956. From 1985 to present date is the Modern Age.

3. Batman Family is an informal name given to characters associated with Batman (both aliases and villains). *DC Rebirth* (2016) currently has ongoing titles with the Batman Family including *Batman, Detective Comics, Batgirl, Batwoman, Nightwing, All-Star Batman, Birds of Prey, Trinity, Titans, Teen Titans, Harley Quinn, Red Hood and the Outlaws, Suicide Squad,* and *Batman Beyond.*

4. Batman's rogue's gallery consists of villains has faced over the years of publication. Joker first appears in *Batman* #1 (April 1940). Catwoman first appears in *Batman* #1 (April 1940). Scarecrow first appears in "World's Finest #3" (Spring 1940). Two-Face first appears in "Detective Comics #66" (August 1942). Riddler first appears in "Detective Comics #140" (October 1948). Poison Ivy first appears in "Batman #181" (October 1948). Bane first appears in "Batman: Vengeance of Bane #1" (January 1993). This list of Batman villains is by no means comprehensive.

WORKS CITED

Ackermann, Hans W., and Jeanine Gauthier. "The Ways and Nature of the Zombi." *Journal of American Folklore* 104.414 (1993): 466–94. Print.

"All the Happy Families Are Alike." *Gotham.* Dir. Danny Cannon. Perf. Ben McKenzie, Robin Lord Taylor, and Nicholas D'Agosto. New York: Fox. 4 May 2015. Television.

The Amazing Spider-Man. Dir. Marc Webb. Perf. Andrew Garfield, Emma Stone, and Rhys Ifans. Sony, 2012. Film.

Batman. Dir. Tim Burton. Perf. Michael Keaton, Kim Basinger, and Jack Nicholson. Warner Bros., 1989. Film.

Batman Begins. Dir. Christopher Nolan. Perf. Christian Bale, Katie Holmes, and Michael Caine. Warner Bros., 2005. Film.

Batman Returns. Dir. Tim Burton. Perf. Michael Keaton, Michelle Pfeiffer, and Danny DeVito. Warner Bros., 1992. Film.

Bluestone, George. *Novels into Film: The Metamorphosis of Fiction into Cinema.* 1957. Berkeley: University of California Press, 1968. Print.

Booker, Christopher. *The Seven Basic Plots: Why We Tell Stories.* London: Continuum, 2006. Print.

Burke, Liam. *The Comic Book Film Adaptation: Exploring Hollywood's Leading Genre.* Jackson: University Press of Mississippi, 2015. Print.

Dixon, Chuck, and Nolan Graham. "Batman: Vengeance of Bane Vol. 1 #1." *Detective Comics.* New York: DC Comics, 1993. Print.

Dixon, Chuck, and Tom Lyle. "Electric City: Part 1 #644." *Detective Comics.* New York: DC Comics, 1992. Print.

Finger, Bill, and Dick Sprang. "Detective Comics #140." *Detective Comics.* New York: DC Comics, 1948. Print.

Genette, Gérard. *Narrative Discourse: An Essay in Method.* Trans. Jane E. Lewin. Ithaca: Cornell University Press, 1980. Print.

Harris, Jack C. "Foreword." *The Dark Age: Grim, Great, & Gimmicky Post-Modern Comics.* By Mark Voger. 4–5. Canada: Post-Modern Comics, 2006. Print.

Hutcheon, Linda. *A Theory of Adaptation.* New York: Routledge, 2006. Print.

Johnson, Jeffery K. *Super-History: Comic Book Superheroes and American Society 1938 to the Present.* Jefferson, NC: McFarland, 2012. Print.

Kane, Bob, and Bill Finger. "Batman #1." *Detective Comics.* New York: DC Comics, 1940. Print.

_____. "Detective Comics Vol. 1 #66." *Detective Comics.* New York: DC Comics, 1942. Print.

Kanigher, Robert, and Sheldon Moldoff. "Batman Vol. 1 #181." *Detective Comics.* New York: DC Comics, 1966. Print.

Leitch, Thomas. *Film Adaptation and its Discontents: From* Gone with the Wind *to* The Passion of the Christ. Baltimore: John Hopkins University Press, 2007. Print.

"Lovecraft." *Gotham.* Dir. Guy Ferland. Perf. Ben McKenzie, Robin Lord Taylor, and Nicholas D'Agosto. New York: Fox. 24 Nov. 2014. Television.

Lovecraft, H.P. "Herbert West—Reanimator." *Zombies! Zombies! Zombies!* Ed. Otto Penzler. 226–44. New York: Vintage, 2011. Print.

Lytle, Paul. "The Madness of Arkham Asylum." *Batman Unauthorized: Vigilantes, Jokers, and Heroes in Gotham City.* Ed. Dennis O'Neil. 109–120. Dallas: BenBella Books, 2008. Print.

MacCabe, Colin. "Bazinian Adaptation: *The Butcher Boy* as Example." *True to the Spirit: Film Adaptation and the Question of Fidelity.* Ed. Colin MacCabe, Kathleen Murry, and Rick Warner. 3–26. Oxford: Oxford University Press, 2011. Print.

Metz, Christian. *Film Language: A Semiotics of Cinema.* Trans. Michael Taylor. Chicago: University of Chicago Press, 1974. Print.

Miller, Frank, and David Mazzucchelli. *Batman: Year One.* New York: DC Comics, 2005. Print.

Morrison, Grant, and Dave McKean. *Arkham Asylum: A Serious House on Serious Earth.* New York: DC Comics, 1989. Print.

Night of the Living Dead. Dir. George A. Romero. Perf. Judith O'Dea, Duane Jones, and Marilyn Eastman. Image Ten, 1968. Film.

O'Neil, Dennis. "Batman #258." *Detective Comics.* New York: DC Comics, 1974. Print.

Penzler, Otto, ed. *Zombies! Zombies! Zombies!* New York: Vintage, 2011. Print.

"Pilot." *Gotham.* Dir. Danny Cannon. Perf. Ben McKenzie, Robin Lord Taylor, and Nicholas D'Agosto. New York: Fox. 22 Sept. 2014. Television.

Pretty Woman. Dir. Gerry Marshall. Perf. Julia Roberts and Richard Gere. Touchstone, 1990. Film.

"Rogue's Gallery." *Gotham.* Dir. Oz Scott. Perf. Ben McKenzie, Morena Baccarin, and Christopher Heyerdahl. New York: Fox. 19 Jan. 2015. Television.

Ryan, Marie-Laure. "Toward a Definition of Narrative." *The Cambridge Companion to Narrative.* Ed. David Herman. 22–35. Cambridge: Cambridge University Press, 2007. Print.

Siegel, Jerry and John Sikela. "World's Finest #5." *Detective Comics.* New York: DC Comics, 1941. Print.

Sin City. Dir. Robert Rodriguez and Frank Miller. Perf. Bruce Willis, Clive Owen, and Mickey Rourke. Miramax, 2005. Film.

Spider-Man. Dir. Sam Raimi. Perf. Tobey Maguire, William Defoe, and Kirsten Dunst. Sony, 2002. Film.

Stam, Robert. "Beyond Fidelity: The Dialogics of Adaptation." *Film Adaptation*. Ed. James Naremore. 54–76. New Brunswick: Rutgers University Press, 2000. Print.

Stam, Robert, Robert Burgoyne, and Sandy Flitterman-Lewis. *New Vocabularies in Film Semiotics: Structuralism, Post-Structuralism, and Beyond*. London: Routledge, 1992. Print.

The Walking Dead. Dir. Robert Kirkland. Perf. Andrew Lincoln, Jon Bernthal, and Sarah Wayne Callies. Georgia, United States, AMC, 2010. Television.

"What the Little Bird Told Him." *Gotham*. Dir. Eagle Egilsson. Perf. Ben McKenzie, Robin Lord Taylor, and Nicholas D'Agosto. New York: Fox. 19 Jan. 2015. Television.

Finding Value
through "Personal Baggage"

CHARLES R. HAMILTON

Beyond the stylishly designed syllabus, the research-based learner-centered pedagogy, or the contemporary survey of literature text remains a question that is a constant with educators; how do I help learners find value in what they are reading, make that personal connection with the literature that aids in their understanding of what they read? Too many educators respond to the previous question in a rather surprised manner. They are puzzled and ask: "What does a learner's personal connection with the literature have to do with understanding? Why can't they just learn by memorizing the 'correct' meaning I give them and repeating it on a test?" The answers to these questions and more become clear through an understanding of Transactional theory, developed by Louise Rosenblatt in 1937 and discussed in depth in her essential text *Literature as Exploration,* first published a year later. She describes this transaction as

> the reader approaches the text with a certain purpose, certain expectations or hypotheses that guide his choices from the result of past experiences. Meaning emerges as the reader carries on a give-and-take with the signs on the page. As the text unrolls before the reader's eyes, the meaning made of the early words influences what comes to mind and is selected for the succeeding signs. But if these do not fit in with the meaning developed thus far, the reader may revise it to assimilate the new words or may start all over again with different expectations. For the experienced reader, much of this may go on subconsciously, but the two-way, reciprocal relation explains why meaning is not "in" the text or "in" the reader. Both reader and text are essential to the transactional process of making meaning [26–27].

Literary critic Wayne C. Booth further explains Rosenblatt's intensions in the foreword to the 1995 fifth edition, saying that "she cared more about turning all learners into better readers than about turning a few learners into disciples of the one right reading or kind of reading" (ix). Booth goes on to say that she instructed educators to consider the relationship of the reader to the book, "that is, of the transaction between potentially powerful texts and readers whose emotional engagement should be 'read' as closely as the text itself" (viii).

Rosenblatt's ideas help to form a connection between educators, individual learners, and the class as a whole. One of the primary rules taught for success in writing is "know your audience." While disseminating this notion to learners, sometimes we forget that learners are also an audience. One of the first pedagogical concepts taught in instructional education classes for new educators is the idea that learners need to feel "safe" in the classroom, both physically and conversationally. College learners in the early years of their education are at times shy or nervous about expressing themselves or offering comments during classroom discussions. Many come from public schools in which they were not encouraged to offer personal opinions but only to listen to, remember, and regurgitate the comments and meanings offered by the educator. Thus, an educator's first task becomes helping learners feel safe when expressing their opinions. *Know your audience.*

Utilizing Rosenblatt's concept of "a transaction between the reader and the literature," brings new life to the "safe" classroom, even if it involves more work for the educator who tries to guide readers in finding value in what they are reading or viewing. Booth proclaims, "I doubt that any other literary critic of this century [20th] has enjoyed and suffered as sharp a contrast of powerful influence and absurd neglect as Louise Rosenblatt.... She has probably influenced more educators in the ways of dealing with literature than any other critic. But the world of literary criticism and theory has only recently begun to acknowledge the relevance of her arguments" (vii). The educator's job is to provide such conditions in the classroom as to allow that "transaction" to happen. This type of teaching allows the reader to relate personally to a situation unique to that reader and maybe to understand what they are reading in a more personal way. Rosenblatt's title, *Literature as Exploration,* is very fitting. She emphasizes that "the importance of a relationship between educator and learners that will permit the learner to respond intimately and spontaneously to literature" (73).

The next step in helping learners obtain value and understanding from literature is through helping them understand themselves. They begin to develop self-confidence and an awareness that their answers are as valuable as anyone else's. Early in the process classroom discussions begin slowly, but develop quickly once learners understand the basic purpose of informational and experiential purposes and self-growth. Learners begin their own personal quest of self-understanding by first examining their ideologies. Self-questioning, a form of metacognition, is encouraged throughout the semester.

Learners should answer the following questions to begin their self-questioning process:

> 1. Why do I reason the way I do? Where did my ideology come from?
> 2. Why do I believe what I believe?
> 3. How does my past experience influence my ideology?
> 4. How do the stories and characters of past texts relate to me and my current culture and environment?

The answers to these and other personally generated questions reveal to the reader how an ideology/value system is constructed. Through classroom discussion, learners see different perspectives, and by understanding what others think about like topics, are able to compare those perspectives with their own, sometimes modifying their personal ideologies. This process of developing understanding begins by discussing topics of local interest that are of contemporary interest. Such techniques help with learner understanding of the transactional process and help them get to know the educator's teaching style which, in turn, lets them understand what to expect in class. Rosenblatt states that "we can create in our classrooms an atmosphere of give-and-take and mutual challenge; through this, we shall surely find indirect evidence of the real literary experiences, the sources of growth" (273). Understanding the values other learners see can sometimes help clarify personal value.

To make this process work, learners also need to be open-minded enough to consider new and different ideas without instant rejection or dismissal. Discussing the following questions and using them as a guide helps foster rational, logical discussion:

> 1. Are you willing to listen without tuning out?
> 2. Could you allow a new idea to replace or modify an old one?
> 3. Are your prejudices too great to overcome?
> 4. Is it possible for you have civil discourse with an "enemy?"
> 5. Without open-minded learners, classroom discussion can be non-productive.

It is apparent that Rosenblatt prioritizes the learner and the "transaction between the reader and the text" in the learning process (*Exploration* 101). As a simplistic example: if a story is about Bob, who happened to be wearing a red shirt, should the question be "What color was Bob's shirt?" or "Why do you think Bob liked red shirts?" or "What does the color red suggest to you about Bob?" What is important here: only knowledge level learning within the cognitive domain or critical thinking with an outcome in the affective domain? Using transactional methods helps to draw out an affective response. Rosenblatt asserts that "since literature involves the whole range of human concerns, it is impossible to avoid assuming some attitude toward them" (8). She continues: "Moreover, because the implied moral attitudes and unvoiced systems of social values are reinforced by the persuasiveness of art, the educator should bring them out into the open for scrutiny" (8).

Rosenblatt's ideal, to get the learner to find value by connecting personally with literature, is a difficult process that requires a learner-centered teaching style. She also suggests that educators must not go too far in offering external examples of connections between the reader's life and the text while encouraging transaction: "What he [the learner] brings to the text is not only an external environment and special dialect but also fundamental human emotions and relationships" (270). From my first experience as a college learner in the late 60s and early 70s, I found many educators trying to explain what they believed was the central meaning of the text. They expected we should follow their example through multiple-choice tests and short-answer essays. Learners' opinions were not welcome, especially if they differed from those of the educator. They were leading me, and my thinking to a predetermined end. I only knew what they knew and wanted me to know, thinking those were the only "correct" answers. Rosenblatt observes that "even the search for meaning is reduced too often to paraphrase that simply dulls and dilutes the impact of the work" (271), as a means of checking whether learners have read the literature. "The concern with theme often relies too much on high-level abstractions, while the analysis of techniques becomes a preoccupation with recognizing devices—the scanning of verse, the labeling of types, the listing of symbols, the recognition of recurrent myths" (271). She stresses that "the educator's function is, rather, to help learners realize that the most important thing is what literature means to them and does for them" (64).

Rosenblatt's ideas should fit well within the culture of academia, and with discussions of adaptation studies since Dudley Andrew, who, in the 80s encouraged the move away from primacy of text adaptation studies to adaptation studies based on the quality of the adaptation as a new and separate creation. But, because both Andrew and Rosenblatt are more interested in the value of the personal connection the reader/viewer draws from their experience versus the primacy of what information the text contains, in many English or literature departments the study of the adaptation is dismissed as irrelevant. George Bluestone's argument in favor of the primacy of the novel (*Novels into Film* [1957]) is based on his ideas of the differences in the verbal versus the visual, and the divergent interests of readers versus viewers. He claims that readers have the advantage of reacting and responding to a novel, while a viewer has only visual interpretations to work with. Joy Boyum feels that Bluestone's bias has been shared by those she calls "defenders of high culture," thereby providing "one of the reasons that some quarter of a century after the publication of *Novels into Film* ... no study of adaptations has come along to replace it" (10).

Adaptation studies continued to focus on textual issues throughout the Eighties, although other theorists were beginning to follow Andrew's lead and push for change. Joy Boyum talks of the value of adaptations from a literary standpoint. Her view of the adaptation is partly based upon her long-time association with Louise Rosenblatt, whose Transactional Theory has been adapted into what some might refer to as reader-response theory, but is different in its depth and focus, in that it focuses more on the individual "transaction" between the reader and the text than their assumed group reaction. Boyum feels that approaches to studying the novel and the film should focus more on collaboration and that they both have important, yet different, ways of reaching readers and viewers that have hitherto not been studied in depth: "I had long subscribed to the view that a literary work has no mode of existence in itself—that it comes into being only as a partner in a cooperative venture with the reader who inevitably brings to bear an entire constellation of past experiences, personal associations, cultural biases and aesthetic preconceptions" (xi). She advocates a viewer-response theory to work in conjunction with reader-response theory. This sounds much like the theory of intertextuality, a term first coined in the 1960s by Julia Kristeva, and is, as Graham Allen notes in *Intertextuality* (2000): "a dominant idea within literary and cultural studies, taken up by practically every theoretical movement." Allen explains his concept of the theory of intertextuality, and how it differs from the concept of "extracting meaning from text reading or interpretation":

> Texts, whether they be literary or non-literary, are viewed by modern theorists as lacking in any kind of independent meaning. The act of reading, theorists claim, plunges us into a dense network of textual relations. To interpret a text, to discover its meaning, or meanings, requires us to trace those relations. Reading thus becomes a process of moving between texts, with meaning and value existing between a text and all the other texts to which it refers and relates, moving out from the independent text into a network of textural relations. The text becomes the intertext [Allen 1].

But where does the reader/viewer fit into this model? If value only lies within a variety of texts, are readers supposed to understand texts or films in the same way, with the same connections, only through commonality? Allen's ideas run counter to Rosenblatt's in that Rosenblatt believes in some sort of "universal" meaning, not unlike educators who want learners to know and take possession of their meaning as the "right" meaning. However, Rosenblatt thinks learners only understand value and meaning from a text or film through a personal connection or transaction with the content.

In "Reading Film and Literature," Brian McFarlane tackles the decades-old topic of fidelity in adaptation, not from a viewpoint of irrelevance, but from the viewpoint of a blending of the semiotics of both source and target texts. His theoretical basis is centered in reader-response and/or transactional theory, dispelling the myth that the source text has more value than the target simply because it is perceived as "original," or that both texts can stand alone without reliance on each other. Such arguments eventually lead to a discussion of intertextuality as an alternative to or necessary part of adaptation. McFarlane begins by discussing and countering what he refers to as "shibboleths" (customs or principles now regarded as unimportant) in the study of adaptation. Fidelity should be revaluated in the interests of "understanding or judgment" (15). His emphasis here is on reader-response theory based on the reaction of the reader to the blending of the text with the film to create a new and individual meaning that minimizes the importance of the transaction between the product and the individual. McFarlane cites George Bluestone to support the argument.

The second argument McFarlane challenges is that "film makes fewer demands on the imagination than a book does" (16). He counters with the statement: "However, it may be just as persuasively argued that in coming to serious terms with a film, much more is being required of us" (16) to discover the subtleties and nuances that exist in the adaptation. McFarlane's third argument to challenge is the idea that some literary texts do not lend themselves to or cannot be adapted to film. Here he cites Australian novelist Helen Garner, who insists that filmmakers who attempt to do so are "simply out of their league" (16). McFarlane's answer to her statement is that the task is not impossible; it just requires more talent (17). His fourth point is that adaptation is perhaps not the only relationship formed between source and target texts. His answer here is that films can explore any aspect of a source text, communicating in-depth studies of perspective and point of view to the viewer, and thereby adding to the power of film and text, in what he calls "[a] recognition of ways in which the interests of literature and film might fruitfully mesh" (17). This sounds very much like intertextuality, which he mentions near the end of his essay.

McFarlane continues to work his way through (and to attack) stereotyped misconceptions in adaptation studies, most of which relate to the "dumbing down" of literature in order to adapt it to film. Considering his earlier observation favoring individualistic meaning derived from an interaction between readers, text, and film this part of the argument seems mundane. Surprisingly, he subsequently draws on an extract from Bluestone's *Novel into Film*, which looks at adaptation from a structuralist point of view, and cites Roland Barthes inviting readers to draw on the semiotics of the text to construct meaning. By doing so he says that readers are liberated, giving them the power to construct value systems of their own in their interpretation, even if such interpretations might be of less value than "official" (i.e., critical) opinion. Also, countering those early statements is the very disturbing and ambiguous comment that "No one is suggesting that viewer-readers will not have opinions about whether they prefer the film or novel. Opinions, though, are private reactions that don't necessarily forward the discourse about film and literature" (27). Here it seems he denigrates the viewers' opinions as not serious enough to include in the discourse on literature and film, in favor of the use of the techniques of structuralism, which seems to be a mixed message when it comes to how meaning is generated. In the end McFarlane has blurred adaptation studies with the indistinct qualities of intertextuality. He lists the strategies of structuralism as an appropriate method for studying adaptation and even favors considering a new era of fidelity studies (a re-hashing, if you will). If he is trying to make a new point about values I cannot find it, but he did name his 1996 book on adaptation *Novel to Film*, in true "Bluestonian" fashion.

Another limiting factor in discussions of the value of adaptations is a refusal, by some professors in English or literature departments, to consider the study of texts outside the recognized literary canon as possessing value. From personal experience, many professors continue to focus on the primacy of text in Bluestonian fashion—especially if the text is part of the literary canon. Film studies, and especially adaptation studies (from text to film), are often spoken of as by these professors as peripheral, leading them to overlook the importance and other specific qualities present within the cinematic text. Their discussions focus on specific differences (or what is missing) from text to film that create an inferior product, not a separate and new piece that should be considered on its own merits.

Returning to college (28 years after my first degree) I was expecting a newer version of those close-minded professors I had experienced from the 60s and 70s. Fortunately I was happily surprised to find my educators teaching more from Rosenblatt's philosophy, although, at the time I knew nothing of her or transactional theory. Because I was not being pressured to memorize the professor's "correct" meaning of a text, I soon began to feel that personal connection between reader and literature, to find my own meaning and value within the text. This feeling intensified while taking two undergraduate reading courses for my teaching credentials in language arts. I was so impressed with what I learned about learner-created meaning that I decided to take a minor in Reading during my graduate work in English. Much of Rosenblatt's philosophy was included on these syllabi and it instantly made sense. As other learners offered their opinions, I was sometimes amazed at how their perspectives were so different from my own. At the same time, I realized that I was participating in an unlimited learning process, and that my opinions mattered, although different from those of my peers and educators. I gained self-confidence, and understood how my personal connection to the literature was valuable in constructing meaning from the text. I now follow Rosenblatt's example constantly with great learner success.

She writes about looking at the reader's reaction to the whole text, and stresses that each reaction relies on all other reactions to generate an over-all impression (47). She also understands how a reader's comprehension of a text derives from the "baggage" (background experience) the reader brings with them (74). Rosenblatt says that "[the reader] should be encouraged to bring to the text whatever in his [or her] past experience is relevant: ... sensuous awareness, ... feeling for people and practical circumstances, ... ideas and information, as well as ... feeling for the sound and pace and texture of the language" (270). Through this method of analysis individual value depends on the meaning created by the learner, not the educator or the text. Rosenblatt describes the process metaphorically as an infinite circle; you must experience life to get the most from literature, and you must experience literature to get the most from life (52). We should not prioritize the reader understanding the "correct" meaning of the text; its meaning depends on what the reader takes from it or how the reader transacts with it.

Another important connection that influences understanding and value is in the relationship between the situations in the text and the reader's socio-economic situation (SES). Rosenblatt notes that the reader is in a constant state of change and must adjust to changes in social life and society. As these changes occur, the reader's reactions to literary texts constantly change, rendering definite answers to the question "What does it mean?" impossible (84). She suggests that the educator must be aware of what might influence learners' needs and be ready to lead them toward a "fuller participation in what the text offers" (74). Learners, as a result, become aware that many different plausible interpretations of the text exist other than their own. The educator's responsibility at this point is to act as facilitator; to introduce or emphasize the elements of pluralistic thinking that help learners better understand their interpretations. They compare their views to those of their classmates and educators and subsequently may even revise their own opinions. This provides a method of understanding the reasoning behind their interpretations of a text. In "Transactional Theory in the Teaching of Literature," R.E. Probst discusses the transaction between reader and poem, placing "a great deal of emphasis on the role of the reader. If meaning resides not in the text but rather in the enactment by the reader, then the discussion of literature demands consideration of the mind of the individual reader or groups of readers" (1–2). As learners acquire self-confidence, they might also develop hitherto undiscovered knowledge of themselves. Probst suggests: "If learners are to deal with these matters, many of which will be personal, the literature classroom must be cooperative rather than combative…. Discussions should encourage learners not to win but to clarify and define" (3).

Under the topic of "Implications for Teaching" Probst lists the following principles of instruction:

1. Invite response. Make clear to learners that their responses, emotional and intellectual, are valid starting points for discussion and writing.

2. Give ideas time to crystallize. Encourage learners to reflect upon their responses, preferably before hearing others.

3. Find points of contact among learners. Help them to see the potential for communication among their different points of view.

4. Open the discussion to the topics of self, text, and others. The literary experience should be an opportunity to learn about all three.

5. Let the discussion build. Learners should feel free to change their minds, seeking insight rather than victory.

6. Look back to other texts, other discussions, other experiences. Learners should connect the reading with other experiences.

7. Look for the next step. What might they read next? About what might they write? (4–5)

He closes by discussing the responsibility of the learner: "The epistemology at the base of transactional theory returns the responsibility for learning to the learner. Knowledge—especially knowledge of literature—is not something to be found, not something the educator can give to the learner. Rather, it is to be created by the individual through exchanges with texts and other readers" (5).

In *Reading Texts: Reading, Responding, Writing,* authors McCormick, Waller, and Flower also clearly believe in an approach to reading that involves the transaction between reader and text, which also draws meaning from culture and history, as have more traditional methods of teaching literature. But, in discussing what they refer to as methods of teaching literature that are interactive, they go further, "to make the *reader's* social and cultural views part of the investigation" (71), with what they call a "response statement" that asks the reader about his or her personal response to a text.

But what these authors and texts are asking from their learners is more than a simple personal response to a poem, a short story, or a novel. They are asking the reader to stop and consider their personal socio-economic situation when investigating a text. As readers explore a text, they define vocabulary, social situations, culture, all through their views of personal experience, and then make comparisons with their own existences to come up with a value system that is exclusively theirs. This type of study now requires us to adopt an affective taxonomy to find personal meaning and value, and that does get personal.

These authors rely on a version of "reader-response" theory that moves more toward Rosenblatt's transactional theory in discussing the methods they feel readers use to create the most meaning from reading. "When you read, you create a text of your own" (McCormick et al. 151). The reader brings parts of this theory into play automatically as well as intentionally for personal understanding and personal value received. In discussing the reading of poetry through the "reader-response" method, the theory comprises a series of phases the reader experiences in making sense of a text. The first, and most obvious, question the reader asks is "What effect does this poem have on me?"—a question related to personal background, culture, and history. This immediately affects meaning for each reader, evoking a sense of personal connection. After this initial reading, the reader needs to understand how this personal understanding of the text was created. These preliminary steps outlined above form the basis for a different and personal reading, based on personal information and interpretation. For example, and as a basic difference between readers of different societies and cultures, a learner of 18 years of age has a different reading, writing, and speaking vocabulary than a learner of 35. This seems obvious, but based on this simple fact it is easy to see why different learners come away with a variety of meanings for the same text. Taking into consideration some other factors—history, location, age, educational background, and a variety of other personal characteristics and conditions of the reader—it is even more obvious that no two readers will generate the same meaning from the same poem. A reader from New York City who knows first-hand the history of Harlem will have a better understanding of the poetry of Langston Hughes than a learner who grew up on a rural farm, who may have never been to a large city, and who (as strange as it may sound) may never have heard of Harlem. On the other hand, a reader who grew up on a rural farm may have a better chance of understanding what Robert Frost describes in "The Death of the Hired Hand" than a reader from New York City, who has never experienced rural farm life. Although these situations seem very simplistic, they are part of what helps a reader create value.

Gerald Graff, in *Beyond the Culture Wars*, discusses how he changed his method of teaching Joseph Conrad's *Heart of Darkness*. Graff says that he had not considered what the reaction of African American learners might be to Conrad's view of Africa and Africans. After reading an essay by Chinua Achebe, in which Conrad's view of Africa appeared racist, Graff says he began to see what effect race and culture had on the way learners looked at a text. Previously he had taught *Heart of Darkness* as if Conrad and his novel were what mattered most. Now, after reading Achebe's essay, he identified with an African: Conrad's representation of Africa is how Africa and Africans were reconstructed by imperialist Europe. Graff has now added Achebe's novel

Things Fall Apart and his essay on Conrad as required reading when he teaches *Heart of Darkness.* He assigns and discusses the readings without trying to influence learners toward a right or wrong choice of understandings, but lets them form their own opinions after looking at different perspectives. He refrains from prejudicing learners toward his point of view. Graff says that *Things Fall Apart* and Achebe's essay have added a perspective he had not considered. He adds that Achebe's novel provided a sharp contrast to *Heart of Darkness* making Conrad's view of Africa and Africans not so universal (26–31). He now relies on the "transaction" between reader and text to make meaning—to create value.

In her preface to the fifth edition of *Literature as Exploration,* Rosenblatt emphasizes her idea "that there is no poem, no literary work, unless there has been an aesthetic reading and ... that there can be no absolute, single 'correct' meaning of a text" (xviii–xvx). Her hope is that through the transaction between reader and text readers will "nourish both aesthetic and social sensitivities and can foster the development of critical and self-critical judgement." Wayne Booth agrees, and adds further emphasis to what he sees as Rosenblatt's hopes for future readers.

> To survive as the kind of people Rosenblatt would have us become, the learners we have in classrooms today need something more than education in conducting transaction with books, they need what seems to be the more difficult art ... : slowing down the image, recognizing that living with the flow of images and talking back to them is, as Rosenblatt says of reading literature, a "mode of living" (264), a training for the life that occurs after the images are turned off" [xiv].

Louise Rosenblatt never fully received the recognition she deserved for her application of Transactional Theory, and her emphasis on the meaning each reader makes. In *The Reader, the Text, the Poem: The Transactional Theory of the Literary Work* her original theory is again clearly defined in the new preface to this edition when she declares the premise to be "that a text, once it leaves its author's hands, is simply paper and ink until a reader evokes from it a literary work—sometimes, even, a literary work of art" (ix). Her argument continues against the dualistic view that some reader-response theorists hold relating to the lack of value given to the reader's response and the idea that the value of the work lies in the words of the text (183).

Her ideas of the reader as an active participant in discerning meaning and value clearly go against traditional theories of the reader as passive, looking for the one correct meaning of a text. "My insistence that there is no such thing as a generic reader, that each reading involves a particular person at a particular time and place, underlines the importance of such factors in the transaction as gender, ethnic and socioeconomic background, and cultural environment" (viii).

Rosenblatt's idea is that the reader's purpose is not to focus only on a search for the author's meaning, but to form one's own meaning from the interaction of reader and text, essentials of transactional theory (12). This wide variety of responses is also part of what defines transactional theory. "The concept of the reader's stance in the efferent-aesthetic continuum, as well as the transactional paradigm, differentiates my theory both from the traditional and New Critical approaches and from the other so-called reader-response, structuralist, and poststructuralist theories" (184).

Her ideas about the value of the reader's response coincide partially with reader-response theorists, but differ in the amount of weight given to the reader's response. In her challenge to develop her theory she found through her classroom experience that the reader benefits more from the response if allowed to focus more on a personal reaction with the text rather than a traditional text-oriented translation handed down by a teacher. "And I had observed the value of interchange among learners as a stimulant to the development of critical and self-critical reading ..." (179).

Although Rosenblatt considers the reader, the text, and the poem as essential elements for the understanding of meaning, she does not go as far as considering all readings as valid. Her view is that all serious responses are worth exploration, but that some are better than others. Her classroom experiences support this. She found that as learners completed multiple readings of a text their responses changed based on their self-critical reading (*Exploration* x–xi).

The elements of transactional theory are clearly reader centered and have the potential to provide the personal connection between text and reader that has been missing in all too many literature classes. The reader can now feel a kind of ownership, knowing that personal meaning is as valid as any other stated by teachers or critics. Applying Rosenblatt's theory not only helps clarify meaning, but also encourages self-confidence in the reader, which in turn encourages classroom discussion and stimulates critical thinking. Transactional theory does away with the teacher-centered literature classroom and allows the reader to create meaning and value through personal transaction in response to the text. After all, "a text, once it leaves its author's hands, is simply paper and ink until a reader evokes from it a literary work—sometimes, even, a literary work of art" (Rosenblatt ix).

WORKS CITED

Achebe, Chinua. *Things Fall Apart*. 1958. New York: Penguin, 2006. Print.
Allen, Graham. *Intertextuality*. New York: Routledge, 2007. Print.
Andrew, Dudley. "Adaptation." *Film Adaptation*. Ed. James Naremore. 28–37. New Brunswick: Rutgers University Press, 2000. Print.
Bluestone, George. *Novels into Film*. Berkeley: University of California Press, 1957. Print.
Boyum, Joy Gould. *Double Exposure: Fiction into Film*. 1985. New York: Signet, 1989. Print.
Conrad, Joseph. *Heart of Darkness*. 1899. London: Penguin, 2014. Print.
Frost, Robert. "Death of a Hired Man." 1915. *The Poetry Foundation*, 2017. Web. 7 Mar. 2017.

Graff, Gerald. *Beyond the Culture Wars.* New York: W.W. Norton, 1993. Print.

Kristeva, Julia. *Desire in Language: A Semiotic Approach to Literature and Art.* Oxford: Blackwell, 1980. Print

McCormick, Kathleen, Gary Waller, and Linda Fowler. *Reading Texts: Reading, Responding, Writing.* Boston: D.C. Heath, 1987. Print.

McFarlane, Brian. "Reading Film and Literature." *The Cambridge Companion to Literature on Screen.* Ed. Deborah Cartmell and Imelda Whelehan. 15–28. Cambridge: Cambridge University Press, 2007. Print.

Probst, R.E. "Transactional Theory in the Teaching of Literature." *ERIC Digest* ED284274 (1987): 1–6. Web. 30 Oct. 2009.

Rosenblatt, Louise M. *Literature as Exploration.* 5th ed. New York: The Modern Language Association, 1995. Print.

_____. *The Reader, the Text, the Poem: The Transactional Theory of the Literary Work.* 1978. Preface to the paperback ed., vii–viii. Carbondale: Southern Illinois University Press, 1994. Print.

Adaptation and Transformative Learning in an Undergraduate History Class

Lisa Bunkowski

In the 24 years that I have been teaching history at the post-secondary level, I have often used film and literature to augment standard history texts to improve learner engagement. The first course I taught, as a graduate teaching assistant working on my master's degree in history, was a multidisciplinary class offered for history, anthropology, and English credit. That course started me down the path of a using a transdisciplinary (Raw and Gurr) approach as well as the strategy of incorporating different types of texts (including material culture) into how I taught and interpreted the past in my own professional work. Many of my early attempts were limited to helping learners make the connections between literary interpretations and the past or helping them root out fact from fiction in film and literature based on historical events. In my doctoral program, studying the work of postmodern anthropologists and literary critics transformed my approach to history, and how I interpreted texts. It opened up the notion of perspective and challenged the idea of authenticity and the "Truth" in history. This is a concept that I still apply to my teaching, and one that I find both disconcerts and stimulates the thinking of undergraduate learners.

Background of the Problem

In my U.S. women's history course last spring (2016), I focused on the concept of adaptation (Raw and Gurr), and required the learners to work with multiple adaptations in their final projects. In addition, we explored the idea of primary historical documents as adaptations (Marcus et al.) as well, which reinforced the importance of critically reading all evidence. The course was developed to study the history of women in America from the colonial period through 1877, with particular emphasis on women's roles in public and private life as well as the historical role of women in the development of the nation. Due to learner interest, and the artificiality of the chronological timeframe, we extended the end date to include historical subjects who were born within the original time-frame, but whose lives extended beyond it. The course was designed to provide the information necessary for undergraduate-level history learners to better understand women's roles and the historical role of women in the development of the United States before the end of Reconstruction. There were a series of course-level learning outcomes:

1. Demonstrate factual knowledge concerning U.S. Women's History to 1877, and Apply course materials to improve historical/critical thinking;

2. Work collaboratively to identify and evaluate online resources concerning U.S. Women's History to 1877;

3. Locate, analyze, and critically evaluate primary and secondary sources, major arguments, and points of view concerning U.S. Women's History to 1877;

4. Critically evaluate the roles of gender, diversity, and "difference" in U.S. Women's History to 1877; and

5. Demonstrate skill in written and oral expression consistent with undergraduate history learners.

The generic stems for these outcomes were taken from the course outcome language on the IDEA Center Learner Ratings of Instruction system. The IDEA ratings survey instruments are learner evaluations that address the course objectives, instructor's teaching methods, and the course and instructor in general. I developed the specific details to align with the undergraduate history program, and the course goals. The primary outcome for working with adaptations was to improve historical/critical thinking. The unwritten goal, from my point of view as the instructor, was to evoke a lasting change in the learners' approach to historical thinking. In other words, to use adaptation to bring about transformative learning in how learners approach the discipline of history (Mezirow; Hoggan).

I could tell the class members were on the right track with regard to transformative learning and the use of adaptation based on learner participation and comments during the class, the feedback through course evaluations, and a few learner email messages immediately following the end of the term. However, to gauge the longer term effect, I needed to assess their perceptions of the impact of class activities with adaptation after the passage of time (Hoggan; Hullender). This chapter addresses that challenge; it reports on a small study that examined the value of transformative learning and adaptation in an undergraduate history class.

Purpose Statement and Research Objectives

The purpose of this small, qualitative case study was to examine learner attitudes and perspectives about the transformative learning impact of the use of adaptation in this undergraduate history course. The research objectives guiding this study were to obtain learner perceptions of the impact of transformative learning through adaptation, and to evaluate the alignment of learner perceptions with my perceptions (as the instructor) of the efficacy of adaptation as a strategy for teaching history and achieving the learning objective: to improve historical thinking.

Rationale or Significance of the Study

To a degree this study was intended to help me systematically improve the structure of my course materials and instructions for working with adaptation in teaching history. As faculty members, we are often too busy to take the time to adequately reflect on our experiences. Even less often do we collect reflections from our learners about the impact of the classroom, particularly their perceptions of the value of teaching and learning strategies six months after a course has ended. Such a practice is necessary to begin to understand the transformative impact of a learning experience. In addition, this study makes a contribution to the literature through this small, empirical study of the potential transformative learning impact of adaptation.

Assumptions

Assumptions for this study involved the participants' integrity. Participation in the open-ended survey was voluntary and the survey was designed to keep participants' identities confidential. In addition, because the pool of participants consisted of former learners in my class, I knew them to be trustworthy.

Limitations/Delimitations

Participation in the open-ended survey was limited to learners who completed my spring U.S. Women's History through 1877 course; that would be 21 of the 22 learners who had enrolled. This case study, based on the experiences of one class, while valuable, is limited. The data simply do not provide the scope needed to generalize the results.

Definitions

Transformative learning—The foundation for understanding transformative learning and its educational value for this study is Jack Mezirow's 2003 definition, "learning that transforms problematic frames of reference—sets of fixed assumptions and expectations (habits of mind, meaning perspectives, mindsets)—to make them more inclusive, discriminating, open, reflective, and emotionally able to change" (58). Chad D. Hoggan's more focused definition of transformative learning was used in the conclusions section to evaluate the transformative impact of using adaptation. Hoggan maintains that "*transformative learning* refers to processes that result in significant and irreversible changes in the way a person experiences, conceptualizes and interacts with the world" (71).

Historical thinking—In class we used a variety of approaches to historical thinking, including the concept of the "five C's of historical thinking" by Thomas Andrews and Flannery Burke: "change over time; causality; context; complexity; and contingency" (Andrews and Burke 32). In addition, as part of this broad concept, we devoted time to exploring what Alun Munslow has explained as the epistemological, ontological, and authorial decisions and judgments made by historians (Munslow). The learners explored the discipline and what it can mean to engage in its practice. On the open-ended survey questionnaire, however, as a prompt for the learner, I used the concise definition offered by AP/College Board frame of reference for the concept of critical thinking skills applied to history: analyzing evidence—content and sourcing; interpretation; comparison; contextualization; synthesis; causation; patterns of continuity and change over time; periodization; argumentation. By introducing adaption, learners' epistemic assumptions about historical thinking and the nature of their work as budding historians were challenged.

Review of Related Literature

There are three main bodies of scholarship that provide a foundation for this study: adaptation and history; history and film; and transformative learning. There is some overlap between the first two sections, however much of the history and film literature does not overtly address the concept of adaptation. Guiding the review of the literature was the need for practical application with history learners—translating theory into practice.

Adaptation and History

Of particular use for my class was the scholarship that supported the use of adaptation to evoke critical analysis and its use beyond the field of literature. The foundational work for this project was a collection of essays edited by Laurence Raw and Defne Ersin Tutan, *The Adaptation of History*. In their introduction, Raw and Tutan discussed two critical points for this study. The first was the notion, building from the work of E. H. Carr that the past—as told through narrative or film—can be used to convey different meanings to different generations (Raw and Tutan 8). The second point was found in their discussion of two schools of historical thinking: Conventional and Interpretive. The former group, like many undergraduate learners, tended to look for an immutable version of the past. The latter, viewed history as an interpretation of the past. Raw and Gurr explained that "rather than engaging in debates about the way history should be approached (either adaptively or interpretively), we propose that all historical documents should be treated as adaptations" (Raw and Gurr 11). This concept supported my approach to working with all historical evidence in the classroom.

It is clear from much of the literature that adaptation and film are effective teaching tools. However, a shortcoming of the literature is the paucity of empirical studies. In her recent article, Sara Djamàa examined the impact of reading literature and film adaptations on the critical thinking skills of adult learners in Algeria. Although her findings regarding the efficacy of the use of film proved less promising, she did find that "teaching cinematic adaptation of literature hand in hand with the source text nurtured critical thinking dispositions" (Djamàa 260), as did teaching literature on its own. She observed that teaching strategies employed for the study, which included lecturing with questioning, discussion, debates and reading circles, all promoted critical thinking. Djamàa concluded that the critical component was the instruction the learners received and their practice to nurture developing critical thinking skills.

In his discussion of the use of adaptations of *The Scarlet Letter* and *Billy Budd*, Nazmi Al-Shalabi also emphasized developing learners' critical thinking skills. Al-Shalabi's cites the film adaptation literature in making this connection to critical thinking (Anderson, Connor-Greene, Dewey, & O'Connor), yet he neglects to provide a definition or description of what he means by critical thinking. He does, however, provide a description of the application of skills that learners developed as a result of employing adaptation in the classroom. These skills included reflection, abstract thinking, and empathy. These skills align with the broad concept addressed by Michael Scriven and Richard Paul, who maintained that "critical thinking is the intellectually disciplined process of actively and skillfully conceptualizing, applying, analyzing, synthesizing, and/or evaluating information gathered from, or generated by, observation, experience, reflection, reasoning, or communication, as a guide to belief and action" (Scriven and Paul). Al-Shalabi's work underscored the idea that film is "an educational tool whose effectiveness is determined by the way it's used, and that it is our duty [as educators] to prepare ourselves to make the best use of it not only in American literature but also in other fields of knowledge" (Al-Shalabi 63).

Allen Schwab and Carrol Fry provided a more nuanced discussion of the adaptation of *Billy Budd*. They also raise the issue of learner desire for "'definitive' answers and judgements on complex circumstances" (Schwab and Fry 95), of course they were referring to the analysis of literature, but this is a challenge faced by undergraduate history educators as well. Their strategies for teaching with adaptation and fostering critical thinking transfer well to the type of assignment used for the final group project in my class. Schwab and Fry encouraged their readers and learners to analyze the source, adaptations as well as the historical context of each. Jeffrey Jackson's book-history concept is a good approach as well. Jackson reminds us that books, rather than being "original texts," were themselves adaptations of spoken words and the ideas in the minds of the authors. This concept resonates with the idea that even primary source historical documents are filtered through at least one adaptation by the recording of the event by a human actor. In their examination of the topic, *Adaptation Studies and Learning: New Frontiers*, Laurence Raw and Tony Gurr included a chapter on history that explored the construction of history, which supports this notion of multiple perspectives—multiple adaptations of historical events or periods. They noted the challenge for classroom instructors working with learners on a project like this, is how to properly assess it. This brief study demonstrates several ways to evaluate the impact of teaching with adaptations.

Teaching History with Film

The focus of the literature on teaching history with film is the pedagogy component. To have an impact on learners the instructors need to provide adequate and appropriate instruction for the learners to feel confident in working with the materials. In addition they need to manage class discussion and learner assessment in effective ways. In his examination of historical films and pedagogy, Scott Alan Metzger emphasized the concept of historical literacy. Although not stated as a separate learning outcome for the course, historical literacy competencies (content knowledge; narrative analysis; historical-cultural positioning; historical empathy; discernment of presentism) (Metzger 67), align well with the language of the first and third course objectives: factual knowledge, historical/critical thinking, analyze and critically evaluate sources. Metzger was focused on historical feature films, and though his study included qualitative assessment of secondary educators, he addressed the post-secondary environment in his conclusions. The goal, he stressed, is to guide the learners "toward treating movies as arguments or interpretations of the past to be examined and debated" (Metzger 73). To accomplish this, he concluded, we must shift from educator-centered instruction to "adventurous, at times risky, teaching" (Metzger 74). Bryan Jack explored the use of film in the history class as well. Jack discussed the use of film with post-secondary learners, and like Metzger emphasized the importance of teaching methodology and fully understanding the films' strengths and weaknesses (Jack 3).

There is a lot that has been written about the use of film in history classes at the secondary level. For this study, I referred primarily to selections from the limited literature that focused on the post-secondary-level. However, there is one source that targets the secondary-level that has proven to be invaluable, Alan Marcus et al., *Teaching History with Film*. Marcus et al. provided history educators with a handbook to effectively utilize film in the classroom. The questions raised throughout the book provide a template. For example:

> Why is a history movie telling a story about an era or event in a particular way?
> Why are certain perspectives emphasized or ignored?
> Whom does the movie want the audience to cheer for or against?
> What perspectives on the past does the movie encourage the audience to empathize with and why?
> What moral reactions about the past does the movie aim to evoke, or provoke, in the viewers? [Marcus et al. 7].

The book aligns with Metzger's discussion of historical literacy—Metzger was a co-author with Marcus et al. The book contains chapters on using movies as primary documents and as secondary sources, each with strategies and examples to guide educators down an effective instructional path.

A study on British heritage film audiences by Claire Monk holds a key point of comparison with my learners. Although the learners in the class were a very small group working with films they selected for their group projects (rather than films selected strictly for enjoyment), and the films had been critiqued to varying degrees by historians, nevertheless, there was an alignment with Monk's assessment of the two groups in her study, the older National Trust (NT) film group and the younger *Time Out* (TO) group. Monk determined that

> the most significant distinguishing trait of the TO audience, however was critical self-reflection; TOs were far more likely than NTs to think critically about terms such as "quality" and to define them in their own—at times expressly revisionist—terms. The "culture" of the TO audience was further distinguished from that of the NTs by a strong prioritization of narrative engagement and a valuing of complexity—and (in some cases) political or social engagement, and contemporary or personal relevance in the period films TOs enjoyed [68].

Separate groups in the classroom were not distinguished by categories of films or by age, so much as by experience. The approach characterized by critical self-reflection that led to more critical thinking about the films and their understanding of the meaning of them was more visible in the more experienced group of learners—this included learners who had previously taken my Historians Craft course or other courses at the institution that emphasized analytical thinking. The alignment was significant enough to warrant examination in the future.

Transformative Learning

To judge the effectiveness of the instructional path I utilized to examine adaptation and history with my class, I looked for evidence of transformative learning in the qualitative study of their attitudes and perspectives. To understand exactly what transformative learning is, it is best to refer to Jack Mezirow. Mezirow introduced the concept of transformative learning to the field of adult education in 1991. And although his critics offer barbs—too spiritual (Dirkx), too limited (Taylor), too broad (Hoggan), the emphasis on discourse is too soft (Newman "Transformative Learning"), and so on—the theory persists. Transformative learning is an adult learning theory, which makes it suited to our learner population. The learners at our university are all adults—the average age is 34 years old. According to Mezirow's 2003 definition: "Transformative learning is learning that transforms problematic frames of reference—sets of fixed assumptions and expectations (habits of mind, meaning perspectives, mindsets)—to make them more inclusive, discriminating, open, reflective, and emotionally able to change" (58). Mezirow reminded us, like Metzger and Marcus et al., to develop the critical thinking skills of our learners. However, Mezirow took it a step further by telling educators that they "must help learners become aware and critical of their own and others' assumptions" (Mezirow "Transformative Learning" 10). In addition, he reminded educators that they need to provide an environment that fosters effective discourse, and adopt a more learner-centered approach to teaching. In his examination of transformative learning theory, Edward W. Taylor concluded that there is much more to taking a transformative learning theory approach than a simple change in strategy. This approach demands a lot of work from learners and educators. "It means asking yourself," Taylor explained, "Am I willing to transform in the process of helping my learners transform?" (Taylor 13). This study and the modification of the next iteration of the course based on the study results reflect my willingness to assess my instructional strategies and transform as an educator.

A recurring question involves assessment, not only of the learners' work, but of the overall process. As I considered how I would assess the long-range transformative impact, I consulted empirical studies for examples of evidence used to demonstrate transformative learning. Ren Hullender et al. examined evidence of transformative learning in a service-learning mini-course. The evidence in Hullender's phenomenological study was the learners' reflective writing. The questions of the study supported the basic definition of transformative learning. The researchers looked for evidence of: transformative learning in learner perceptions and behavior; "triggers or incidents of disequilibrium"; how the course structure supported learning; and how the experience effected their thinking skills (Hullender et al. 62). In their conclusions, the researchers emphasized that the reconstruction process was often a time-consuming process. They explained that "given time and distance to reflect upon the experience, many of the learners drew new conclusions" (Hullender et al. 77). Jacqueline K. Kuennen also conducted an empirical study. Unlike the qualitative study of Hullender et al., Kuennen's study consisted of a five-item questionnaire, with five-point Likert scale statements. The questionnaire was an evaluation of a critical reflection paper and the instruction provided for that assignment. It offered a valuable approach for a quick read on the effectiveness of the teaching strategy. Kuennen's simplification of transformative learning theory is one of the common critiques of the theory.

Related to over-simplification, is the critique that transformative learning theory lacks a cohesive structure. Chad D. Hoggan addressed this issue by refining the definition, and developing a typology and criteria. Hoggan's work, which was grounded in an extensive literature review, resulted in analytical metatheory for transformative learning with the definition: "Transformative learning refers to processes that result in significant and irreversible changes in the way a person experiences, conceptualizes, and interacts with the world" (Hoggan 71). The typology outcome types included "worldview, epistemology, ontology, and behavior" (Hoggan 71). The criteria included depth/evidence of deep impact; breadth/evidence of impact on multiple life contexts; and relative stability/evidence that change is not temporary (Hoggan 72–73). Hoggan's framework provided a good footing for developing an assessment of learning in this study.

Methodology

The focus of this study was an effort to gauge the longer-term value (Hoggan) of using adaptation, and to formalize the collection of learner perceptions of their learning techniques. The purpose of the modified case study was to examine learner attitudes and perspectives about the transformative learning impact of the use of adaptation in this undergraduate history class. It was important to understand the full context, therefore a modified case study approach was adopted (Creswell *Qualitative*; Creswell *Educational*). This study was approved by the Institutional Review Board of Texas A&M University–Central Texas.

Purpose of the Study and Research Objectives

The principal purpose of the small, qualitative case study was to examine learner attitudes and perspectives about the pedagogical value of the use of adaptation in this undergraduate history class. The research objectives guiding this study were:

RO 1: Obtain learner perceptions of the impact of transformative learning through the use of adaptations.

RO 2: Align learners' perceptions with faculty member's perceptions of the efficacy of adaptations as a strategy for teaching history and achieving the learning objective: apply course materials (adaptations) to improve historical thinking.

Research Design

This qualitative case examined learner attitudes and perspectives about the transformative learning impact of the use of adaptation in this undergraduate history class. By adopting a modified version of the case-study approach (Creswell *Qualitative*; Creswell *Educational*). I was able to evaluate the learner responses within the context of the course, course materials, and the course experience. The data collection methods for this study included multiple forms of data: archival records (course syllabus, assignment instructions, and related documents), and the open-ended survey question responses. (See appendix for survey questions).

Participants and Setting

The setting for this study was a small, state university that is part of a large university system. The university has been an independent entity within the system since 2009, and independently accredited by the Southern Association of Colleges Committee on Colleges since 2013. One unique aspect of the institution is that it only offers upper-level and graduate courses. Having no freshman or sophomore classes contributes to the group of learners mentioned above.

The study was conducted with my spring 2016 course, U.S. Women's History through 1877, which ended in early May 2016. There were 22 learners enrolled in the course, and one dropped after the census date, which left 21 learners eligible to participate in the study. Of the 21 learners, five were men and 16 were women. Although that appears to be heavily weighted toward women in this class, for this institution, and particularly for a women's history course, I considered it a success to have five men enrolled and fully participating. Their participation often promoted deeper discussions about perspective and identity. Because I did not include demographic questions on the survey, nor did the survey questionnaire approved by the IRB include the request to examine this type of learner data, I would not ordinarily even reference this point. However, it was an email message from one of the males in the course after the class had ended that prompted me to conduct the study. In addition, one of the female learners stopped by my office several months later and expressed similar sentiments. One of them evidently spoke to the Provost about the impact of the course because I received an email message from her about the value of this encounter.

The modality of this class was hybrid (or blended), meeting online for six of the 31 sessions. The format of the class was lectures, probing Socratic questioning (Paul and Elder), and general class discussion in which the instructor participates. For the Socratic questioning component, the instructor systematically asks a series of questions designed to help the learners examine the course materials, their thinking or assumptions, and the underlying concepts. Assessments included weekly individual reflection papers over the readings. The topics for the reflection papers were designed to get the learners thinking about assumptions, perspective, and identity. The learners were asked to write to two critical review essays of scholarly journal articles related to our course topic. The midterm and final exams consisted of essay questions that asked learners to find connections in these topics through a topical or historiographic approach based on the course readings (selected scholarly journal articles and two collections of essays). The group project assignment, presented at the end of the semester was the focus of this study.

This qualitative study was designed to solicit feedback from learners about the instructional strategy—the use of adaptation to effect transformative learning. The class worked in groups on final projects. Each group selected a historical event or figure from the late eighteenth through the mid–19th century. This end-point was later extended to the end of the nineteenth century to accommodate a group who wanted to include an important woman who had just begun to achieve prominence in the mid–19th century. Each group reviewed the historical record (according to history textbooks and conventional primary sources), then turned to documentaries and museum exhibits, popular film and television, and literature, including autobiographies, biographies, and historical fiction—all various adaptations of their selected person's or event's history. The groups wrote individual reports about their individual research component and a group presentation about their collaboration. Their presentations were made in class, with supporting documents shared in our learning management system. They covered what they learned from their research—not only about the person or event under study, but also about what each adaptation tells us about society (and the perspective or interpretation of the author, director, developer, etc.) at the time of its creation and presentation to the public. They were to address how and why these interpretations changed over time, and what that process can teach us about historical thinking and how we view the world. There was an individual reflection component as well, examining how the process of this investigation affected each learner's frame of reference for approaching the topic and the discipline.

At the end of October 2016, all 21 eligible learners in the class received an email from me inviting them to participate in the survey. The email message contained a link to the anonymous survey, administered via Qualtrics, an online survey creation collection, and analysis platform. The survey was designed to prevent learner information from being attached to the responses. The survey was sent to the learners using their university email accounts and any personal email account on record with the university. However, I could not be certain that all twenty-one eligible learners would receive a copy of the survey link. Faculty members know that learners do not always check their university email accounts, particularly if they are not currently taking courses, and the status of personal email accounts on record is notoriously unreliable. I put the email addresses I had obtained in the blind courtesy copy (bcc) section of the email address line, to protect learner privacy.

Data Collection/Data Sources

I developed the open-ended survey questions to capture the anecdotal information I had received (email correspondence after the class had ended) and to systematically collect data about the efficacy of the transformative learning impact of the use of adaptation in teaching history. The questions were reviewed by a colleague in the instructional design office. The informed consent form encapsulated the project and included a brief introduction designed to encourage reflection about the course experience and final project. In addition, the main question set was prefaced with this brief prompt (in case they simply accepted the consent and proceeded to the survey), "In the final class projects about specific historical figures or events related to US women's history, your groups utilized conventional history source materials as well as adaptations (for example, historical fiction novels, television, and films). For your individual component, you were also expected to reflect on the use of these different layers of the historical 'story') see full survey questionnaire in the Appendix)."

Of the 21 eligible learners, 19 surveys were returned. Ten of the surveys had completed responses to the question sets; six were only partially completed, and three were blank surveys. In other words, 47.6 percent of the surveys were returned with data that could be analyzed for this study. The responses came back anonymously—not linked to any easily identifiable learner information such as ID numbers, names, or email addresses.

Treatment of the Data/Data Analysis

I utilized a modified version of the case study method, suggested by John W. Creswell (*Educational*). Although the open-ended surveys were brief, the supporting data included all of the course materials, correspondence with former learners after the course ended, my class notes, and my reflections about the experience. To preserve confidentiality of the survey respondents' identities, I removed any identifying information from their comments and assigned pseudonyms (Learner B through Learner T). The hard copies of the data were stored on the university desktop computer in my university office, where I coded the responses. Because the survey was administered electronically, the informed consent forms and original responses are all password protected in the university Qualtrics account.

After reading through each set of responses several times, I transferred the material into a spreadsheet and sorted by question. I employed a combination of open and axial coding (Hopewell) to develop a set of themes for analysis (Creswell *Qualitative Inquiry & Research Design*; Lofgren). I verified patterns from the responses and documents associated with the case to corroborate the accounts (Creswell *Qualitative Inquiry & Research Design*). At the end of the study, I utilized Hoggan's chart to further analyze the data, and to visually convey the analysis and meaning for the reader.

Provisions of Trustworthiness

I adopted research methods suggested by Creswell (*Qualitative, Educational*), Kent Lofgren (*Qualitative*) and demonstrated by Thomas M. Hopewell (*Risks*). These methods included triangulating participants' responses with each other and with related course materials and document. In addition, I employed a measure of member checking by discussing the project with one of the most interested participants after the survey had closed to get her input on what had emerged from analysis of the data.

Epoche

I was the instructor for this class, I acknowledge opinions and interests that influenced me in selecting this topic for investigation. It is important to note, however, that because the survey was conducted long after the semester had ended (which was necessary given the research goal), learner participation or lack thereof could have no impact on their grades. Moreover, I am not teaching this year, so it is highly unlikely given the university's upper-level-only status, that the learners would be in a position to have me as their instructor again.

Findings

The data analysis process was conducted within the framework of Alan Bryman's four stages filtered through approaches of Graham R. Gibbs ("Coding") and Kent Lofgren. A combination of open and axial coding (Hopewell) helped me to connect the research objectives with emerging themes related to learner attitudes and perspectives about the transformative learning impact of the use of adaptation in this class.

Themes

The learners' comments demonstrated their attitudes and their perspectives on the impact of using adaptation on their learning experience. Their responses encompassed four extremely interconnected themes: clearer understanding; learner satisfaction; reflective understanding; and historical thinking.

Clearer Understanding

Three of the ten learners specifically connected the use of adaptation to a clearer understanding of the material. For example, Learner B explained: "The adaptations simplified my understanding of the topic; made it easier to understand exactly what I was looking for." And in response to another question, the learner reiterated "adaptations made it easier to understand a topic."

Others in the class shared this point of view. Learner F noted that adaptations "helped me to more easily think about historical events from the viewpoints of the people that existed about that time"—addressing historical thinking as well. In addition, Learner H concurred that adaptations, "connected the dots between the topic[s] and made it easier to analyze."

Table 1. Clearer understanding. Summary of key learner responses that demonstrate learner perceptions that working with adaptation resulted in a clearer understanding of the course topics, materials, and concepts.

Summary of key student responses regarding clearer understanding as a result of working with adaptations*

- Adaptations simplified my understanding of the topic (B)
- Made it easier to understand exactly what I was looking for (B)
- Adaptations made it easier to understand a topic (B)
- Helped me to more easily think about historical events from the viewpoints of the people that existed about the time (F)
- Connected the dots between the topic and made it easier to analyze (H)

*underlining added to emphasize relationship to themes; letters in parentheses indicate the pseudonym of the student that made the comments included here

Learner Satisfaction

Part of what we are seeing with "clearer understanding" is that the learners found the use of adaptation provided more satisfaction in that it made the study of history more engaging and enjoyable. Four learners emphasized how engaging they found the adaptations. Learner K explained that "the use of adaptations made me more curious to look into the topic we covered." Learner C described the experience: "I feel that adaptations are an important and interesting layer when it comes to studying history. Especially when there are several different adaptations from different time periods." In response to another question, Learner C exclaimed: "we really enjoyed working together on our project." Learner J found that the project/use of adaptation "made you put yourself in the time period itself to truly understand it. I learned a great deal." This concept of putting "yourself in time period" also speaks to historical literacy, a thread running through many responses and themes. Learner F noted: "it was fun too, which also made it memorable." Memorable—that is a key point for transformative learning, that it have a lasting impact. Five other learners made specific comments about the use of adaptations making history more tangible for them. For example, Learner B explained: "unlike a traditional history source, such adaptation, like a movie, provided a tangible source in the sense that I can see for myself exactly what the source is telling me." The learner conceded: "Whether or not the adaptations are completely accurate historically, that is debatable." Learner E explained the concept this way: "The adaptations gave a much more human feel to the historical figures that we studied. When you're able to find a way to relate to a historical figure, it is much easier to write about their life." In response to another question, Learner E elaborated in way that overlaps with the historical thinking theme as well: "Most people think history is boring and bland, but these adaptations find a way to spice up history, of course adaptations aren't completely accurate, and fine to show people that these historical figures were normal people placed upon a pedestal, so it really isn't that hard to relate to them" (Learner E). For Learner E and others in the class, the adaptations were a good bridge. As Learner G put it: "The use of adaptations brought the evidence to life." Learner H suggested: "I think it should be used more to teach history. It will make history come alive, and the learners that experience it will be happier than using some of the other methods that seem boring." Coming back to Learner J's position, the transformative impact is evident: "The way it [the class] was set up was relevant and encouraged active and reward type of thinking way after the class was over. The discussions in class were great, and were sometimes heated."

Table 2. Learner satisfaction. Summary of key learner that demonstrate learner perceptions that the use of adaptation made learning more engaging and/or fun.

Summary of key student responses regarding **learner satisfaction** as a result of working with adaptations*

- Adaptations are an important and <u>interesting</u> layer when it comes to studying history (C)
- We <u>really enjoyed working together</u> on our project (C)
- It was <u>fun</u> too, which also made it <u>more memorable</u> (F)
- The use of adaptations <u>made me more curious</u> to look into the topic (K)
- Made you <u>put yourself into the time period</u> to truly understand it (J)
- Provided a <u>tangible</u> source in the sense I can <u>see for myself</u> exactly what the source is telling me (B)
- Adaptations <u>gave a much more human feel</u> to the historical figures that we studies (E)
- Adaptations find a way to <u>spice up history</u> (E)
- Use of adaptations <u>brought the evidence to life</u> (G)
- <u>Make history come alive</u>, and the students that experience it will be <u>happier</u> (H)
- <u>Relevant</u> and encouraged <u>active</u> and reward type of thinking (J)

*underlining added to emphasize relationship to themes; letters in parentheses indicate the pseudonym of the student that made the comments included here

Reflective Understanding

Nine of the learners reflected on how the use of adaptations enhanced their understanding of the history. Learner B stated that "the use of adaptations made me realize just how important traditional sources are." The learner elaborated in response to another question, explaining, "I feel that I achieved an understanding between the historical contexts [of the original event] and contexts of the adaptations." Learner F described the process:

> Adaptations exposed me to various points of view about the topic that I might not have seen otherwise. Seeing fictional versus nonfictional adaptations of my topic also helped me to see how it had been romanticized, and therefore gave me a better idea of how it had affected our nation at the time. Finally, exposure to various adaptations had the benefit of repeated re-exposure, which helped me to firmer cement my learning about the topic [Learner F].

Learner C and Learner E both wrote at length about their groups' projects and the relationship of the historical topics they investigated and subsequent adaptations of them, and what they learned. Learner D expressed this perspective more succinctly: "These methods gave me a more [in-]depth understanding." Learner G was similarly concise: "It had a profound impact because it helped me to go deeper into the subject." Learner I emphasized the value and complexity derived from working with adaptation as well and explained: "I haven't [have] never experienced this type of methodology to teach history.

**Table 3. Reflective understanding. Summary
of key learner responses that demonstrate learner
reflections on their perceptions of enhanced
understanding of course topic, materials,
and concepts as a result of working with adaptation.**

Summary of key student responses regarding **reflective understanding** as a result of working with adaptations*

- These methods gave a <u>more [in-]depth understanding</u> (D)
- Adaptations <u>exposed me to various points of view about the topic that I might not have seen otherwise</u> (F)
- Finally, exposure to various adaptations had the benefit of <u>repeated re-exposure</u>, which helped me to <u>firmer cement my learning</u> about the topic (F)
- It gave me a <u>well-rounded understanding</u> of the topics we were researching (I)
- It helped me to <u>go deeper</u> into the subject (I)
- It had a profound impact because it helped me to <u>go deeper</u> into the subject (G)
- Use of adaptations made me realize just how important traditional sources are (B)
- The <u>constant re-exposure</u> to the subject through reviewing the various adaptations helped me to commit what I learned about my topic to <u>permanent memory</u> (F)

*underlining added to emphasize relationship to themes; letters in parentheses indicate the pseudonym of the student that made the comments included here

It gave me a well-rounded understanding of the topics we were researching. It helped me to go deeper into the subject."

Historical Thinking

Eight of the learner responses addressed the theme of historical thinking. They directly discussed the positive impact of using adaption to develop their historical thinking skills. For some, it was as simple as gauging historical accuracy within the adaptation. For example, Learner C noted that "it helped us to realize how Hollywood can try to tweak history (romanticize, dramatize) to make money." Learner I emphasized the issue of historical accuracy as well, taking it a bit further: "The adaptations helped us to analyze evidence critically, because we had to determine fact from fiction. We had to understand how the historical figure changed over time through the adaptation and why. We also had to interpret the changes and compare those to changes that were made in the past or through other adaptations" (Learner I). Learner B's comments supported those of Learner I. Learner B also noted that

> what adaptations forced me to do is analyze them critically, and look for the mistakes and historical inaccuracies. They are bound to spring up. Now is this a bad thing? Probably not because by analyzing the adaptation, I am, more or less, checking my understanding of the topic. Essentially, adaptations improved my ability to think critically because I realized that if you genuinely look hard enough, you begin to analyze something without actually knowing it [Learner B].

This notion of lasting impact (such as beginning to implement critical analysis as one's reflexive response), was expressed by Learner J as well. Given the specific topic of this class, Learner J noted: "I did think differently about some groups of women after this class, I also thought differently about those who wrote about them." Learner K commented on enhanced skepticism: "the adaptations affected the way I think about traditional historical evidence by making me view the adaptation in a more critical light." Others, like Learner E, found that the adaptation project "made me think about things that usually would not be touched upon," Learner E explained, which led to the determination "that there is always a way to connect past figures and their problems to the people of today." Likewise, Learner G, commented that the project helped them to demonstrate the characteristics of historical thinking: "It made me think of history from the side of those who lived it. To think of history in today's modern culture would cause bias to the one that was studying history in which they were studying [presentism]." This application was echoed in the comments of Learner F, who also wrote: "Adaptations helped me to better understand and identify public reactions concerning various events, how these possibly correlated to future events of historical significance." Learner F concluded that "something I took away from this course that I have not in courses similar is that we can better understand and analyze historical events if we do our best to understand and analyze those events throughout the viewpoints of the people whom lived through those times." Highlighting the transformative impact of adaptation on historical thinking, Learner H explained: "This class changed the perspective I had, and completely overturned many things I thought were only a certain way. It made me see the subject from many angles giving me a better understanding of the topic at hand."

Table 4. Historical thinking. Summary of key learner responses regarding learner perceptions that historical thinking skills improved as a result of working with adaptation.

Summary of key student responses regarding **historical thinking** as a result of working with adaptations*

- Affected the way I think about traditional historical evidence by making me view the adaptions in a more critical light (K)
- We can better understand and analyze historical events if we do our best to understand and analyze those events throughout the viewpoints of the people whom lived through those times (F)
- I did think differently about some groups of women after this class, I also thought differently about those who wrote about them (J)
- It made me think of history from the side of those who lived it (G)
- This class changed the perspective I had, and completely overturned many things I thought were only a certain way at hand (H)
- It changed the way I viewed history among other subjects as a whole (G)
- Adaptations helped me to better understand and identify public reactions concerning various events, how these possibly correlated to future events of historical significance (F)
- It made me think about things that usually would not be touched upon (E)
- It helped us to realize how Hollywood can try to tweak history (romanticize, dramatize) to make money (C)
- [what] Adaptations forced me to do is analyze them critically, and look for the mistakes and historical inaccuracies (B)
- Essentially, adaptations improved my ability to think critically (B)
- The adaptations helped us to analyze the evidence critically (I)

*underlining added to emphasize relationship to themes; letters in parentheses indicate the pseudonym of the student that made the comments included here

Discussion

The learners who responded to the open-ended survey demonstrated an awareness of the value of adaptations on their learning processes and an appreciation for the efficacy of adaptation as a strategy for improving their historical thinking skills. When reviewing learner responses and emerging themes in the context of the scholarly literature, the overlapping nature of the themes became clear. The research objective of investigating learner perceptions of the impact of the use adaptations on their historical thinking emerged as a major theme, and the research objective of assessing learner perceptions of transformative learning through the use of adaptations emerged as well.

Conclusions

Although a minor theme, several learners specifically noted a *Clearer Understanding*. They described the usefulness of the adaptations in making the historical materials easier to understand and analyze. The idea of this approach "connect[ing] the dots between the topic[s] and ma[king it easier to analyze" the evidence is supported by Marcus and Metzger. The learner comments that reflected the theme of *Learner Satisfaction* were similar. Learner satisfaction encompassed the hook that often captured and held learner interest. The potential danger, as Al-Shalabi, Jack, Marcus et al., and Metzger pointed out, is to not let it stop there. The instructor must have a carefully crafted instructional strategy to move the learners past the "pedagogical potential" (Metzger 67), and through to effective practice. That the learners experienced—and could recall six months later having worked with multiple adaptations and having enjoyed the project, and learned a lot—is encouraging. The most prevalent theme was *Reflective Understanding*. The learner responses are supported by the work of Marcus et al. Feature films in particular helped the learners to better visualize the past and to challenge their previous, simplistic understandings of the past (Marcus et al. 13). The final theme, and the most strongly connected to the second research objective of this study, *Historical Thinking* was addressed by most of the learners. Their comments demonstrated they had retained the skills they had developed in the course. The learners' detailed responses aligned with Metzger's explanation of historical literacy concepts, the critical skills outlined by Marcus et al., Jack, and Djamàa. For example: "We had to understand how the historical figure changed over time through the adaptation and why. We also had to interpret the changes and compare those to changes that were made in the past or through other adaptations" as explained by Learner I.

Transformative Learning

Using Hoggan's transformative learning typology and criteria to evaluate the transformative impact of the learners' learning experience, it is evident

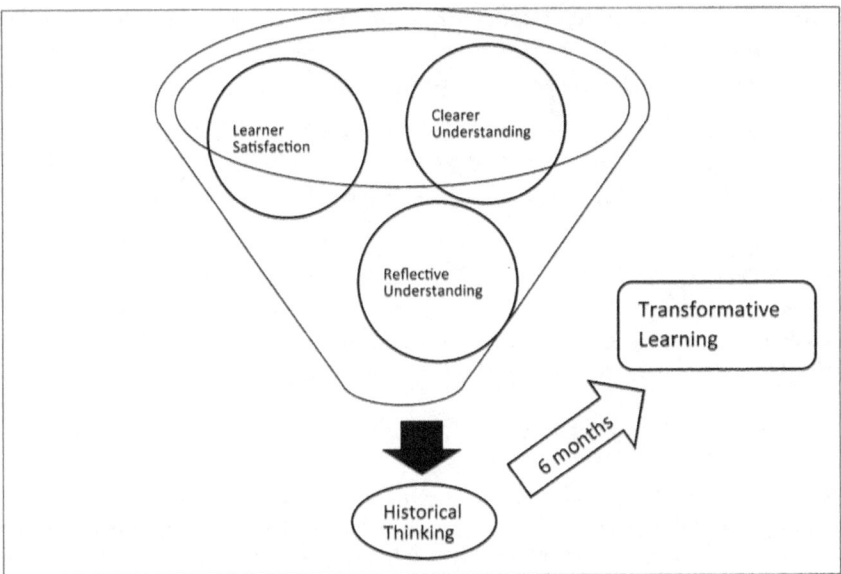

Fig. 1 Themes. Depiction of learner response themes funneling into major theme of historical thinking, and assessment of transformative impact.

that the limited qualitative study did not probe deeply enough to obtain the evidence necessary to fully complete the typology and criteria chart. There is enough information for the data to show promise, however, and to demonstrate that learner perspectives of the impact of the use of adaptation to improve historical thinking and to achieve transformative learning was positive. As Learner G expressed it, "I would recommend this class to everyone no matter their major. I often think there should have been a part II [chronologically, to the class]. It changed the way I view history among other subjects as well." And as Learner F explained, "The constant re-exposure to the subject through reviewing the various adaptations helped me to commit what I learned about my topic to permanent memory."

Implications

The literature clarifies the need for educators to be adequately prepared (Al-Shalabi, Jack, Marcus et al., Metzger), to guide learners through the process of "treating movies [and other adaptations] as arguments or interpretations of the past to be examined and debated]" (Metzger 73). This study, although small and limited, suggests that the instructional strategy of using adaptation along with conventional historical sources can be very successful

Outcome	Deep Impact	Multiple Life Contexts*	Relative Stability
Worldview			
Assumptions, etc.	B, C, E, G, H, J, K	[Not assessed]	G, H, J, K
More Inclusive	C, E, F, J	[Not assessed]	F, J
Epistemology			
More Discriminating	B, C, E, F, G, H, I, J, K	[Not assessed]	F, G, H, J, K
More Open	B, C, G, H, J	[Not assessed]	G, J
More Reflective	B,,E, F, G, I, J	[Not assessed]	F, G, J
Ontology			
Capable of Change	C, F, G, H, J	[Not assessed]	F, G, H. J
More Self-Directed	B, E, G, H, J, K	[Not assessed]	F, G, J, K
Behavior**	[Not assessed]	[Not assessed]	[Not assessed]

Chart 1. Hoggan's Typology of Transformative Learning. Data from learner responses to the open-ended survey, assessed using Hoggan's typology. Learner pseudonym letters are referenced in each category to which their comments aligned. *Multiple life contexts were not assessed, although one learner referenced application of the impact on his/her approach to other academic areas. **The study did not include observation of learner behavior or questions that addressed self-reporting of behavior.

in helping learners achieve learning goals. It demonstrates the efficacy of using adaptation as a strategy for teaching history as well as transformative learning.

Future Research

To more effectively evaluate this approach, the study should be conducted over several more semesters using the same instructional strategy—integrating adaptation into undergraduate history coursework—the instruments for the study should be further refined to more fully include Hoggan's definition of transformative learning as well as his typology and criteria from the initial stages of research design. The open-ended survey questions should be reviewed by scholars with expertise in adaptation and its application to the discipline of history, such as Raw, Gurr, and Tutan. In addition, the open-ended surveys should be followed up with qualitative interviews to collect more in-depth and useful data.

In addition, further research on teaching with adaptation in a paired course environment would be useful. Much of the literature focuses on the use of film in history classes (Jack, Marcus et al., and Metzger) or on the use of film and/or literature in literature classes (Al-Shalabi, Jackson, Schwab and Fry). Pairing a course from each discipline in a truly transdisciplinary approach, would make for an engaging learning environment, and would make a fascinating study on transformative learning and the use of adaptation.

Appendix

Survey Questions from the open-ended Survey Questionnaire, delivered via Qualtrics

*Note, although we do not offer sophomore-level courses, some learners transfer in with sophomore standing due to number of credit hours completed.

Section 1: *Background*

1. Which title best describes your academic classification in spring 2016—when you were enrolled in U.S. Women's History to 1877 with Dr. Bunkowski?

- Sophomore*
- Junior
- Senior
- Other _____

2. What is your academic major? _____

Section 2: *Adaptation and U.S. Women's History*. In the final class projects about specific historical figures or events related to U.S. women's history, your groups utilized conventional historical source materials as well as adaptations (for example, historical fiction novels, television, and films). For your individual component, you were also expected to reflect on the use of these different layers of the historical "story."

1. What impact do you feel that the use of adaptations had on your understanding of your topic that might not have been achieved through the use of traditional historical source materials alone?
2. In what ways did the use of adaptations affect the way you think about traditional historical evidence?
3. One of the goals of this project was to make connections in our understanding between the historical context of our research subjects and the contexts of each adaptation. To what degree do you feel you achieved this? What do the connections reveal about social and cultural history over time?

4. One of our course objectives was to apply course materials to improve historical thinking. In what ways did the use of adaptations affect your ability to think historically? [critical thinking skills applied to History: analyzing evidence content and sourcing; interpretation; comparison; contextualization; synthesis; causation; patterns of continuity and change over time; periodization; argumentation] AP/College Board.

5. Is there anything you wish to share about the project/use of adaptations in our U.S. Women's History class?

WORKS CITED

Al-Shalabi, Nazmi. "Using Film to Teach American Literature: Roland Joffe's Adaptation of Hawthorne's *The Scarlet Letter* and Peter Ustinov's Adaptation of Herman Melville's *Billy Budd* as Two Case Studies." *Teaching American Literature: A Journal of Theory and Practice* 4.2 (2011): 53–66. Print.

Anderson, D.D. "Using Features Films as Tools for Analysis in a Psychology and Law course." *Teaching of Psychology* 19.3 (1992): 155–58. Print.

Andrews, Thomas, and Flannery Burke. "What Does It Mean to Think Historically? *Perspectives on History* 45.1 (2007): 32–35. Print.

Connor-Greene, Patricia A. "Interdisciplinary Critical Inquiry: Teaching about the Social Construction of Madness." *Teaching of Psychology* 33.1 (2006): 6–13. Print.

Creswell, John W. *Educational Research: Planning, Conducting, and Evaluating Quantitative and Qualitative Research*. 5th ed. New York: Pearson, 2015. Print.

_____. *Qualitative Inquiry & Research Design: Choosing Among Five Approaches*. 3rd ed. Thousand Oaks: Sage, 2013. Print.

Dewey, John. *Democracy in Education: An Introduction to the Philosophy of Education*. New York: Macmillan 1916. Electronic Text Center, University of Virginia Library. Web. 5 Feb. 2017.

Dirkx, John M. "Self-Formation and Transformative Learning; A Response to 'Calling Transformative Learning Into Question: Some Mutinous Thoughts,' by Michael Newman." *Adult Education Quarterly* 62.4 (2012): 399–405. Print.

Djamàa, Sara. "Reading the Book versus 'Reading' the Film: Cinematic Adaptations of Literature as Catalyst for EFL Learners' Critical Thinking Dispositions." *Journal of Language Teaching & Research* 7.2 (2016): 252–263. Print.

Gibbs, Graham R. "Coding Part 1: Alan Bryman's 4 Stages of Qualitative Analysis." YouTube. 24 October 2011. Web. 6 Feb. 2017.

Hoggan, Chad D. "Transformative Learning as a Metatheory: Definition, Criteria, and Typology." *Adult Education Quarterly* 66.1 (2016): 41–50. Print.

Hopewell, T.M. "Risks Associated with the Choice to Teach Online." *Online Journal of Distance Learning Administration* 15.4 (2012). Web. 3 Feb. 2017.

Hullender, Ren, et al. "Evidences of Transformative Learning in Service-Learning Reflections." *Journal of the Scholarship of Teaching and Learning* 15.4 (2015): 58–82. Print.

IDEA Center. "Objectives." Faculty Information Form [Legacy], 1998. *IDEA Center*. Web. 2 Feb. 2017.

Jack, Bryan. "Feature Films as History." *The Councilor: A Journal of the Social Studies* 76.1 (2015): 1–8. Print.

Jackson, Jeffrey E. "Apples to Apples: A Book-History Approach to Film Adaptations in the Classroom." *The CEA Critic* 77.4 (2015): 295–99. Print.

Kuennen, Jacqueline K. "Critical Reflection: A Transformative Learning Process Integrating Theory and Evidence-Based Practice." *Worldviews on Evidence-Based Nursing* 12.5 (2015): 306–08. Print.

Lofgren, Kent. "*Qualitative Analysis of Interview Data: A Step-by-step Guide.*" YouTube, 19 May 2013. Web. 3 Feb. 2017.

Marcus, Alan S., et al. *Teaching History with Film: Strategies for Secondary Social Studies.* New York: Routledge, 2010. Print.

Metzger, Scott Alan. "Pedagogy and the Historical Feature Film: Toward Historical Literacy." *Film & History* 37.2 (2007): 67–75. Print.

Mezirow, Jack. "Transformative Learning as Discourse." *Journal of Transformative Education* 1.1 (2003): 58–63. Print.

_____. "Transformative Learning: Theory to Practice." *New Directions for Adult and Continuing Education* 74 (1997): 5–12. Print..

Monk, Claire. *Heritage Film Audiences: Period Films and Contemporary Audiences in the UK.* Edinburgh: Edinburgh University Press, 2011. Print.

Munslow, Alun. "Genre and History/Historying." *Rethinking History* 19.2 (2015): 158–76. Print.

Newman, Michael. "Michael Newman's Final Comments in the Forum on His Article 'Calling Transformative Learning into Question: Some Mutinous Thoughts.'" *Adult Education Quarterly* 62.4 (2012): 406–11. Print.

_____. "Transformative Learning: Mutinous Thoughts Revisited." *Adult Education Quarterly* 64.4 (2014): 345–55. Print.

O'Connor, John E. "Reading, Writing, and Critical Viewing: Coordinating Skill Development in History Learning." *The History Teacher* 34.2 (2001): 183–92. Print.

Paul, Richard, and Linda Elder. *The Thinker's Guide to the Art of Socratic Questioning.* New York: Foundation for Critical Thinking, 2006. Print.

Raw, Laurence, and Tony Gurr. *Adaptation Studies and Learning: New Frontiers.* Lanham: Scarecrow, 2013. Print.

Raw, Laurence, and Defne Ersin Tutan. "Introduction: What Does 'Adapting' History Involve?" *The Adaptation of History: Essays on Ways of Telling the Past.* Ed. Laurence Raw and Defne Ersin Tutan, 7–23. Jefferson: McFarland, 2013. Print.

Schwab, Allen, and Carrol Fry. "Journey to the End of Life Lessons from Teaching Melville's *Billy Budd, Sailor* and Peter Ustinov's *Billy Budd.*" *Eureka Studies in Teaching Short Fiction* 11/12 (2015): 95–110. Print.

Scriven, Michael, and Richard Paul. "Critical Thinking as Defined by the National Council for Excellence in Critical Thinking, 1987." *The Critical Thinking Community.* Web. 4 Feb. 2017.

Taylor, Edward W. "Transformative Learning Theory." *New Directions for Adult and Continuing Education* 119 (2008): 5–15. Print.

Faiblesse des Deux Côtés

Adaptation and Value
in Sexual Subjectivation

JILLIAN SAINT JACQUES

"There are ... transsexuals who dislike transvestites as well
as homosexuals. Intolerance can be found in strange quarters"
> —Benjamin *Transsexual Phenomenon* 53

"Weakness on both sides is, as we know, the motto of all
quarrels"
> —Voltaire *Philosophical Dictionary* 200

You often hear it said that "people never really change," but it seems to
me that all 58 years of my life have been characterized by change. I am certainly not the person I was when I started, physically or ideologically, though
I am—and have always been—me. Some of these changes and their inevitable
remainders, vestiges of my life as a transsexual and post-transsexual, were
manifested of my own accord, while other changes, like the loss of my mother,
were visited on me through no choice of my own. Until I get to the end of
the road, it is difficult for me to say what these changes add up to, and even
then it will only be a matter of perspective—but here's something I know for
certain: through the shaping process of time, which is little more than an
ongoing milieu of birth, eradication and resistance, many of the aforemen-
tioned changes, intentional or not, have been inscribed on my body, resulting
in a transdisciplinary physical and psychic text as pointed and opaque as any
other, a nebulous transposition of identities yielding an intimate mélange of
scars, syntax, memories and mannerisms. Viewing a series of photographs
that depicts various sexual subject positions I've inhabited since infancy, this

essay will consider my own body as a corpus of study, not merely in a flesh-and-blood sense, but as a body of work, a compendium of textual, theoretical and physical facts that form a works-in-progress that continues to resist quantification against the normative grain.

Consider, for example, the set of images depicting my childhood. In the first photo (plate 1), infant-me nestles between his apparently doting parents; my father, a Freudian analyst, my mother, a professional painter. And there I am several years later, in 1962, sitting in the lap of a roly-poly Santa whose skin smelt like powdered dough [plate 2]). A third photo depicts a malcontent teenager lounging at home (plate 3), while a fourth image finds me home on leave from the U.S. Air Force in 1979, attempting to strike a heraldic pose in Britannia jeans, gripping a cutlass

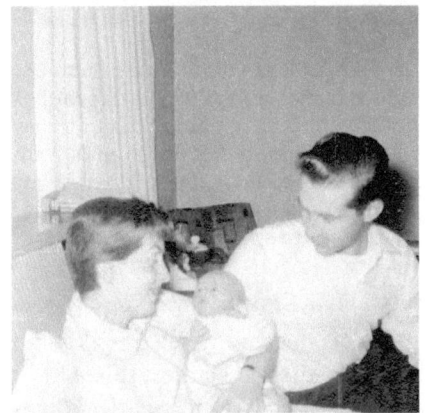

Left: **Plate 1: One month old, nestled between mom and dad in Detroit, Michigan, 1957. Photographer unknown, family photograph.** *Below, left:* **Plate 2: Posing with Santa at J.L. Hudson on Woodward Avenue, 1961. Photographer unknown, family photograph.** *Below, right:* **Plate 3: The author as spaced-out teenager in Santa Fe, New Mexico, 1972. Photographer unknown, family photograph.**

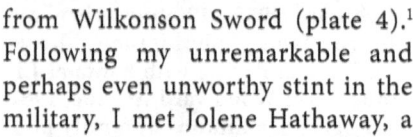

Left: Plate 4: Home on leave from the U.S. Air Force, 1979. Photographer unknown, family photograph. *Above:* Plate 5: A sunny day on Jolene's farm in Durango, Colorado, kissing my favorite ducklings, 1981. Photographer unknown, property of the author.

from Wilkonson Sword (plate 4).[1] Following my unremarkable and perhaps even unworthy stint in the military, I met Jolene Hathaway, a massage therapist who was perhaps the most violent lover I ever had. She owned a cherry orchard, and this picture depicts me among the trees kissing a tribe of newborn ducks several months before their execution (plate 5).

If I examine these initial snapshots in terms of my own *sexual acclimatization*—I will argue in this essay that individual human beings, in a singular sense, cannot be said to sexually *adapt*—this set of images underscores the influence of parents, culture and socioeconomic circumstances on my first 25 years of life. In my compendium of childhood memories, homophobic, violent men weren't the exception, they were the rule, and the overbearing regime of patriarchal oppression, which provided the ontological support for their privileges, was bolstered at every turn by an ages-old interlacement of teachers, church, medicine and the state. This overarching ontological apparatus considered sexual difference of any kind—particularly homosexuality and anything connected to it—as a disease calling for treatment by psychiatrists or exorcism by priests—and it was in reaction to this normativity-machine that my own "sexual identity" was formed, a lexicon of assimilations and reactions to patriarchal prohibitions that influenced my own attempts to negotiate the turbulent waters of sexual subjectivation. As Judith Butler (and Sigmund Freud) might argue, sexual identities are not born, they're made—and the script for their making, a script composed of "thou shalt nots" and their enforcement in a legitimized code of social injustice, existed long before I or any of us came into this world.

Looking at these images of my own body as a body of work, then, I think I can at least make the claim that my relationship to the theoretical confluence of sexuality and adaptation is deeply personal: lived knowledge. Considering each of the influences and changes that have shaped the subjective contours of my physical and ideological corpus, along with the fact that I am still, at the end of the day, myself, I can only concur with Freud and Lacan in their observations that adaptation, in a psychological sense at least, does not and cannot exist, inasmuch as the individual human psyche, in its organic state, does not and cannot survive. As Freud often noted, it wasn't his objective to transform unhappy subjects into happy little sprites in Santa's Great Workshop; psychoanalysis was never intended to *adjust* neurotics and psychopaths into harmonious cogs in a grand machine. Its purpose was to assist organic human beings in acclimating to the ongoing trauma of life, which at best is chaotic, emergent and arbitrary. Viewed in this sense (ultimately, a Darwinian sense), the individual human can never be said to adapt; instead, the solo organism merely acclimates to the conditions of its existence for a time. This semantic difference bears emphasis; to put a fine point on it, adaptations to organisms and species only occur over transgenerational spans of time, through the development and eradication of discrete characteristics and traits that result in extensive alterations to a group, with acclimation as the in-transit process through which adaptations can be said to emerge. There is much hope here; namely, if we work hard as a species—an incalculable number of individuals sharing a common space, through a process of continued and various individual acclimations—we can create more habitable spaces in which our species may adapt, not only to survive longer, but to survive better.

Nevertheless, in a biological sense, adaptation only provisionally belongs to the individual, inasmuch as adaptations consist of long-term transformations manifested in the community, not the singleton, no matter how bold, utilitarian or unusual those manifestations might be. Until discrete manifestations take on a larger level, they are simply isolated modifications, mutations, aberrations. This does not in any way devalue the intense relationship of psychoanalysis and adaptation—instead, it places a specific and even rarified value on both of them, particularly if we dream of adapting our culture to accommodate more difference rather than less. Psychoanalysis for the individual subject might be a temporary or provisional palliative, but if you have a terrible headache, a temporary palliative is better than no palliative at all. Indeed, if we agree that more progressive cultures in turn support more progressive human beings, the wider efficacy of a temporary analytic palliative, whether our analysis be cultural or critical, bears more than the possibility of improving our collective living conditions. It opens a corridor for us to change the conditions of our existence to the extent that we will no longer be dependent on that specific elixir to heal our cultural ills—although I suspect we will never be free from psychic or intellectual palliatives altogether. Analysis of any kind is a glass onion. You strip away one layer of neurosis only to encounter another: the analysis interminable.

"Me-search," Sexual Identities, Valuations of the Isolated Phase

In their highly prescriptive book, *Me-Search and Re-search: A Guide for Writing Scholarly Personal Narrative Manuscripts* (2011), authors DeMethra Bradley and Robert Nash claim the praxis of writing scholarly personal narratives was "a genre created over 15 years ago by *Robert*"—the Robert in question being the Nash at hand (3, emphasis mine). Setting this preposterous assertion aside, Nash and Bradley kick off their project by identifying several interesting questions for "me-searchers" who are new to the game of autobiography as scholarship. "Where exactly is the 'me' in my writing," the authors ask, "and why is the 'me' [so] important in advancing my ideas to others?" (6). It's a decent enough rhetorical question, though Bradley and Nash answer it in the most obvious direction (how can one harness the quality of personal narrative to advance their scholarly aims?). The question they beg is far more productive, and part of a larger existential query: Where exactly is the "me" in the general emergence of life? While it's not surprising that a tightly structural enterprise as *Mesearch and Research*, which seeks to reduce "the complex method of SPN [scholarly personal narrative] writing into bite-sized steps," steers clear of this post-structuralist dilemma—given their tendency to aggrandize the most banal of topics, it's probably best for Bradley and Nash to leave the deconstruction of the speaking subject to post-structuralists like Judith Butler or Michel Foucault, who had something intelligent to say about it (x).

I would like to linger for a moment on how Nash and Bradley set the word "me" in quotes. In performing this form of rhetorical shorthand, their grammatical bookending of "me" is suspicious, like those compendium pronouns (s/he) so popular in the '90s or the more recent gender-neutral compressions that comprise their semantic offspring ("Xena ate hir food because ze was hungry"). In their usage, the word "me" becomes a one-size-fits-all that tries to do too much too fast. Is the framing of "me" in quotes a gesture towards intertextuality, a quick nod to identity politics or lip-service to an entire discourse of human subjectivation? It's impossible to tell. But the question within a question is axiomatic for this section of my chapter, inasmuch as the "me" that advances through an aggressively reductive process of "life,"

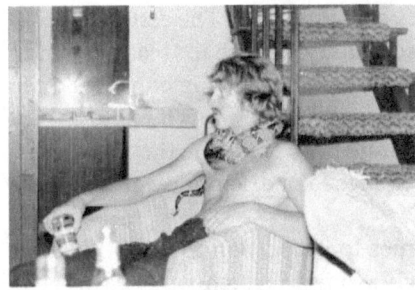

Above: Plate 6: Bare-chested with Gus at The Iron Horse Inn in Durango, 1983. Photograph by Bonnie Gibbs. *Right:* Plate 7: Returning to the Four Corners as a punk rocker, Mesa Verde, 1985. Photograph by Lisa Russell.

resisting the onslaught of forces beyond its control as it emerges into diffusion, is the same intertextual location that anoints itself with the process of valuation. Because this same kernel of sentience is the "me" who values things, typically in positive and negative terms: this thing was a failure, that thing was a success, glad I did that one, definitely regretted the other. The third flavor lacked panache, the fourth was an utter bore.

And the voices of many "me"s in unison creates a mighty roar, a verdict, a "way" (*we don't do things that way around here*), common knowledge, collective conclusion. Yet while value is solidified by the "me," whether singular (an individual person) or plural ("us," i.e., the human race), it remains a distinctly *human* value.[2] But the problem with this system of valuation often results in binaries that are easily falsifiable, inasmuch as they are too simplistic to account for the variety of interactions at play in complex operations like adaptation. The binary division of factual vs. "personal" writing in one obvious example, as can be witnessed in the system of "me-search" Nash and Bradley describe:

> Some research projects require methodologies that result in testable, factual, data-driven answers, all guided by a *cool dispassion*. Other research projects require personal leaps of faith, intuition, emotion, all guided by a *warm passion*. Dispassion calls for research residing in the cool waters of objective reason, disciplined empirical investigation, and logic; passion calls for research residing in the warm waters of self-disclosure, story-telling, artistic innovation, and empathy. We will argue that both languages have a rightful (and justifiable) place in this world of research [82].

I do not believe that forcing passion and dispassion into a binary relationship is productive, however—particularly if we view "testable, factual, data-driven answers" as property of the dispassionate, with "faith, intuition, [and] emotion" belonging to the impassioned. In this swift gloss, Nash and Bradley are trading in intellectual compressions that elbow strange bedfellows into binary lodgings, closing down routes of exploration. The essential problem with such thinking is it's not interdisciplinary enough to treat the matter at hand, not the least because disparate and even conflicting concepts often result in the most interesting and fantastic progeny if we allow them to cohabitate a bit, and do not value them into separate beds or shame them for refusing to comply with our commands to disengage for a discipline-specific sense of propriety.

This seems doubly true when it comes to adaptation theories, particularly if we take our lead from works such as Linda Hutcheon's *A Theory of Adaptation*, which follows a similar methodology as *Meserach and Research* by attempting to force-feed the adaptation process through a series of "generalizable insights into theoretical issues," rather than giving breathing room to the objects onto which an adaptation discourse has been applied (xv). As I have argued elsewhere, this approach turns objects into one-dimensional "examples" or "illustrations" of a neat theory the author seeks to espouse, while effectively throttling anything the object might say on its own behalf. Theoretical compartmentalizations can rob adaptive objects of their multifaceted and constantly shifting sets of meaning as well as their most productive copulations with the scholarship at hand. This lip-service to the object shuts down corridors for cross-pollination and eliminates possibilities to examine a set of objects as a larger body of work rather than a selected image of the body in bits and pieces. In her review of *A Theory of Adaptation*, Dianne F. Sadoff succinctly criticizes Hutcheon's "generalizable theory" and her efforts to supplant the fidelity debates of the 90s:

> Borrowing a model from the biological sciences, then, [Hutcheon] posits "cultural transmission" as "analogous to genetic transmission," but, instead of genes, "memes," that, like genes, are "replicators" and enable a text to compete for "survival in the meme pool." The fittest stories undergo "cultural selection" and not only survive but also "flourish"; the qualities necessary for "high survival value" are "longevity," "fecundity," and "copying-fidelity." Here, Hutcheon smuggles back into her theory the notion of fidelity that she had promised to discount, for "copying-fidelity" is, as she defines it, a replication that "chang[es] with each repetition, whether deliberate or not" [172].

As I observed in *Adaptation Theories*, Hutcheon over-prioritizes the relationship between source text (or its replicators) and authorial intent in the adaptation process. Clearly, authors select tokens or features to keep, others to reject, this much is known. But in a more holistic sense, adaptations open things up, perforating the arbitrary boundaries that contain things, police things, guard citadels of representation. The exciting possibilities for adaptation don't so much concern the replication or reproduction of strong or weak features. Those are simply isolated instances of permutation, the difference between one *Hamlet* and the next. The truth claim is enough. What is more exciting for me is the outer edge of adaptation.

Much in the same way that Benjamin, in "The Task of the Translator," suggested any speech act posits the inherent translatability of its statements, to produce a text is (1) to already engage in an adaptive act (the adaptation of the meta-text and its pre-referents) and (2) to already posit the adaptability of the "new" text, which, through the multifarious and provisional quality of language, is open to adaptation and maladaptation before it escapes the pen, the camera, the computer animation software, or the body itself (88). In fact, adaptation was happening before the piece was touched; since the first utterance, the adaptive cycle has been constantly opening up, from "simplex" languages of paramecium and earthworms to bee dances, wolf packs and ultimately (within our own frame of reference, at least, which accounts for just about nothing) the multifarious languages of the human race. Throughout this larger cycle of adaptation, nothing exists and continues to adapt because it is inherently stronger than something else—it exists because a place has been opened for it to do so, and it has seized the opportunity and capitalized on it. Without the opening, nothing. As Thomas Van Parys suggests in "Against Fidelity: Contemporary Adaptation Studies and the Example of Novelisation," we would do well to mind the gap (158).

Méconnaisance and the Zero-Point of Recognition

Let us turn back to my own set of images as a body of work, an emergent unfolding, not simply as isolated and carefully circumscribed events or "phases." As I have suggested, this set of images is not inherently linear unless it has been constrained to that mode of perception. Taking a tip from Nash and Bradley, and endorsing the spirit of this current collection, viewing the unfolding of the aggregate "me" might yield some interesting "temporal questions of value: how conceptions of value change over time and space"—a possibility that became particularly crucial for me when I became a post-transsexual, and the thing that I sought to do with my identity appeared to exceed the space for its reception.

The images in Plates 8 through 12 depict me from the time I decided to begin doing drag in a public way through my ten years living as a transsexual. The photographs in Plates 13 and 14 were taken during my "stealth years," when I was living in upstate New York and binding down my breasts with surgical elastics in order to keep my job at the conservative newspaper that employed me under the impression that I was a man. Plates 15 through 17 followed my decision to stop living as a transsexual in 1999. It was after this decision that I had the good fortune to publish a chapter in *The Journal*

Left, top: Plate 8: A Mission District drag queen in a red satin robe, San Francisco, California, 1988. Photograph by Sharon Beth Greenberg. *Right, top:* Plate 9: Posing with lace gauntlets at San Francisco Art Institute, 1990. Photograph by Leah Polishook. *Left, middle:* Plate 10: At home with my drawings in my San Francisco artist loft, 1991. Photograph by Leah Polishook. *Right, bottom:* Plate 11: Photograph shoot in Los Angeles, California, during the Green Iguana Phase, 1993. Photograph by Grete Dalum. *Left, bottom:* Plate 12: My 40th birthday party, and the last time I'd wear a dress, Rochester, New York, 1997. Photograph by Cynthia Young.

of Visual Culture (2007) entitled "Retro-translations of Post-Transsexuality, Notions of Regre," which treats the topic of post-transsexuality far more thoroughly than time allows here. Suffice it to say that "Retrotranslations" drew on the studies of Judith Butler, Homi K. Bhabha and Michel Foucault to critique the legal, clinical and theoretical mistranslations of the

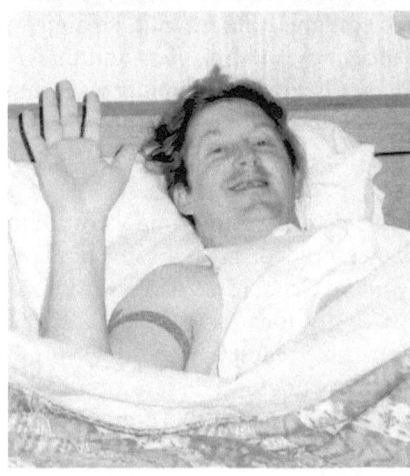

Left, top: Plate 13:Upstate PR man with camera, Honeoye Falls, New York, 2000. Photographer unknown, plate property of the author. *Left, bottom:* Plate 14: Bedridden after surgery with an ice pack on my chest, Lake Tahoe, California, 2000. Photographer anonymous, plate property of the author. *Right, top:* Plate 15: Sitting on a train platform in Amsterdam with Charles, The Netherlands, 2007. Photograph by Charles Karubian. *Right, middle:* Plate 16: Holding my baby boy, Corvallis, Oregon, 2008. Photograph by Jennie Greene. *Right, bottom:* Plate 17: Celebrating my successful dissertation defense at The Amsterdam School for Cultural Analysis, University of Amsterdam, 2014. Photograph by Kat Willie.

post-transsexual enterprise, particularly the notion that post-transsexuals can only translate forward through going back.

In light of the images before you, I would like to cordially discuss how, at different points in my life, specific viewers regarded my sexual identity as "ambiguous," and were troubled, puzzled, angered or delighted by the relationship of that ambiguity to their own points of sexual determination. Before proceeding, I hasten to add that, like numerous intersexuals, transsexuals, transvestites and androgynes, sissyboys and tomboys, poofs and queers, I *never* regarded my own sexuality as ambiguous—not even when I found it confusing myself. Fluidity and open-endedness are different than ambiguity, which is typically defined as vagueness, obscurity, doubtfulness and uncertainty. I was never in any doubt about my own sexuality. It simply was what it was, even if I did not know precisely what it was at that moment—even in its lack of clarity, it was always quite specific, from my own frame of reference, at least.

For the remainder of this essay—and this is far more important than my perceptions and opinions about the "meaning" of my own sexual identity—I will (following Butler's work in *Undoing Gender* in a haphazard fashion) refer to intersubjective efforts to sexually locate a subject, and the discursive nexus wherein such negotiations take place, as the *zero-point of sexual recognition*. As I discussed at length in my doctoral dissertation, "Sexual Ambiguity: Narrative Manifestations in Adaptation" (2014), this fraught and contentious zero-point is a trans-subjective interstice at which sexual lives and livable lives are arbitrated and apportioned. And the discourse of *sexual valuation* takes place within this turbulent fulcrum, as people evaluate and (re)evaluate the sexual subject position of the other so as to identify, verify, vouchsafe and in some cases even negotiate their own. On an elemental level, like bats in a cave, others respond to the sexual script they perceive embodied in you. As I quickly discovered as a transsexual who did not want to "pass" as a "real woman," people did not always know what to make of that refusal to locate in a recognizable identity (within their framework of recognition), and I did not always know what to do when they did not know what to make of it.

But I always regarded this moment of encounter as tremendously valuable, precisely because it is here that the negotiation of recognizable identity palpably takes place. And in ways that seem almost inevitable, this discursive interstice is often more defined by misrecognition (*méconnaisance*) than recognition, which can be both a positive and negative value, depending on its manipulation and interpretation—in short, its valuation—on the part of the receiver. Indeed, the zero-point of misrecognition is ripe for sexual adaptation in a holistic sense, even as it simultaneously presents an opportunity for the acclimation of individuals. The deepest adaptation, after all, is often proportionate to the deepest embrace of the unfamiliar. As the title of my essay suggests, with its clever reference to Voltaire, the ability to (mis)recognize is weak at both ends. But in weakness there is strength, for the weakness presents an opening for adaptation. To enact a preposterous metaphor, both good and bad things can happen when the viewers of a sexual subject—like grandparents trying to identify a child while desperately fishing for their spectacles—lack the ontological basis for recognition. In a worst case scenario, faced with a sexuality he "just doesn't get," gramps chokes on his sexual dentures and unleashes a hurricane of recrimination and rebuke, spoiling Thanksgiving dinner. But in the best of times, when parity of (mis)recognition is reached, gramps and progeny realize they love each other no matter how confusing they are, and the family moves forward into life with increased solidarity.

If that sounds like a prescription for the family of man, then it is. With stakes so high, we cannot afford to shrink from sexual misrecognition, which provides an opportunity to adapt our sexual culture to be more valuable for all of us, instead of select individuals. In the fulcrum of sexual *méconnaisance*, we might alternately re-stabilize our love for one another and de-stabilize the regimes that actively prevent this love. Yet before proceeding on this adventure, we must acknowledge that sexual misrecognition—the ability to not cognize again—can also lead to panic, and terror, when one is surrounded by an overarching cultural regime that, through its relentless refusal to recognize ("as far as we're concerned, you're still a man") and incorrect but overwhelming misinterpretation ("I see you are no longer a transsexual, you must be returning to manhood"), seeks to fix or force one into a discrete sexual position they might reject as undesirable, even toxic.

Resistance Is Not Folly

I had a crisis when it came time to present my thesis work for my Master's degree at the California Institute of the Arts (around the time of Plate Eleven). The technology didn't work. I intended on screening footage from a 45-minute stage performance I'd done at The Whore Academy in Helsinki, Finland (1995). But the performance had been documented using PAL video technology instead of NTSC, which was the only technology the video equipment supported. Because it'd taken so much energy to convene all the members of my defense committee in one place, I decided to suggest an alternate route for discussion. "We can talk about my body," I said. The committee looked at me aghast, none more so than my graduate mentor, Leslie Dick, whose mouth dropped open, eyes wide with shock. They were entirely flummoxed by my suggestion, but it seemed quite reasonable to me; the French artist, Orlan, had recently been in the news with the work she had done with her own plastic surgeries as well as Bob Flanagan's intensive work with body politics in *Supermasochist* (Vale and Juno). I had approached my own body modifications with no less intentionality than those artists, so why not? But the committee at hand did not recognize the value of this idea. We rescheduled the defense, and a month later, I passed.

The notion of body as authorship remained on my mind, however, nagging at me with more energy when I broached adaptation studies during my doctoral program at University of Amsterdam. In the CFP for the collection of essays you are currently reading, one of the possible threads for examination included "the role of the author in shaping questions of value; the value placed on 'creativity'; the creation of canons in literature, film, and other media; how canons shape issues of value." In that sense, as artists like Orlan and Flanagan have indicated, the body can be, with the correct amount of authorial intention (the truth claim that it is "work"), another type of text that is as plastic as anything else, within certain parameters. Like a chunk of bronze, the body melts into a puddle of liquid if you apply enough heat. But given the right amount of structural rigidity, it can be sculpted and molded into any variety of representational and/or abstract forms, depending on the ontological basis of the receiver.

Within the zero-point of sexual recognition—and more specifically, within the zero-point of sexual misrecognition as it occurs in force relations—the outcome of this shaping enterprise depends on strength, support, and agency on either side of the viewing coin. If you shape yourself into sufficient intelligibility (or unintelligibility as the case may be), you might have some say in the way your body representations are received. But, as Foucault emphasizes in *Herculine Barbin*, the overwhelming force of the majority can push back with such force that your own interpretation of your body and its significance comes undone (145).[3]

As a post-transsexual, I've enjoyed ample experience with this. For most people, particularly since I've had children, it's just easier for them to categorize me as somebody's dad. I've got a beard, I wear pants and T-shirts, my voice sounds suitably low—as far as they're concerned, I am not a post-transsexual, I simply went back to being a guy. To argue this point in everyday life would take an infinite amount of energy, requiring me to assert my sexual identity in the most banal of conversations ("no goddamnit, I am not a man, I am a post-transsexual!"), thereby requiring the need for infinite recapitulations of backstory. Engaging in that amount of explanation would make me late for my kids' karate practices, and I don't really see the percentage. At a certain point, you've gleaned what you needed to glean in conversation and it's time to get the adaptation moving. Kathy Acker once called me insane for doing a performance in which I tried to live as a transsexual Catholic martyr saint for 40 days and 40 nights, fasting and scourging myself by walking naked through the Mojave desert: "Just do it in the writing," she said.

Easy words for a woman who wrote while giving herself orgasms with a vibrator—and there were priceless things that I learned through working things out in the flesh, things I never would've encountered "in the writing," things I carry with me to this day; I could not do this writing without having lived it first. And seen from this point of view, the vantage point of my post-transsexual body, I know one thing for certain: when it comes to the meaning of our own temporary acclimatization to the onslaught of life, whether that acclimation be written or lived (as if those two are separate), the final mis-interpretation, the one that remains behind after all other parties are gone, will belong not to some resilient meme or "replicant" within the text or the author, but to whoever has the most power to solidify and bolster its contin-uation. And even that interpretation remains open to modification, eradica-tion, and even complete reversal further down the temporal line, when none of the original players remain on the playing field, in which any "play" at hand—any chance for change or modification—occurs through a process of opening and resistance. Indeed, the more I examine the adaptation process, the more I see the concept of resistance as axiomatic, though it is an entangled resistance in which object and context are entwined. On both sides of the fence, the resistance is contingent on value: What do we choose to resist or not to resist? What is valuable enough to fight for? Do we choose to give in to the contextual pressures of force relations, and, if we do not choose to give in, when is it nevertheless advantageous to retreat in the face of overwhelming forces, seeking a safe haven from whence to resist again?

Yet our own valuation is not the only valuation at play, just as our own resistance isn't the only game in town. Always as we proceed, we are aware of the contextual resistance that surrounds us. Giving way before our footsteps sometimes, yielding to our efforts, while other times it suddenly drops into pits, runs into walls, seals off in dead ends, embrasures, enclosures. But when we do make the effort, holding our values tightly to our chest, how exhila-rating it is when everything yields suddenly into light.

As I have mentioned here, adaptation is not merely the emergence of new organs, new perceptions, new forms of discourse—the most interesting of which are often the least faithful to the source. Adaptation also involves eradication and vestigiality: the things that have disappeared or remnants caught in the process of eroding in time. Although the Mexican Tetra became blind and smaller brained as it acquired its lodgings in caves, it still retains the semblance of eyes, as well as the presence of brain, and each of these objects could re-manifest if they were valuable enough and the context opened into the possibility for their (re)adaptation. On a physical level, there is much of the vestigial in human beings as well: we have the coccyx, the appendix, body hair, wisdom teeth, goosebumps, all of which are vestigial but not completely valueless. While they no longer serve their original function, they still function in a modified way. Goosebumps, for example, are no longer responsible for flexing copious body hair, allowing us to appear bigger and scare off predators—but they still inform us when it is cold and alert us when creepy or menacing things are near. Although it exists in much smaller patches than it used to, we enjoy looking at lustrous swatches of body hair on people, and hair can be useful for making things. Wisdom teeth remain useful to chew with, although we don't chew as much (or as hard) as we did 35,000 years ago, when our fibrous foods contained more grit and sand. And while each of these vestigial organs have resisted complete obliteration, it is possible, no matter what the proponents of Dollo's Law say, that they could come back again—just as it is possible, particularly through the intervention of genetic modification, for us to develop new organs that, by twentieth-century standards, might seem the stuff of fantasy: slots for insert GPS microchips, gills to breathe underwater, taste buds to make Pabst Blue Ribbon seem like decent beer.

And our lives are full of vestigial value; the memories, stories and justifications we carry with us in our efforts to acclimate to our rapidly shifting moral-ethical and physical terrain. Yet the way in which we are valued—as a species and as individuals—is not altogether in our hands, our control. What we are "meant to be" will never be decided until we are spent, and even then, that valuation could be subject to change, even if it's not "us" who change it. But either way, it is the contextual weakness of "existence"—which could more effectively be defined as a lack of resistance, and in fact could be existence's greatest strength—on either side of the existential core that provides the opportunity for individual strengths and weaknesses to emerge and perhaps resolve into large-scale adaptations.

Who knows? On an individual level, perhaps even I've had my strengths. Not necessarily because of me, but because of me and others like me, our heterocentric culture has opened into more sexual possibility—more possibility for desire and its adaptive effects—and I am a part of that moment, the moment when a heterosexist lexicon opened to account for more, and eventually if only provisionally transformed to include it. But now that I am here, on the post-transsexual side of the street, I can also see why it's important not only to make room for the new and unfamiliar, but to rekindle and revitalize gendered locations long considered stable or "set"—locations like girlhood, fatherhood, motherhood, even heterosexual white dude. Just as we resist the silencing of troubling bodies in sexual discourse, we must resist these easy encapsulations with all our might. In sweeping those nodes of identification under the sexual determinacy of the "familiar," and thereby (mis)recognizing their adaptive potential, much productive terrain for adaptation is dismissed to the status of un-queer, ancient history, has-been.

It's not so much that both ends of the candle are alive and lit. The problem with Voltaire's quote, and its critique of weakness on both sides, is that it creates a binary spectrum of weakness that comprises only two sides; always a dangerous affair in a multifarious discourse of sexual valuation. There is weakness everywhere, and through such weakness we stand a chance of resistance, and with it, adaptation. This is not to say the adaptation of human cultures will produce the survival of our species as the fittest in the universe. It won't. Yet within our brightly numbered days, we have the opportunity to resist in new directions, to carve out a plane of social justice not only for transsexuals and post-transsexuals—or sexualities long deemed static and even dead—but for sexualities that do not exist yet because we haven't emancipated a place for them to sound off and thrive. My visibly post-transsexual body is only one body, and it will never truly adapt—but despite the many challenges it faces and the impact of counter-translation in many directions, it continues to be a body of resistance. Despite all the blows and scars, and thanks to many libidinal rewards, my me-search—ultimately, little more than an accretion and distribution of resistance—continues. And that makes all the difference.

Notes

1. Another possible corpus of study for future papers might be the identity of Wilkonson Sword, a company that adapted from manufacturing swords to razor blades and gardening equipment.

2. Quentin Meillassoux digs at the subject of human valuation wonderfully in *Before Finitude*, noting that informing readers "the Earth was hot" during the accretion of the solar system only makes sense within a human valuation of temperature—within the frame of its own emergence, the Earth was no hotter or colder than it needed to be (11).

3. In exploring the adaptive critical reception of *Herculine* at length in "Sexual Ambiguity," and availing myself of Rancière's work in *The Politics of Aesthetics*, I expressed skepticism concerning Butler's criticism of Foucault's editorial mission in that work, which in the end, I asserted, was identical to her own aims in *Gender Trouble*. Ultimately, Foucault was right: the process of political emancipation, to borrow a term from Rancière, takes place in a volatile crucible of force relations (Rancière 19–29, 86–90). And Butler was right: the emancipation of abjectified bodies in sexual discourse does create the opportunity for us to recognize more, to recognize better. In their approaches to *Herculine*, both scholars were weak on both sides, inasmuch as they inadequately engaged with the object at hand (opting to transpose their own views over it) but they were strong on both sides as well.

Works Cited

Benjamin, Harry. The Transsexual Phenomenon. Dusseldorf: Symposium Publishing: 1999. Web. 18 Apr. 2016.

Benjamin, Walter. "Task of the Translator." *Illuminations*. Trans. Harry Zohn. Ed. Hannah Arendt. New York: Schocken Books, 1968. Print.

Bhabha, Homi K. *The Location of Culture*. London: Routledge, 1994. Print.

_____. *Nation and Narration*. London: Routledge, 1990. Print.

Bloom, Harold. *Poetics of Influence: New and Selected Criticism*. New Haven: H.R. Schwab, 1988. Print.

Butler, Judith. *Gender Trouble: Feminism and the Subversion of Identity*. New York: Routledge, 1990. Print.

_____. *Undoing Gender*. New York: Routledge, 2004. Print.
De Lauretis, Teresa. *Figures of Resistance: Essays in Feminist Theory*. Urbana: University of Illinois Press, 2007. Print.
Foucault, Michel. *Abnormal: Lectures at the College de France, 1974–1975*. Trans. Graham Burchell. New York: Macmillan, 2004. Print.
_____. *Herculine Barbin: Being the Recently Discovered Memoirs of a French Hermaphrodite*. Trans. Richard McDougall. New York: Pantheon, 1980. Print.
_____. *The History of Sexuality: An Introduction, Volume I*. Trans. Robert Hurley. New York: Pantheon Books, 1978. Print.
Hutcheon, Linda. *A Theory of Adaptation*. New York: Routledge, 2006. Print.
Kristeva, Julia. "'Nous Deux' or a (Hi)Story of Intertextuality." *Romanic Review* 93.1 (2002): 7–14. Print.
_____. *Powers of Horror: An Essay on Abjection*. Trans. Leon Roudiez. New York: Columbia University Press, 1982. Print.
Leitch, Thomas. "Everything You Always Wanted to Know about Adaptation Especially if You're Looking Forwards Rather than Back." *Literature Film Quarterly* 33.3 (2005): 233–245. Print.
_____. "Twelve Fallacies in Contemporary Adaptation Theory." *Criticism* 45.2 (2003): 149–71. Print.
Nash, Robert J., and DeMethra LaSha Bradley. *Me-Search and Re-Search: A Guide for Writing Scholarly Personal Narrative Manuscripts*. Charlotte, NC: Information Age Publishing. 2011. Print.
Rancière, Jacques. *The Politics of Aesthetics*. Trans. Gabriel Rockhill. New York: Continuum, 2004. Print.
Sadoff, Dianne. "*A Theory of Adaptation* (review)." *University of Toronto Quarterly* 78.1 (2009): 172–173. Web.
St. Jacques, Jillian. *Adaptation Theories*. Maastricht: Jan van Eyck Academie Press, 2011. Print.
_____. "Retrotranslations of Post-Transsexuality, Notions of Regret." *Journal of Visual Culture* 6.1 (2007): 77–90. Print.
_____. "Sexual Ambiguity: Narrative Manifestations in Adaptation." Diss. U. of Amsterdam, 2014.
Silverman, Kaja. *The Threshold of the Visible World*. New York: Routledge, 1996. Print.
Vale, Andrea, and A. Juno. *Bob Flanagan—Supermasochist: Interviews*. Los Angeles: Re/Search Publications, 1993. Print.
Van Parys, Thomas. "Against Fidelity: Contemporary Adaptation Studies and the Example of Novelization." In Saint Jacques, *Adaptation Theories*. 144–70. Maastricht: Jan van Eyck Academie Press, 2011. Print.
Voltaire. *The Works of Voltaire: A Contemporary Version with Notes, Vol. 14*. Trans. William Fleming. New York: E.R. Dumont, 1901. Print.
Wilkerson, William. *Ambiguity and Sexuality: A Theory of Sexual Identity*. Basingstoke: Palgrave Macmillan, 2010. Print.

About the Contributors

Dorota **Babilas** works at the Institute of English Studies at the University of Warsaw, Poland. Her academic interests include Victorian, Gothic, and film studies. Her doctoral studies focused on the literary status of *The Phantom of the Opera*. She is the author of a book on the cultural afterlife of Queen Victoria (University of Warsaw, 2012).

Lisa **Bunkowski** is a lecturer in the Humanities Department at Texas A&M University–Central Texas. Her historical research focus is on the mid-19th century Western United States, with emphasis on issues of violence and gender. She is also the director of the Faculty Center for Teaching & Learning at Texas A&M University–Central Texas. Her research focus in this area is on faculty mentoring and online teaching.

Wickham **Clayton** is a lecturer at the University for the Creative Arts, Farnham, United Kingdom. He is the editor of *Style and Form in the Hollywood Slasher Film* (Palgrave Macmillan, 2015) and the co-editor of *Screening Twilight: Critical Approaches to a Cinematic Phenomenon* (I. B. Tauris, 2014).

Suzanne **Diamond** is a professor of English at Youngstown State University. Her publications have focused on British literary figures, film adaptations, confessional narration, collective memory, and writing pedagogy. She regularly teaches undergraduate and graduate courses dealing with British literature, film studies, mythology, and writing.

Ela İpek **Gündüz** is a lecturer at the English Language and Literature Department, Faculty of Science and Letters, Gaziantep University, Turkey. Her research interests include women writers, gender studies, postcolonial literature, postmodernism, cinema, and adaptation studies. She teaches undergraduate courses on women's literature, postcolonial literatures, modern drama and introduction to literature.

Charles R. **Hamilton** is a professor of English at Northeast Texas Community College, where he teaches film, literature, and composition courses, and an adjunct professor at Texas A&M University–Central Texas, where he teaches communications and liberal studies courses. He is the co-editor of *Clint Eastwood's Cinema of Trauma* (McFarland, 2017).

Agata **Hołobut** is a lecturer in translation studies at the Institute of English Studies, Jagiellonian University, Kraków, Poland. Her main areas of interest include translation studies, cognitive linguistics, and visual arts. She has published several articles on audiovisual and literary translation as well as a book-long interview with a renowned Polish poster designer Mieczysław Górowski titled *Drzwi do plakatu* ("A door to a poster," Universitas, 2009).

Kenneth A. **Longden** is a lecturer in critical approaches to television at the University of Salford, United Kingdom, and a lecturer in film and media at the University of Central Lancashire. He is a published author for Palgrave, Intellect Books, JAST, and various academic journals.

Leslie **McMurtry** teaches radio theory at the University of Salford. She has published on radio drama, podcasts, Gothic, adaptation studies and *Doctor Who*. She writes and produces audio drama and was an artist in residence at the Badlands National Park in 2017.

Özlem **Özmen** is a research assistant at Muğla Sıtkı Koçman University. Her research is on the contextual analysis of contemporary rewritings of Shakespeare's plays in British drama. Other areas of interest include British women playwrights, political drama, and postcolonial literature.

Rebecca M. **Pauly**, recently retired, was a professor languages at West Chester University. Her interest in adaptation goes back to the 80s, when she was teaching French and Italian at the University of Delaware and completing a doctorate in both languages. Her research interests include French and Italian film studies, 19th and 20th century French literature, text and image theory.

Allen H. **Redmon** is an associate professor of English and film studies at Texas A&M University–Central Texas. He is the author of *Constructing the Coens: From Blood Simple to Inside Llewyn Davis* (Rowman & Littlefield, 2015) and the co-editor of *Clint Eastwood's Cinema of Trauma* (McFarland, 2017). He regularly publishes articles on adaptation, popular film, and religion and film.

Dennis **Rothermel** is emeritus professor of philosophy at California State University, Chico. His research interests lie in the intersection of Continental philosophy and cinema studies. His recent publications include "Slow Food, Slow Film," and "Heroic Endurance," in the *Quarterly Review of Film and Video*. He co-edited a volume of essays on peace studies, *Remembrance and Reconciliation* (Rodopi, 2011) and *A Critique of Judgment in Film and Television* (Palgrave Macmillan, 2014), a collection of theoretical essays in film and media theory.

Jan **Rybicki** is an assistant professor at the Institute of English Studies, Jagiellonian University, Kraków, Poland. His interests include literary translation, comparative literature, and digital humanities, especially stylometry and distant reading. He is also an literary translator, with some thirty translated novels.

Jillian **Saint Jacques** is a senior instructor in the School of Writing, Literature and Film at Oregon State University. He is the editor/author of *Adaptation Theories*

(Jan van Eyck Academie, 2011). His published articles include work on transsexuality and post-transsexuality, the artwork of Monet Clark, Adel Abidin, Cynthia Young, Abdul Mati Klarwein and others. He also writes fiction.

Hui **Wu** is a professor of media art at Communication University of China in Beijing and a member of the International Shakespeare Association. Her main published works include two books as well as numerous academic articles. Her research interests include Western movie culture and adaptation studies.

Christopher **Wydler** is a graduate teaching assistant and doctoral candidate in English at Texas A&M University–Commerce, where he teaches first-year composition and introductory literature courses. Wydler's research interests gauge transdisciplinary applications in multimodal texts. He is also the chief editor of the student-run literary journal *The Mayo Review*.

Hülya **Yağcıoğlu** is an assistant professor in the English and Writing Studies Department at Zayed University, UAE. She published in the field of comparative literature, specifically on the interaction between material culture and literature, and her research areas include comparative literature, cultural studies, literary criticism, and modern Turkish and American fiction.

The contributors would like to acknowledge the efforts
and influence of the editor, Laurence Raw,
who passed away before final production of this volume.

Index

www.ingramcontent.com/pod-product-compliance
Lightning Source LLC
Chambersburg PA
CBHW021419110726
47901CB00008B/2225